MODERN HUMANITIES RESEARCH ASSOCIATION

TUDOR & STUART TRANSLATIONS

VOLUME **8**

General Editors
ANDREW HADFIELD
NEIL RHODES

ELIZABETHAN SENECA

THREE TRAGEDIES

ELIZABETHAN SENECA
THREE TRAGEDIES

Edited by

James Ker and Jessica Winston

MODERN HUMANITIES RESEARCH ASSOCIATION
2012

Published by
The Modern Humanities Research Association,
1 Carlton House Terrace
London SW1Y 5AF

First published 2012

ISBN 978-0-947623-98-2

Copies may be ordered from www.tudor.mhra.org.uk

MHRA TUDOR AND STUART TRANSLATIONS

For details of published and forthcoming volumes please visit our website:

http://www.tudor.mhra.org.uk

TABLE OF CONTENTS

GENERAL EDITORS' FOREWORD

The aim of the *MHRA Tudor & Stuart Translations* is to create a representative library of works translated into English during the early modern period for the use of scholars, students and the wider public. The series will include both substantial single works and selections of texts from major authors, with the emphasis being on the works that were most familiar to early modern readers. The texts themselves will be newly edited with substantial introductions, notes, and glossaries, and will be published both in print and online.

The series aims to restore to view a major part of English Renaissance literature which has become relatively inaccessible and to present these texts as literary works in their own right. For that reason it will follow the same principle of modernisation adopted by other scholarly editions of canonical literature from the period. The series will have a similar scope to that of the original *Tudor Translations* published early in the last century, and while the great majority of the works presented will be from the sixteenth century, like the original series it will not be rigidly bound by the end-date of 1603. There will, however, be a very different range of texts with new and substantial scholarly apparatus.

The *MHRA Tudor & Stuart Translations* will extend our understanding of the English Renaissance through its representation of the process of cultural transmission from the classical to the early modern world and the process of cultural exchange within the early modern world.

Andrew Hadfield
Neil Rhodes

ACKNOWLEDGEMENTS

Many people helped us in the completion of this volume. We are grateful to the *MHRA Tudor and Stuart Translations* editors and advisory board, especially Neil Rhodes and Louise Wilson for their encouragement and timely assistance with methodological and practical questions. Robert Miola provided important comments on the initial proposal, and Fred Schurink and Gordon Kendal helped with literary contexts and linguistic issues. Other scholars also contributed useful input on sixteenth-century contexts, including Jane Griffiths, as well as Mike Pincombe and Curtis Perry, both of whom kindly shared work still in manuscript.

Members of the ISU Department of English and Philosophy provided valuable responses to an early draft of the introduction; Susan Goslee and Sonja Launspach offered encouragement and helped with specific conceptual or linguistic issues. Jim Skidmore helped to check the texts and also generously gave other important practical and intellectual support. At Penn, Jo Park as well as members of the Classical Studies Department were willing interlocutors throughout the process.

Staff at the following libraries gave generous assistance: the Oboler Library at Idaho State University (especially Jim Teliha and Teresa Warren), the Department of Rare Books and Special Collections at Princeton University, the Princeton Theological Seminary Library (Kate Skrebutenas), the Rare Book and Manuscript Library at the University of Pennsylvania (John Pollack, Bob Walther), the Codrington Library at All Souls College, Oxford, and the Bodleian Library, Oxford.

Research for this edition was supported by a one-semester sabbatical leave from the ISU College of Arts & Sciences, by a grant from the ISU Humanities and Social Sciences Research Committee, and by ongoing support from the School of Arts and Sciences at the University of Pennsylvania.

INTRODUCTION

In 1559, a classical tragedy appeared in print for the first time in England. This was Jasper Heywood's *Troas*, a translation of Seneca's *Troades* (Trojan Women), a play about the women and children who survived the fall of Troy. Today, *Troas* is not often read, and without biographical and literary context it can seem like little more than a typical example of mid-Tudor verse. *Troas* was, however, a turning point in English Renaissance literature. Most immediately, the translation established Heywood as a significant writer of the day. Contemporaries praised his 'smooth and filed style', 'perfect' and 'thundering' verse, and 'learned and painful [i.e. painstaking] translation'.[1] Perhaps because of this appreciation, *Troas* drew attention to Seneca's plays generally, beginning a vogue for Senecan translation and adaptation that profoundly shaped the subject matter and style of English drama through the rest of the century and into the next.[2]

Remarkably, by the late 1560s nine of Seneca's ten plays had been translated into English, by Heywood, Alexander Neville, John Studley, and Thomas Nuce. These translations were:

1559	Heywood	*Troas* (also known as *Troades*, 'Trojan Women')
1560	' '	*Thyestes*
1561	' '	*Hercules Furens* ('Hercules Insane')
1563	Neville	*Oedipus*
1566	Studley	*Agamemnon*
1566	' '	*Medea*

---

[1] See 'T. B. to the Reader', lines 1–2 below in *Agamemnon*. Also 'R. W. to the Reader' in John Drout, *The Pityfull Histori[e] of Two Loving Italians* (London: Henry Bynneman, 1570), sig. A3ᵛ; Arthur Hall, trans., *Ten Books of Homers Iliades, Translated out of French* (London: [Henry Bynneman for?] Ralph Newbery, 1581), sig. A2ᵛ.

[2] See, for example, John W. Cunliffe, *The Influence of Seneca on Elizabethan Tragedy* (London: Macmillan, 1893; repr. Hamden, CT: Archon Books, 1965); H. B. Charlton, *The Senecan Tradition in Renaissance Tragedy: A Re-Issue of an Essay Published in 1921* (Manchester: Manchester University Press, 1946); T. S. Eliot's introduction to *Seneca: His Tenne Tragedies*, ed. by Thomas Newton, 2 vols, Tudor Translation Series (London: Constable and Co., 1927), I, v–liv; Robert S. Miola, *Shakespeare and Classical Tragedy: The Influence of Seneca* (Oxford: Clarendon Press, 1992).

1566?	'	'	*Hercules Oetaeus* ('Hercules on Oeta')
1567	'	'	*Hippolytus* (also known as *Phaedra*)
c. 1566	Nuce		*Octavia*

In 1581, Thomas Newton translated the remaining play, *Thebais* (also known as *Phoenissae*, 'Phoenician Women') and combined all of the translations in *Seneca: His Tenne Tragedies* (1581),[3] the first complete collection of plays printed in England, prefiguring the *Works* of Ben Jonson (1616) and the first folio of Shakespeare (1623).[4]

As much as the translations started a lasting trend, by themselves they mark a distinct phase in the English reception of Seneca. As far back as the fourteenth century, English authors knew at least some of Seneca's writings,[5] and sayings from his plays and prose regularly appeared in collections of *florilegia* on the continent and in England.[6] Yet, prior to 1559, there was little direct interest in Seneca's works, with only a few of his prose writings and excerpts of his plays appearing in Latin or English.[7] By contrast, in the three decades after the *Tenne Tragedies*, the English engagement with Seneca was to be entirely different. While no one undertook a translation of an entire work, authors and playwrights routinely alluded to and reworked his *sententiae*, ideas, characters, and plots in their own writings. Why was there such interest in translating Seneca in the early Elizabethan period? This initial flurry of Seneca translations can be attributed to a number of factors, including the popularity of classical translation, Seneca's reputation, the view that Seneca's plays in particular reflected contemporary concerns about the prerogatives of royal power, and

---

[3] Thomas Newton, ed., *Seneca: His Tenne Tragedies Translated into English* (London: Thomas Marsh, 1581).

[4] On the influence of the *Tenne Tragedies* on these later collections, see Tara Lyons, 'English Printed Drama in Collection before Jonson and Shakespeare' (unpublished doctoral thesis, University of Illinois, Urbana-Champagne, 2011).

[5] On Chaucer's references to Seneca, see Harry Morgan Ayres, 'Chaucer and Seneca', *Romanic Review*, 10 (1919), 1–15.

[6] Jerome Bertram Cohon, 'Seneca's Tragedies in *Florilegia* and Elizabethan Drama' (unpublished doctoral thesis, Columbia University, 1960); Roland Mayer, 'Personata Stoa: Neostoicism and Senecan Tragedy', *Journal of the Warburg and Courtauld Institutes*, 57 (1994), 151–74 (pp. 156–57).

[7] On the translation of Seneca before 1559, see Jessica Winston, 'Seneca in Early Elizabethan England', *Renaissance Quarterly*, 59 (2006), 29–58 (p. 30). Translated passages from the plays also appeared in *Tottel's Miscellany* (1557). See Don Share, ed., *Seneca in English* (London: Penguin, 1998), pp. 3–5.

the backgrounds and goals of the individual translators themselves.[8]

The present edition emphasizes this last and less studied aspect of the translations: the aims of the individual translators and how these aims are manifested in specific stylistic choices in each work. Critics tend to look at the translations as a group, viewing them as a Seneca 'project',[9] in which the translators are 'midwives to the birth of English tragedy', or oppositional writers with a 'serious commitment to political resistance in an era of religious repression and censorship'.[10] These arguments offer ways of understanding the early Elizabethan interest in Seneca as a whole. Indeed, the translators after Heywood knew of and responded to his work and they shared broadly similar backgrounds and interests, especially in the relationship between kingship and tyranny. Yet their proximate publication and later consolidation in *Tenne Tragedies* make the translations look more like a 'project' than they were. Each one was shaped by separate circumstances and styled to meet specific aims, and each one responded in new ways to the challenges of translating Senecan drama into English.

By focusing on each translation as a distinct text, we hope to provide readers with a sense of the ways in which the dramatic translators approached their work and as a result shaped and reshaped Seneca's legacy as it would be known to later Elizabethan and Jacobean writers. We include three plays that are milestones in Senecan translation: the first English translations by the two most prolific translators of Seneca: *Troas* by Heywood and *Agamemnon* by Studley, and what critics have come to see as the most important Senecan translation of the period, Heywood's *Thyestes*.[11]

---

[8] See C. H. Conley, *The First English Translators of the Classics* (New Haven: Yale University Press, 1927), W. A. Armstrong, 'The Elizabethan Conception of the Tyrant', *Review of English Studies*, 22 (1946), 161–81 and 'Influence of Seneca and Machiavelli on the Elizabethan Tyrant', *Review of English Studies*, 24 (1948), 19–35, Gordon Braden, *Renaissance Tragedy and the Senecan Tradition: Anger's Privilege* (New Haven: Yale University Press, 1985), esp. pp. 28–62, Winston, ibid., and Linda Woodbridge, *English Revenge Drama: Money, Resistance, Equality* (Cambridge: Cambridge University Press, 2010), pp. 130–38.

[9] O. B. Hardison, *Prosody and Purpose in the English Renaissance* (Baltimore: Johns Hopkins University Press, 1989), pp. 148–53.

[10] See respectively B. R. Rees, 'English Seneca: A Preamble', *Greece and Rome*, 2nd ser., 16 (1969), 119–33 (p. 133), and Woodbridge, p. 131.

[11] Heywood's *Thyestes* is the only one of the translations that has appeared in a free-standing edition: Joost Daalder, ed., *'Thyestes': Translated by Jasper*

The plays also make for an interesting trio, since in its plot *Agamemnon* is a sequel to the other plays.

Seneca also wrote prose essays and letters, and some of these writings were translated in the Elizabethan period as well. *De Beneficiis* appeared twice in translation, first in 1569 in a partial version by Nicholas Haward not attributed to Seneca, then in 1578 in complete form, translated by Arthur Golding. Edward Aggas's *Certain Collections Gathered out of Seneca* (1576) includes Seneca's writings about death by way of an original French anthology of passages by Philippe de Mornay. Yet the plays and the prose works were translated in different phases, and the translators of each also operated with significantly different assumptions about their author. The plays appear in the early to mid-1560s, while the two main Elizabethan prose translations are a decade later. More importantly, the prose translators are not in conversation with the earlier playwrights, or even with each other, and they appear not to have regarded their Seneca as the same person as the tragedian (discussed below). For this reason, although we refer to these prose translations in what follows, our focus is on the Elizabethan reception of Seneca's life and legacy as a tragedian.

Below we begin with a general discussion of Senecan tragedy before focusing on the particulars of each translator and each translation. We conclude with some general discussion of these works' early reception and influence.

TRAGIC SENECA: ANCIENT, ELIZABETHAN, AND PRESENT-DAY

The translators might first have encountered Seneca's works in school, for instance in performance at a grammar school, or at Oxford and Cambridge.[12] Alongside Erasmus's celebrated edition

---

Heywood (1560) (London: Ernest Benn, 1982). It is also the only play in translation with its own chapter in the *Oxford Handbook of Tudor Drama*. See Mike Pincombe, 'Tragic Inspiration in Jasper Heywood's Translation of Seneca's *Thyestes*: Melpomene or Megaera?', in *The Oxford Handbook of Tudor Drama*, ed. Tom Betteridge and Greg Walker (Oxford: Oxford University Press, 2012), pp. 531–46.

[12] There were productions of Seneca at English schools and universities, for instance, a probable performance of *Hippolytus* at Westminster in 1546, and a 1580s production of a combined version of Neville's translation of *Oedipus* and

of Seneca's prose works (1529), they had access to major editions of his tragedies published on the continent, especially Gryphius's 1541 edition, which would supply the main Latin text from which they made their translations (see the Appendix on 'The Translators' Latin Sources'). And they read Senecan tragedy far more than Greek tragedy – indeed, at this time Seneca defined the paradigm of classical tragedy.

Who and what did the translators understand the tragic Seneca to be? The simple answer is that they understood him to be a statesman and philosopher whose plays offered an education in moral and political conduct. But this view is best approached by tracing the Senecan tradition from antiquity into the sixteenth century and by reviewing more recent developments in the interpretation of Senecan tragedy.

Seneca's Life and Works. Present-day readers know with certainty that the author of the tragedies was Lucius Annaeus Seneca, the

---

Newton's translation of *Thebais*, based on the versions published in Newton's *Tenne Tragedies* in 1581. See Yale Elizabethan Club, '*Oedipus* Manuscript', <www.yale.edu/elizabethanclub/oedipus.html> [accessed 30 November 2011], as well as productions in Latin at Cambridge in the 1560s and in the 1580s at Oxford. On productions of Seneca in the period, see Bruce R. Smith, 'Toward the Rediscovery of Tragedy: Productions of Seneca's Plays on the English Renaissance Stage', *Renaissance Drama*, n.s., 9 (1978), 3–37, and Winston, 'Seneca', p. 30 at nn. 5–6. Seneca's plays were also important dramatic models for plays at Jesuit colleges and universities on the continent. See Mayer, pp. 159 and 166, and N. H. Griffin, *Jesuit School Drama: A Checklist of Critical Literature,* Supplement 1, Research Bibliographies and Checklists (London: Grant & Cutler, 1985). There is no direct evidence for Seneca's place in Latin language teaching in grammar school, yet at least some viewed Seneca as an important part of early education. In a letter 'To His Son', Thomas Wyatt recommends he read 'moral philosophers, among whom I would Senec were your study and Epictetus, because it is little to be ever in your bosom' [i.e. a little goes a long way]. See *Life and Letters of Sir Thomas Wyatt*, ed. by Kenneth Muir (Liverpool: Liverpool University Press, 1963), p. 43. Also Lawrence Humphrey, in section on educating nobles in his treatise *The Nobles or Of Nobilitye*, recommends reading 'Seneca's tragedies' along with the comedies of Plautus and Virgil's *Georgics* for the 'stateliness of the matter and style' (London: Thomas Marsh, [1563]), sig. Y4ʳ. The example of Queen Elizabeth is also suggestive. She translated part of *Hercules Oetaeus* (*c.* 1589) and *Epistulae Morales* 107 (*c.* 1567). Her *Sententiae* (*c.* 1563) includes eleven citations of Seneca. Although dated to her mid-twenties or later, these works reflect the kinds of exercises in translation and common-placing she would have completed in her studies as a youth. See Janel Mueller and Joshua Scodel, eds, *Elizabeth I: Translations, 1544–1589* (Chicago: University of Chicago Press, 2009), pp. 5–7; 341.

Roman statesman and writer of works on Stoic philosophy. Seneca was born to a Roman equestrian family in Cordoba, Spain around 4–1 BCE and as a child was brought to Rome, where he was educated in rhetoric and philosophy. After beginning a tumultuous career in the Roman senate under the emperors Caligula and Claudius that resulted in his being banished to Corsica for the years 41–49 CE, he was recalled to Rome to serve as advisor to the young Nero, who became emperor in 54. The relationship with Nero eventually soured: Seneca was accused of involvement in the Pisonian conspiracy in April 65 and was forced to commit suicide.[13]

During his career, Tacitus tells us, Seneca enjoyed 'renown for his studies' (claritudo studiorum, *Annals* 12.8.2), and this is what brought him to the attention of Agrippina, Nero's mother, when she was looking for someone to instruct her son. The rhetorician Quintilian, writing in the generation after Seneca's death, celebrates and laments Seneca's stylistic influence on the young orators of his day: he acknowledges him as a 'distinguished attacker of vices' (egregius vitiorum insectator) and applauds his 'many distinctive aphorisms' (multae claraeque sententiae, *The Orator's Education* 10.1.129–30), yet he also draws attention to features that support the verdict of Caligula that Seneca's sententious style was 'sand without lime' (harena sine calce, Suetonius, *Caligula* 53.2). In ancient accounts of Seneca, ambivalence is a constant theme both in assessments of his rhetorical style and in attitudes to his career as a moralist who enjoyed the heights of wealth and power.[14]

Seneca's surviving works fall into two groups:[15] (1) prose works that deal with topics of moral philosophy and natural science mostly from a Stoic point of view. These include *On Anger, On Clemency, On Benefits, Moral Letters, Natural Questions*, along

---

[13] On Seneca's life and political career, see Miriam T. Griffin, *Seneca: A Philosopher in Politics*, 2nd edn (Oxford: Oxford University Press, 1992).

[14] On Quintilian's assessment of Seneca, see William J. Dominik, 'The Style is the Man: Seneca, Tacitus and Quintilian's Canon', in *Roman Eloquence: Rhetoric and Society in Literature*, ed. by William J. Dominik (London: Routledge, 1997), pp. 50–68. On Seneca as a model for his contemporaries, see Thomas N. Habinek, 'Seneca's Renown', *Classical Antiquity*, 19 (2000), 264–303.

[15] On Seneca's varied oeuvre, see James Ker, 'Seneca, Man of Many Genres', in *Seeing Seneca Whole: Perspectives on Philosophy, Poetry and Politics*, ed. by Katharina Volk and Gareth D. Williams (Leiden: Brill, 2006), pp. 19–41.

with the mock encomium *Apocolocyntosis,* on the 'pumpkinification' of the emperor Claudius; and (2) eight tragedies on famous mythological themes from the Greek and Roman dramatic tradition: *Hercules* (also known as *Hercules Furens*), *Troades* (Trojan Women, also known as *Troas*), *Phoenissae* (Phoenician Women, also known as *Thebais*), *Medea, Phaedra* (also known as *Hippolytus*), *Oedipus, Agamemnon,* and *Thyestes.* Two additional ancient 'Senecan' tragedies likely also from the first century were attributed to Seneca until the sixteenth century, but are probably not by him: *Hercules Oetaeus* (Hercules on Oeta) and *Octavia,* the latter an historical play focusing on Nero's divorce of his first wife Octavia and his marriage to Poppaea. It is difficult to link many of these works in specific ways to Seneca's career, and it is important not to automatically assume that the tragedies were intended principally to teach Nero or indeed to criticize him. None of the tragedies can be securely dated, though they probably belong to the years between Seneca's exile and his death, and of the three tragedies in this volume *Agamemnon* is probably the earliest and *Thyestes* the latest – an ordering based primarily on stylistic grounds.[16]

Despite these problems and the complexity introduced by the coexistence of the prose works and the tragedies, Seneca's identity as statesman, philosopher, and tragedian is now safely established. This Seneca is often referred to as 'Seneca the Younger', to distinguish him from his father (Seneca the Elder), whose surviving works are two collections of rhetorical exercises, or declamations (*Controversiae* and *Suasoriae*).

Sixteenth-Century Seneca. The translators in this volume were inheritors of a tradition in which the tragic Seneca usually had been thought to be a different person from the statesman-philosopher. This confusion arose in part from a reference to 'two Senecas' by the Roman poet Martial (*Epigrams* 1.61.7–8). Martial likely meant (1) the statesman-philosopher-tragedian (Seneca the Younger) and (2) the rhetorician (Seneca the Elder). Yet already before the Middle Ages most writers assumed that this referred to (1) a statesman-philosopher-rhetorician (conflating Seneca the Elder and Seneca the Younger into a single person who lived over 100 years)

---

[16] On this chronology, see John G. Fitch, *Seneca: Tragedies,* 2 vols, Loeb Classical Library (Cambridge, MA: Harvard University Press, 2002), I, pp. 12–13.

and (2) a tragedian (Boccaccio identified him as 'Marcus Seneca'). This false division was reinforced by other factors in the reception of Seneca's life and in the transmission of his texts.[17]

In the manuscript tradition, the tragedies were transmitted separately from the prose works. Commentators and biographers of the Middle Ages and Renaissance knew Seneca in part through the biographical sketch by St Jerome (*De Viris Illustribus* 12), which portrayed Seneca as a friend to Christianity, due to the existence of letters supposedly exchanged between Seneca and St Paul (still extant, but now regarded as a fourth-century forgery), but this sketch was only ever attached to manuscripts of the prose works. Some scholars also perceived basic differences in style or in quality between the tragedies (or at least some of the tragedies) and the prose works. Furthermore, *Octavia*, transmitted together with Seneca's tragedies and generally accepted at that time as all being by the same author, portrayed Seneca the statesman as a character – surely not an autobiographical perspective. Biographers such as Sicco Polenton (*c.* 1437) identified the tragedian as a son of Seneca who wrote the tragedies to avenge his father by criticizing Nero. When Erasmus published his major edition, *L. Annei Senecae Opera* (Brussels, 1529), a collection that includes the declamations (of Seneca the Elder) along with the philosophical works (of Seneca the Younger), he excluded the tragedies. As it happens, Erasmus's view was that the tragedies were by more than one author, and this view persisted on the continent at least until the end of the sixteenth century.[18]

In the latter half of the sixteenth century in England, however, many of the common understandings of Seneca were in transition. Earlier in the century it was recognized (indeed, by Erasmus) that Seneca could not have converted to Christianity, and most English authors accepted this. (Only a few, such as William Baldwin writing in the late 1540s, still referred to the forged letters between

---

[17] Another complication was the fact that the declamations were not recognized as the work of Seneca the Elder until the end of the sixteenth century. On the reception of Seneca's philosophical works, see G. M. Ross, 'Seneca's Philosophical Influence', in *Seneca,* ed. by C. D. N. Costa (London: Routledge, 1974), pp. 116–65, and on Senecan biographies, Lutezia A. Panizza, 'Biography in Italy from the Middle Ages to the Renaissance: Seneca, Pagan or Christian?', *Nouvelles de la république des lettres*, 2 (1984), 47–98.

[18] Mayer, pp. 152–53.

Seneca and Paul as fact.)[19] But the new consensus was that Seneca was a proto-Christian or 'Christian ethnic', as he is called by Neville and Studley in the 1560s.[20] This made Seneca's example not less but more relevant to Christian audiences: Edward Aggas observes that Christians ought to be inspired by Seneca's attitude toward death, since he espoused it even without possessing the assurances of Christian doctrine.[21] In his 1614 translation of Seneca's prose works Thomas Lodge describes how Seneca, with his 'divine sentences, wholesome counsels, serious exclamations against vices, in being but a heathen, may make us ashamed being Christians'.[22]

On the question of the 'two Senecas', authors of this period exhibit more than one view. Lodge, writing in 1579, states that 'Seneca, though a stoic, would have a poetical son',[23] and the division between the prose and tragic Senecas, whether or not it is explicitly stated, appears to be common to most authors who were concerned primarily with translating Seneca's prose writings, such as Aggas and Golding. On the other hand, some of the translators of Seneca's tragedies clearly view their author as the same person as the philosophical writer. In his preface to *Oedipus*, Neville explains that the play was 'written by the most grave, virtuous and Christian ethnic Seneca (for so doubteth not *Erasmus* to term him) Lucius Annaeus Seneca'.[24] Newton also links the two, writing in the dedicatory epistle to the *Tenne Tragedies* that Seneca's 'philosophical sentences [...] beateth sin down', like Neville linking the plays and the prose.[25]

---

[19] William Baldwin, *Treatise of Morall Phylosophie* (London: [Edward Whitchurch, 1547]), sig. H6ᵛ.
[20] Alexander Neville, *Lamentable Tragedie of Oedipus* (London: Thomas Colwell, 1563), sig. A3ʳ; John Studley, *Seuenth Tragedie of Seneca, Entituled Medea* (London: Thomas Colwell, [1566]), sig. A2ᵛ.
[21] Edward Aggas, *Defence of Death Contayning a Moste Excellent Discourse of Life and Death* (London: John Allde for Edward Aggas, 1576), sig. A4ʳ.
[22] Thomas Lodge, *Workes of Lucius Annaeus Seneca, both Morrall and Naturall* (London: William Stansby, 1614), sig. B4ʳ.
[23] Thomas Lodge, 'Protogenes Can Know Apelles' [Reply to *School of Abuse*] ([London: H[ugh] Singleton?, 1579]), sig. A1ʳ.
[24] Neville, *Oedipus*, sig. a3ʳ.
[25] Newton, 'To the Right Worshipful Sir Thomas Heneage Knight' in *Tenne Tragedies*, sig. A4ʳ. Seneca, a character in Matthew Gwinne's neo-Latin play *Nero* (1603), quotes lines from the plays and prose; Gwinne perhaps felt that the philosopher and tragedian were one and the same. By the 1670s, Milton held that

For the dramatic translators, Seneca's tragedies were closely tied to his style of moralizing prose. In a poem 'to the Reader' printed as a preface to Studley's *Agamemnon*, W. Parker lauds Seneca, '[w]hose saws profound, whoso thereon do look, / To virtue's race do show a ready way' (ll. 22–24). Newton also links the tragedies with virtuous 'saws':

> I doubt whether there be any among all the catalogue of heathen writers that with more gravity of philosophical sentences, more weightiness of sappy words, or greater authority of sound matter beateth down sin, loose life, dissolute dealing, and unbridled sensuality, or that more sensibly, pithily, and bitingly layeth down the guerdon of filthy lust, cloaked dissimulation and odious treachery, which is the drift whereunto he leveleth the whole issue of each one of his tragedies.[26]

This approach to the tragedies is in tune with contemporary assumptions about the moral purpose of the prose works. Arthur Golding, for example, in the dedicatory epistle to *De Beneficiis*, remarks: '[Seneca's] sentences are short, quick and full of matter; his words sharp, pithy and unaffected; his whole order of writing grave, deep and severe; fitted altogether to the reforming of men's minds and not to the delighting of their ears'.[27]

Sixteenth-century English writers also built on the image of Seneca as someone who tried to hold in check the worst impulses of Nero, and the tragedies as veiled political commentary on the excesses of Nero and other Julio-Claudian rulers. Thomas More's *Utopia* (1516) favourably mentions Seneca as he is represented in *Octavia* – that is, as an outspoken counsellor to Nero.[28] In a brief biography of Seneca, William Baldwin mentions Nero's tyranny three times, noting that Seneca chose to kill himself when he saw

---

the philosopher wrote at least some of the tragedies, writing in the 'Preface' to *Samson Agonistes* that 'Seneca the philosopher is by some thought the author of those tragedies (at least the best of them) that go under that name'; see *Complete Poetry of John Milton*, rev. edn, ed. by John T. Shawcross (New York: Anchor Books, 1963), p. 574.

[26] Newton, sigs. A3ᵛ–A4ʳ.

[27] Arthur Golding, 'To the Right Honourable Sir Christopher Hatton, Knight' in *The Woorke of the Excellent Philosopher Lucius Annaeus Seneca Concerning Benefyting* (London: [John Kingston for] John Day, 1578), sig. *2ᵛ.

[28] Thomas More, *Utopia*, 3ʳᵈ edn, ed. and trans. by George M. Logan (New York: W. W. Norton, 2011), p. 33.

that Nero's 'tyranny could not be appeased'.[29] In *Discourses upon Seneca the Tragedian* (1601), Sir William Cornwallis comments on the moral and political sayings in the plays, copying out lines on kingship and then explicating their meaning. By the end of the sixteenth century, it was this latter aspect of Seneca's legacy that was arguably most important, as poetic treatises came to describe tragedy as a form of political guidance (see 'Reception and Influence' below).

This understanding of the moral and political purpose of the tragedies was tied in a general way to Seneca's profile as a moralist, but not specifically to his Stoicism. The notion that the tragedies' ethics and metaphysics corresponded in a direct way to Stoic doctrine did not arise until the writings of the Jesuit Martin Delrio (1551–1608) at the end of the sixteenth century – and then only as part of Delrio's criticism of Senecan tragedy as irreconcilable with Christianity, especially given the Jesuits' use of drama for didactic purposes.[30]

Specific traditions of textual transmission, commentary, and translation also shaped the translators' understanding of Seneca and his writings. A discussion of these traditions, as well as notes on instances where they help to explain differences between the Elizabethan translations and modern versions of Seneca's plays, appears in the Appendix on 'The Translators' Latin Sources'.

Senecan Tragedy and Criticism. Seneca's plays were different in type from their Greek originals, and it is a matter of great consequence that the Elizabethan dramatists learned tragedy primarily through Seneca rather than through Aeschylus, Sophocles, and Euripides. Greek tragedy did not have the rigid five-act structure that Seneca passed on to the Elizabethans; its choruses were more likely to be participants or close observers than the more detached commentators found in Seneca, and certain stage conventions that are frequent in Seneca are rare or non-existent in Greek tragedy, such as the aside spoken by a character who is entering.[31] The distinctive structural and thematic elements of Senecan tragedy include the relative absence of the gods and of

---

[29] Baldwin, *Treatise*, sig. H7ᵛ.

[30] On the influence of Delrio's *Syntagma tragoediae latinae* (1594–95), see Mayer, esp. pp. 159–67.

[31] On these and other distinctive features, see R. J. Tarrant, 'Senecan Tragedy and Its Antecedents', *Harvard Studies in Classical Philology*, 82 (1978), 213–63.

the social world, with a tighter focus on underworld forces, moral psychology, the power of rhetoric, and fortune (often personified as Fortune, evoking the Roman goddess 'Fortuna'). Seneca's preoccupation with the supernatural and with revenge is evident in the three plays in the present volume, all of which feature a vengeful ghost in a prologue (*Thyestes, Agamemnon*) or early in the play (*Troas*). These Senecan elements were all taken seriously by Elizabethan readers as defining the anatomy of classical tragedy, and their influence continues to this day.

Elizabethan views of Senecan tragedy bear only a qualified resemblance to the traditions of interpretation that have developed since then. In the nineteenth century, for example, Senecan tragedy came to be unfavourably compared with Greek tragedy as derivative bombast. The distinctive elements of Senecan dramatic technique mentioned above began to be used by critics as a framework for drawing contrasts between Greek and Latin drama, with questions raised about whether Seneca's tragedies could be considered tragic drama at all, being seen as declamatory dramas on trite themes. Such views are evident in T. S. Eliot's observation: 'In the plays of Seneca, the drama is all in the word, and the word has no further reality behind it. His characters all seem to speak with the same voice, and at the top of it; they recite in turn'.[32] Seneca's reputation as a dramatist has been undermined in part by the absence of decisive evidence that his tragedies were performed in antiquity rather than being written only for recitation or private reading.[33]

Even as some critics disparaged Senecan drama, however, others began the process of assessing them in more positive ways, paying particular attention to their literary-historical context and their style and technique. For example, in a pivotal 1930 essay Otto Regenbogen sought to explain Seneca's focus on suffering and death as catering to first-century Romans' anxieties about their social world. An essay on 'Senecan Tragedy' by C. J. Herington (1966) set out to describe the schematic architecture of Seneca's plays: in the course of each play he sees a movement from 'The

---

[32] Eliot, p. ix.

[33] For a review of the debate see Cedric J. Littlewood, *Self-Representation and Illusion in Senecan Tragedy* (Oxford: Oxford University Press, 2004), pp. 1–7; John G. Fitch, 'Playing Seneca', in *Seneca in Performance*, ed. by George W. M. Harrison (London: George Duckworth & Co., 2000), pp. 1–12.

Cloud of Evil' to 'The Defeat of Reason by Passion' to 'The Explosion of Evil'.[34] In the decades since, Senecan tragedy has come to be taken more seriously as a chapter in the history of ancient drama, and indeed of Latin poetry. The supposedly threadbare aesthetics of Seneca's dramas have been appreciated anew as the independent creative endeavours that they are; their motifs borrowed from the poetry of the Augustan poets Virgil and Ovid are recognized as sophisticated exercises in intertextuality, just as their reworkings of the mythic plots, with their insights on the psychology of the 'self', are understood as probing explorations of evil and human suffering. Seneca's self-consciously belated characters whose dark interior feelings are writ large on the chaotic cosmic landscape, characters rhetorically adept at rationalizing their wrong and violent acts, are now read as cultural productions responsive to the interests of elite audiences in the Early Imperial period – a world dominated by the Julio-Claudian court, the city of Rome, and the geopolitics of empire.[35]

There have also been efforts recently to articulate more subtly the relationship between Seneca's tragedies and his philosophical prose. For some scholars, the tragedies are meant to reinforce Stoic rationalism and providentialism by negative example, showing what happens when someone allows fortune (or Fortune) to exercise power over his or her state of mind; for others, the tragedies are a separate sphere of literary endeavour with no necessary philosophical status; for others again, the tragedies implicitly or even explicitly subvert the ideal of moral invulnerability projected in the prose works.[36] The nature of the Senecan chorus, too, has been vigorously debated: it is now difficult to argue that its moralizing voice is to be identified directly with Seneca's, as often the chorus seems as misguided as some of the characters. And in the choral odes Seneca's complex

---

[34] Otto Regenbogen, 'Schmerz und Tod in den Tragödien Senecas', in *Kleine Schriften* (Munich: Beck, 1961), pp. 409–62; C. J. Herington, 'Senecan Tragedy', *Arion*, 5 (1966), 422–71 (pp. 449–57).

[35] For a sample of these approaches see 'Further Reading' below.

[36] See especially Thomas G. Rosenmeyer, *Senecan Drama and Stoic Cosmology* (Berkeley: University of California Press, 1989). But for a thorough (and sceptical) scrutiny of the Stoic aspect of the tragedies, see Mayer, pp. 151; 174; Harry M. Hine, '*Interpretatio Stoica* of Senecan Tragedy', in *Sénèque le tragique*, ed. by Margarethe Billerbeck and Ernst A. Schmidt (Geneva: Fondation Hardt, 2004), pp. 173–220.

reworking of lyric form (especially that of Horace) is now understood to be in service of varying goals in each play, and indeed in each ode.[37]

This renewed critical energy is evident in the burgeoning of recent modern commentaries on Seneca's plays, as well as translations and productions.[38] As indicated above, this renaissance is not identical to the Elizabethan Renaissance. The Elizabethan translators' sense of the moral and political purpose of the tragedies was more unified than in present accounts which point up the heterogeneity of Seneca's activities.

Studies of Early Elizabethan Seneca. The recent interest in Seneca among classicists has been accompanied by a new appreciation of the significance of Seneca's dramatic legacy in early Elizabethan England. While the translations have long been recognized as drawing new attention to Seneca in the period, recent critics have begun to emphasize the early translators' cultivation of Senecan tragedy as a mode for politically engaged dramatic counsel and commentary.[39] These thematic studies are important, since they help us to see the Senecan translations as precursors to later Elizabethan dramatic politics in new ways. (See sections on 'Reception and Influence' and 'Further Reading' below.)

The translators, however, made numerous micro-level decisions as they developed broader themes, political and otherwise. In terms of understanding these decisions, T. S. Eliot's introduction to the 1927 reprinting of the *Tenne Tragedies* continues to offer a valuable approach to the translations. Even as Eliot perpetuated nineteenth-century views of Seneca's plays as undramatic, he offered qualified appreciation of the distinctive features of Senecan tragedy and took seriously the translators' poetic enterprise.

For example, in describing their work, Eliot fastens upon the choruses as an area of 'less scrupulous' – that is, more creative – innovation, while also identifying other emphases overall:

---

[37] See Peter J. Davis, *Shifting Song: The Chorus in Seneca's Tragedies* (Hildesheim: Olms-Weidmann, 1993).

[38] On one modern production and the challenges involved, see several of the essays in *Seneca in Performance,* ed. by George W. M. Harrison (London: George Duckworth & Co., 2000).

[39] See n. 8 above and the discussion of 'Reception and Influence' below.

When they translate the dialogue they are literal to the best of their ability – occasional inaccuracies or mistranslations being admitted – but in the choruses they will sometimes lengthen or shorten, sometimes omit altogether, or substitute an invention of their own. On the whole, their alterations tend to make the play more dramatic; sometimes they may be suspected of adding a political innuendo to the Senecan moralising on the vanity of place and power. And it is especially in the choruses that we find, now and then, flashes of that felicity which is present in Tudor translation more perhaps than in the translations of any period into any language.[40]

It is striking that Eliot sees the translators as restoring some of the dramatic aspect that he finds wanting in Seneca. For Eliot, the 'literary value' of such particularities is inseparable from the translations' historical importance in mediating the influence of Senecan tragedy on Elizabethan tragedy.[41] But tracing this influence requires the reader to pay heed to the individual moments and larger patterns in the translations, since in Eliot's words, 'the distortion' – what we might call the adaptation – 'of Seneca begins in his translation'.[42]

In our notes on the texts, we follow Eliot's lead and offer a detailed guide to this process. Our goal is to aid readers in reading the three selected translations not only with clear comprehension but also with an understanding of how each work functions both as an exercise in translation and as an individual poetic work in its own right. For as much as the dramatic translators echoed, furthered, and gave force to medieval and early Renaissance views of and debates about Seneca's life and works, each one also shaped and constructed Seneca for a new time, making his works relevant to themselves and for English readers in the mid-sixteenth century. In so doing, they shaped the texts in relation to their specific backgrounds (religious, educational, and literary) as well as their own interests and aims. And it is to these individual translators and texts that we now turn.

---

[40] Eliot, pp. lii–liii.
[41] Ibid., esp. p. vi.
[42] Ibid., p. xlix.

JASPER HEYWOOD'S *TROAS* AND *THYESTES*

With *Troas* in 1559, Jasper Heywood became the first writer to publish a translation of one of Seneca's plays in England. His unprecedented interest in Seneca developed out of his taste for moralizing literature as well as a personal interest in the themes of Seneca's plays, and also perhaps his Catholicism; and each translation helped him to represent himself in different ways as a scholar and tragic poet.

Life. Jasper Heywood was born in London in 1535, part of a notable Catholic intellectual and literary family. He was the grandson of the law printer John Rastell, grand-nephew of Thomas More, and the son of the playwright and epigrammatist, John Heywood. His older brother was Ellis Heywood, who preceded Jasper as a Jesuit exile and published the treatise *Il Moro* in praise of their great-uncle Thomas in Florence in 1556. (Their youngest sister was Elizabeth Heywood, the mother of John Donne.)[43]

With these family connections, it is not surprising that Heywood was well-educated and a committed Catholic. Since his father was a musician and playwright in the court of Henry VIII, Heywood shared a tutor with Princess Elizabeth,[44] and in 1547, at the age of twelve, he proceeded to Oxford, where at Merton he took his BA in 1553 and his MA in 1558.

Heywood's next few years were tumultuous. In Dennis Flynn's words, 'conflict with authority was a hallmark of Heywood's career'.[45] In 1558, having been warned several times by John Reynolds, the warden of the College, about behavioural misdemeanours perhaps related to his position as the College's Christmas Lord of Misrule, he resigned his fellowship. Probably with the help of Sir John Mason, the privy councillor and Oxford chancellor to whom he would dedicate *Thyestes*, Heywood then

---

[43] Biographical information is from Dennis Flynn, 'Heywood, Jasper (1535–1598)', *DNB*, <http://www.oxforddnb.com/view/article/13182> [accessed 4 October 2011].

[44] Dennis Flynn, 'The English Mission of Jasper Heywood, S. J.', *Archivum historicum societatis Jesu*, 54 (1985), 45–76 (p. 45).

[45] Flynn, 'The English Mission of Jasper Heywood, S. J.', p. 45. On Heywood's temperament, as well as an overview of his writings in the context of his life, see also Flynn's *John Donne and the Ancient Catholic Nobility* (Bloomington: Indiana University Press, 1995), esp. pp. 36–53.

took a fellowship at All Souls.[46] Here, he completed his three Senecan translations. In 1561, he left Oxford because of conflicts with the College, this time because, as a devout Catholic, he refused to comply with Elizabethan religious reforms.

Heywood lived briefly with his uncle, William Rastell, at Gray's Inn in London, but in 1562 left England for Rome, where he became a Catholic priest. His later life continued to be marked by conflicts with authority; for instance, he refused to participate in the public disputation required for the doctorate at the University of Dillingen. Heywood joined the Jesuit mission of Edmund Campion and Robert Persons to England in 1581, but fell out with Persons after theological disagreements. He died in Naples in 1598.

Literary Activities. Heywood's interest in Seneca was in concert with his other verse. While at Oxford, he wrote shorter poems, earning a reputation as a 'quaint poet'.[47] His surviving poems appear in the *Paradise of Dainty Devises* (1576–1606). These are typical of the mid-Tudor period: serious, admonitory, monosyllabic, and deliberately lacking in intricate internal rhythms and elaborate conceits. Such 'plain' style has a moral dimension, in G. K. Hunter's words, 'stressing above all things the common lot that holds individual egotism in check'.[48]

In these poems, the narrators are not individuals; they are ventriloquists of paternalistic commonplaces. In one, the narrator advises readers to 'know thyself in each degree', 'Be friend to all, familiar to few', and warns 'Too light of credit, see thou never be'.[49] Several of these maxims probably derive from the *Disticha Catonis* (Couplets of Cato),[50] but the injunction to 'know thyself'

---

[46] In his 'Preface' to *Thyestes*, dedicated to Mason, Heywood mentions that Mason 'failed not to help and succour' him (line 174). This aid possibly involved Heywood's move to All Souls.

[47] Anthony à Wood, *Athenae Oxonienses* (London: Thomas Bennet, 1691), column 251.

[48] G. K. Hunter, 'Drab and Golden Lyrics of the Renaissance', in *Forms of Lyric: Selected Papers from the English Institute*, ed. by Reuben A. Brower (New York: Columbia University Press, 1970), pp. 1–18.

[49] *Paradise of Dainty Devises, 1576–1606*, ed. by Hyder Edward Rollins (Cambridge, MA: Harvard University Press, 1927), poem 12 (p. 15, ll. 6–8). Rollins restarts the line numbers on every page (instead of for every poem); thus further references to this volume are to numbered poems followed by the page and line numbers where the quoted passage appears.

[50] *Paradise*, p. 190 at n. 15.6

was a sixteenth-century commonplace, and the whole poem may have been a source for Polonius's advice to his son Laertes in *Hamlet*. Heywood's other verse is similarly admonitory, and a favourite theme concerns the caprices of fortune for those in positions of authority. In 'Who Waiteth on this Wavering World', one learns that 'who so climbs above the mean, there is no hope of stay, / The higher up the sooner down and nearer his decay'. He thus advises those in power: 'Then you that here in pomp or place to guide the golden mace, / Let crown and sceptre both obey the mean of virtue's race'.[51]

In view of Heywood's aesthetics, it is not surprising that he sought to translate Seneca, a writer also known for his sententiousness. Moreover, Seneca's plays often deal with fortune, and key terms in Heywood's own verse such as 'wavering', 'pomp' and 'sceptre' appear as well in his translations (see *Troas*, *'Translation Style'* below).

Heywood may have identified with these subjects on a personal level: he translated Seneca during a time when he experienced reversals of fortune related to his conflicts with the heads of his Colleges (see *'Life'* above). His run-ins with authority echoed, albeit in a distant way, Seneca's experiences at court, as well as the experiences of the title characters of the three plays he chose to translate. All of them cope with terrible misfortune, suffered in whole or in part at the hands of someone else.[52]

Yet, as similar as Heywood's chosen plays are in theme and tone, they are striking for the differences they demonstrate in Heywood's approach, style, and aims. Here we look more closely at the two texts included in this volume, *Troas* and *Thyestes*.

Troas

While *Troas* was a turning point in Renaissance literary history, most immediately for Heywood it was a bid for recognition through literary innovation in a strongly political genre. He sought

---

[51] Poem 100 (p. 100, ll. 3–4).

[52] In choosing to translate Seneca, Heywood may also have been influenced by the dramatic tradition at Jesuit colleges and universities on the continent, where neo-Latin plays modelled on Seneca were an important part of the curriculum. See n. 12 above.

to turn *Troas* into something more than the original, adding passages to shape the play into a 'speculum principis' (mirror for the prince), a genre of writing that seeks to instruct rulers in appropriate rule or behaviour by providing specific examples to imitate or avoid. Some of these passages were his own, but often he used Seneca's other plays as a source. Below we introduce Seneca's play, its mythological background and plot, and then return to these points in sections on Heywood's prefatory materials, influences, and translation style.

Seneca's 'Troades' (Trojan Women). The play is set in the aftermath of the fall of Troy, as queen Hecuba and the other Trojan women react to their past, present, and future sufferings at the hands of the Greeks. It culminates in the sacrifices of Astyanax and Polyxena, two children of the Trojan royal household whom the Greeks believe they must kill in order to return home safely. The theme had been dealt with many times before in Greek and Roman tragedy, most notably in Euripides' *Trojan Women* and *Hecuba*, but Seneca appears to have innovated in treating the Astyanax and Polyxena stories in close parallel within one play.

Seneca's work was part of the broader revival of Trojan themes in Roman literature and art of the Augustan and Imperial periods that is most conspicuous in Virgil's *Aeneid*, which traced how the fugitive Trojan Aeneas came to found the city of Rome as well as the Julian household through which the Julio-Claudian emperors down to Nero would trace their descent. As a tragedy, however, *Troades* explored Troy's aftermath in a less teleological mode. It is a study in the collective experience of destruction and grief caused by arbitrary powers, and in the limited forms of resistance available to victims in the form of self-consolation or by dying nobly. As in much first-century Latin literature, these experiences are presented with a particular emphasis on spectacle, inviting implicit comparisons to the experience of victims and spectators in the Roman amphitheatre. Heywood takes this spectacular aspect one step further, turning the play into a 'mirror' and inviting the queen to consider the play's examples of kingly misfortune.[53]

---

[53] On *Troades* and its modern interpretation, see 'Further Reading' below.

Mythological Background. The play unfolds in the aftermath of the Trojan War, and characters regularly allude to some of the war's causes and major events.

The war's origins go back at least to the birth of Paris, the son of the Trojan king and queen, Priam and Hecuba. When Hecuba was pregnant with Paris, she dreamed she would give birth to a fire-brand which would be the ruin of Troy. As a young man, Paris judged the beauty contest between the three goddesses Hera, Athena, and Aphrodite (the Judgement of Paris), and for giving the prize of a golden apple to Aphrodite he was awarded Helen. Paris took Helen away from her husband Menelaus in Sparta and brought her back to Troy (with or without her consent – the accounts vary).

Menelaus and his brother Agamemnon, King of Argos, retaliated by raising a Greek fleet against the Trojans. When the Greeks could not set sail owing to a lack of wind, Agamemnon sacrificed his daughter Iphigenia on the instructions of the prophet Calchas. The Greek force included Ulysses, King of Ithaca, known for his cunning, and Achilles, the greatest Greek warrior, known also for his melancholy reluctance to fight. (Even before arriving in Troy, Achilles had hidden, disguised as a woman, on the island of Scyros). During the ten-year war, Agamemnon was forced to give up Chryseis, daughter of Chryses, priest of Apollo, after Apollo sent a plague against the Greeks. Agamemnon then took Briseis, Achilles' prize, as compensation, prompting Achilles to withdraw from battle; he returned only after his friend, Patroclus, was killed by Hector, the son of Priam. Once Achilles re-entered the war, the tide of battle turned, decisively so when Achilles killed Hector and dragged his body behind his chariot around the walls of Troy. At the request of Priam, Achilles ransomed Hector's body back to the Trojans. Achilles himself died later, although not in battle: when he had been promised the hand of Polyxena, daughter of Priam and Hecuba, he was ambushed by Paris.

The Trojans were finally defeated after they took inside their walls the Trojan Horse, filled with Greek soldiers who emerged at night to raze the city. During the night of Troy's destruction, Priam sought safety at the altar of Jove but was killed by Achilles' son, Pyrrhus. Foremost among the surviving Trojans were Hecuba and her daughter Polyxena, as well as Andromache, Hector's wife, and her son Astyanax, whom the Greeks feared would grow up to avenge his father. After the events presented in *Troades*, Hecuba, allotted to Ulysses, was turned into a snarling dog.

Plot. Seneca's play begins after Troy's destruction, as the Trojan women reflect on their misfortune and the Greeks prepare to sail home. In the outline here, we note Heywood's major structural additions and deletions in italics.

Act 1: Hecuba laments the destruction of Troy.

Chorus: In responsion, Hecuba and the Chorus of Trojan women mourn Hector and Priam. *Heywood retains this chorus within Act 1 as 'Scene 2' and adds a new chorus on the vulnerability of all kings to misfortune.*

Act 2: *Heywood adds a scene in which the ghost of Achilles appears.* Talthybius, a Greek herald, reports having seen the ghost of Achilles rise up and threaten storms against the Greeks' voyage home if they do not sacrifice Polyxena on his grave. The demand is debated by Agamemnon and Pyrrhus. The prophet Calchas adjudicates, confirming the demand for Polyxena and reporting that Astyanax also must die.

Chorus: The Chorus expresses doubt about the existence of ghosts and whether there is life after death.

Act 3: Andromache, having been warned by the dead Hector in a dream, seeks to conceal Astyanax in Hector's grave. Ulysses arrives to retrieve Astyanax. Andromache pretends that Astyanax is dead, but when Ulysses threatens to destroy Hector's grave she gives him up.

Chorus: The Chorus of Trojan women speculate on the different parts of the Greek world to which they will each be taken by their captors. *Heywood replaces this chorus with a section from Seneca's 'Phaedra', together with some freely composed lines, on the vulnerability of all things to fortune.*

Act 4: Helen retrieves Polyxena, pretending that she is to be married to Pyrrhus, but soon divulges the truth, including information about the Greeks to whom the other Trojan women have been allotted.

Chorus: The Chorus of Trojan women seek comfort in one another as they prepare to be shipped off to different destinations.

Act 5: A Messenger reports on the deaths of the two children, which were watched with equal admiration and sympathy by Trojans and Greeks: Astyanax nobly jumped from the top of a tower before he could be thrown, and Polyxena threw herself to the ground while being butchered on Achilles' grave. The Greeks prepare to set sail.

Prefaces. Heywood altered Seneca's *Troades* in significant ways. The three original prefaces suggest a motive for these interventions, signalling that the translation is a hesitant but nonetheless ambitious attempt to garner recognition as a tragic poet.

This combination of hesitance and ambition is present in the first two prefaces, a dedication to Queen Elizabeth and a 'Preface to the Readers'. Downplaying any ambition, Heywood describes himself as 'a simple scholar' and 'a rash young man' (Dedication, lines 12–13), and *Troas* as a mere 'private exercise' (Preface, line 11). He also conveys ambitions well beyond what a mere 'exercise' might imply.[54] He dedicates the work to the monarch and draws attention to ways in which the text is also his own, listing his substantial changes (see *'Plot'* above). Such changes are consistent with translation practices in the period, but they alert the reader that Heywood altered the text to his own ends.

In his 'Preface to the Readers', Heywood espouses a dynamic and capacious conception of what translation *is*: he sought 'to keep touch with the Latin, not word for word or verse for verse as to expound it, but neglecting the placing of the words observed their sense'. In keeping with the humility topos, this statement serves as an excuse for the flaws in the translation, which he says are due variously to his youth, the translation's origin as an 'exercise', his lack of eloquence, the poverty of the English language, his failure 'to touch at full in all points the author's mind (being in many places very hard and doubtful and the work much corrupt by the default of evil printed books)', Seneca's excellence as 'the flower of all writers', and 'the royalty of speech' needed in a tragedy. Yet in observing 'sense' and neglecting correspondences at the level of word and verse, Heywood also claims significant creative licence as a translator. One indication of this licence is his account of the things he has added and changed because the play is 'in some places unperfect' or because some passages 'should have no grace

---

[54] Heywood's audacity is slightly less than it might initially seem. Heywood knew Elizabeth from his boyhood at court (see *'Life'* above) and presented *Troas* to her at New Year, a time when people of many different ranks gave gifts to the queen. He also justifies this presentation of Seneca in particular: the queen, he notes, delights in the 'sweet sap of fine and pure writers' (line 26), and especially enjoys Seneca (lines 32–33). See n. 12 above.

in the English tongue, but be a strange and unpleasant thing to my readers' (see further below on *'Translation Style'*).

Another assertion of creative licence is Heywood's invocation of a fury as muse, which he does in his 'Preface to the Tragedy', an original poem of nearly 100 lines in *rime royale* in which he more explicitly presents himself as a tragic poet. Consistent with the other prefaces, Heywood initially emphasizes the modesty of his enterprise. He lists authors, including Homer and Virgil, who have written about the Trojan War, stating that he will 'overpass' tales of 'targe and shield' to develop a more personal theme: 'mothers' tears' and 'blood of babes that guiltless have been slain' (38–42). Yet Heywood also elevates himself and this subject matter, aligning the translation with Chaucer's *Troilus and Criseyde* (*c.* 1380s), a poem that also concerns a more personal story of the Trojan War. He invokes a similar muse to Chaucer, who appeals to 'Thesiphone', one of three avenging furies, to help him to write 'woful vers', which makes him 'wepen' as he writes.[55] Using similar language of weeping and woefulness, Heywood asks a 'fury fell' to 'guide' his 'hand and pen' to write 'in weeping verse of sobs and sighs'.[56] Chaucer may be wryly hyperbolic, but Heywood is serious. Seneca is the original author, but Heywood presents himself as a solemn, tragic poet in his own right.[57]

Influences. Heywood's additions are part of the project of fashioning himself as a tragic poet, allowing him to transform the play into a 'speculum principis' (mirror for the prince). Two additions illustrate this larger pattern. In an added chorus, Heywood states that Hecuba '[a] mirror is to teach you what you are, / Your wavering wealth, O princes, here is seen' (1.Cho.55–56). Later, Agamemnon observes, also in an added line, that Priam is 'a cause of pride, a glass of fear, a mirror for the nones' (3.3.74).

In developing this 'mirror', Heywood emphasizes the theme of kings' vulnerability to fortune, and in his 'freely composed' passages on this theme he frequently uses lines from elsewhere in Seneca. We indicate many of these debts in the notes, but here is one telling example: in the third chorus, Heywood writes: 'Chance

---

[55] See Book 1, 6–7. References to Chaucer are to *The Riverside Chaucer*, 3rd edn, ed. by Larry D. Benson (Boston: Houghton Mifflin, 1987).
[56] Ibid., lines 50–56.
[57] Studley also echoes *Troilus and Criseyde,* see n. at *Agamemnon* 5.5.19–20.

beareth rule in every place, / And turneth man's estate at will' (3.Cho.15–16). The line is a reworking of Seneca's *Phaedra*: 'Res humanas ordine nullo / Fortuna regit' (Fortune rules human affairs with no semblance of order, *Pha.* 978–79). The number of Senecan references shows that Heywood not only interprets *Troas* as a play about fortune, but also feels justified in drawing on the rest of Seneca's oeuvre to enhance the theme.[58]

Heywood's emphasis on the 'unfortunate prince' aspect of *Troas* likely relates to the contemporaneous publication of the *Mirror for Magistrates*. Compiled by William Baldwin and a group of seven other writers in the 1550s, the *Mirror* contains didactic tragedies about the downfalls of English kings, nobles, and pretenders to power between the reigns of Richard II and Edward IV. Originally conceived as an extension of John Lydgate's massive *Fall of Princes* (*c.* 1431–39), itself a translation and expansion of Boccaccio's *De casibus virorum illustrium* (*c.* 1358) via Laurent de Premierfait's French prose translation, *Des cas des nobles hommes et femmes* (*c.* 1409), the *Mirror* appears as an admonition to princes, nobles, and others in positions of power and authority. Baldwin thus explains to nobles in an opening preface: 'For here as in a looking glass, you shall see (if any vice be in you) how the like hath been punished heretofore, whereby admonished, I trust it will be a good occasion to move you to the sooner amendment'.[59] The *Mirror* was an immediately important and influential work, appearing in a revised and expanded version in 1563 and in further expanded editions through the rest of the sixteenth century. Heywood knew the *Mirror*: in his 'Preface' to *Thyestes* (95–96), he praises it by name. Since the *Mirror* appeared in print in 1559, the same year as *Troas*, Heywood could have known the work in earlier form.[60]

Heywood's additions align *Troas* with the *Mirror*, especially in terms of the central theme of the latter work, the capriciousness of fortune. For instance, in the *Mirror's* tragedy of Thomas of Woodstock, Duke of Gloucester, the duke complains that '[w]hen

---

[58] See Winston and Ker, 'A Note on Jasper Heywood's "Free Compositions" in *Troas* (1559)', forthcoming in *Modern Philology*, 110:4 (2013).

[59] Lily B. Campbell, ed., *Mirror for Magistrates*, (New York: Barnes and Noble, 1938), pp. 65–66. Further references will be to line numbers in this edition.

[60] The *Mirror* is a revision of *A Memorial All Such Princes*, which was suppressed by the Privy Council on its initial publication *c.* 1554. Only a few sheets of it survive today.

forward Fortune list for to frown', a person who seems to be firmly established and secure in his high position 'may in a moment turn upside down'.[61] Heywood likewise accentuates this theme, writing for instance, at the end of his newly composed first chorus, about the 'stealth' (i.e. the unpredictability) of fortune, which he terms 'chance':

> Who weeneth here to win eternal wealth,
> Let him behold this present perfit proof,
> And learn the secret step of Chance's stealth,
> Most near alas when most it seems aloof.
> In slipper joy let no man put his trust;
> Let none despair that heavy haps hath passed. (33–38)

The first four lines are freely composed, while the last two are direct translations from Seneca's *Thyestes* (615–16). All six echo the *Mirror*, casting the theme of fortune as a lesson for anyone, but especially those who seek 'wealth' and high rank.

Heywood echoes the *Mirror* through his metre as well. The predominant metre in the translation is fourteener couplets, but Heywood also employs *rime royale*, a seven-line scheme (ababbcc), which in England goes back at least to Chaucer (who used the metre in *Troilus*) and to Lydgate, who used the metre in the *Fall*. It is also the most common verse form in the *Mirror*, where it appears in all of the tragedies of the 1559 edition except, intriguingly, those of the three monarchs (Richard II, Henry VI, Edward IV). Heywood uses the metre in the 'Preface to the Tragedy', the added speech of Achilles (2.1), the second chorus, and fourth chorus, all passages that emphasize fluctuations in rulers' fortunes beyond the control of mere mortals.

Translation Style. As he shaped *Troas* into a 'mirror', Heywood made significant choices concerning how to 'set forth' Seneca's Latin tragedy in English verse. As he explains in his 'Preface', Heywood gave priority to Seneca's 'sense' and tragedy's 'royalty of speech' rather than to translating 'word for word or verse for verse'. In practice this means that the translation adds material in order to explain, enhance, or complete the play, often taking its

---

[61] Lily B. Campbell, ed., *Mirror for Magistrates*, p. 91.

inspiration – and indeed whole passages – from other Senecan plays.[62]

At a basic level, Heywood's *Troas* corresponds fairly directly to Seneca's play. With a few notable exceptions, the characters and the Chorus speak at the same time and say the same things in the same order. Heywood conveys Senecan style and the 'royalty of speech' that distinguishes tragedy through his Latinate diction and syntax and also by rhetorical features such as alliteration, anaphora, and sententious brevity. The mythological and metaphysical structures of the original are retained – the pagan gods, the role of fortune, and the mythological background. In a number of instances (indicated in the notes), Heywood diverges from Seneca because he apparently misunderstood the Latin. In other cases, the difference from Seneca's play as it is presented in modern editions is due to his using the Gryphius edition, which rested on the A branch of the manuscript tradition (see the Appendix on 'The Translators' Latin Sources'). Often, however, his additions, subtractions, and substitutions on a line-by-line basis are deliberate attempts to make the play more accessible to his audience. Most basically, for example, 'Troy' is his standard translation of Seneca's various terms 'Troia', 'Ilium', and 'Pergamum'.

Yet Heywood uses linguistic and literary devices inventively to approximate Seneca's drama. Daalder observes that, 'like other excellent translators, Heywood works on the principle that where one cannot retain the original's effect in one's own language in one place, one will try to do so in another'.[63] An example is his approach to metre. Heywood approximates Seneca's use of iambic trimetres (usually twelve syllables) in his choice of iambic fourteeners for dialogue, and also follows Seneca in using other, varied metres for choral passages or lyric passages uttered by main characters (Hecuba, 1.2; Andromache, 3.2). At the same time, he

---

[62] Here we build on analyses of *Troas* by Ernst Jockers, 'Die englischen Seneca-Uebersetzer des 16. Jahrhunderts' (doctoral thesis, Strassburg, Druckerei der Strassburger Neuesten Nachrichten A.-G., 1909), pp. 1–40; Evelyn Spearing, *The Elizabethan Translations of Seneca's Tragedies* (London: W. Heffer and Sons, 1912), pp. 13–19; H. de Vocht, *Jasper Heywood and His Translations of Seneca's 'Troas', 'Thyestes', and 'Hercules Furens'* (Louvain: A. Uystpruyst, 1913), pp. xxvii–xxxiii; and John O'Keefe, 'An Analysis of Jasper Heywood's Translations of *Troas, Thyestes,* and *Hercules Furens*' (unpublished doctoral thesis, Loyola University, Chicago, 1974), pp. 54–115.

[63] Daalder, p. xliii.

draws upon specific metrical forms and rhyming patterns which are an existing part of English tradition with no direct correlate in Latin poetry or in Seneca's given phrasing.[64] In doing so, he 'translates' Seneca's verse techniques into comparable, but not identical, English forms.

Heywood exaggerates those formal and thematic elements that are most important to him. Below we illustrate some of his most consequential choices – as we will do also in our discussions of *Thyestes* and *Agamemnon* – by comparing the opening lines of the original and the translation, then by considering several representative moments from later in the play.

Here are the opening lines of Seneca's *Troades* spoken by Hecuba, followed by Heywood's translation, where words that lack a direct correlation in the Latin have been given in italics:

Quicumque regno fidit et magna potens
dominatur aula nec leves metuit deos
animumque rebus credulum laetis dedit,
me videat et te, Troia: non umquam tulit
documenta fors maiora, quam fragili loco
starent superbi.   (1–6)

Whoso in *pomp of proud estate or* kingdom sets delight,
Or who that *joys* in *prince's* court *to* bear *the sway of* might,
Ne dreads *the fates which from above* the wavering gods *down
     flings*,
But fast affiance *fixèd* hath in *frail and fickle* things,
Let him *in* me *both* see *the face of Fortune's flattering joy*,
And *eke respect the ruthful end of* thee (*O ruinous* Troy),
For never gave she plainer proof *than this ye present see*:
How frail *and brittle* is th'estate of pride *and high degree*. (1–8)

Most obviously, Heywood's translation is bigger, going from five-and-a-half lines to eight, nearly doubling the number of syllables (60 > 112) and tripling the number of words (33 > 91). Seneca's style, famously, is concentrated far beyond the inherent concision of the Latin language, but Heywood's English is itself unusually expansive.

We can explain some of Heywood's expansion in terms of verse technique. Although the fourteener itself is not much longer than

---

[64] On Heywood's metrical technique see Hardison, pp. 148–69.

Seneca's iambic trimetres (three pairs of iambic feet, so at least twelve syllables long), which sometimes 'resolve' into thirteen or fourteen syllables, he inflates phrases to fill whole lines. Seneca's first three words, for example, become a whole line in Heywood, and Heywood does not preserve Seneca's enjambments in lines 4–5 and 5–6. Heywood also adopts poetic techniques that were common in English, including line-by-line rhyming (not a feature of Latin poetry) and alliteration (here especially *p* and *f*), both of which fuel the proliferation of words.

Heywood's expansions are not simply formalistic. They stem from his effort to convey – even to write large – Seneca's sense. Several 'seed words' in Seneca inspire recurring language in Heywood: the adjectival doublets 'frail and fickle' and 'frail and brittle' correspond to the single word 'fragili' that comes late in the Seneca passage. 'Superbi' is Seneca's only reference to pride, but Heywood turns it into a framing emphasis, adding 'proud' in the first line and 'pride' in line eight, an instance of 'ring composition'. Heywood exaggerates divine agency to similar effect. In Seneca the gods are simply 'leves' (fickle, 'wavering'), whereas in Heywood they 'fling down' the 'fates'. He similarly intensifies fortune. Seneca mentions 'fors' once (5), but Heywood has Hecuba point to herself emphatically as an embodiment of fortune and misfortune.

Heywood is most active as an interpreter when he seeks to convey that the play can teach a lesson. Just as Heywood adds passages to emphasize the 'mirror' aspects of the play, he also adds similar emphases on the micro-level. In Seneca, Hecuba addresses 'anyone who trusts in a kingdom' (quicumque regno fidit) and 'in what a fragile place the proud stood' (quam fragili loco starent superbi). In Heywood, she elevates her reference to persons of high 'estate', a noun perhaps corresponding to 'starent' (stand) but perhaps alluding more directly to English society. Moreover, Hecuba's address to the audience, in the key phrase 'than this ye present see', is a bold intervention. Self-conscious metatheatrical reference is a recognized characteristic of Senecan tragedy, but Heywood makes this address far more explicit. He initiates a line of communication with the audience that is built upon in the later references to the play as a mirror discussed above.

Heywood's approach to other typical features of Senecan tragedy is equally interventionist. One recurring element in tragedy is stichomythia, line-for-line verbal repartee, in conflicts between two speakers, and in Seneca stichomythia is the prime venue for his characteristic *sententiae*. A representative passage occurs in the dialogue between Pyrrhus and Agamemnon over whether to sacrifice Polyxena to the dead Achilles:

> PYR. Mortem misericors saepe pro vita dabit.
> AGA. At nunc misericors virgines busto petis?
> PYR. Iamne immolari virgines credis nefas?   (*Tro.* 329–31)

> PYR. A point of mercy sometime is what lives in care to kill.
> AGA. But now your mercy moveth you a virgin's death to will?
> PYR. Account ye cruel now her death whose sacrifice I crave?
>   Your own dear daughter once ye know yourself to
>   th'altars gave.   (2.3.127–30)

Heywood seeks only partially to capture the concision and wordplay of the debate. For example, he conveys the parallel repetition of 'misericors' (merciful) and the use of rhetorical questions, but not the repetition of 'virgines'. His term 'cruel' only weakly renders 'nefas' (unspeakable crime against divine law), one of the central articulations of moral transgression in Senecan tragedy. Heywood's priorities lie elsewhere – for instance, in adding a line to clarify Pyrrhus's allusion to Agamemnon's earlier sacrifice of his daughter Iphigenia.

In Seneca, the choral passages are not only metrically different but also more markedly poetic, and Heywood adjusts his own style of translation accordingly, writing more freely there (as Eliot noted).[65] Here is a stanza from the second chorus, comparing the dissolution of the soul after death to the scattering of smoke or clouds:

> For as the fume that from the fire doth pass,
> With turn of hand, doth vanish out of sight,
> And swifter than the northern Boreas,
> With whirling blast and storm of raging might,
> Driv'th far away and puts the clouds to flight,
> So flee'th the sprite that rules our life away,
> And nothing tarry'th after dying day.
>   (2.Cho. 29–35 = *Tro.* 392–97)

---

[65] See pp. 14–15 above.

In these lines Heywood produces 'poetry of rough beauty'.[66] Some of the syntax, images, and words directly correspond to Seneca's, including 'fume' (fumus), 'vanish' (vanescit), and 'sprite' (spiritus). But Heywood adds images of his own (for example 'With turn of hand'), reorders clauses, and expands Seneca's five-and-a-half lines into the structure of the seven-line *rime royale*. This results in some striking reformulations: for example, where Seneca writes 'post mortem nihil est ipsaque mors nihil' (literally, 'after death there is nothing, and death itself [is] nothing', *Tro.* 397), in a paradoxical formulation underlined by the repetition of 'mors' (death). Heywood's final line instead compresses the separate phrases into one thought and gets this across without using the word 'death' even once.[67]

Heywood sometimes downgrades in importance whole lines that modern readers of Seneca have understood as key indicators of a characters' psychology. An example is in Act 5, where Andromache encourages the Messenger to describe the children's deaths, saying 'gaudet animus aerumnas meas / tractare totas' (my mind enjoys going over my woes in full, *Tro.* 1066–67). Heywood, perhaps uncomfortable with Andromache's seemingly perverse pleasure, elides the comment (5.1.10). Other interpreters, however, might see the line as a convincing characterization of Andromache's traumatized mind, and it certainly coheres with the focus on spectacle throughout Senecan tragedy. Heywood recognizes the spectacle focus overall, but he channels it in a different direction with his emphasis on the didactic role of the play as mirror.

The two aspects that Heywood most greatly amplifies in the play are, as noted above, the scene in which Achilles' ghost appears (2.1) and the choral passages that he either adds (1.Cho.), supplements (2.Cho.), or replaces by substitution (3.Cho.) – all of which he regards as remedies to imperfections, and all of which draw on materials from other Senecan plays. The ghost scene allows Heywood to give a greater degree of realism to the otherwise tacit presence of Achilles within the play, drawing on the

---

[66] O'Keefe, p. 101.

[67] This emphasis on the finality of death in this chorus posed significant interpretive problems for those who sought to reconcile Seneca with Christian theology; on varying approaches from Mussato to Delrio, see Mayer, pp. 156; 163.

ghost prologues of other Senecan plays (*Thyestes, Agamemnon*), as if to make *Troas* conform to an established Senecan pattern (for specific echoes, see the notes). This provides a starker metaphysical apparatus for *Troas*, dramatizing the theme of revenge more explicitly in a play where revenge would otherwise play a peripheral role.[68]

When Heywood remarks in the 'Preface to the Readers' that 'the Chorus is no part of the substance of the matter' (line 50), he thereby asserts that he is not changing the play itself, but rather the interpretive packaging that surrounds it. This line of thinking has interesting consequences. For example, it seems to inform his sense that the lyric exchange between Hecuba and the Chorus of Trojan women in Act 1 does not constitute a genuine choral ode (even if he does translate it in a lyric metre); this leads him to add a whole new ode by a more anonymous 'Chorus'. Likewise, the substituted chorus in Act 3 displaces the perspectives of the Trojan women who speculate on the places to which they will be taken, instead offering a more general perspective on the instability of fortune. In these changes Heywood makes the Chorus in *Troas* conform to the more detached choruses of Seneca's *Medea*, *Thyestes*, and *Phaedra*, who offer examples and observations that serve more as an interpretive sounding board than as a direct intervention in the action. At the same time, however, some of Heywood's additions to the chorus adopt a meta-spectatorial position: they allude to the function of the play as a mirror displaying the capriciousness of fortune (1.Cho.55), and the stanzas added to the end of Act 2 address 'Good Ladies' (2.Cho.64–70) – ostensibly the Trojan women, but an open-ended reference – and prepare them for further grief as they watch the following act.

With these techniques Heywood shaped *Troas* into a generalized instantiation of Senecan tragedy, incorporating features that were sometimes more characteristic of other plays in the Senecan corpus than of this individual play. In the process, he

---

[68] On the exaggeration of revenge, and ghosts, see Frederick Kiefer, 'Seneca Speaks in English: What the Elizabethan Translators Wrought', *Comparative Literature Studies*, 15 (1978), 372–87 (p. 385), and Daalder, pp. xxxiv–xxxvii. G.K. Hunter provides an alternative view: 'The ghosts who appear in Elizabethan plays may come from heaven or hell, but their interest is not (like Seneca's) in degrading and destroying humanity, but in achieving the satisfaction of justice seen to be done'. 'Seneca and English Tragedy', in *Seneca*, ed. by Costa, 166–204 (p. 179).

established a model for 'set[ting] forth' a Senecan tragedy that he and others would revise and refine.

Thyestes

For Heywood, *Thyestes* is a transition between the freely translated *Troas* and the more literally rendered *Hercules Furens*.[69] Yet it also seems part of another transition, his move from Oxford to the Inns of Court. In 1560, Heywood was at odds with Oxford authorities over his refusal to comply with religious reforms (see '*Life*' above). Although it would be another year before he left, one can see *Thyestes* as a valediction to his Oxford dedicatee and patron, Sir John Mason, and as an effort to connect with the literary network at the Inns, described at length in the 'Preface'. As we did with *Troas*, below we introduce Seneca's play, background, and plot, and then develop these points in discussions of the prefatory materials, influences, and translation style.

Seneca's 'Thyestes'. The play presents Atreus, the king of the Greek city of Argos, taking revenge against his exiled brother Thyestes by welcoming him back home and then deceiving him into eating his own children. Although many plays entitled *Thyestes* or *Atreus* existed in the Greek and Roman dramatic tradition, Seneca's play is the only one that survives whole.[70]

The story is part of a rich mythological and dramatic tradition concerning the royal household of Tantalus, in which the same themes recur across multiple generations: deception, cannibalism, adultery, disputed paternity, fraternal rivalry, tyranny, revenge, and guilt inherited from preceding generations. A focus on kingship in Seneca's play gave it a strong resonance in first-century Rome dominated by the Imperial court. Seneca's two Tantalid plays, *Thyestes* and *Agamemnon,* which concern two successive generations, are a distinctive pair in that each begins with a prologue spoken by an ancestor who returns from the underworld as a ghost and sees the action to come as the continuation of his own crime and punishment. Within Seneca's dramatic oeuvre,

---

[69] O'Keefe, p. 152.

[70] On Seneca's *Thyestes* and its modern interpretation, see P. J. Davis's *Seneca: 'Thyestes'*, Duckworth Companions to Greek and Roman Tragedy (London: Duckworth, 2003), and other works in 'Further Reading' below.

however, *Thyestes* is most similar in type to *Medea*: in both, the protagonist is concerned with surpassing all prior crimes – in Medea's case, her own crimes; in Atreus's case, the crimes of his ancestors – and both characters stage-manage their acts of revenge, and the victim's realization of the truth, as a cruel theatrical spectacle.

Mythological Background. The play alludes to a rich storehouse of prior Tantalid crimes: Tantalus sought to trick the gods at a banquet by serving them the flesh of his son Pelops. Detecting this deception, the gods restored Pelops to life and severely punished Tantalus, placing him in Hades to be tormented (hence 'tantalized') by perpetual hunger and thirst. As a young man, Pelops won the hand of Hippodamia by cheating in a chariot race against her father, King Oenomaus of Olympia – or, in some versions, of Pisa. Pelops bribed King Oenomaus's charioteer, Myrtilus, into sabotaging his master's chariot, so that he could win the hand of Hippodamia. When Myrtilus claimed a reward, Pelops killed Myrtilus and threw his body into the sea (thenceforth named the 'Myrtoan' sea).

When Pelops died, his sons, Atreus and Thyestes, battled over who would be King of Argos. Atreus gained the crown, but Thyestes seduced Atreus's wife Aerope, bringing into doubt the paternity of Atreus's children Agamemnon and Menelaus, and also stole the golden ram whose fleece supplied the gold for the royal sceptre. Taking over the kingship, Thyestes banished Atreus. But Atreus, regaining the upper hand, in turn banished Thyestes from Argos.

Plot. When the play begins, Thyestes is still in exile but Atreus desires a greater revenge.

Act 1: The ghost of Tantalus is brought back to the earthly world by a Fury and is forced to renew in his household the same madness he himself once exhibited.

Chorus: A Chorus of Argives prays to the gods that Argos will break the cycle of crimes and punishments initiated by Tantalus.

Act 2: Atreus outlines his planned revenge against the protests of his attendant: he will send his own sons as messengers to lure Thyestes and his sons back to Argos.

Chorus: The Chorus celebrates the apparent peace between the rival kings, and discourses on the nature of true kingship: not power and wealth, but freedom from fear and desire.

Act 3. As Thyestes returns to Argos, in dialogue with one of his sons he expresses a sense of dread and repudiates ambition, but his son convinces him to continue. Atreus welcomes Thyestes back.

Chorus: The Chorus again celebrates the apparent end to civil war, but also warns of the instability of fortune.

Act 4: A Messenger describes to the Chorus (or a chorus-member) how Atreus took Thyestes' sons into the innermost sanctum of the palace and killed them sacrificially, then roasted and boiled them and served them to Thyestes to eat. He also describes how the sun reversed its course in horror at the crime.

Chorus: The Chorus (apparently unaware of the revelations of Act 4) observes the sun's reversed course and expresses shock and a sense of responsibility, predicting that the courses of all the heavenly bodies will go into disorder.

Act 5: Atreus appears alone, enjoying his deed; then Thyestes appears alone (though watched by Atreus), enjoying his meal. Atreus gradually reveals the truth, to which Thyestes reacts in horror, calling on the gods to take revenge. *Heywood adds a scene in which Thyestes recognizes himself as a monstrous descendant of Tantalus and seeks fitting punishment in the underworld.*

Prefaces. Heywood composed significant original verse for this play in the three prefaces, which together suggest the nature of the translation as an attempt to close one chapter of his life and open a new one.

Heywood's first two prefaces are a dedication to privy councillor and Oxford Chancellor, Sir John Mason (*c.* 1503–66), and a poem 'To His Book'. These give the impression of *Thyestes* as a book end, a concluding thanks to Mason for past assistance. Heywood states that Mason 'failed not to help and succour' him ('Preface' 174), perhaps helping Heywood to move to All Souls, after his resignation from Merton in 1558. Possibly echoing Seneca's *De Beneficiis*, Heywood emphasizes that his translation is a small but well-considered gift (Dedication, 1–8). Although it will never equal Mason's generosity, it is nonetheless a meaningful attempt to recognize the kindness of a man Heywood refers to as a 'wight of honour' ('To his Book', 1) and his 'daily orator' (Dedication), and its thoughtful nature is reinforced in 'To his Book', where he tries to imagine the right time at which to draw Mason's attention to his gift.

Even as Heywood presents *Thyestes* as a humble token, he signals its literary importance. This emphasis may be part of the presentation of the book as a well-considered gift (it is something crafted with care), but it is also a way to garner attention as a writer, most notably from the men involved in the literary network of the Inns.

All three of the prefaces are in verse, a choice that calls attention to the book as a *literary* work. Moreover, 'To his Book' aligns Heywood with classical and medieval poets. The conceit of the book as messenger is an occasional theme in earlier literature. Heywood most closely echoes Ovid's *Tristia* 1.1, where the exiled poet sends his book to the emperor Augustus to plead for his pardon and recall (a motif taken up by other Latin poets such as Martial). Heywood's opening 'Thou little book' (1) also evokes *Troilus and Criseyde*, where Chaucer sends his 'little book' to 'kiss the steps' of literary predecessors, including Homer, Virgil, and Ovid.[71] (On Heywood's awareness of *Troilus*, see *Troas, 'Prefaces'* above.)

In his 'Preface' (the title of the 391-line original poem), Heywood more overtly establishes the significance of his translation, linking himself to famous forbears and to the contemporary literary network of the Inns of Court. This effort is evident initially in the plot. Heywood dreams that the ghost of Seneca visits him, praising his *Troas* and asking him to put *Thyestes* into English. Heywood demurs, but Seneca insists, giving him an authoritative manuscript of his tragedies, written at Parnassus, the home of the Muses, and uncorrupted by scribes and printers. Heywood agrees to translate the play. Upon waking, he is inspired by the fury Megaera (a spirit of revenge and herself a character in the play) to begin work. Thus, Heywood presents himself as Seneca's chosen English heir and the translation as the product of quasi-divine inspiration.

Heywood signals the book's importance through genre too. The 'Preface' is a dream vision, a type of poem in which the narrator falls asleep and dreams the events which he then recounts. Popular in the medieval period, dream visions were less common by the 1560s. Utilizing the genre, Heywood aligns himself with previous authors, including Chaucer and Lydgate, whose *Fall of Princes* is a series of dream visions, including one in which Thyestes asks the poet to write his story.[72] More directly, the 'Preface' seems to refer

---

[71] Geoffrey Chaucer, *Troilus and Criseyde*, 5.1786–92.
[72] On possible allusions to Thomas Sackville, see n. at *Thyestes*, 'Preface', line 91.

to John Skelton's *Book of the Laurel* (1523), a dream vision that celebrates Skelton's own poetic abilities, defending his right to a place at the court of Fame, alongside famous authors, including Chaucer and Lydgate.[73] Like Skelton, Heywood begins with a specific reference to the date and time, as well as an allusion to changeable weather.[74] In addition, like Skelton, he intricately describes a *locus amoenus*, an ideal place for poetry (a theme first found in the proem of Hesiod's *Theogony*). Heywood's *locus* is Parnassus and the ornate Temple of the Muses (lines 209–80). Skelton's is the elaborate pavilion of Pallas and garden of poetry. Both have an enclosed garden with a fountain, arbours of roses, a laurel tree, and dancing muses.[75] In other ways, Heywood's dream echoes the 'Prologue' to Book 13 of Gavin Douglas's translation of Virgil (1513), where the ghost of the poet Mapheus Vegius (1407–58) visits Douglas in a dream, demanding that he translate his continuation of the *Aeneid*.[76] By recalling all of these earlier dream visions, Heywood places himself in a line of 'laureate' poets.

Heywood also aligns himself with contemporary poets. At one point, Heywood tells Seneca to find someone else to translate

---

[73] John Skelton, *Book of the Laurel*, ed. by F. W. Brownlow (Newark: University of Delaware Press, 1990). Further references will be to line numbers in this edition.

[74] Skelton opens with a complicated astrological description, which establishes a specific date and time for his writing (Brownlow, p. 175). Heywood's opening lines establish that he begins his work at sunset on Friday, 24 November 1558 (lines 1–2). *Laurel* begins with a description of changeable weather, although for Skelton the weather is a metaphor: fortune 'varyeth in an hour / Now clear weather, forthwith a stormy shower' (lines 11–12). For Heywood, the weather is literal ('And clouds from high began to throw their dreary tears adown', line 9), but also an external projection of his state of mind, since it 'well became the pensive pen' (line 5).

[75] Skelton, *Laurel*, lines 38–41 and 645–706.

[76] There are many similarities between Heywood's dream and Douglas's. Like Seneca (at 'Preface' 15–20), Vegius is advanced in years and wears a long gown and laurel crown. See Gavin Douglas, *The Aeneid* (1513), ed. by Gordon Kendal, MHRA Tudor and Stuart Translations (London: Modern Humanities Research Association, 2011), 13.76–88. There are differences: Vegius's gown is threadbare and his manner disagreeable, while Seneca is 'comely' and 'sweet' ('Preface', 18–19). But the texts end similarly, with each author agreeing to translate his ghostly visitor's work. See Beverly Jane Pugh, 'Jasper Heywood's Translation of Seneca's *Thyestes,* with Particular Reference to the Latter's Sixteenth and Seventeenth-Century Reception of the Themes of Tyranny, Kingship and Revenge', 2 vols (unpublished doctoral thesis, University of Warwick, 1997), II, 32–33.

Thyestes, directing him to the Inns of Court, the London legal societies which were a hub of literary activity at the time, exclaiming: 'go where Minerva's men and finest wits do swarm' (83–84). Heywood then lists by name Inns-of-Court men who would be well-qualified to translate Seneca, including Barnabe Googe, Thomas Sackville, and Thomas Norton. In so doing, Heywood praises a major literary community of the day, perhaps attempting to flatter the writers at the institution to which he would soon move. At the same time, this passage elevates Heywood's status: in having Seneca insist that he, Heywood, is the best person for the job, the translator suggests that he is more suited to the task of translating Seneca than his celebrated contemporaries.

Influences. In his 'Preface', Heywood implicitly makes a case for translation as a mode of literary accomplishment, and this may also be part of the attempt to connect himself with the Inns. Between 1558 and 1572, the Inns were the hub of a large network of translators, who sought to render classical and continental works into English.[77] (This fact is apparent in Heywood's list of works at the Inns, which are mostly translations.) In defending the arts of translation, Heywood builds on the writings of John Lydgate and, more explicitly, his contemporary Barnabe Googe, to suggest the cultural value of this prime genre of literary production.

In spirit, Heywood follows the example of Lydgate in the *Fall of Princes*, a work he must have known since it was the model for the *Mirror for Magistrates*, which Heywood echoed in his translation of *Troas* (see *Troas*, '*Influences*' above). In his prologue to Book One of the *Fall*, Lydgate describes translators as 'artificers', who:

> May change and turn by good discretion
> Shapes and forms and newly them devise,
> Make and unmake in many a sundry wise,
> As potters which to that craft intend
> Break and renew their vessels to amend.[78]

Specifically, translators are potters who break their wares in order to improve them (an image that suggests a precedent for Heywood's 'improvements' to the 'unperfit' passages in *Troas*).

---

[77] Conley, esp. pp. 23–27.
[78] John Lydgate, *The Fall of Prynces* (London: John Wayland, [1554?]), sig. A1^r.

For Lydgate, translation is a way of 'changing and turning by good discretion' in order to 'newly [...] devise'. Translations are 'new'.

Lydgate perhaps inspires Heywood's view of translation as an achievement in its own right, but he is almost certainly in conversation with Barnabe Googe, who translated the first three books of the *Zodiac of Life* (1560), a twelve-book Latin poem (published 1543) by the Italian poet Marcellus Palingenius Stellatus.[79] Heywood and Googe composed and published their translations at about the same time, and for this reason it is difficult to establish a direction of influence,[80] but the two writers certainly knew each other's work.[81]

The most obvious similarity lies in the plots of their prefaces. In *Thyestes* (as we have seen), Heywood is 'at book' (11) when Seneca appears, urging him to translate the play. Although Heywood resists, telling Seneca to find another, he eventually relents. In the *Zodiac*, Googe similarly is 'crouched for cold' among his books, when the Muses arrive, exhorting him to translate a text, although which text is debated.[82] When Calliope recommends the *Zodiac* of Palingenius, the Muses agree. Like Heywood, Googe initially resists, for 'In England here a hundred heads more able now there be'. As Seneca with Heywood, the Muses insist on Googe: 'Take thou this same in hand they cry, thou hast none other choice'.[83]

Both 'Prefaces' present translation as a worthy enterprise, important enough for Seneca to return from the afterlife to urge it and the only literary activity the Muses propose. Moreover, by introducing the *Zodiac* (although not itself heroic poetry) as the chosen poem of Calliope, the muse of epic, Googe aligns the *Zodiac*, but also translation more generally, with the highest form of literary achievement of the time. The 'Prefaces' elevate as well the status of the translator: Googe is the hand-picked poet of the muses; Heywood is the heir of Seneca himself, a defender of the

---

[79] Barnabe Googe, *Firste Three Bokes of the Most Christia[n] Poet Marcellus Palingenius, Called the Zodyake of Lyfe* (London: John Tisdale for Ralph Newbery, 1560).
[80] Both prefaces are unusually specific about dates of composition. Judging from these, Heywood began his work later than Googe, but published it sooner.
[81] In *Zodiac*, Googe praises Heywood, without mentioning a specific text (sig. *iiii^r^). In *Thyestes*, Heywood praises *Zodiac* by name ('Preface', line 102).
[82] Googe, sig. *v^v^.
[83] Googe, sigs. *vii^r^ and *vii^v^.

arts of translation, and a peer of some of the most notable writers of the day, especially Googe.

Heywood signals the importance of *Thyestes* in another way, by framing the 'Preface' with echoes of Atreus's lines in the play. In the opening, Heywood observes that an initially fair Friday has turned rainy and stormy, a statement that echoes Act 2, where Atreus, working himself up to revenge, comments, 'The day so fair with thunder sounds' (88). At the end of the 'Preface', Heywood, 'enflamed with force' of the fury Megaera declares that he will translate *Thyestes*: 'it should be done' (341), recalling Atreus, who having been 'enflamed' to revenge (implicitly by the fury Megaera, who appears in Act 1), resolves: 'it must be done' (2.1.109). In aligning himself with Atreus, Heywood links his artistic creation to Atreus's 'great' deeds, translating the protagonist's vengeful fury into poetic fury.

Translation Style. Heywood's second translation retains many of the features found in his first, but for a work translated by the same author so soon after *Troas*, *Thyestes* is remarkable for its differences.[84]

Heywood translates more directly, adhering more closely to the verse units, word order, syntax, and diction of Seneca's text. For example, he uses many more directly anglicized Latin terms ('stadies' for Lat. 'stadia', 3.1.6; 'fulgent face' for Lat. 'fulgore', 3.1.12; 'impotent ambition' for Lat. 'ambitio impotens', 2.Cho.15) – *Troas* has far fewer such instances.[85] Sometimes this increased directness results in denseness and even obscurity. More often, however, even as it makes for a more faithful representation of Seneca, it advertises Heywood's own literary skills by showing his ability to write poetry within tighter constraints, conveying the sense of the original using fewer words and retaining more of Seneca's structures.

Some of the differences between *Troas* and *Thyestes* appear to have been motivated by Heywood's concerns about the transmission of Seneca expressed in the 'Preface'. In the dream-encounter with Seneca, Heywood describes *Troas* as an overly ambitious project for a young man and acknowledges that in its

---

[84] Here we build on useful analyses by O'Keefe, pp. 116–228, Daalder, pp. xxxviii–xlv, and Hardison, pp. 158–70.

[85] For a full list, see O'Keefe, pp. 210–15.

published form it had so many faults that for a while he refused to translate more plays (114–135). He undertakes *Thyestes* only because of the perfect manuscript shown him by the dream-Seneca and because, having been dismayed by the number of errors in Tottel's printing of *Troas*, he has now found a new printer, Thomas Powell.

After this apparent renewal of confidence in the accuracy of his text, Heywood's *Thyestes* represents a transition toward a more direct mode of translation. We cannot be certain about all the reasons for this shift, though the dream-encounter with Seneca in the 'Preface' points to a new kind of respect for the author, one that entails a heightened concern with the specific sequencing of words, ideas, and images in the original. This concern is raised to the level of guiding principle in Heywood's third translation, *Hercules Furens* (1561), which presents the Latin and English on facing pages. There Heywood shows an editor's concern for presenting a 'diligently corrected' Latin text, as he announces on the title-page, and in the translation there is a clear pedagogical motive: to help students to learn Latin by comparing a translation with the original. Indeed, the translation of *Hercules Furens* is so tightly bound to the phrasing of the Latin words that it is often unintelligible without consulting the Latin. On the other hand, the reader of *Hercules Furens* also stands to gain a relatively unmediated introduction to the form and content of a single play with all its idiosyncrasies. *Thyestes* already represents a significant step in this direction: although Heywood adds a final scene, in other respects he strives for a more disciplined rendering of Seneca's play.

Below we illustrate Heywood's changed approach to *Thyestes* first by comparing the opening lines of the original and the translation, then by considering several representative moments from later in the play.

Thyestes begins with the ghost of Tantalus, who is surprised by his own presence in the world of the living. Again, Heywood's added words have been given in italics:[86]

> Quis me furor nunc sede ab infausta abstrahit
> avido fugaces ore captantem cibos?
> quis male deorum Tantalo vivas domos
> ostendit iterum? peius inventum est siti

---

[86] Hardison, pp. 158–59, also discusses these opening lines in detail.

arente in undis aliquid et peius fame
hiante semper? (*Thy.* 1–6)

What fury *fell* enforceth me to flee th'unhappy seat
That gape *and gasp* with greedy jaw the fleeing food *to eat*?
What god to Tantalus the bowers *where* breathing *bodies dwell*
Doth show again? Is aught found worse than burning thirst *of
hell*
In lakes *alow*? Or yet worse *plague* than hunger is there *one*,
In vain that ever gapes *for food*? (1.1.1–6)

As in *Troas*, the translation is 'bigger', but now by a smaller degree: the word count is doubled (34 > 63), but the syllable count is only slightly greater (69 > 78), a greater proportion of Heywood's words now being monosyllabic. The most revealing formal feature here is the versification: Heywood translates with exactly the same number of lines, and he embraces Seneca's use of enjambment for dramatic effect.

This more mimetic approach extends to the ordering of components within sentences. Thus 'Doth show again' is postponed to the same position in the line and sentence that it occupies in Seneca (ostendit iterum), even though this distorts the normal English order of Subject-Verb-Object. Heywood continues to privilege rhyme and alliteration as he did in *Troas*, exploiting opportunities for a doublet where possible ('gape and gasp'), but only within the constraints imposed by his observing line-for-line correspondences. Details without any direct correlations to the Latin are few and brief. Unlike in *Troas*, these additions do not serve to introduce additional themes or an interpretive apparatus. They reinforce the central image of Tantalus's mouth 'gaping' for food and drink, or they clarify the basic situation. '[T]he bowers where breathing bodies dwell' unpacks an otherwise opaque Senecan phrase, 'vivas domos' (living abodes); and 'of hell' and 'alow' help the audience to understand that the ghost has come up to the land of the living from the underworld – a fact Seneca had left for his better-informed audience to infer for themselves.

Heywood's more direct approach also has consequences for how he deals with the various elements of Seneca's tragic style. In the stichomythia between Atreus and his Servant (2.1) about whether Thyestes should be punished, the English matches the Latin phrase for phrase:

ATR.   Sanctitas pietas fides
        privata bona sunt: qua iuvat, reges eant.
SAT.   Nefas nocere vel malo fratri puta.
ATR.   Fas est in illum quidquid in fratrem est nefas.

(Thy. 217–20)

ATR.   Such holiness, such piety and faith
        Are private goods. Let kings run on in that that likes their
        will.
SER.   The brother's hurt a mischief count, though he be ne'er so
        ill.
ATR.   It is but right to do to him that wrong to brother were.

(2.1.42–45)

Most of the distinctive features of Heywood's rendering, such as the remarkable frequency of monosyllabic words, serve his goal of keeping within the same verse structure. The final line also matches the mirror-like structure of Seneca's word order with its own ABBA structure ('is [...] right [...] wrong [...] were'). Still, the carry-over is not entirely direct: Heywood varies strikingly Seneca's term 'nefas' (unspeakable crime against divine law), translating it first with 'mischief' then with 'wrong' and losing its formal contrast with 'fas', here translated 'right' – a reminder that, just as in *Troas*, Heywood is relatively uninterested in mapping precisely the same moral landscape of Seneca's play.

In the choral passages of *Thyestes*, Heywood makes no substantial additions or changes of the sort he had made in *Troas*. And although Seneca's lyric metres are just as varied as in *Troas*, Heywood translates these all with pentametre crossed rhyme (ABAB), avoiding larger rhyme-patterns entirely. As a result, the choral passages, although still lyrical, are more directly rendered:

Regem non faciunt opes,
non vestis Tyriae color,
non frontis nota regia,
non auro nitidae trabes   (*Thy.* 344–47)

Not riches make a king or high renown,
Not garnished weed with purple Tyrian dye,
Not lofty looks or head enclosed with crown,
Not glittering beams with gold and turrets high   (2.Cho.9–12)

In these lines from the second chorus, on true kingship, Heywood puts 'Not' first even in the initial line, in an exaggerated adherence to Seneca's anaphoric repetition. Although Seneca's shorter verse form allows Heywood to amplify his language here to an extent that is rare elsewhere in *Thyestes*, he does not do so redundantly but in a way that brilliantly distinguishes the several meanings of Seneca's terms: for example, Lat. 'opes' evokes 'riches' and 'renown', and Lat. 'frontis nota regia' (literally, 'royal insignia on the forehead') suggests both the 'crown' and 'lofty looks' characteristic of kings. Heywood carefully unpacks the Latin in a way that fully exploits its semantic potential, yet with more discipline than he had shown in the amplifications of *Troas*.

Heywood renders the one lyric passage spoken by a character in Seneca's play with similar fidelity and thoughtfulness. In his 'song' at the banquet in Act 5, Thyestes expresses his sense of foreboding. Heywood's translation conveys the musical and emotional qualities of the original. It is 'perhaps more expressive than any other tragic speech written before the 1580s'.[87] The closing lines illustrate some of Heywood's technique:

> I, wretch, would not so fear, but yet me draws
> A trembling terror. Down mine eyes do shed
> Their sudden tears, and yet I know no cause.
> Is it a grief or fear? Or else hath tears
> Great joy itself?   (5.2.46–50 = *Thy.* 965–69)

The translation corresponds exactly to the verse structure in Seneca, down to the final half-line, and Heywood follows Seneca in modelling Thyestes' puzzlement over his emotional symptoms – in other words, self-observation without self-understanding. Heywood spotlights the failure in self-knowledge, recasting Seneca's 'nec causa subest' (nor is the cause apparent) as a first-person formulation 'and yet I know no cause'. He also adds a poetic overlay in the rhyming scheme (ABAB) which heightens the oddity of the final enjambment; his recurring assonance in 'fear [...] tears [...] fear [...] tears' gives cogent simplicity to the series of four different Latin terms 'terror [...] fletus [...] metus [...] lacrimas'.

Heywood's major addition is the soliloquy by 'Thyestes alone' at the end of Act 5, of which Heywood made no mention in the prefaces. In his speech, Thyestes calls upon the forces of the

---

[87] Hardison, p. 169.

underworld both to punish him for a crime worse than Tantalus's and to take revenge on Atreus for perpetrating the crime. Though not technically a ghost scene, its form and content closely parallel Tantalus's appearance in the prologue of *Thyestes*, thereby bringing the play full circle, and the scene also looks ahead to the prologue of *Agamemnon*, where the ghost of Thyestes will anticipate the punishment of Atreus's son. Where Seneca's *Thyestes* had ended with a conspicuously weak gesture toward future revenge, Heywood integrates the play more obviously within the broader Tantalid tradition and, as we saw with his additions to *Troas*, within the Senecan corpus as a whole. This has been referred to as a 'narratorial' tendency: both Heywood and Studley (who adds a final scene to *Agamemnon*) cultivate a 'now-read-on' effect, as '[t]he particularity of the single play is absorbed into, and softened by, the longer perspectives of destiny'.[88]

Comparison of 'Troas' and 'Thyestes'. The differences between *Troas* and *Thyestes* have resulted in competing assessments of their merits. Heywood's 'Preface' makes clear that he has higher ambitions for *Thyestes* and it is not uncommon for scholars to refer to it as 'Heywood's masterpiece'.[89] In *Thyestes,* we certainly see a closer adherence to qualities of the original that are only partially conveyed in *Troas*, while the play still precedes Heywood's descent, as it were, into the counter-productive literalism of *Hercules Furens*. It is also relevant that the play and its plot proved the most fascinating to Elizabethan audiences.[90] Furthermore, in present-day classical studies *Thyestes* is often regarded as *Seneca's* masterpiece – a judgement that is perhaps not unrelated to the fact that it is the only play of Seneca for which a Greek model does not survive, giving the play a greater air of originality. Others, however, have seen *Troas* as Heywood's most profoundly 'literary' work: its freer form appears to give greater scope to 'real poetic feeling', and it is 'less servile to Seneca's text'.[91] The debate is a reminder of the contingency of our criteria for evaluating a translator's art.

Heywood's incorporation of several lines from *Thyestes* in *Troas* provides us with an opportunity to compare the translations.

---

[88] Hunter in *Seneca,* ed. by Costa, p. 189.
[89] Hardison, p. 170.
[90] See Daalder, pp. xix–xxxviii.
[91] Vocht, p. xxviii; cf. Spearing, *Elizabethan Translations*, p. 15 and Jockers, p. 6.

Consider, for example, his translation of 'ponite inflatos tumidosque vultus' (*Thy.* 609): first 'Lay down your lofty looks, your pride appease' (*Troas* 1.Cho.3), then 'Lay ye your proud and lofty looks aside' (*Thyestes* 1.Cho.64). The second version is more literal, maintaining its focus on the concrete 'looks' (Seneca's 'vultus') without adding a paraphrase. We may also compare his two renderings of Seneca's strikingly parallel two lines, 'quem dies vidit veniens superbum, / hunc dies vidit fugiens iacentem' (*Thy.* 613–14). In *Troas* Heywood translates 'Whom dawn of day hath seen in high estate, / Before sun's set, alas, hath had his fall' (1.Cho.57–58), whereas in *Thyestes* he translates 'Whom dawn of day hath seen in pride to reign, / Him overthrown hath seen the evening late' (3.Cho. 68–69). Heywood does not in either instance replicate completely Seneca's parallel structure between the two lines, and indeed in the second version he imposes his own temporal structure to have the first line begin with dawn and the second end with evening. But the repetition of 'seen' in the second version reflects Heywood's greater adherence to Seneca's precise phrasing, and this consistency arguably creates a more powerful image. More importantly, however, the variation between versions demonstrates Heywood's own restlessness as a poetic creator, seeking ever new ways to meet the challenge of conveying Seneca in English verse.

JOHN STUDLEY'S *AGAMEMNON*

In *Agamemnon*, John Studley follows the tradition launched by Heywood, but with some significant innovations in manner and method. While emulating a 'stately style' much as Heywood had done,[92] he assists readers to a greater degree by including, within his translation, fuller clarifications of the mythological references. Here, again, we provide some background on Studley's life and writings as well as Seneca's play before turning to Studley's prefaces, influences, and translation style.

Life and Literary Activities. Born *c.* 1545, Studley attended Westminster School and Trinity College, Cambridge, where he proceeded to his BA in 1566 and took a fellowship in 1567. In

---

[92] 'H. C. to the Reader' (5) in *Agamemnon.*

1566, he seems to have been admitted to one of the Inns of Court, probably Barnard's Inn, associated with Gray's Inn (see further below). Although Heywood was Catholic and Studley Protestant, they were similar in their rebellious personalities, especially when it came to religious controversy. In 1572, Studley signed a petition opposing the master John Whitgift's imposition of new university statutes against Puritans. In 1573, because of this opposition, he was forced to vacate his fellowship. Little is known of Studley's later life; he is reputed to have died at the siege of Breda in 1590.[93]

While at Cambridge, Studley produced four translations of Seneca, of which *Agamemnon* (1566) is the first. It was followed by *Medea* later in 1566, *Hercules Oetaeus* (*c.* 1566, published 1581), and *Hippolytus* (1567, although the surviving print version is in Newton's *Tenne Tragedies* of 1581). Described in the later seventeenth century as 'a noted poet',[94] Studley must have written other English poetry at this time, but it does not survive. He did contribute Latin verses on the death of Nicholas Carr, published with Carr's translation of Demosthenes in 1571.[95] Later, he translated John Bale's *Acta pontificum Romanorum* as *The Pageant of Popes* (1574), which he dedicated to Thomas Radcliffe, Earl of Sussex. These writings earned the praise of at least one contemporary. Echoing Heywood's praise of the Inns of Court in 'The Preface' to *Thyestes* as well as early approval of Studley's 'stately style' in a preface to *Agamemnon*, Richard Robinson in 1574 wrote that 'Th' Inns of Court' have 'a sort of gentlemen' who can write with 'stately style', including 'Studley, Hake, or Fulwood'.[96]

Seneca's 'Agamemnon'. The play centres on the return of Agamemnon, King of Argos, from the Trojan War and his murder by his wife Clytemnestra and her lover Aegisthus. The theme is

---

[93] T. P. J. Edlin, 'Studley, John (*c.* 1545–1590?)', *DNB*, <http://www.oxforddnb.com/view/article/26742> [accessed 5 Oct 2011].
[94] Wood, column 289.
[95] J. W. Binns, *Intellectual Culture in Elizabethan and Jacobean England* (Leeds: Francis Cairns, 1990), p. 45.
[96] Richard Robinson, *Rewarde of Wickednesse* ([London: William Williamson [1574]]), sig. Q3ʳ. A later entry in the *Admissions Register* of Gray's Inn suggests that Studley attended Barnard's Inn. See *Studley's Translations of Seneca's 'Agamemnon' and 'Medea': Edited from the Octavos of 1566*, ed. by Evelyn M. Spearing (Louvain: A Uystpruyst, 1913), p. xxii. Conley (p. 133) lists Studley's admission to Barnard's Inn as 1566.

best known from Aeschylus's *Agamemnon*, the first play in the *Oresteia* trilogy. In the context of Seneca's oeuvre, however, the play resonates with the other two plays in this volume: *Troades*, because it is set in the aftermath of the Trojan War and Agamemnon is a character in both plays; and *Thyestes*, because it chronicles an episode from the house of Tantalus – Agamemnon and Aegisthus being sons of Atreus and Thyestes respectively. Seneca's version is different from Aeschylus's, not least in its use of a dual chorus (being sometimes a generalized group of Greek men, sometimes Trojan women) and in the fact that Cassandra, the Trojan princess whom Agamemnon brings home with him and who is a major character in both plays, is still alive at the end of Seneca's play, whereas in Aeschylus her death is reported before the end. In Seneca, also, Aegisthus is more prominent, and Clytemnestra is more hesitant to plot against her husband.[97]

Mythological Background. In addition to the events described above as background to *Troades* and *Thyestes*, such as the Judgement of Paris, the sacrifice of Iphigenia, and the Trojan Horse, the play alludes to events connected directly with Aegisthus, Cassandra, and Clytemnestra.

Aegisthus was born from the union of Thyestes and his own daughter Pelopia. Thyestes perpetrated this incest after being told by the oracle of Phoebus Apollo that it would bring forth a son who could avenge him against Atreus and his line.

Cassandra, daughter of Priam and Hecuba, was the prophetess of Apollo, but because she refused Apollo's sexual advances her predictions of Troy's downfall were doomed not to be believed. During the war Cassandra rejected the advances of suitors, such as the warrior Coroebus; at the war's end she was raped by Ajax the Lesser in the temple of Athena, before being given to Agamemnon as a war-prize.

Clytemnestra was from Sparta, the daughter of Tyndareus and Leda; she was the half-sister of Helen, whose father, Zeus, appeared to Leda in the form of a swan. (The two sisters, one mortal and one divine, were the twins of corresponding mortal and divine brothers, Castor and Pollux.) At the beginning of the Trojan

---

[97] On Seneca's *Agamemnon* and its modern interpretation, see 'Further Reading' below.

War, Agamemnon made possible the sacrifice of Iphigenia at Aulis by telling Clytemnestra to send her there to be married to Achilles.

Plot. The play is set in Argos. The Trojan War is over but the Greek fleet has not yet arrived home:

Act 1: The ghost of Thyestes appears, recounting his monstrous banquet and his incest with his daughter and anticipating his revenge when Aegisthus will kill Agamemnon.

Chorus: The Chorus warns about fortune as a deceiver of kings, whose wealth and power makes them more vulnerable, not less.

Act 2: Clytemnestra speaks first with her Nurse, who counsels her toward moderation, then with Aegisthus, who reminds her of her reasons for taking revenge.

Chorus: The Chorus celebrates the arrival of the Greek fleet, singing a hymn to Apollo, Juno, Athena, Diana, and Jupiter.

Act 3: The soldier Eurybates announces the arrival of the Greeks but describes the massive storm that almost destroyed them on their way home.

Chorus: The Chorus, now representing the Trojan women who have arrived with Cassandra, observe that the only safe haven from human woes is death, and they recount the destruction of Troy which they had observed at first hand. *Studley treats this chorus and the dialogue between the Chorus and Cassandra in Act 4 as a continuation of Act 3 and uses the fourteeners of regular dialogue; the translation thus lacks a clearly delineated choral ode.*

Act 4: Cassandra, speaking with the chorus, repudiates them for their sympathy toward her. In an ecstatic vision Cassandra foresees what is to come: a repetition of the fall of Troy, with Aegisthus as a new Paris and Clytemnestra as a new Helen. Agamemnon appears, but fails to apprehend Cassandra's words of warning. *Studley begins and ends the dialogue of Act 4 with the single scene involving Agamemnon and Cassandra.*

Chorus: The Chorus praises Argos for having added Hercules to the ranks of the gods, and catalogues Hercules' labours.

Act 5: Cassandra narrates the killing of Agamemnon. Electra entrusts her brother Orestes to Strophius of Phocis, a friend of their father's, for safekeeping. Electra and Cassandra show contempt for the threats of Clytemnestra and Aegisthus. *Studley adds a scene in which Eurybates castigates the Furies for perpetuating the crimes of the household; he describes the death of Cassandra and Electra's banishment from the house, and foretells Orestes' later revenge on Clytemnestra and Aegisthus.*

Prefaces. As in Heywood, the prefaces to *Agamemnon* signal Studley's literary ambitions, marking the translation as a momentous publication. It was not uncommon for a work to appear in print with several commendatory poems or letters. For instance, Barnabe Googe recently published the first book of occasional poems by a living author in English, the *Eglogs, Epytaphes, and Sonnettes* (1563). Googe sought to shield himself from criticism with three prefaces by fellow writers. This set an example for Studley in the sheer number of prefaces, yet Studley surpasses Googe: the *eight* (!) poems in *Agamemnon* give the impression that the translation is an unusually important work.

Like Heywood's 'Preface', these prefaces authorize and elevate Studley in relation to contemporary literary networks. The poems are by literary notables of the day, such as Thomas Nuce, translator of Seneca's *Octavia*, and Thomas Peend, a translator of Ovid among other work. These legitimate Studley as a participant in the contemporary literary scene. T. B.'s verse (perhaps the translator Thomas Blundeville) extends this network, comparing Studley with yet other accomplished translators, including Heywood and Alexander Neville, as well as Thomas Phaer, Barnabe Googe, and Arthur Golding. In his own prefaces, Studley invites further comparison, mentioning Heywood and Alexander Neville who made 'Seneca himself to speak in English'. Although Studley suggests that his translation is 'barbarous' compared to others' 'eloquency' ('Preface to the Reader'), the total effect of the prefaces is to suggest that he is an 'apt and feat' translator ('Verses upon the Same', 6), pre-eminent among his contemporaries.

The prefaces also shield Studley from criticism, attempting to dissuade, even threaten, potential critics. They emphasize Studley's youth, urging readers to recognize *Agamemnon* as a remarkable achievement for one so young. Perhaps following Heywood (who mentions 'Zoilus' in his 'Preface'), the poems in Studley disparage fault-finders as 'Zoili' or 'Momes' (plurals of 'Zoilus' and 'Momus'), meaning carping detractors.[98] Thomas Nuce even

---

[98] Heywood's *Thyestes* appears to be the first use of 'Zoilus' in English (see Neologisms). On references to Zoilus and Momus in the period, see H. S. Bennett, *English Books and Readers, 1558–1603* (Cambridge: Cambridge University Press, 1965), esp. pp. 6–10, and Heidi Brayman Hackel, *Reading Material in Early Modern England: Print, Gender, and Literacy* (Cambridge: Cambridge University Press, 2005), esp. pp. 122–25.

threatens potential censurers, drawing a parallel between Agamemnon's fate and those of 'carping critics'. The parallel may seem far-fetched, but the underlying idea is that anyone who judges Studley's brain-children, as it were, commits a crime equal to Atreus's offence against Thyestes and his children, and thus risks bringing upon his lineage the sort of destruction wrought upon Atreus's son, Agamemnon ('In Agamemnona', 9 and 11 and 'Verses upon the Same', 39–74).

In his own two prefaces (a dedication and a letter to the reader) Studley shields himself further from criticism, constructing himself less as an ambitious writer than as a member of the community of scholars. His dedicatee is the privy councillor William Cecil, praised for his learning, his 'hearty goodwill and friendly affection' towards students at the queen's Westminster School, and for his role as chancellor of Cambridge, where Studley himself was a student or fellow at the time. In his letter to readers, Studley presents himself as carrying on Cecil's example: the work is intended for 'the use of such young students as thereby might take some commodity'.

Influences. Studley's most important influence was Heywood. By the time Studley wrote, Heywood was the measure of literary accomplishment, having defined the paradigm for English tragedy. One preface praises Heywood's 'perfect verse and doleful tune' ('T. B. to the Reader', 1) and another promises that Studley's tragic material will illustrate 'fickle Fortune's wavering wiles' ('W. R. to the Reader', 19) – a phrase that recollects the opening lines of *Troas*, where the words 'fickle', 'Fortune', and 'wavering' also appear. Whereas Heywood is the standard, the prefaces elevate Studley and other translators, such as Neville, to Heywood's level ('T. B. to the Reader', 11–21). They point out that it was the 'muses' who, as they did with Heywood, moved Studley in '[t]he stately style of Senec sage in vulgar verse to write' ('H.C. to the Reader', 4).

Yet the prefaces further explain how Studley develops – and to some extent also departs from – the purposes and methods established by Heywood. While Heywood does not mention emotional or moral impact in his prefaces, the prefaces to *Agamemnon* regularly emphasize the blend of 'pleasure and commodity' ('H. C.', 2) to be derived by the reader, whose 'wavering mind' may be 'set on fire' by a poetically crafted tragedy ('W. R.', 4–5). Studley himself underscores his moral purpose in his brief preface, mentioning 'furtherance of virtue, and abolishment of vice' (Epistle to William Cecil).

Studley also emphasizes 'the advancement and increase of learning' (Epistle to William Cecil), perhaps influenced by Heywood's *Hercules Furens*, which was designed 'for the profit of young scholars', as announced on its title-page. Studley's efforts in this regard are more extensive, however, and less about language than theme. Nuce describes how Studley 'hidden stories oft [...] shows [i.e. elucidates] to make his poet plain' ('Upon the Same', 7). As a clarifier, Studley seeks to discharge a 'double office [...] as sometime barely to expound, to comment sometime eke, / So that to understand this book, ye need no farther seek' (8–10). Some Elizabethan readers of Seneca in Latin would have benefited from the Latin commentary in Ascensius' 1514 edition (see Appendix on 'The Translators' Latin Sources'); Studley's translation performs a comparable service, only now in English and within the poetic text itself.

Translation Style. In *Agamemnon* Studley took many of the stylistic and metrical conventions established by Heywood as a point of departure, but his poetry has its own distinctive emphases.[99]

Like Heywood in *Troas*, Studley produced a more expansive translation, but his imagery and language are far more colourful. Where Heywood amplified Seneca in his search for a more elevated speech register and exaggerated the role of fortune and the function of the text as a mirror, Studley's main goals include jolting the reader's emotions as well as clarifying mythological allusions. Heywood's main sources for his added scenes were other plays by Seneca himself, but Studley occasionally introduces material from further afield. And whereas Heywood's career culminated in the strictly direct translation of *Hercules Furens*, Studley would continue to make decisive interventions throughout his career, for example giving extra lines to Phaedra in his *Hippolytus*, changing the first chorus in *Medea*, and making strategic cuts to *Hercules Oetaeus*.

---

[99] Here we build on the useful analyses by Spearing, *Elizabethan Translations*, pp. 30–40, and Jockers, pp. 76–128.

Below, as with Heywood, we examine the beginning of *Agamemnon* and then several other illustrative passages in the play. In the opening lines the ghost of Thyestes speaks alone:

Opaca linquens Ditis inferni loca,
adsum profundo Tartari emissus specu,
incertus utras oderim sedes magis:
fugio Thyestes inferos, superos fugo.
En horret animus et pavor membra excutit:
video paternos, immo fraternos lares.   (*Aga.* 1–6)

Departing from the darkened dens, *which* Ditis low *doth keep*,
Lo, here I am sent out *again* from Tartar dungeon deep.
Thyestes, I, that whither coast to shun *do stand* in doubt,
Th'infernal *fiends* I fly, the folk of earth I chase about.
My conscience, lo, abhors *that I should hither passage make*,
Appallèd sore with fear *and dread*, my trembling sinews shake.
My father's house or rather yet my brother's I espy.   (1.1.1–7)

Here the increase in words (32 > 74) and syllables (76 > 98) is far more restrained than in Heywood's *Troas* and is comparable to *Thyestes*. For the most part Studley maintains a strict line-for-line correspondence.

Studley follows Heywood in elevating his language through alliteration (*d* in the first line) and through artificial word order. The sentence final phrases 'do stand in doubt' and 'I espy' do not in fact correspond to those of the corresponding Latin terms (incertus; video), but in their position at the ends of lines, they maintain a Latinate – really, a hyper-Latinate – order.

Studley's word choice reflects his sense of the emerging tragic lexicon in English – at least for presenting ghost scenes, since several expressions here are seen already in Heywood: 'deep dens' (*Troas* 2.1.2), 'Lo' (5), 'dungeon' (*Thyestes* 5.4.1), 'abhor' (9), and 'th'infernal fiends' (48). The term 'again' gives us pause, in that it has no correlate in the Latin text. But Studley was aware that readers of Heywood's translations would have remembered the ghosts of Achilles and Tantalus; and 'again' echoes the fourth line of Heywood's *Thyestes* (where it translates 'iterum', Sen. *Thy.* 4). Readers may also have recalled that Heywood's *Thyestes* concluded with the added scene in which Thyestes began his passage to the underworld – in other words, that the present appearance of Thyestes' ghost had a recent prequel.

One feature of Studley's translation stands out: his sudden shift from a line-for-line translation to give an intense and controlled expansion of Seneca's line 5, which concerns the ghost's psychological reaction. This is the first instance of Studley's strategic amplifications of selected lines for specific purposes, in this case engaging the reader through a character's more complex psychological profile ('conscience', for example, is more loaded than Seneca's term 'animus', mind).

In his approach to *sententiae* and stichomythia, Studley shifts conspicuously between expansive and direct translation. The dialogue in Act 2 in which the Nutrix seeks to dissuade Clytemnestra from adding crime to crime, begins with an almost mathematical duplication of every line:

NUT. Tuta est latetque culpa, si pateris, tua.
CLY. Perlucet omne regiae vitium domus.　　　(*Aga.* 147–48)

NUT. In silent shore thou sailest yet, thy trespass we may hide.
　　　If thou thyself detect it not, nor cause it be descried.
CLY. Alas it is more blazed abroad, and further is it blown,
　　　Than any crime that ever in this princely court was sown.
　　　　　　　　　　　　　　　　　　　　　　　(2.1.64–67)

Studley paraphrases Seneca by introducing several new domains of imagery. The images, however, are not necessarily random: the maritime metaphor, for example, allows Studley to prefigure the storm of Act 3. Later in the same dialogue, Studley changes gear:

NUT. Quod metuit auget qui scelus scelere obruit.
CLY. Et ferrum et ignis saepe medicinae loco est.　　(151–52)

NUT. The thing he fears he doth augment, who heapeth sin to
　　　　sin.
CLY. But fire and sword, to cure the same, the place of salve
　　　　supply.　　　　　　　　　　　　　　　　(2.1.71–72)

These line-for-line renderings preserve the singular directness and proverbial encapsulation in Seneca's *sententiae*, and are closer to Heywood's method in *Thyestes*. Studley adds dramatic intensity, however, precisely through his transition from the doubling mode to the direct mode.

Studley's approach to lyric passages is less varied than Heywood's and in some ways less adventurous. In Seneca's *Agamemnon*, Act 3 concludes with an extensive lyric exchange between the Chorus and Cassandra, but Studley chooses to treat this as dialogue and presents it in fourteeners; indeed, he uses fourteeners for the remaining lyric passage also (4.Cho.). When he does change metres, which is only in the choruses of Acts 1 and 2, he uniformly uses twelve-syllable rhyming couplets. Like Heywood, though, he also seems to exercise greater poetic licence in the choral passages, as in these opening lines of the first chorus:

> O regnorum magnis fallax
> > Fortuna bonis,
> in praecipiti dubioque locas
> > excelsa nimis.
> Numquam placidam sceptra quietem
> certumve sui tenuere diem   (*Aga.* 57–61)

> O Fortune that dost fail the great estate of kings,
> On slippery sliding seat thou placest lofty things,
> And set'st on tottering sort where perils do abound,
> Yet never kingdom calm, nor quiet could be found.
> No day to sceptres sure doth shine that they might say,
> 'Tomorrow shall we rule as we have done today'.

> (1.Cho.1–6)

After compressing Seneca's first two lines into one line without seeking to convey the sense of deception that is implicit in Latin 'fallax' (his rendering with the cognate term 'fail' results in a different sense), Studley expands the later lines and introduces whole phrases of his own, such as 'Yet never kingdom calm', which among other things uses 'Yet' to make explicit the contrast that is characteristically left implicit by Seneca. The notion of an uncertain day that occupies only a phrase in Seneca (Numquam [...] certum [...] diem) is elaborated with the image of shining and with the direct speech attributed to kings, contrasting 'tomorrow' and 'today'.

As noted above, Studley's most strategic amplifications are gauged at affecting the reader's emotions or elucidating the mythological background. In the preface by W. R., the reader is promised 'troublous toils most tragical' and 'bloody broils of envious ire' that will set heart and mind on fire, and at moments that involve violence and/or heightened passions Studley will sometimes multiply single phrases in order to maximize the linguistic and imagistic possibilities. Thus, four lines spoken by Clytemnestra in Seneca become *eight* in Studley:

Maiora cruciant quam ut moras possim pati;
flammae medullas et cor exurunt meum;
mixtus dolori subdidit stimulos timor;
invidia pulsat pectus, ...   (*Aga.* 131–34)

So grievous is my careful case, which plungeth me so sore,
That deal I cannot with delay, nor linger anymore.
The flashing flames and furious force of fiery fervent heat,
Outraging in my boiling breast, my burning bones doth beat.
It sucks the sappy marrow out, the juice it doth convey,
It frets, it tears, it rents, it gnaws my guts and gall away.
Now feeble fear still eggs me on, with dolour being pressed,
And cankered hate with thwacking thumps doth bounce
    upon my breast.   (2.1.34–41)

Studley takes Seneca's physical and psychological details as
opportunities for free composition. The formulaic phrases he uses
here, such as 'thwacking thumps', 'boiling breast', and 'cankered
hate' will have their own life in his tragic repertoire, translating
different terms of Seneca's later in the play (cf. 3.2.8; 3.1.166, 176)
and recurring in the final scene (5.5.3).

The final scene is Studley's one major addition to *Agamemnon*.
Bringing the character Eurybates back on-stage to call upon the
Furies to avenge Agamemnon's death, Studley follows Heywood's
example in the *Thyestes* of using a final soliloquy to reincorporate
the drama within the cycle of vengeance already sketched out in
the prologue. Also as in Heywood, several of the components of
the speech, such as the description of the *locus horridus* in which
Electra is incarcerated (5.5.58–68), appear to draw on Senecan
type-scenes. But much of the content of Eurybates' speech,
particularly the description of Cassandra's death and her
comparison to a dying swan (5.5.37–40), appears to be drawn from
Aeschylus (*Aga.* 1444–45). In remedying the perceived deficiency
of Seneca's play, in which Cassandra's fate is left unmentioned,
Studley supplies what Seneca himself had altogether lost from the
Greek tradition. To this extent Studley's notion of translation may
be said to include 'restoration'.

Studley is particularly concerned to provide the reader with
fuller versions of myths which are often only alluded to in Seneca
and sometimes not mentioned at all. Thus, in the final scene
(5.5.48) Studley evokes Cassandra's courage in death by saying
she embraced death as if she were being married to Corebus (i.e.

Coroebus), the suitor who is mentioned in Virgil's *Aeneid* (2.341–46). This technique of fleshing out Seneca's use of myth can be seen throughout *Agamemnon*, where even Seneca's bare term 'cupido' (desire) is hyper-classicized to describe Cupid ('the blinded boy that lovers' hearts doth reave', 2.1.42).

Comparison of Heywood and Studley. Our best opportunities to compare the translation styles of Heywood and Studley come in those passages from *Medea* and *Phaedra* that Studley went on to translate as part of his whole versions of those plays, but Heywood already incorporated in *Troas*. Thus, for example, compare these two versions of Seneca's *Medea* 625–33 describing the death of Orpheus:

> Whose songs the woods hath drawn and rivers held,
> And birds to hear his notes did theirs forsake,
> In piecemeal thrown amid the Thracian field
> Without return hath sought the Stygian Lake.
>
> (*Troas* 2.Cho.17–20)

> That Orpheus Calliope's son, who stayed the running brook,
> While he records on heavenly harp with twangling finger fine,
> The wind laid down his pipling blasts. His harmony divine
> Procured the woods to stir themselves, and trees in trains along
> Came forth with birds that held their lays and listened to his
>   song.
> With limbs asunder rent in field of Thrace he lieth dead.
> Up to the top of Heber flood, eke halèd was his head.
> Gone down he is to Stygian damps, which seen he had before,
> And Tartar boiling pits from whence return he shall no more.
>
> (*Medea* 3.Cho.)

Admittedly, Heywood extracts these lines for his own purposes in *Troas*, but his translation does not omit much that is in Seneca. Studley, by contrast, transforms Seneca's allusive sketch into a wholesale recounting of the myth. The translation does not, however, lapse into the prosaic language of a footnote or an encyclopaedia entry, but enlarges the account within the poetic framework.

RECEPTION AND INFLUENCE

The early Elizabethan dramatic translations were immediately well-received. Although there is no direct record of performance,[100] the translations were read and praised, especially Heywood's.[101] Neville and Studley also received accolades. In a preface to *Agamemnon*, T. B. asserts that Neville 'gives no place' (i.e. is equal to) Heywood (line 15). In *Medea*, W. F. lauds Studley, urging readers to give 'praise unto the painful pen that hath deservèd so', and in 1570, one R. W. asserts that Studley was 'inferior not' to Heywood or Googe.[102] Having had their works brought together in the *Tenne Tragedies* in 1581, the translators were also praised as a group. In 1586, William Webbe commended 'the laudable authors of Seneca in English',[103] and a few years later, Thomas Nashe suggested that the translations made Seneca too accessible, complaining that unlatined contemporary dramatists relied too much on 'English Seneca read by candlelight'.[104]

Yet there is little evidence to support Nashe's claim that later Elizabethan playwrights relied on the translations of Seneca as opposed to the Latin editions. Critics have documented a limited number of echoes of the translations in later drama. In our notes,

---

[100] Some translations may have been written for performance (Eliot, p. liii, and O'Keefe, pp. 111–15). Neville's preface to *Oedipus* indicates that he had the stage in mind. He 'thought to have put it [the translation] to the very same use that Seneca himself in his invention pretended, which was by tragical and pompous show upon stage [...]' (A3^v).

[101] For praise of Heywood, see n.1 above. It is difficult to gauge the dissemination of the tragedies. Library inventories in the period are scarce, but Heywood's *Troas*, possibly his *Hercules Furens*, as well as the *Tenne Tragedies* appear in some private collections. See *A Collection and Catalogue of Tudor and Early Stuart Books Lists*, ed. by Joseph Black and E. S. Leedham-Green, 7 vols, (Tempe: Arizona Center of Medieval and Renaissance Studies, 1992–2009), entries on *Troas* 133.199; *Hercules Furens* ad4.109; and *Tenne* ad4.411 and ad 3.66.

[102] 'W. F. in the Translator's Behalf', sig. A4^r; 'R. W. to the Reader' in Drout, sig. A3^r.

[103] William Webbe, *A Discourse of English Poetrie* (London: John Charlewood for Robert Walley,1586), sig. C4^r.

[104] Nashe's statement appears in his preface to Robert Greene's play *Menaphon* (c. late 1580s). The preface is a lengthy complaint about contemporary writers who lack originality and offer up only bad imitations of classical authors. See *Works of Thomas Nashe*, ed. by Ronald B. McKerrow, rev. by F. P. Wilson, 5 vols, (London: Barnes and Noble, 1966), 3, 315.

we draw attention to some of these, especially echoes of John Studley's *Agamemnon* in *Macbeth* (*c.* 1606). Also, *A Tragedie called Oedipus*, a school play in manuscript from later in the Elizabethan period, cribs many lines from Neville's *Oedipus* as well as Newton's *Thebais*.[105] Yet most quotations of and allusions to Seneca in later Renaissance drama appear to refer directly to the Latin, since in most cases characters either cite the Latin or paraphrase it in a way that does not reflect the specific phrasing in the translations.[106]

It is clear, however, that the translations drew new attention to Seneca's works, and in this way influenced the form, subject matter, and style of later Renaissance drama. As G. K. Hunter writes, 'the etymology of *influence* suggests no single link, but rather a stream of tendency raining down upon its object'.[107] It is difficult to find a later Elizabethan or early Jacobean tragedy without some echo of Seneca – in the five-act division of the play, in a character's bombastic speech, in a scene of sparring dialogue, in the presence of a ghost, or in a call for revenge. In two tragedies, characters carry copies of Seneca with them onto stage, quoting Latin lines from the plays and prose as they plot revenge.[108]

The translations seem to have influenced Elizabethan tragedy in a different way, helping to focus the views of contemporary writers on a traditional sense of the genre – and Senecan tragedy in particular – as commentaries on kingship or, more specifically, tyranny. As we have seen, the early Elizabethan translators describe Seneca in terms of his serious tone and moral guidance. Yet there was another, more political reading of the tragedies, which partly stemmed from *Octavia*, where Seneca appears as an outspoken advisor to Nero. Although the translators did not describe their works in overtly political terms, they seem to have been influenced by contemporary political concerns, including contemporary resistance theory.[109] Thus, although not at all a call to arms, Heywood's *Troas* demystifies kingship by emphasizing

---

[105] Yale Elizabethan Club, para. 4.

[106] See the lists of 'Latin quotations from Seneca in Elizabethan Tragedies' and 'Imitations of Seneca' in Cunliffe, pp. 127–29; 130–55.

[107] G. K. Hunter, 'Seneca and the Elizabethans: A Case-Study in "Influence"'. *Shakespeare Survey*, 20 (1967), 17–26 (p. 18).

[108] Thomas Kyd, *Spanish Tragedy*, Act 3, Scene 13, and John Marston, *Antonio's Revenge*, Act 2, Scene 3.

[109] e.g. Winston, 'Seneca', and Woodbridge, pp. 129–66.

the ways that rulers can fall. Several neo-Senecan plays of the Elizabethan period, most notably Thomas Sackville and Thomas Norton's *Gorboduc* (1561–62), the multi-authored *Gismond of Salern* (1568), and the multi-authored *Misfortunes of Arthur* (1587–88), exploit Senecan form to offer politically motivated criticism of Elizabeth's handling of monarchic prerogative, more specifically her personal refusal to settle the succession, as well as her imperial ambitions.[110]

Writers before 1560 expressed the view that tragedy comments on tyranny. The idea is evident in the arrogant tyrant figures of Greek and Roman tragedy, and it is given explicit expression earlier in the sixteenth century in *The Governor* (1531), where Thomas Elyot writes that 'in reading tragedies' one will 'execrate and abhor the intolerable life of tyrants'.[111] By the early 1570s, we hear more about Seneca's political commentary than his moral guidance, as authors who mention Senecan tragedy focus on its political aspects, emphasizing its potential to curb the autocratic tendencies in rulers. One example is the prologue to *Cambises* (1570), the drama about the ancient Persian tyrant:

> The sage and witty Seneca, his words thereto did frame
> The honest exercise of kings; men will ensue the same.
> But contrary-wise, if that a king abuse his kingly seat,
> His ignominy and bitter shame in fine shall be more great.[112]

Later writers repeat this view, sometimes drawing out its broader implications: the capriciousness of tyrants represents the mutability of the world. In his *Apology for Poetry* (1581), Philip Sidney quotes from Seneca's *Oedipus* to illustrate the role of tragedy, which:

---

[110] See especially Curtis Perry and Melissa Walter, 'Staging Secret Interiors: *The Duchess of Malfi* as Inns of Court and Anticourt Drama', in *The Duchess of Malfi: A Critical Guide*, ed. by Christina Luckyj (London: Continuum, 2011), pp. 85–105; Curtis Perry, '*Gismond of Salern* and the Elizabethan Politics of Senecan Drama', in *Gender Matters*, ed. by Mara R. Wade (forthcoming: Amsterdam: Rodopi); and Perry's 'British Empire on the Eve of the Armada: Revisiting *The Misfortunes of Arthur*', *Studies in Philology*, 108 (2011), 508–37.

[111] Thomas Elyot, *The Boke Named the Governour* (London: Thomas Berthelet, [1531]), fol. 35^v.

[112] Thomas Preston, *A Lamentable Tragedy [...] of Cambises King of Percia* ([London: John Allde, [1570?]]), sig. A2^r.

openenth the greatest wounds and showeth forth the ulcers that are covered with tissue; that maketh kings fear to be tyrants, and tyrants manifest their tyrannical humours; that with stirring affects of admiration and commiseration teacheth the uncertainty of this world, and upon how weak foundations gilden roofs are builded.[113]

Without mentioning Seneca explicitly, George Puttenham (1589) reflects the same idea. Tragedies portray tyrants and in this way:

their infamous life and tyrannies were laid open to all the world, their wickedness reproached, their follies and extreme insolences derided, and their miserable ends painted out in plays and pageants to show the mutability of fortune and the just punishment of God in revenge of a vicious life.[114]

Although such descriptions of tragedy were nothing new, the Elizabethan translators seem nonetheless to have been a pivotal part of the story whereby Seneca's 'moral' tragedies came to be seen more narrowly as a genre that helped playwrights to represent and comment on the extremes of royal power.

In turn, later Elizabethan and Jacobean playwrights developed tragedies that reflected and responded to contemporary political trends, particularly the increasing centralization of power in the figure of the monarch. Characters such as Julius Caesar, King Claudius, and Macbeth figure the real and potential excesses of monarchs and magistrates. With such themes, Shakespeare, as well as other later Elizabethan and Jacobean tragedians, cultivated the political emphasis implicit in ancient tragedy. Yet rather than holding a mirror up to the monarch and magistrates, these later playwrights wrote for a diverse cross-section of people – the noblemen, foreigners, lawyers, apprentices, and masterless men – who frequented the public playhouses of Renaissance London, as well as for the monarch, who might command a performance at court or even, as James did, patronize a company. Later Renaissance English playwrights thus drew upon Seneca's legacy

---

[113] Sir Philip Sidney, *An Apology for Poetry*, ed. by Forrest G. Robinson (Indianapolis: Bobbs-Merrill, 1970), p. 45. On Sidney's reception of Senecan tragedy, see G. Staley, *Seneca and the Idea of Tragedy* (New York: Oxford University Press, 2010).
[114] George Puttenham, *Arte of English Poesie* (London: Richard Field, 1589), sig. F2r.

to represent the excessive passions and personal prerogatives of monarchs, inviting both ruler and subjects to consider, in Sidney's words, what 'maketh kings fear to be tyrants', and indeed where the line was between them.[115]

---

[115] On the ambiguous representation of tyrants on the Renaissance stage, see Rebecca Bushnell, *Tragedies of Tyrants: Political Thought and Theater in the English Renaissance* (Ithaca: Cornell University Press, 1990).

FURTHER READING

The bibliography of Seneca is vast, and for 'English Seneca' it is large as well. Here we list important texts and studies that will help to orient readers to Seneca's works, life, and the reception and influence of his tragedy in the English Renaissance.

Seneca: Works and Life, Reception. The standard bilingual edition of Seneca's plays is Seneca, *Tragedies*, ed. by J. G. Fitch, 2 vols, Loeb Classical Library (Cambridge, MA: Harvard University Press, 2002–04). A recommended recent translation in idiomatic English is Emily Wilson's *Seneca: Six Tragedies* (Oxford: Oxford University Press, 2010).

The major biography of Seneca is M. Griffin's *Seneca: A Philosopher in Politics*, 2nd edn (Oxford: Clarendon Press, 1992); a study of his reputation in antiquity is conducted by T. N. Habinek, 'Seneca's Renown: *Gloria, Claritudo*, and the Replication of the Roman Elite', *Classical Antiquity*, 19 (2000), 264–303. Among the various studies of his later reception are James Ker's *The Deaths of Seneca* (New York: Oxford University Press, 2009), which traces the reception of Seneca's death scene and writings on death from antiquity to the present day, and Roland Mayer's 'Personata Stoa: Neostoicism and Senecan Tragedy', *Journal of the Warburg and Courtauld Institutes*, 57 (1994), 151–74, which examines Renaissance understandings of the relationship between Seneca's plays and prose.

Anyone interested in Seneca should also consult several important collections of essays, which provide multiple perspectives on central debates in Seneca studies. A selection of some of the most influential scholarship, including on the tragedies, is presented in J. G. Fitch, ed, *Seneca*, Oxford Readings in Classical Studies (Oxford: Oxford University Press, 2008). See also K. Volk and G. Williams, eds, *Seeing Seneca Whole: Perspectives on Philosophy, Poetry, and Politics* (Leiden: Brill, 2006) and *Seneca*, ed. by C. D. N. Costa, (London: Routledge & Kegan Paul, 1974). A more specific thematic approach is taken in the collection by S. Bartsch, and D. Wray, eds, *Seneca and the Self* (Cambridge: Cambridge University Press, 2009). The tragedies in particular are the focus of *Seneca Tragicus: Ramus Essays on Senecan Drama*, ed. by A. J. Boyle (Berwick: Aureal Publications,

1983) and *Sénèque le tragique* ed. by Margarethe Billerbeck and Ernst A. Schmidt (Geneva: Fondation Hardt, 2004). On the performance of the tragedies, see *Seneca in Performance*, ed. by George W. M. Harrison (London: Duckworth, 2000).

Important studies of the tragedies include the now classic essay by C. J. Herington, 'Senecan Tragedy', *Arion*, 5 (1966), 422–71. The relationship to Greek tragedy is examined by R. J. Tarrant in 'Senecan Drama and Its Antecedents', *Harvard Studies in Classical Philology*, 82 (1978), 213–63. Overall studies of Senecan tragedy include A. J. Boyle's *Tragic Seneca: An Essay in the Tragic Tradition* (New York: Routledge, 1997), and C. Littlewood's *Self-Representation and Illusion in Senecan Tragedy* (Oxford: Oxford University Press, 2004).

Further background on the three plays by Seneca focused on in this edition can be found in several editions, commentaries, and studies. On *Troades*, see E. Fantham's *Seneca's 'Troades': A Literary Introduction with Text, Translation, and Commentary* (Princeton: Princeton University Press, 1982) and A. J. Boyle's edition of *Seneca's 'Troades': Introduction, Text, Translation and Commentary* (Leeds: Francis Cairns, 1994). On *Thyestes*, see R. J. Tarrant's *Seneca's 'Thyestes': Edited with Introduction and Commentary* (Atlanta: Scholars Press, 1985). P. J. Davis's, *Seneca: 'Thyestes'* in the Duckworth Companions to Greek and Roman Tragedy Series (London: Duckworth, 2003) offers a very helpful survey of the major themes of *Thyestes* as well as its later Renaissance reception; and the play has also been the focus of a major recent monograph by A. Schiesaro, *The Passions in Play: 'Thyestes' and the Dynamics of Senecan Drama* (Cambridge: Cambridge University Press, 2003). On *Agamemnon*, see R. J. Tarrant, *Seneca: 'Agamemnon': Edited with a Commentary* (Cambridge: Cambridge University Press, 1976).

Senecan Tragedy in Renaissance England. There is to date no complete scholarly edition of the first English translations of Seneca's plays. In 1927, Thomas Newton's *Seneca: His Tenne Tragedies Translated into English* (1581) was reprinted as part of the Tudor Translations Series (London: Constable and Co., 1927). In the introduction, T. S. Eliot offers his important appraisal of the early translations (pp. v–liv). This was later reprinted as 'Seneca in Elizabethan Translation' in his *Selected Essays* (New York: Harcourt, Brace and Co., 1932), pp. 51–88. H. de Vocht reproduces the first quartos of Heywood's three translations and provides an extensive and informative introduction and notes in *Jasper Heywood and His Translations of Seneca's 'Troas', 'Thyestes', and 'Hercules Furens'*, Materialien zur Kunde des alteren Englischen Dramas (Louvain: A. Uystpruyst, 1913). As part of the same series, Evelyn Spearing edits Studley's first two plays in *Studley's Translations of Seneca's 'Agamemnon' and 'Medea': Edited from the Octavos of 1566* (Louvain: A. Uystpruyst, 1913). Joost Daalder's edition of *Thyestes*, New Mermaids Series (London: Ernest Benn, 1982) is a modern-spelling edition of that play. An appendix on Heywood's sources, 'The Latin Texts Used by Heywood' (pp. 83–88), is especially valuable.

The introductions to these editions emphasize Seneca's influence on later Elizabethan and Jacobean drama. There are many critical studies of this topic. The most important of these include: J. W. Cunliffe's *The Influence of Seneca on Elizabethan Tragedy* (London: Macmillan, 1893); H. B. Charlton's *The Senecan Tradition in Renaissance Tragedy*, an essay originally published as an introduction to vol. 1 of *The Poetical Works of William Alexander, Earl of Stirling*, ed. by L. E. Kastner and H. B. Charlton (Manchester: The University Press, 1921; repr. Manchester: Manchester University Press, 1946); Gordon Braden, *Renaissance Tragedy and the Senecan Tradition: Anger's Privilege* (New Haven: Yale University Press, 1985); and Robert Miola, *Shakespeare and Classical Tragedy: The Influence of Seneca* (Oxford: Oxford University Press, 1992). In addition, P. J. Davis traces the influence of *Thyestes* in particular in his chapter on 'Reception' in *Seneca: 'Thyestes'* (London: Duckworth, 2003), pp. 81–133. Don Share's *Seneca in English* is an anthology of translations of Seneca in English poetry and drama (London: Penguin, 1998), especially in the Renaissance.

G. K. Hunter questions the nature and extent of Seneca's impact in two important articles: 'Seneca and the Elizabethans: A Case Study in "Influence"', *Shakespeare Survey*, 20 (1967), 17–26, and 'Seneca and English Tragedy' in *Seneca*, ed. by C. D. N. Costa (London: Routledge and Kegal Paul, 1974), pp. 166–204.

There are fewer studies of the translation and reception of Seneca in the early Elizabethan period specifically. One early book is Evelyn M. Spearing, *The Elizabethan Translations of Seneca's Tragedies* (Cambridge: W. Heffer and Sons, 1912). Frederick Kiefer looks at the emphasis on fortune and revenge in the translations in 'Seneca Speaks in English: What the Elizabethan Translators Wrought', *Comparative Literature Studies*, 15 (1978), 372–87, which is also the seed of the chapter 'The Elizabethan Translations of Seneca' in *Fortune and Elizabethan Tragedy* (San Marino, CA: Huntington Library, 1983), pp. 60–82. Dennis Flynn provides a helpful overview of Heywood's translations in the context of his life in *John Donne and the Ancient Catholic Nobility* (Bloomington: Indiana University Press, 1995). Gordon Braden provides a helpful discussion in his chapter on 'Tragedy' in *The Oxford History of Literary Translation in English, Volume 2, 1550–1660*, ed. by Gordon Braden, Robert Cummings, and Stuart Gillespie (New York: Oxford University Press, 2010), pp. 262–79. Mike Pincombe describes Heywood's attitude toward tragedy and tragic inspiration in 'Tragic Inspiration in Jasper Heywood's Translation of Seneca's *Thyestes*: Melpomene or Megaera?', in *The Oxford Handbook of Tudor Drama*, ed. by Tom Betteridge and Greg Walker (Oxford: Oxford University Press, 2012), pp. 531–46. Jessica Winston, in 'English Seneca: Heywood to *Hamlet*' (*The Oxford Handbook of Tudor Literature, 1485–1603*, ed. by Mike Pincombe and Cathy Shrank, Oxford: Oxford University Press, 2009, pp. 472–87), contrasts the early and later Elizabethan reception of Seneca.

Recently, critics have begun to explore the politics of the early Elizabethan translation and adaptation of Seneca, looking at the works as offering politically engaged counsel and comment. See especially Jessica Winston, 'Seneca in Elizabethan England', *Renaissance Quarterly*, 54 (2006), 29–58, Linda Woodbridge's chapter '"A Special Inward Commandment": The Mid-Sixteenth Century' in *English Revenge Drama: Money, Resistance, Equality* (Cambridge: Cambridge University Press, 2010), pp. 129–66, and Curtis Perry, '*Gismond of Salern* and the Elizabethan Politics of Senecan Drama' in *Gender Matters*, ed. by Mara R. Wade (forthcoming: Amsterdam: Rodopi).

JASPER HEYWOOD
TROAS (1559)

To the most high and virtuous princess, Elizabeth, by the grace of God, Queen of England, France, and Ireland, defender of the faith, her highness's most humble and obedient subject, Jasper Heywood, student in the University of Oxford, wisheth health, wealth, honour, and felicity.[1]

If consideration of Your Grace's goodness toward us all your loving subjects, which flying fame by mouths of men resounds, had not fully in me repressed all dread of reprehension° (most noble princess and my dread sovereign lady); if the wisdom that God at these years in Your Highness hath planted had not seemed to me a strong defence against all bite of shameless arrogance (reproach whereof, flung with disdainful words from ireful tongues, as adders stings should strike me); finally, if the learning with which God hath endued° Your Majesty had not been to me a comfortable
10 persuasion of your gracious favour toward the simple gift and duty of a scholar, I would not have incurred so dangerous note of presumption in attempting a subject to his princess, a simple scholar to so excellently learnèd, a rash young man to so noble a queen, by none other sign to signify allegiance and duty toward Your Highness save by writing, when oft times is the pen the only accuser in some points of him that therewith doth indite.°[2] But now to see (most gracious lady) that thing come to pass, which to the honour of Him and for the wealth of us God hath ordained, a princess to reign over us, such one to whom great freedom is for us
20 to serve, what joy may serve to triumph at that blissful day, or what should we spare with pen to preach abroad that inward gladness of heart that floweth from the breasts of us your most loving subjects? Beseeching God that it may please Him to grant Your Grace long and prosperous governance of the imperial crown of England, then well understanding how greatly Your Highness is delighted in the sweet sap of fine and pure writers, I have here presumed to offer unto you such a simple New Year's gift[3] as neither presenteth gold nor pearl, but duty and good will of a scholar, a piece of Seneca

---

[1] wisheth health, wealth, honour, and felicity] A standard expression. See also dedications to *Thyestes* and *Agamemnon*.

[2] is the pen [...] therewith doth indite] i.e. 'a written text is the only thing that brings censure upon the writer'.

[3] New Year's gift] On New Year's gifts, see Miller. Although the calendar year began in March, New Year's Day was January 1.

30 translated into English, which I the rather enterprise to give to Your Highness, as well for that I thought it should not be unpleasant for Your Grace to see some part of so excellent an author in your own tongue (the reading of whom in Latin I understand delights greatly Your Majesty) as also for that none may be a better judge of my doings herein than who best understandeth my author.[4] And the authority of Your Grace's favour toward this my little work may be to me a sure defence and shield against the sting of reprehending tongues, which I, most humbly beseeching Your Highness, end with prayer to God to send us long the fruition° of so excellent and gracious a lady.

---

[4] On Elizabeth and Seneca, see Introduction, nn. 12 and 54.

The Preface to the Readers

Although (gentle reader) thou may'st perhaps think me arrogant for
that I only, among so many fine wits and towardly° youth (with
which England this day flourisheth), have enterprised to set forth in
English this present piece of the flower of all writers, Seneca, as
who say not fearing what graver heads might judge of me in
attempting so hard a thing, yet upon well pondering what next
ensueth, I trust both thyself shalt clear thine own suspicion and thy
changed opinion shall judge of me more rightful sentence. For
neither have I taken this work first in hand, as once intending it

10   should come to light (of well doing whereof I utterly despaired),
and being done but for mine own private exercise, I am in mine
opinion herein blameless, though I have (to prove° myself)
privately taken that part which pleased me best of so excellent an
author. For better is time spent in the best than other, and at first to
attempt the hardest writers shall make a man more prompt to
translate the easier with more facility. But now since by request
and friendship of those to whom I could deny nothing, this work
against my will extorted is out of my hands,⁵ I needs must crave
thy patience in reading, and facility of judgement, when thou shalt

20   apparently° see my witless lack of learning, praying thee to
consider how hard a thing it is for me to touch at full in all points
the author's mind (being in many places very hard and doubtful
and the work much corrupt by the default of evil printed books),⁶
and also how far above my power to keep that grace and majesty of
style that Seneca doth, when both so excellent a writer hath passed
the reach of all imitation, and also this our English tongue (as many
think and I here find) is far unable to compare with the Latin. But
thou (good reader) if I in any place have swerved from the true
sense, or not kept the royalty of speech meet° for a tragedy, impute

30   the tone to my youth and lack of judgement, the other to my lack of

---

⁵ But now since [...] extorted is out of my hands] A commonplace mocked in a
letter 'To the Reader' in a 1660 translation of *Troades* by one S.P.: 'If thou ask'st
why I have offered it [the translation] to public view, I will not answer thee with
that trivial and palliating come-off that the entreaties of friends have forced me
contrary to my will to tumble into press, where after so desperate a squeeze I
appear so misshapen and besmeared with black blood. No truly, I freely jumped
in' (sig. A2ᵛ–A3ʳ).
⁶ evil printed books] Heywood complains about printers in *Thyestes* ('Preface'
116, 287–88, and 307–10).

eloquence. Now as concerning sundry places augmented and some altered in this my translation. First, for as much as this work seemed unto me in some places unperfect° (whether left so of the author or part of it lost as time devoureth all things I wot° not), I have (where I thought good) with addition of mine own pen supplied the want of some things, as the first Chorus after the first act beginning thus, 'O ye to whom', etc. Also in the second act, I have added the speech of Achilles' spright,° rising from hell to require the sacrifice of Polyxena beginning in this wise, 'forsaking
40   now' & etc. Again the three last staves° of the Chorus after the same act, and as for the third Chorus which in Seneca beginneth thus, 'Quae vocat sedes?',[7] for as much as nothing is therein but a heaped number of far and strange countries, considering with myself the names of so many unknown countries, mountains, deserts, and woods should have no grace in the English tongue, but be a strange and unpleasant thing to the readers (except° I should expound the histories of each one, which would be far too tedious), I have in the place thereof made another beginning in this manner, 'O Jove that lead'st' & etc., which alteration may be borne withal,
50   seeing that the Chorus is no part of the substance of the matter. In the rest I have for my slender learning endeavoured to keep touch with the Latin, not word for word or verse for verse as to expound° it, but neglecting the placing of the words observed their sense. Take gentle reader this in good worth, with all his faults. Favour my first beginnings and amend rather with good will such things as herein are amiss, than to deprave or discommend my labour and pains for the faults, seeing that I have herein but only made way to other that can far better do this or like, desiring them that as they can, so they would. Farewell gentle reader, and accept my good
60   will.

---

[7] 'Quae vocat sedes?'[...] mountains, deserts, and woods] In S. (814–60), the Chorus asks 'Quae vocat sedes habitanda captas?' (What place summons us captive women, forcing us to live there?) and then lists Greek cities and regions.

PREFACE TO THE TRAGEDY[8]

The ten years' siege of Troy, who list° to hear,
And of th'affairs that there befell in fight,
Read ye the works that long since written were
Of all th'assaults and of that latest night
When turrets' tops in Troy they blazèd bright.
Good clerks they were that have it written well.
As for this work, no word thereof doth tell.

But Dares Phrygian well can all report,
With Dictys eke° of Crete in Greekish tongue,[9]
10   And Homer tells to Troy the Greeks' resort
In scannèd° verse, and Maro hath it sung.
Each one in writ hath penned a story long.
Who doubts of aught and casteth° care to know,[10]
These antique authors shall the story show:

The ruins twain of Troy,[11] the cause of each,
The glittering helms,° in field the banners spread,
Achilles' ires and Hector's fights they teach.
There may the jests of many a knight be read:
Patroclus, Pyrrhus, Ajax, Diomed,
20   With Troilus, Paris, many other more
That day by day there fought in field full sore;°

And how the Greeks at end an engine made,
A hugie horse where many a warlike knight
Enclosèd was, the Trojans to invade
With Sinon's craft, when Greeks had feignèd flight,

---

[8] The preface is in *rime royale*; see Introduction, p. 25.

[9] 8–9] Dares Phrygius, a priest of Hephaestus in Homer's *Iliad*, supposedly wrote the (now lost) poem on the fall of Troy which was translated into Latin in the fifth century and became a primary source on the Trojan War for medieval authors, including Boccaccio and Chaucer; it was first published in England in an English translation by Thomas Paynell (by way of Mathurin Heret's French translation) as *The Faythfull and True Storye of the Destruction of Troye, Compyled by Dares Phrigius* (1553). Dictys of Crete is the legendary author of a fourth-century Latin fiction purporting to be a diary, *Ephemeris belli Troiani* ('Chronicle of the Trojan War'), which was no less influential than the poem of Dares.

[10] casteth care] i.e. 'desires'.

[11] ruins twain of Troy] Troy was sacked twice by the Greeks, by Hercules during the childhood of Priam and then at the end of the Trojan War. See also 1.2.72–3 and 3.2.17–24.

While close they lay at Tenedos from sight;
Or how Aeneas else, as other say,
And false Antenor did the town betray.[12]

But as for me, I nought thereof indite.°
30   Mine author hath not all that story penned.
My pen his words in English must recite
Of latest woes that fell on Troy at end,
What final fates the cruel gods could send,[13]
And how the Greeks when Troy was burnt gan° wreak°
Their ire on Trojans, thereof shall I speak.

Not I, with spear who piercèd was in field,
Whose throat there cut or head ycorvèd° was,
Ne° bloodshed blows that rent° both targe° and shield,
Shall I recite; all that I overpass.
40   The work I write more woeful is alas.
For I the mothers' tears must here complain,°
And blood of babes that guiltless have been slain,

And such as yet could never weapon wrest,
But on the lap are wont° to dandled° be,
Ne yet forgotten had the mother's breast,
How Greeks them slew alas, here shall ye see.
To make report thereof, ay woe is me.
My song is mischief, murder, misery,
And hereof speaks this doleful° tragedy.

50   Thou Fury fell° that from thy deepest den[14]
Could'st cause this wrath of hell on Troy to light,
That workest woe, guide thou my hand and pen
In weeping verse of sobs and sighs to write,
As doth mine author them bewail° aright.
Help woeful Muse, for me beseemeth° well
Of others' tears with weeping eye to tell.

When battered were to ground the towers of Troy,
In writ as ancient authors do recite,
And Greeks again repaired to seas with joy,

---

[12] 25–28] Sinon (a Greek) and Aeneas and Antenor (Trojans) assisted in the defeat of Troy, in various versions of the story.
[13] cruel] Disyllabic here and often (also 'prayer', 'oar'). See further pp. 289–90.
[14] 50–56] On Heywood's invocation, see Introduction, p. 23.

60 Up riseth here from hell Achilles' spright.°
  Vengeance he craves with blood his death to quit,°
  Whom Paris had in Phoebus' temple slain,
  With guile betrapped° for love of Polyxene.[15]

  And wrath of hell, there is none other price
  That may assuage, but blood of her alone.
  Polyxena he craves for sacrifice,
  With threatenings on the Grecians many one
  Except° they shed her blood before they gone.[16]
  The sprights, the hell, and deepest pits beneath,
70 O Virgin dear, alas, do thirst° thy death.

  And Hector's son, Astyanax, alas,
  Poor silly° fool,° his mother's only joy,
  Is judged to die by sentence of Calchas.
  Alas the while to death is led the boy,
  And tumbled down from turrets' tops in Troy.
  What ruthful° tears may serve to wail the woe
  Of Hector's wife that doth her child forgo?

  Her pinching pang of heart, who may express,
  But such as of like woes have borne a part?
80 Or who bewail her ruthful heaviness°
  That never yet hath felt thereof the smart?
  Full well they wot° the woes of heavy heart,
  What is to leese° a babe from mother's breast,
  They know that are in such a case distressed.

  First how the queen laments the fall of Troy,
  As hath mine author done, I shall it write;
  Next how from Hector's wife they led the boy
  To die, and her complaints I shall recite;
  The maiden's death then must I last indite.
90 Now who that list the Queen's complaint to hear,
  In following verse it shall forthwith appear.

---

[15] 62–63] In the temple of Apollo, Paris killed Achilles, who had expected to marry Polyxena.
[16] 68] i.e. 'Unless they sacrifice Polyxena before they leave'.

THE SPEAKERS[17]

HECUBA, QUEEN OF TROY

A COMPANY OF WOMEN[18]

THE SPRIGHT° OF ACHILLES

TALTHYBIUS, A GRECIAN

AGAMEMNON, KING OF GREEKS

CALCHAS

PYRRHUS

CHORUS

ANDROMACHA

[SENEX],[19] AN OLD MAN TROJAN

ULYSSES

ASTYANAX

HELENA[20]

---

[17] Speakers] Non-speaking parts include soldiers (3.1) and Polyxena (4.1).
[18] Company of Women] Chorus of Trojan women, S.'s only Chorus. Heywood's new Choruses (Acts 1 and 3) are more anonymous.
[19] Senex] Lat. 'old man'.
[20] Helena] Helen.

THE FIRST ACT

HECUBA

Whoso in pomp of proud estate or kingdom sets delight,
Or who that joys in prince's court to bear the sway of might,
Ne° dreads the fates which from above the wavering gods down
    flings,
But fast affiance° fixèd hath in frail and fickle things,
Let him in me both see the face of Fortune's flattering joy,[21]
And eke° respect the ruthful° end of thee, O ruinous Troy,
For never gave she plainer proof than this ye present see:
How frail and brittle is th'estate of pride and high degree.[22]

The flower of flowering Asia, lo, whose fame the heavens[23]
    resound,[24]
10   The worthy work of gods above, is battered down to ground,[25]
And whose assaults they sought afar,[26] from west with banners
    spread,
Where Tanais cold her branches seven abroad the world doth shed
With hugie host, and from the east, where springs the newest day,
Where lukewarm Tigris' channel runs and meets the ruddy sea,
And which from wandering land of Scythe the band of widows
    sought: [27]
With fire and sword thus battered be her turrets down to nought.
The walls but late of high renown, lo here, their ruinous fall:
The buildings burn and flashing flame sweeps through the palace
    all.
Thus every house full high it smokes of old Assarac's land,

---

[21] flattering] Fortune 'flatters' by granting high status and wealth only to take them away.

[22] 1–8] On Heywood's s translation style here, see Introduction, pp. 27–28.

[23] heavens] Monosyllabic here and often (also 'driven', 'even', 'over', 'seven'). See further pp. 289–90.

[24] flower of flowering Asia] i.e. Troy. Studley perhaps echoes this phrasing in *Agamemnon* 4.1.3.

[25] work of gods] Apollo and Neptune built Troy's walls. See also 3.1.67.

[26] 11–15] S. introduces a catalogue of armies with 'ad cuius arma venit [...]' (To [Troy's] defence came [...]), rendered obscurely as 'And whose assaults they sought afar' (11). The list alludes to Troy's allies: Rhesus, King of Thrace ('from west'), Memnon, King of Ethiopia ('from the east'), and Penthesilea, Queen of the Amazons (from 'land of Scythe').

[27] band of widows] Unmarried Amazons.

20   Ne yet the flame withholds from spoil the greedy victor's hand.
The surging smoke the azure sky and light hath hid away,
And, as with cloud beset, Troy's ashes stains the dusky day.
Through pierced with ire and greedy of heart, the victor from afar
Doth view the long assaulted Troy, the gain of ten years' war;
And eke the miseries thereof abhors to look upon,
And though he see't yet scant himself believes it might be won.
The spoils thereof, with greedy hand, they snatch and bear away;
A thousand ships would not receive aboard so huge a prey.

The ireful might, I do protest, of gods adverse to me,[28]
30   My country's dust and Trojan king I call to witness thee,
Whom Troy now hides and underneath the stones art overtrod,
With all the gods that guide thy ghost, and Troy that lately stood,
And you also ye flocking ghosts of all my children dear,
Ye lesser sprights:° whatever ill hath happened to us here,
Whatever Phoebus' waterish face in fury hath foresaid
At raging rise from seas, when erst° the monsters had him
    frayed,°[29]
In childbed bands° I saw it yore and wist° it should be so,[30]
And I in vain before Cassandra told it long ago.
Not false Ulysses kindled hath these fires, nor none of his;[31]
40   Not yet deceitful Sinon's craft that hath been cause of this;
My fire it is wherewith ye burn and Paris is the brand[32]
That smoketh in thy towers, O Troy, the flower of Phrygian land.
But ay alas, unhappy age,[33] why dost thou yet so sore°
Bewail° thy country's fatal fall? Thou knew'st it long before.[34]
Behold thy last calamities and them bewail with tears.[35]

---

[28] 29–34] Hecuba invokes as witnesses the gods, the 'Trojan king' (Priam), the dust of Troy, and her children's ghosts. At 32 Heywood misses a reference to Hector.

[29] 35–36] Heywood misses S.'s first reference to Cassandra, 'Phoebas ore lymphato furens' (the priestess of Phoebus, frenzied, her mouth inspired by madness). Heywood perhaps thinks of 'lympha' (water) and adds 37 referring to the sea to rationalize this image.

[30] 37–44] Hecuba dreamt that Paris would be a fire-brand who destroyed the city.

[31] nor none of his] An allusion to Diomedes, who with Ulysses conducted a midnight raid instrumental to Troy's defeat.

[32] Paris is the brand] A typical clarifying addition by Heywood.

[33] unhappy age] i.e. old age; metonym for Hecuba.

[34] thou knewest it long before] Heywood's addition, highlighting prophecy motif.

[35] last] S. 'recentes' (latest).

Account as old Troy's overturn and passed by many years.
I saw the slaughter of the king and how he lost his life
By th'altar's side (more mischief was) with stroke of Pyrrhus'
    knife,[36]
When in his hand he wound his locks and drew the king to ground,

50   And hid to hilts his wicked sword in deep and deadly wound,   [50]
Which when the gorèd king had took, as willing to be slain,
Out of the old man's throat he drew his bloody blade again.
Not pity of his years, alas, in man's extremest age,
From slaughter might his hand withhold, ne° yet his ire assuage.
The gods are witness of the same, and eke the sacrifice,
That in his kingdom holden° was that flat on ground now lies.[37]
The father of so many kings, Priam, of ancient name,
Untombèd lieth and wants in blaze of Troy his funeral flame.

Ne yet the gods are wreaked,° but lo his sons and daughters all,[38]

60   Such lords they serve as doth by chance of lot to them befall.
Whom shall I follow now for prey? Or where shall I be led?
There is perhaps among the Greeks that Hector's wife will wed,
Some man desires Helenus' spouse, some would Antenor's have,
And in the Greeks there wants not some that would Cassandra
    crave.
But I alas most woeful wight,° whom no man seeks to choose,
I am the only refuge° left and me they clean° refuse.[39]

[To Chorus][40]

Ye careful, captive company, why stints your woeful cry?
Beat on your breasts and piteously complain° with voice so high

---

[36] more mischief was] S. describes Pyrrhus's killing of Priam at the altar of Jove as 'maius scelus' (a worse crime) than the rape of Cassandra by Ajax, son of Oileus.

[37] 53–56] Heywood partially conveys three things that, in S., did not deter Pyrrhus: 1) Priam's old age (here omitted); 2) divine witnesses (here given accurately); and 3) 'quoddam sacrum regni iacentis' (a certain sacred reverence for a kingdom laid low), here rendered as 'the sacrifice that in his kingdom holden was'.

[38] his sons and daughters all] S. refers only to Priam's 'daughters-in-law and daughters'.

[39] refuge] i.e. refugee? S. 'sola sum Danais metus' (I alone am a source of fear to the Greeks).

[40] A sudden transition from act to choral ode typical of S. Less typical is Hecuba's interaction with the Chorus (though compare *Agamemnon* 3.2).

As meet° may be for Troy's estate; let your complaints rebound
70   In tops of trees and cause the hills to ring with terrible sound.[41]

The Second Scene

THE WOMEN HECUBA

[WOMEN]

Not folk unapt, nor new to weep, O Queen,
Thou will'st to wail; by practice are we taught:
For all these years, in such case have we been,
Since first the Trojan guest Amyclas sought,[42]
And sailed the seas that led him on his way,
With sacred ship to Cybele dedicate,[43]
From whence he brought his unrepining° prey,
The cause alas of all this dire debate.[44]
Ten times now hid the hills of Idey be[45]
10   With snow of silver hue all overlaid,
And barèd° is for Trojan roges° each tree;
Ten times in field the harvest man afraid
The spikes of corn hath reaped; since never day
His wailing wants, new cause renews our woe.[46]
Lift up thy hand, O Queen, cry well away.
We follow thee, we are well taught thereto.

HECUBA

Ye faithful fellows of our casualty,[47]
Untie th'attire that on your heads ye wear
And, as behoveth state of misery,
20   Let fall about your woeful necks your hair.

---

[41] trees […] hills] Heywood generalizes S.'s reference to Mt Ida, 'iudicis diri domus' (home to the fatal judge), an allusion to the Judgement of Paris.

[42] Trojan guest Amyclas sought] Paris was the guest of Menelaus at Sparta (near Amyclae) when he seduced Helen ('prey' at 7).

[43] 6] i.e. 'with ship holy to Cybele (the Great Goddess)', since its wood comes from her sacred home, Mt Ida.

[44] 7–8] Heywood's addition, clarifying the beginnings of the Trojan War.

[45] Idey] Mt Ida.

[46] 13–14 since never day […] renews our woe] i.e. for ten years, not a day has passed that does not give cause for grieving.

[47] of our casualty] S. 'casus nostri' (of our misfortune).

In dust of Troy rub all your arms about
In slacker° weed,° and let your breasts be tied[48]
Down to your bellies; let your limbs lie out.
For what wedlock should you your bosoms hide?
Your garments loose, and have in readiness
Your furious hands upon your breasts to knock.
This habit well beseemeth° our distress.
It pleaseth me: I know the Trojan flock.[49]
Renew again your long accustomed cries,
30   And more than erst° lament your miseries.
We bewail Hector.

WOMEN

Our hair we have untied, now everychone,°
All rent for sorrows of our cursèd race,
Our locks out spreads; the knots we have undone,   [100]
And in these ashes stainèd is our face.

HECUBA

Fill up your hands and make thereof no spare,
For this yet lawful° is from Troy to take.
Let down your garments from your shoulders bare
And suffer not your clamour so to slake.[50]
40   Your naked breasts wait for your hands to smite.
Now dolour° deep, now sorrow, show thy might;
Make all the coasts that compass Troy about
Witness the sound of all your careful cry;
Cause from the caves the Echo to cast out,
Rebounding voice of all your misery,
Not as she wonts° the latter word to sound,[51]
But all your woe from far let it rebound;
Let all the seas it hear and eke the land.[52]

---

[48] breasts] i.e. (as in S.) the folds of the women's garments, tied down to expose their shoulders and chests.
[49] know] S. 'agnosco' (recognize). Hecuba recognizes the mutilated women and dishevelled women as fully manifesting their condition as victims.
[50] 39] Heywood's free composition, corresponding to an uncertain text in S. (line 105).
[51] 44–46] Compare Thomas Hughes et. al., *Misfortunes of Arthur* (1587–1588): 'Thou Echo shrill that haunt'st the hollow hills / Leave off that wont to snatch the latter word' (4.2.1–2) (Maxwell, p. 171).

Spare not your breasts with heavy stroke to strike;
50   Beat ye your selves, each one with cruel hand,
For yet your wonted cry doth me not like.[53]
We bewail Hector.

WOMEN

Our naked arms thus here we rent for thee,
And bloody shoulders, Hector, thus we tear.
Thus with our fists our heads, lo, beaten be,
And all for thee behold we hale° our hair.
Our dugs,° alas, with mothers' hands be torn,
And where the flesh is wounded roundabout,
Which for thy sake we rent thy death to mourn,
60   The flowing streams of blood they spring there out.
Thy country's shore° and destiny's delay,
And thou to wearied Trojans wast an aid.
A wall thou wast and on thy shoulders Troy:
Ten years it stood, on thee alone it stayed,
With thee it fell, and fatal day alas
Of Hector both and Troy but one there was.

HECUBA

Enough hath Hector. Turn your plaint° and moan,
And shed your tears for Priam everychone.

WOMEN

Receive our plaints, O lord of Phrygian land,
70   And old twice captive king receive our tear.[54]
While thou wert king Troy hurtless then could stand,
Though shaken twice with Grecian sword it were,
And twice did shot of Herc'les' quivers bear.[55]
At latter loss of Hecuba's sons all,
And roges for kings that high on piles° we rear,
Thou father shut'st our latest funeral,[56]

---

[52] the seas it hear and eke the land] S. 'pontus et aether' ('sea and sky').

[53] 51] S. 'I am not content with the accustomed sound'.

[54] twice captive] i.e. captured by Hercules and later killed by Pyrrhus.

[55] 72–73] See 'Preface to the Tragedy', n. at line 15.

[56] 74–76] i.e. 'after ('at latter') the loss of Hecuba's children and funerals for princes ('roges for kings') raised on high pyres, you, Priam ('father'), come at the very end of our ('shut'st our latest') funeral procession'.

And beaten down to Jove for sacrifice,
Like lifeless block in Troy thy carcass lies.

HECUBA

Yet turn ye once your tears another way:
80   My Priam's death should not lamented be.
O Trojans all full happy is Priam say,[57]
For free from bondage down descended he
To the lowest ghosts and never shall sustain
His captive neck with Greeks to yokèd be.[58]
He never shall behold the Atrids twain,
Nor false Ulysses ever shall he see,
Not he a prey for Greeks to triumph at,   [150]
His neck shall subject to their conquests bear,
Ne give his hands to tie behind his back
90   That to the rule of sceptres wonted were,
Nor following Agamemnon's chair in band,
Shall he be pomp to proud Mycenas land.

WOMEN

Full happy Priam is, each one we say,
That took with him his kingdom then that stood;
Now safe in shade he seeks the wandering way
And treads the paths of all Elysius wood;
And in the blessèd sprights full happy he
Again there seeks to meet with Hector's ghost.
Happy Priam, happy who so may see
100   His kingdom all at once with him be lost.

CHORUS

Added to the tragedy by the translator

O ye to whom the lord of land and seas,
Of life and death hath granted here the power,
Lay down your lofty looks, your pride appease.[59]

---

[57] O Trojans all] S. 'Iliades' (Trojan women).
[58] 83–84 never shall sustain [...] to yokèd be] i.e. 'will never bear the yoke of Greeks upon his conquered neck'.
[59] 1–3, 37–39, 57–58] From the third Chorus of *Thyestes* (607–09, 615–17, and 613–14). On Heywood's retranslation of these lines in *Thyestes*, see Introduction, p. 45 and O'Keefe, 'Analysis', p. 74.

The crownèd king flee'th not his fatal hour.
Whoso thou be that lead'st thy land alone,
Thy life was limit° from thy mother's womb.
Not purple robe, not glorious glittering throne,
Ne crown of gold redeems thee from the tomb.[60]

A king he was that, waiting for the veil
10   Of him that slew the Minotaur in fight,
Beguiled with blackness of the wonted sail,
In seas him sunk and of his name they hight.°[61]
So he that willed to win the golden spoil
And first with ship by seas to seek renown,
In lesser wave at length to death gan° boil,[62]
And thus the daughters brought their father down.
Whose songs the woods hath drawn and rivers held,
And birds to hear his notes did theirs forsake,
In piecemeal thrown amid the Thracian field
20   Without return hath sought the Stygian Lake.[63]
They sit above that hold our life in line,
And what we suffer down they fling from high –
No cark,° no care that ever may untwine
The threads that woven are above the sky.[64]
As witnessed he that sometime King of Greece
Had Jason thought in drenching seas to drown,
Who 'scaped both death and gained the Golden Fleece:[65]
Whom Fates advance, there may no power pluck down.

---

[60] 7–8] Echoes S. *Thy.* 344–47.

[61] 9–12] The 'king' is Aegeus of Athens: when Theseus failed to fly a white sail on his return voyage from Crete indicating that he was alive, his father Aegeus threw himself into the sea (thence named 'Aegean').

[62] 13–15] A lightly adapted translation of S.'s *Medea* 664–67, part of the third choral ode on deaths associated with the Argonauts. King Pelias sent Jason and the Argonauts to retrieve the Golden Fleece, but Pelias's own daughters boiled him to death, thinking this would rejuvenate him. Line 16 is a free composition.

[63] 17–20] Translation of S.'s *Medea* 628–30 and 632–33 (the same ode as 13–15 above). S. contrasts the good fortune of the singer Orpheus, the legendary poet and an Argonaut, with his death (being torn apart by women of his native Thrace). Orpheus once visited the underworld and returned, but could not reverse his death. On Studley's rendering of these lines, see Introduction, p. 56.

[64] 24] The Fates spin the threads of people's lives, which they lengthen or cut as they desire.

[65] 25–27] Reference to Pelias, who 'thought [...] to drown' Jason, but died instead in boiling waters (see n. at 13–15 above).

The highest god, sometime that Saturn hight,[66]
30   His fall him taught to credit their decries.°
The rule of heavens he lost it by their might,
And Jove, his son, now turns the rolling skies.

Who weeneth° here to win eternal wealth,[67]
Let him behold this present perfit° proof,
And learn the secret step of Chance's stealth,
Most near alas when most it seems aloof.
In slipper° joy let no man put his trust;
Let none despair that heavy haps° hath passed.
The sweet with sour, she mingleth as she lust,
40   Whose doubtful web pretendeth nought to last:
Frail is the thread that Klotho's rock hath spun,
Now from the distaff drawn, now knapped° in twain.
With all the world, at length his end he won,
Whose works have wrought, his name should great remain,
And he, whose travails twelve his name display,[68]
That fearèd nought the force of worldly hurt,
In fine alas hath found his fatal day
And died with smart of Deianeira's shirt.[69]

If prowess might eternity procure,
50   Then Priam yet should live in liking° lust.
Ay portly pomp of pride, thou art unsure;
Lo, learn by him, O kings, ye are but dust.
And Hecuba that waileth now in care,
That was so late of high estate a queen,
A mirror is to teach you what you are:
Your wavering wealth, O princes, here is seen.[70]
Whom dawn of day hath seen in high estate,
Before sun's set, alas, hath had his fall.
The cradle's rock appoints the life his date
60   From settled joy to sudden funeral.

---

[66] 29–32] Another example of fate: Saturn, overthrown by Jove.

[67] 33–38] On these lines, see Introduction, pp. 24–25.

[68] travails] Pronounced 'tra'-vels' (here and throughout).

[69] 45–48] S. *Med.* (634–42) likely prompts Heywood's mention of Hercules. After performing twelve great labours, he was killed with a poisoned shirt, given to him by his second wife, Deianeira.

[70] 53–56] On *Troas* as a mirror for magistrates, see Introduction, pp. 23–25.

THE SECOND ACT

The Spright of Achilles added to the tragedy by the translator[71]

Forsaking now the places tenebrous°
And deep dens of th'infernal region,[72]
From all the shadows of Elysious
That wander there the paths fully many one,
Lo, here am I returnèd all alone,[73]
The same Achill[74] whose fierce and heavy hand
Of all the world no wight might yet withstand.

What man so stout° of all the Grecians' host
That hath not sometime craved Achilles' aid,
10   And in the Trojans who of prowess most
That hath not feared to see my banners splayed?
Achilles, lo, hath made them all afraid,
And in the Greeks hath been a pillar post,
That sturdy stood against the Trojan host.

Where I have lacked, the Grecians went to wrack.
Troy provèd hath what Achill's sword could do.
Where I have come the Trojans fled aback,
Retiring fast from field their walls unto.
No man that might Achilles' stroke foredo:°
20   I dealt such stripes° amid the Trojan rout
That with their blood I stained the fields about.

Mighty Memnon that with his Persian band
Would Priam's part with all his might maintain,
Lo now he lieth and know'th Achilles' hand.

---

[71] In S., Act 2 begins with the report of the appearance of Achilles' ghost by the Greek Herald Talthybius (here moved to 2.2). Heywood may have been inspired by Ovid's *Metamorphoses* (13.441–48), where the ghost of Achilles himself demands Polyxena's sacrifice, although this was itself a source for S. (see n. at 2.2.21–22 and 29–32). Continental commentaries on S. may have influenced Heywood, since each 'emphasizes the importance of the "imago Achilles [sic]"' (O'Keefe, 'Analysis', p. 61). John Partridge's poem on Astyanax and Polyxena (1566) also presents Achilles' ghost, instead of a report (sig. A5ᵛ–6ʳ).

[72] region] Trisyllabic here and often (also 'partial', etc.). See further pp. 289–90.

[73] 1–5] These lines echo Thyestes' ghost in S.'s *Agamemnon* (1–2) and possibly inform Studley's rendering of *Aga.* 1.1.2.

[74] The same Achill] Heywood borrows this phrase and other details of the speech from 2.2.17–32 (See n. at 78–84 below.) The phrase appears also at 2.3.145–48.

Amid the field is Troilus also slain.
Yea Hector great, whom Troy accounted plain°
The flower of chivalry that might be found –
All of Achilles had their mortal wound.[75]

But Paris, lo, such was his false deceit,
30   Pretending marriage of Polyxene,
Behind the altar lay for me in wait,
Where I unwares° have fallen into the train,
And in Apollo's church he hath me slain,
Whereof the hell will now just vengeance have,
And here again, I come my right to crave.

The deep Avern my rage may not sustain,
Nor bear the angers of Achilles' spright.
From Acheront, I rent the soil in twain,
And through the ground I grate again to sight.[76]
40   Hell could not hide Achilles from the light.
Vengeance and blood doth Orcus' pit require
To quench the Furies of Achilles' ire.

The hateful land that worse than Tartar is,
And burning thirst exceeds of Tantalus,
I here behold again, and Troy is this.
O, travail worse than stone of Sisyphus,
And pains that pass the pangs of Tityus,
To light more loathsome fury hath me sent
Than hookèd wheel that Ixion's flesh doth rent.[77]

50   Remembered is alow,° where sprights do dwell,
The wicked slaughter wrought by wily way;
Not yet revengèd hath the deepest hell,
Achilles' blood on them that did him slay.
But now of vengeance comes the ireful day,
And darkest dens of Tartar from beneath
Conspire the fates of them that wrought my death.

---

[75] 22–28] The list of victims (Memnon, Troilus, and Hector) parallels, though in a different order, the mural description in Virgil's *Aeneid* 1.474–89.

[76] grate] Probably from the verb 'grate' meaning 'to wear away by abrasion', suggesting that Achilles clawed his way through the soil, which was 'rent in twain' (line 38). Vocht (p. 324) suggests 'gate', i.e. 'got'.

[77] 43–49] Parallels S.'s list of victims of punishment in the underworld (*Thy.* 4–12 and *Aga.* 12–21).

Now mischief, murder, wrath of hell draw'th near,
And dire Phlegethon flood doth blood require.
Achilles' death shall be revengèd here,
60   With slaughter such as Stygian lakes desire.
Her daughter's blood shall slake the spirits' ire,
Whose son me slew, whereof doth yet remain
The wrath beneath, and hell shall be their pain.

From burning lakes, the Furies' wrath I threat,
And fire that nought but streams of blood may slake.
The rage of wind and seas these ships shall beat,
And Ditis deep on you shall vengeance take.
The sprights cry out, the earth and seas do quake;
The pool of Styx, ungrateful Greeks it see'th.
70   With slaughtered blood, revenge Achilles' death.

The soil doth shake to bear my heavy foot,
And fear'th again the sceptres of my hand,
The poles with stroke of thunderclap ring out,
The doubtful stars amid their course do stand,
And fearful Phoebus hides his blazing brand.
The trembling lakes against their course do flyte°
For dread and terror of Achilles' spright.

Great is the ransom ought° of due to me,
Wherewith ye must the sprights and hell appease.
80   Polyxena shall sacrificèd be
Upon my tomb their ireful wrath to please,
And with her blood ye shall assuage the seas:
Your ships may not return to Greece again
'Till on my tomb Polyxena be slain.[78]

And for that she should then have been my wife,
I will that Pyrrhus render her to me,
And in such solemn sort bereave° her life,
As ye are wont the weddings for to see.
So shall the wrath of hell appeasèd be.
90   Nought else but this may satisfy our ire,
Her will I have and her I you require.[79]

---

[78] 78–84] Corresponds to Talthybius's report at 2.2.29–32.
[79] her I you require] i.e. 'I demand her from you'.

The Second Scene

TALTHYBIUS   CHORUS

[TALTHYBIUS]

Alas how long the lingering Greeks in haven do make delay,
When either war by seas they seek or home to pass their way.

CHORUS

Why show, what cause doth hold your ships and Grecian navy
    stays?
Declare if any of the gods have stopped your homeward ways.

TALTHYBIUS

My mind is mazed,° my trembling sinews quake and are
    afeared,
For stranger news of truth than these I think were never heard.
Lo I myself have plainly seen in dawning of the day,
When Phoebus first gan to approach and drive the stars away,
The earth all shaken suddenly and from the hollow ground,
[Me] thought I heard with roaring cry a deep and dreadful
    sound[80]
That shook the woods and all the trees wrung out with thunder
    stroke.
From Ida hills down fell the stones, the mountain tops were
    broke,
And not the earth hath only quaked, but all the sea likewise
Achilles' presence felt and knew, and high the surges rise.[81]
The cloven ground Erebus' pits then showed, and deepest dens
That down to gods that guide beneath, the way appeared from
    hence.[82]
Then shook the tomb from whence anon in flame of fiery light
Appearèd from the hollow caves Achilles' noble spright,
As wonted he his Thracian arms and banners to display,
And wield his weighty weapons well against th'assaults of Troy.

10

20

---

[80] Me thought I heard] Heywood's addition, perhaps making Talthybius a 'more convincing witness' (O'Keefe, 'Analysis', pp. 77–78).

[81] high the surges rise] Heywood apparently misconstrues S.'s image of deathly calm, 'stravit vada' (levelled the seas).

[82] down to gods that guide beneath] In S., 'ad superos iter' (a path to those above [i.e. the living]).

The same Achilles seemed he then that he was wont to be
Amid the hosts,[83] and easily could I know that this was he[84]
With carcass slain in furious fight that stopped and filled each
    flood,
And who by slaughter of his hand made Xanthus run with
    blood,
As when in chariot high he sat with lofty stomach° stout,
While Hector both and Troy at once he drew the walls about.
Aloud he cried and every coast rang with Achilles' sound,
And thus with hollow voice he spake from bottom of the
    ground:

'The Greeks shall not with little price redeem Achilles' ire.

30   A princely ransom must they give, for so the Fates require.
Unto my ashes Polyxene spousèd shall here be slain
By Pyrrhus' hand, and all my tomb her blood shall
    overstain.'°[85]

This said, he straight sank down again to Pluto's deep region.
The earth then closed, the hollow caves were vanishèd and
    gone.
Therewith the weather waxèd clear, the raging winds did slake,   [200]
The tumbling seas began to rest and all the tempest break.[86]

The Third Scene

PYRRHUS AGAMEMNON CALCHAS

[PYRRHUS]

What time our sails we should have spread upon Sygeon seas,
With swift return from long delay to seek our homeward ways,
Achilles rose,[87] whose only hand hath given Greeks the spoil

---

[83] 19–22] In S., Talthybius alludes to two victims of Achilles: the Thracian Rhesus (misunderstood by Heywood, who refers to Achilles' 'Thracian arms'); and Cygnus son of Neptune (whom Heywood omits).

[84] 21–22] Heywood expands, possibly echoing Ovid's *Metamorphoses* 13.441 that describes Achilles as 'quantus, cum viveret, esse solebat' (as great as he was accustomed to be when alive).

[85] 29–32] Heywood excises the first three lines of the quoted speech in S. (*Tro.* 191–93) to avoid extensive overlap with the ghost scene. S. models Achilles' speech on Ovid, *Metamorphoses* 13.441–48.

[86] all the tempest break] Heywood omits S.'s final line (*Tro.* 202) describing the sound of a marriage song sung by a chorus of sea-deities (Tritons).

90

Of Troia sore annoyed by him and levelled with the soil,
With speed requiting° his abode and former long delay,
At Scyros isle and Lesbos both amid th'Aegean sea.
'Till he came here in doubt it stood of fall or sure estate.[88]
Then though ye haste to grant his will, ye shall it give too late.
Now have the other captains all the price of their manhood,[89]
10   What else reward for his prowess than her all only blood?[90]
Are his deserts° think you but light that when he might have
        fled,
And passing Pelyus' years in peace a quiet life have led,[91]
Detected yet his mother's crafts, forsook his woman's weed,
And with his weapons proved himself a manly man indeed?[92]

The King of Mysia, Telephus, that would the Greeks withstand,
Coming to Troy forbidding us the passage of his land,
Too late repenting to have felt Achilles' heavy stroke,
Was glad to crave his health again, where he his hurt had took.
For when his sore might not be salved, as told Apollo plain,
20   Except° the spear that gave the hurt restorèd help again,
Achilles' plasters cured his cuts and saved the king alive.
His hand both might and mercy knew to slay and then revive.[93]
When Thebes fell, Eetion saw it and might it not withstand,[94]

---

[87] Achilles rose] Perhaps continuing his emphasis on the ghost, Heywood adapts
S. 'excidit Achilles' (Has Achilles fallen from your memory?) to refer to his
'rising' ghost. Earlier commentators on Seneca clearly understood 'fallen from
memory' (O'Keefe, 'Analysis', p. 78).
[88] 1–7] Heywood does not fully convey Pyrrhus's point in S.: the Greeks were
wrong to forget Achilles, who had made Troy's fall inevitable, even if he did not
live to see it.
[89] 9] i.e. 'Each Greek man has taken his own Trojan woman'.
[90] her all only blood] i.e. 'the blood of Polyxena alone'. Compare 2.3.131,
referring to Iphigenia.
[91] Pelyus] Heywood misreads a form of 'Pylian', alluding to Nestor, the old and
wise Greek hero from Pylos.
[92] 13–14] Achilles' mother Thetis hid him, dressed as a woman, on the island of
Scyros (where Pyrrhus was conceived), delaying his arrival at Troy. Ulysses
discovered the deception (referred to at 3.1.165).
[93] 16–23] Expands S.'s account of Achilles' hurting then healing of Telephus,
adding a reference to Apollo, the god of healing.
[94] 23–32] A selective and somewhat confused rendering of S.'s catalogue of cities
and towns overcome by Achilles: Thebes (near Troy, ruled by Eetion,
Andromache's father), Lyrnesos (near Troy), Pedasus (home of Briseis), Chryse
(home of Chryseis), Tenedos (island off the coast of Troy), Thrace (kingdom of

The captive king could nought redress the ruin of his land.
Lyrnesos little likewise felt his hand and down it fell,
With ruin overturnèd like from top of haughty hill,[95]
And taken Briseis' land it is and prisoner is she caught,
The cause of strife between the kings is Chryses come to nought.
Tenedos isle, well known by fame and fertile soil, he took,

30   That fostereth fat the Thracian flocks and sacred Cilla shook.
What boots° to blaze° the bruit° of him, whom trump° of fame
        doth show
Through all the coasts where Caycus' flood with swelling stream
        doth flow?
The ruthful ruin of these realms so many towns beat down,
Another man would glory count and worthy great renown,
But thus my father made his way and these his journeys are,
And battles many one he fought, while war he doth prepare.[96]
As whist° I may his merits more, shall yet not this remain
Well known and counted praise enough, that he hath Hector
        slain,
During whose life the Grecians all might never take the town?

40   My father only vanquished Troy and you have plucked it
        down.[97]
Rejoice I may my parent's praise and bruit abroad his acts;
It seem'th the son to follow well his noble father's facts.°
In sight of Priam, Hector slain and Memnon both they lay,
With heavy cheer his parents wailed to mourn his dying day,[98]
Himself abhorred his handy work in fight that had them slain.
The sons of gods Achilles knew were born to die again.[99]
The woman, Queen of Amazons, that grieved the Greeks full
        sore,[100]

Rhesus), Cilla (near Troy, sacred to Apollo), and Caycus (river in Mysia, where Achilles defeated Telephus).

[95] With ruin overturnèd like] 'overturned with like ruin'.

[96] 34–36] In S., the stark contrast is between what any other man would regard as great battles and what Achilles did merely on his way to Troy.

[97] 40] i.e. Achilles conquered Troy; the rest of the Greeks merely stripped it. Heywood adds 'only', i.e. 'single-handedly'.

[98] 42–43] S. describes the response of Memnon's mother, Dawn (Aurora): 'parens pallente maestum protulit vultu diem' (his parent with pallid face brought forth a gloomy day; *Tro.* 239–40).

[99] 46] In killing Memnon (son of a goddess), Achilles learned that even someone of divine parentage could die – a poignant lesson for him, also the son of a goddess.

Is turned to flight, then ceased our fear, we dread their bows no
    more.
If ye well weigh his worthiness Achilles ought to have,
50   Though he from Argos or Mycenas would a virgin crave.[101]

Doubt ye herein? Allow ye not that straight his will be done,
And count ye cruel Priam's blood to give to Peleus' son?
For Helen's sake your own child's blood appeased Diana's
    ire.[102]
A wonted° thing and done ere this it is that I require.

AGAMEMNON

The only fault of youth it is not to refrain his rage.   [250]
The father's blood already stirs in Pyrrhus' wanton age.[103]
Sometime Achilles' grievous checks I bear with patient heart:
The more thou may'st, the more thou ought'st to suffer in good
    part.[104]
Whereto would ye with slaughtered blood a noble spirit stain?
60   Think what is meet the Greeks to do and Trojans to sustain.

The proud estate of tyranny may never long endure.
The king that rules with modest mean of safety may be sure.
The higher step of princely state that Fortune hath us 'signed,
The more behov'th a happy man humility of mind,
And dread the change that chance may bring whose gifts so
    soon be lost,
And chiefly then to fear the gods while they thee favour most.
In beating down that war hath won, by proof I have been taught,
What pomp and pride in twink° of eye may fall and come to
    nought.
Troy made me fierce and proud of mind, Troy makes me 'fraid
    withal.
70   The Greeks now stand where Troy late fell; each thing may
    have his fall.

---

[100] Queen of Amazons] Trojan ally, Penthesilea.
[101] 50] i.e. 'even if he should demand a woman from Argos or Mycenae' (the home of Agamemnon).
[102] 53] An allusion to the sacrifice of Iphigenia. See 'Mythological Background', p. 20.
[103] 56] S. has a starker contrast between other young men, whose fervour is due to age, and Pyrrhus, who inherits it from his father.
[104] 58] i.e. 'the more you are capable of, the more you ought to restrain yourself'.

Sometime I grant I did myself and sceptres proudly bear;
The thing that might advance my heart makes me the more to
    fear.
Thou Priam perfect proof present'st, thou art to me eftsoons°[105]
A cause of pride, a glass of fear, a mirror for the nones.°[106]
Should I account the sceptres aught but glorious vanity,
Much like the borrowed braided hair the face to beautify?
One sudden chance may turn to nought and maim the might of
    men,
With fewer than a thousand ships and years in less than ten.
Not she that guides the slipper wheel of fate doth so delay,
80   That she to all possession grants of ten years' settled stay.

With leave of Greece I will confess, I would have won the
    town,[107]
But not with ruin thus extreme to see it beaten down.
But, lo, the battle made by night and rage of fervent mind,
Could not abide the bridling bit that reason had assigned.
The happy sword once stained with blood unsatiable is,
And in the dark the fervent rage doth strike the more amiss.
Now are we wreaked on Troy too much, let all that may remain.
A virgin born of prince's blood for offering to be slain,
And given be to stain the tomb and ashes of the dead,
90   And under name of wedlock see the guiltless blood be shed,
I will not grant. For mine should be thereof both fault and
    blame.
Who, when he may forbiddeth not offence, doth will the same?

PYRRHUS

And shall his sprights have no reward, their angers to appease?

AGAMEMNON

Yes, very great, for all the world shall celebrate his praise,
And lands unknown that never saw the man so praised by fame,
Shall hear and keep for many years the glory of his name.
If bloodshed vail° his ashes aught, strike off an ox's head,

---

[105] 72–73] Heywood omits S. *Tro.* 268–69, where Agamemnon explains that the favour of fortune has humbled his spirit.
[106] a glass of fear, a mirror for the nones] Heywood adds the 'glass' and 'mirror' imagery (see also 1.Cho.53–56).
[107] I would have won the town] i.e. 'I wanted the Trojans to be defeated'.

94

And let no blood that may be cause of mothers' tears be shed.
What furious frenzy may this be that doth your will so lead,
100   This earnest careful suit to make in travail for the dead?
Let not such envy toward your father in your heart remain,[108]
That for his sacrifice ye would procure another's pain.   [300]

PYRRHUS

Proud tyrant while prosperity thy stomach doth advance,
And cowardly wretch that shrinks for fear in case of fearful
    chance –
Is yet again thy breast inflamed with brand of Venus' might?
Wilt thou alone so oft deprive Achilles of his right?[109]
This hand shall give the sacrifice, the which if thou withstand,
A greater slaughter shall I make and worthy Pyrrhus' hand.
And now too long from prince's slaughter doth my hand abide,
110   And meet it were that Polyxene were laid by Priam's side.[110]

AGAMEMNON

I nought deny but Pyrrhus' chief renown in war is this –
That Priam slain with cruel sword to your father humbled is.[111]

PYRRHUS

My father's foes, we have them known submit themselves
    humbly,
And Priam presently ye wot° was glad to crave mercy.
But thou, for fear, not stout to rule, liest close, from foes
    upshet,°[112]
While thou to Ajax and Ulysses dost thy will commit.[113]

AGAMEMNON

But needs I must and will confess your father did not fear,

---

[108] 101] In S., Agamemnon warns Pyrrhus of the 'invidia' (more accurately 'ill-will' than 'envy') that others will have toward Achilles.

[109] so oft] Alludes to Agamemnon's feud with Achilles.

[110] Polyxene] In S., Pyrrhus implicitly threatens Agamemnon, not Polyxena.

[111] 112] In S., Priam is more explicitly Achilles' 'supplex' (suppliant), since he entreated Achilles to recover the body of Hector (mentioned at 113–14).

[112] to rule] Heywood apparently reads 'ad regendum' (to rule) rather than the standard reading 'ad rogandum' (to ask, S. *Tro.* 316).

[113] 116] Pyrrhus scolds Agamemnon for having sent an embassy to Achilles (including Ulysses and Ajax), instead of going himself.

When burnt our fleet with Hector's brands and Greeks they
    slaughtered were,
While loitering then aloof he lay, unmindful of the fight,
120   Instead of arms, with scratch of quill, his sounding harp to smite.

PYRRHUS

Great Hector then, despising thee, Achilles' songs did fear,
And Thessale ships in greatest dread in quiet peace yet were.[114]

AGAMEMNON

For why: aloof the Thessale fleet they lay from Trojans' hands,
And well your father might have rest, he felt not Hector's
    brands.[115]

PYRRHUS

Well seems a noble king to give another king relief.

AGAMEMNON

Why hast thou then a worthy king bereavèd of his life?

PYRRHUS

A point of mercy sometime is what lives in care to kill.

AGAMEMNON

But now your mercy moveth you a virgin's death to will?

PYRRHUS

Account ye cruel now her death whose sacrifice I crave?
130   Your own dear daughter once ye know yourself to th'altars
    gave.[116]

AGAMEMNON

Nought else could save the Greeks from seas, but th'only
    blood of her.[117]
A king before his children ought his country to prefer.

---

[114] Thessale ships] i.e. the ships of Achilles.

[115] 123–24] Heywood misreads S. 'nempe isdem in istis Thessalis navalibus pax alta rursus Hectoris patri fuit' (Indeed in these same Thessalian shipyards, there was profound peace – for Hector's father!; *Tro.* 325–26).

[116] 127–30] On Heywood's translation style in these lines, see Introduction, p. 29.

[117] 130–31] Heywood's addition, clarifying the allusion to Iphigenia.

PYRRHUS

The law doth spare no captive's blood, nor will'th their death to stay.

AGAMEMNON

That which the law doth not forbid, yet shame doth oft say nay.

PYRRHUS

The conqueror what thing he list° may lawfully fulfil.

AGAMEMNON

So much the less he ought to list that may do what he will.

PYRRHUS

Thus boast ye these as though in all ye only bare the stroke,[118]
When Pyrrhus loosèd hath the Greeks from bond of ten years' yoke.

AGAMEMNON

Hath Scyros' isle such stomachs bred?

PYRRHUS

                                        No brethren's wrath it knows.

AGAMEMNON

140   Beset about it is with wave.

PYRRHUS

                            The seas it do enclose.[119]
Thyestes' noble stock I know and Atreus' eke full well,
And of the brethren's dire debate perpetual fame doth tell.

AGAMEMNON

And thou a bastard of a maid deflowered privily,
Whom (then a boy) Achilles gate° in filthy lechery.[120]

---

[118] 137] Heywood's addition.
[119] The seas it do enclose] 'it' is the island of Scyros, Pyrrhus's birthplace. In S., Pyrrhus emphasizes his kinship with the 'sea', through Achilles' mother Thetis, the sea-goddess.

PYRRHUS

> The same Achill that doth possess the reign of gods above:
> With Thetis, seas; with Aeacus, sprights; the starrèd heaven,
>> with Jove.[121]

AGAMEMNON

> The same Achilles that was slain by stroke of Paris' hand.

PYRRHUS

> The same Achilles, whom no god durst ever yet withstand.

AGAMEMNON

> The stoutest man, I rather would, his checks he should refrain.
> I could them tame, but all your brags, I can full well sustain,[122]   [350]
> For even the captives spares my sword. Let Calchas callèd be.
> If destinies require her blood, I will thereto agree.
>
> [Enter Calchas]
>
> Calchas, whose counsel ruled our ships and navy hither brought,
> Unlock'st the pole° and hast by art the secrets thereof sought,
> To whom the bowels of the beast, to whom the thunder clap,
> And blazing star with flaming train betokeneth what shall hap,
> Whose words with dearest price I bought, now tell us by what
>> mean,
> The will of gods agree'th that we return to Greece again.

CALCHAS

> The Fates appoint the Greeks to buy their ways with wonted
>> price,[123]
> And with what cost ye came to Troy, ye shall repair to Greece.
> With blood ye came, with blood ye must from hence return
>> again,

150

160

---

[120] then a boy] S. 'nondum viro' (not yet a man), alluding also to Achilles' being disguised as a woman on Scyros.

[121] 146] Divine relatives of Achilles with their own spheres of power.

[122] 149–50] Obscure translation of S. 'compescere equidem verba et audacem malo poteram domare' (I for my part was able to check his words and to tame his audacity in evildoing). Heywood misreads the noun 'malo' (in evil) as a verb (prefer; translated 'I rather would').

[123] with wonted price] Alludes to Iphigenia.

And where Achilles' ashes lieth, the virgin shall be slain,
In seemly sort of habit such as maidens wont ye see,
Of Thessaly or Mycenas else what time they wedded be.
With Pyrrhus' hand she shall be slain, of rite it shall be so.
And meet it is that he the son his father's right should do.
But not this only stay'th our ships: our sails may not be spread,
Before a worthier blood than thine, Polyxena, be shed,
Which thirst the Fates for Priam's nephew:° Hector's little boy
170   The Greeks shall tumble headlong down from highest tower in
    Troy.
Let him there die, this only way ye shall the gods appease,
Then spread your thousand sails with joy, ye need not fear the
    seas.

CHORUS

May this be true or doth the fable feign –
When corpse is dead the sprite° to live as yet,[124]
When death our eyes with heavy hand doth strain,
And fatal day our leams° of light hath shet,°
And in the tomb our ashes once be set?
Hath not the soul likewise his funeral,
But still alas do wretches live in thrall?[125]

Or else doth all at once together die,
And may no part his fatal hour delay,
10   But with the breath the soul from hence doth fly,
Amid the clouds to vanish quite away,
As danky° shade flee'th from the pole by day,[126]
And may no jot° escape from destiny,
When once the brand hath burnèd the body?

Whatever then the rise of sun may see,
And what the west that sets the sun doth know,
In all Neptunus' reign whatever be,
That restless seas do wash and overflow,

---

[124] live as yet] 'remain alive'.

[125] 5–6] In S., a starker question: 'non prodest animam tradere funeri, sed restat miseris vivere longius?' (Is it useless to confer the soul to death, and must we wretches still live for a longer time?).

[126] As danky] Heywood's addition (Vocht, p. 327) or a skewed sense of S. 'halitu' (exhalation), which is otherwise untranslated.

With purple waves still tumbling to and fro,
20   Age shall consume: each thing that liv'th shall die,
With swifter race than Pegasus doth fly.

And with what whirl the twice six signs do fly,[127]
With course as swift as rector of the spheres,
Doth guide those glistering globes eternally,
And Hecate her changèd horns repairs,
So draw'th on death, and life of each thing wears,
And never may the man return to sight[128]
That once hath felt the stroke of Parcas' might.[129]

For as the fume that from the fire doth pass,
30   With turn of hand, doth vanish out of sight,
And swifter than the northern Boreas,
With whirling blast and storm of raging might,
Driv'th far away and puts the clouds to flight,
So flee'th the sprite that rules our life away,
And nothing tarry'th after dying day.[130]

Swift is the race we run, at hand the mark,
Lay down your hope that wait here aught to win,[131]
And who dreads aught, cast off thy careful cark,
Wilt thou it wot what state thou shalt be in,
40   When dead thou art, as thou had'st never been?
For greedy time it doth devour us all,
The world it sways to Chaos' heap to fall.   [400]

Death hurts the corpse and spareth not the sprite,
And as for all the dens of Taenar deep,
With Cerberus' kingdom dark that knows no light,
And straightest gates that he there sits to keep,
They fancies are that follow folk by sleep.

---

[127] 22–25] Three comparisons for the speed (the 'whirl') of death's approach: the zodiac ('twice six signs'), sun ('rector of the spheres'), and moon ('Hecate').

[128] 27–28] Heywood omits S.'s description of the dead man descending to the river Styx.

[129] Parcas' might] i.e. 'the might of the Fates' (S. 'fata', without mention of Parcae).

[130] 29–35] On Heywood's translation style in these lines, see Introduction, pp. 29–30.

[131] that wait here aught to win] i.e. 'you who expect to gain anything more in life'; S. 'avidi' (greedy people).

Such rumours vain, but feignèd lies they are,
And fables like the dreams in heavy care.

These three staves° following are added by the translator.

50   O dreadful day, alas, the sorry time,
Is come of all the mother's ruthful woe:
Astyanax, alas, thy fatal line
Of life is worn – to death straight shalt thou go.
The Sisters have decreed it should be so.[132]
There may no force, alas, escape their hand.
The mighty Jove their will may not withstand.

To see the mother her tender child forsake,
What gentle heart that may from tears refrain,
Or who so fierce that would not pity take,
60   To see alas the guiltless infant slain.
For sorry heart the tears mine eyes do stain,
To think what sorrow shall her heart oppress,
Her little child to leese° remediless.

The double cares of Hector's wife to wail,
Good Ladies have your tears in readiness,[133]
And you with whom should pity most prevail
Rue° on her grief, bewail her heaviness,°
With sobbing heart lament her deep distress,
When she with tears shall take leave of her son,
70   And now, Good Ladies, hear what shall be done.

THE THIRD ACT

Andromacha Senex Ulysses[134]

[ANDROMACHA]

Alas ye careful company, why hale ye thus your hairs?
Why beat you so your boiling breasts and stain your eyes with
    tears?[135]

---

[132] Sisters] Fates.

[133] Good Ladies] On this phrase, see Introduction, p. 31.

[134] Astyanax also appears. Ulysses enters with soldiers at 112.

[135] 2–3] Omits a sentence in S. (*Tro.* 411–12) contrasting the Trojans' present woes with their more grievous past.

The fall of Troy is new to you, but unto me not so;
I have foreseen this careful case ere this time long ago,[136]
When fierce Achilles Hector slew and drew the corpse about,
Then, then me thought, I wist it well, that Troy should come to
    nought.

In sorrows sunk, I senseless am and wrapped alas in woe,
But soon, except this babe me held, to Hector would I go.
This silly° fool° my stomach tames amid my misery,
10   And in the hour of heaviest haps permits me not to die.
This only cause contstrain'th me yet the gods for him to pray,
With tract of time prolongs my pain, delays my dying day.
He takes from me the lack of fear, the only fruit of ill,
For while he lives yet have I left whereof to fear me still.
No place is left for better chance, with worse we are oppressed.
To fear alas and see no hope is worst of all the rest.

SENEX

What sudden fear thus moves your mind and vexeth you so sore?

ANDROMACHA

Still, still alas of one mishap there riseth more and more;
Not yet the doleful° destinies of Troy be come to end.

SENEX

20   And what more grievous chances yet prepare the gods to
    send?[137]

ANDROMACHA

The caves and dens of hell be rent for Trojans' greater fear,
And from the bottoms of their tombs, the hidden sprights appear.
May none but Greeks alone from hell return to life again?
Would god the Fates would finish soon the sorrows I sustain.[138]
Death thankful were,[139] a common care the Trojans all oppress,

---

[136] careful case] i.e. 'lamentable incident'.

[137] 20] S. is stronger: 'et quas reperiet, ut velit, clades deus?' (What [further] disasters will [i.e. can] the god invent, even if he wants to?).

[138] 24] Heywood's addition, highlighting the Fates (O'Keefe, 'Analysis', p. 87).

[139] Death thankful were] Heywood misconstrues S. 'certe aequa mors est' (Death is certainly equal [for all]).

But me alas amazeth most the fearful heaviness,
That all astonied° am for dread and horror of the sight,
That in my sleep appeared to me, by dream this latter night.

SENEX

Declare what sights your dream hath showed and tell what
    doth you fear.

ANDROMACHA

30 Two parts of all the silent night almost then passèd were,
And then the clear seven clustered beams of stars were fallen to
    rest,[140]
And first the sleep so long unknown my wearied eyes oppressed
– If this be sleep: the astonied maze of mind in heavy mood –
When suddenly before mine eyes the spright of Hector stood,
Not like as he the Greeks was wont to battle to require,
Or when amid the Grecians' ships he threw the brands of fire,
Nor such as raging on the Greeks with slaughtering stroke had
    slain,
And bare indeed the spoils of him that did Achilles feign,[141]
His countenance not now so bright, nor of so lively cheer,
40 But sad and heavy like to ours, and clad with ugly hair. [450]
It did me good to see him though, when shaking then his head:
'Shake off thy sleep in haste', he said, 'and quickly leave thy
    bed.
Convey into some secret place our son, O faithful wife.
This only hope there is to help find mean to save his life.
Leave off thy piteous tears', he said, 'Dost thou yet wail for
    Troy?
Would god it lay on ground full flat,[142] so ye might save the
    boy.
Up stir', he said, 'thyself in haste, convey him privily,
Save if ye may the tender blood of Hector's progeny.'

---

[140] 31] A loose translation; S.'s reference is to the Plough (i.e. the Wain),
indicating midnight.
[141] him that did Achilles feign] Patroclus, who wore Achilles' armour in battle and
was killed by Hector.
[142] full flat] Because Astyanax is to die by being thrown from the tower (as
stipulated at 2.3.170).

Then straight in trembling fear I waked, and rolled mine eyes
    about,
50   Forgetting long my child, poor wretch, and after Hector sought.
But straight, alas I wist not how, the spright away did pass,
And me forsook before I could my husband once embrace.

O child, O noble father's brood and Trojans' only joy,
O worthy seed of th'ancient blood and beaten house of Troy,
O image of thy father, lo thou lively bear'st his face,
This countenance, lo, my Hector had, and even such was his
    pace.
The pitch of all his body such, his hands thus would he bear,
His shoulders high, his threatening brows, even such as thine
    they were.[143]
O son, begot too late for Troy, but born too soon for me,[144]
60   Shall ever time yet come again, and happy day may be
That thou may'st once revenge and build again the towers of
    Troy,
And to the town and Trojans both restore their name with joy?

But why do I, forgetting state of present destiny,
So great things wish? Enough for captives is to live only.
Alas what privy place is left my little child to hide?
What seat so secret may be found, where thou may'st safely
    bide?
The tower that with the walls of gods so valiant was of might,[145]
Through all the world so notable, so flourishing to sight,
Is turned to dust, and fire hath all consumed that was in Troy,
70   Of all the town not so much now is left to hide the boy.
What place were best to choose for guile, the holy tomb is here
That th'enemy's sword will spare to spoil, where lieth my
    husband dear,
Which costly work his father built, King Priam, liberal,
And it upraised with charges great for Hector's funeral.
Herein the bones and ashes both of Hector, lo they lie.
Best is that I commit the son to his father's custody.

---

[143] 58–59] Heywood omits other points of resemblance in S. (e.g. hair and neck).
[144] 59] Astyanax is 'too late' (i.e. too young) to defend Troy, but 'too soon', since he is now vulnerable to the Greeks.
[145] tower] i.e. Troy. S. 'arx' (citadel). See also n. at 1.1.10.

A cold and fearful sweat doth run throughout my members all;
Alas I careful wretch do fear what chance may thee befall.

SENEX

80
Hide him away: this only way hath savèd many more,
To make the enemies to believe that they were dead before.
He will be sought, scant any hope remaineth of safeness,
The peise° of his nobility doth him so sore oppress.

ANDROMACHA

What way were best to work that none our doings might
    bewray?°

SENEX

Let none bear witness what ye do, remove them all away.

ANDROMACHA

What if the enemies ask me where Astyanax doth remain?

SENEX

Then shall ye boldly answer make that he in Troy was slain.

ANDROMACHA

What shall it help to have him hid? At length they will him
    find.

SENEX

At first the enemy's rage is fierce; delay doth slake his
    mind.

ANDROMACHA

But what prevails, since free from fear we can him never
    hide?

SENEX

90
Let yet the wretch take his defence more careless° there to
    bide.[146]

---

[146] 90] Heywood apparently misreads S.: the idea is that beggars can't be choosers when it comes to seeking protection.

ANDROMACHA

> What land unknown, out of the way, what unfrequented place
> May keep thee safe? Who aids our fear? Who shall defend our
>   case?
> Hector, Hector, that evermore thy friends did'st well defend,   [500]
> Now chiefly aid thy wife and child and us some succour send.
> Take charge to keep and cover close the treasures of thy wife,[147]
> And in thy ashes hide thy son, preserve in tomb his life.
> Draw near my child unto the tomb. Why fliest thou backward
>   so?
> Thou tak'st great scorn to lurk in dens; thy noble heart I know.
> I see thou art ashamed to fear. Shake off thy princely mind,
> And bear thy breast as thee behoves, as chance hath thee
>   assigned.
> Behold our case, and see what flock remaineth now of Troy:
> The tomb, I woeful captive wretch, and thou a silly boy.
> But yield we must to sorry Fates; thy chance must break thy
>   breast.
> Go to, creep underneath thy father's holy seats to rest.
> If aught the Fates may wretches help, thou hast thy safeguard
>   there.
> If not, already then poor fool, thou hast thy sepulchre.

SENEX

> The tomb him closely hides, but lest your fear should him
>   betray,
> Let him here lie, and far from hence go ye some other way.

ANDROMACHA

> The less he fears that fears at hand,[148] and yet if need be so,
> If ye think meet, a little hence for safety let us go.

SENEX

> A little while keep silence now; refrain your plaint and cry.
> His cursèd foot now hither moves the Lord of Cephalle.

[Enter Ulysses with soldiers]

---

[147] Treasures] S. 'furtum' (theft), registering Andromache's deceit in hiding Astyanax.
[148] The less he fears that fears at hand] 'one fears less when close by'.

106

ANDROMACHA

[Aside]

Now open, earth, and thou my spouse from Styx rent up the
        ground,
Deep in thy bosom hide my son that he may not be found.
Ulysses comes with doubtful pace and changèd countenance.
He knits in heart deceitful craft for some more grievous chance.

ULYSSES

Though I be made the messenger of heavy news to you,
This one thing first I shall desire: that ye take this for true,
That though the words come from my mouth and I my message
        tell,
120   Of truth yet are they none of mine, ye may believe me well.
It is the word of all the Greeks and they the authors be,
Whom Hector's blood doth yet forbid their countries for to
        see.[149]
Our careful trust of peace unsure doth still the Greeks detain,
And evermore our doubtful fear yet draw'th us back again,
And suffereth not our wearied hands our weapons to forsake,
In child yet of Andromacha while Trojans comfort take.

ANDROMACHA

And say'th your augur Calchas so?

ULYSSES

                                    Though Calchas nothing said,
Yet Hector tells it us himself, of whose seed are we frayed.°
The worthy blood of noble men, oftimes we see it plain,
130   Doth after in their heirs succeed and quickly springs again.
For so the hornless youngling yet of high and sturdy beast,
With lofty neck and branchèd brow doth shortly rule the rest.
The tender twig that of the loppèd stock doth yet remain,
To match the tree that bare the bough in time starts up again;
With equal top to former wood, the room it doth supply,
And spreads on soil alow the shade to heaven his branches high.
Thus of one spark by chance yet left, it happeneth so full oft,

---

[149] blood] i.e. progeny. In S., Ulysses says also that 'the fates demand' Astyanax
(fata expetunt).

The fire hath quickly caught his force and flam'th again aloft.
So fear we yet lest Hector's blood might rise ere it be long.
140   Fear casts in all th'extremity and oft interprets wrong.
If ye respect our case, ye may not blame these old soldiers,
Though after years and months twice five, they fear again the
        wars,
And other travails, dreading Troy not yet to be well won:
A great thing doth the Grecians move, the fear of Hector's son.   [550]

Rid us of fear. This stay'th our fleet and plucks them back
        again,
And in the haven our navy sticks, 'till Hector's blood be slain.
Count me not fierce for that by fates I Hector's son require,
For I as well, if chance it would, Orestes should desire.[150]
But since that needs it must be so, bear it with patient heart,
150   And suffer that which Agamemnon suffered in good part.[151]

ANDROMACHA

Alas, my child, would god thou wert yet in thy mother's hand,
And that I knew what destinies thee held or in what land.
For never should the mother's faith her tender child forsake,
Though through my breast the enemies all their cruel weapons
        strake,°
Nor though the Greeks with pinching bands of iron my hands
        had bound,
Or else in fervent flame of fire beset my body round.
But now my little child, poor wretch, alas, where might he be?
Alas, what cruel destiny, what chance hath happed to thee?
Art thou yet ranging in the fields and wanderest there abroad?
160   Or smothered else in dusty smoke of Troy or overtrod?
Or have the Greeks thee slain, alas, and laughed to see thy
        blood?
Or torn art thou with jaws of beasts or cast to fowls for food?

ULYSSES

Dissemble not. Hard is for thee Ulysses to deceive.
I can full well the mother's crafts and subtlety perceive.

---

[150] 148] i.e. if he had to, Ulysses would kill even Agamemnon's own son; S.
'petissem Oresten' (I would have sought Orestes).
[151] Another reference to Iphigenia.

The policy of goddesses Ulysses hath undone.[152]
Set all these feignèd words aside. Tell me, where is thy son?

ANDROMACHA

Where is Hector? Where all the rest that had with Troy their fall?
Where Priamus? You ask for one, but I require of all.

ULYSSES

Thou shalt constrainèd be to tell the thing thou dost deny.

ANDROMACHA

170   A happy chance were death to her that doth desire to die.

ULYSSES

Who most desires to die would fainest° live when death draw'th
    on.
These noble words with present fear of death would soon be
    gone.

ANDROMACHA

Ulysses, if ye will constrain Andromacha with fear,
Threaten my life,[153] for now to die my chief desire it were.

ULYSSES

With stripes, with fire, tormenting death, we will the truth
    out wrest,
And dolour shall thee force to tell the secrets of thy breast,
And what thy heart hath deepest hid, for pain thou shalt
    express:
Oftimes th'extremity prevails much more than gentleness.

ANDROMACHA

Set me in midst of burning flame, with wounds my body rent,
180   Use all the means of cruelty that ye may all invent,
Prove° me with thirst and hunger both, and every torment try,
Pierce through my sides with burning irons, in prison let me lie,
Spare not the worst ye can devise (if aught be worse than this),
Yet never get ye more of me: I wot not where he is.

---

[152] See n. at 2.3.13–14.
[153] Threaten my life] S. 'vitam minare' (Threaten *me* with *life*).

ULYSSES

It is but vain to hide the thing that straight ye will detect.°
No fears may move the mother's heart, she doth them all
　　neglect.
This tender love ye bear your child, wherein ye stand so stout,
So much more circumspectly warn'th the Greeks to look about,
Lest after ten years' tract of time and battle borne so far,

190　　Someone should live that on our children might renew the war.
As for myself, what Calchas say'th, I would not fear at all,
But on Telemachus I dread the smart of wars would fall.

ANDROMACHA

Now will I make Ulysses glad and all the Greeks also.[154]
Needs must thou woeful wretch confess, declare thy hidden
　　woe.
Rejoice ye sons of Atreus, there is no cause of dread:
Be glad, Ulysses, tell the Greeks that Hector's son is dead.

ULYSSES

By what assurance prov'st thou that? How shall we credit thee?

ANDROMACHA

Whatever thing the enemy's hand may threaten, hap to me.　　　[600]
Let speedy Fates me slay forthwith, and earth me hide at
　　once,[155]

200　　And after death from tomb again remove yet Hector's bones,
Except my son already now do rest among the dead,
And that except Astyanax into his tomb be led.

ULYSSES

Then fully are the Fates fulfilled with Hector's child's decease.
Now shall I bear the Grecians word of sure and certain peace.

[Aside]

Ulysses why what dost thou now? The Greeks will everychone
Believe thy words. Whom credit'st thou? The mother's tale
　　alone.

---

[154] Heywood omits 'invita' (against my will).
[155] 199–202] Andromache swears an oath, wishing death for herself and
desecration of Hector's tomb if Astyanax is not dead.

Think'st thou for safeguard of her child the mother will not lie,
And dread the more the worse mischance to give her son to die?
Her faith she binds with bond of oath the truth to verify;
210   What thing is more of weight to fear than so to swear and lie?
Now call thy crafts together all, bestir thy wits and mind,
And show thyself Ulysses now the truth herein to find.[156]
Search well the mother's mind. Behold, she weeps and waileth
    out,
And here and there with doubtful pace she rangeth all about.
Her careful ears she doth apply to hearken what I say.
More 'fraid she seems than sorrowful. Now work some wily
    way.
For now most need of wit there is and crafty policy.
Yet once again by other means I will the mother try.

[To Andromacha]

Thou wretched woman may'st rejoice that dead he is: Alas,[157]
220   More doleful death by destiny for him decreed there was,
From turret's top to have been cast and cruelly been slain,
Which only tower of all the rest doth yet in Troy remain.

ANDROMACHA

[Aside]

My sprite fail'th me, my limbs do quake, fear doth my wits
    confound,
And as the ice congeals with frost, my blood with cold is bound.

ULYSSES

[Aside]

She trembleth, lo this way, this way, I will the truth out wrest.
The mother's fear detecteth all the secrets of her breast.
I will renew her fear.

[To soldiers]

Go sirs, bestir ye speedily

---

[156] show thyself Ulysses] i.e. be your usual cunning and deceitful self.
[157] 218–19] Heywood omits a detail from S. contrasting other parents, whom 'it is fitting to console in their grief', with Andromache, who should rejoice her son has already died (S. *Tro.* 619–20).

To seek this enemy of the Greeks wherever that he lie.
Well done, he will be found at length. Go to, still seek him
out.[158]

[To Andromacha]

230   Now shall he die. What dost thou fear? Why dost thou look
about?

ANDROMACHA

Would god that any cause there were yet left that might me
fray.°
My heart at last, now all is lost, hath laid all fear away.

ULYSSES

Since that your child now hath ye say already suffered death,
And with his blood we may not purge the hosts, as Calchas
say'th,
Our fleet pass not (as well inspired doth Calchas prophesy)
'Till Hector's ashes cast abroad the waves may pacify,
And tomb be rent. Now since the boy hath scaped his destiny,
Needs must we break this holy tomb where Hector's ashes lie.

ANDROMACHA

[Aside]

What shall I do? My mind distracted is with double fear,
240   On th'one my son, on th'other side my husband's ashes dear.
Alas, which part should move me most? The cruel gods I call
To witness with me in the truth, and ghosts that guide thee all,[159]
Hector, that nothing in my son is else that pleaseth me,
But thou alone; god grant him life, he might resemble thee.
Shall Hector's ashes drownèd be? Bide° I such cruelty
To see his bones cast in the seas? Yet let Astyanax die?   [650]
And can'st thou wretched mother bide thine own child's death
to see,
And suffer from the high tower's top that headlong thrown he
be?

---

[158] Well done [...] seek him out.] In S., Ulysses feints that Astyanax has been
apprehended.
[159] ghosts that guide thee all] S. 'veros [...] manes' (true departed spirits [of
Hector]); these are called on as witnesses along with the 'cruel gods'.

I can and will take in good part his death and cruel pain,
250   So that my Hector after death be not removed again.
The boy that life and senses hath may feel his pain and die,
But Hector, lo, his death hath placed at rest in tomb to lie.
What dost thou stay?° Determine which thou wilt preserve of
        twain.
Art thou in doubt? Save this, lo here thy Hector doth remain.
Both Hectors be, th'one quick of sprite and drawing toward his
        strength,
And one that may perhaps revenge his father's death at
        length.[160]
Alas, I cannot save them both, I think that best it were
That of the twain I savèd him that doth the Grecians fear.

ULYSSES

It shall be done that Calchas' words to us doth prophesy,
260   And now shall all this sumptuous work be thrown down
        utterly.[161]

ANDROMACHA

That once ye sold?[162]

ULYSSES

                        I will it all from top to bottom rend.

ANDROMACHA

The faith of gods I call upon. Achilles us defend,
And Pyrrhus aid thy father's right.[163]

ULYSSES

                                    This tomb abroad shall lie.[164]

ANDROMACHA

O mischief, never durst° the Greeks show yet such cruelty.
Ye strain the temples and the gods that most have favoured you,

---

[160] 255–56] In S., both lines clearly refer to Astyanax as the living 'Hector'.

[161] this sumptuous work] In S., simply 'busta' (the tomb).

[162] sold] Refers to the ransoming of Hector's body to Priam.

[163] aid thy father's right] S. 'genitoris tui munus tuere' (protect your father's gift), alluding to Achilles' decision to return Hector to Priam.

[164] abroad shall lie] Heywood omits S. 'campo [...] toto' (over the whole field).

The dead ye spare not on their tombs; your fury rageth now.[165]
I will their weapons all resist myself with naked hand,
The ire of heart shall give me strength their armour to
    withstand,
As fierce as did the Amazons beat down the Greeks in fight,
270   And Maenad once inspired with god in sacrifice doth smite,
With spear in hand, and while with furious pace she treads the
    ground,[166]
And wood° as one in rage, she strikes and feeleth not the
    wound;
So will I run on midst of them and on their weapons die,
And in defence of Hector's tomb among his ashes lie.

ULYSSES

[To soldiers]

Cease ye? Doth rage and fury vain of woman move ye aught?
Dispatch with speed what I command and pluck down all to
    nought.

ANDROMACHA

Slay me rather here with sword, rid me out of the way,
Break up the deep Avern and rid my destiny's delay.
Rise Hector and beset thy foes. Break thou Ulysses' ire.
280   A spright art good enough for him, behold he casteth° fire,
And weapon shakes with mighty hand. Do ye not Greeks him
    see,
Or else doth Hector's spright appear but only unto me?

ULYSSES

[To soldiers]

Down quite withal.

ANDROMACHA

[Aside]

           What wilt thou suffer both thy son be slain,
And after death thy husband's bones to be removed again?

---

[165] your fury rageth now] Differs from S. 'busta transierat furor' (your rage had
[up till now] left tombs alone).
[166] spear] S. 'thyrsus', the foliage-tipped staff wielded by Maenads.

Perhaps thou may'st with prayer[167] yet appease the Grecians all,
Else down to ground the holy tomb of Hector straight shall fall.
Let rather die the child, poor wretch, and let the Greeks him
    kill,[168]
Than father and the son should cause the tone° the other's ill.[169]

[To Ulysses]

Ulysses, at thy knees I fall, and humbly ask mercy.
290   These hands that no man's feet else knew, first at thy feet they
    lie.
Take pity on the mother's case and sorrows of my breast.
Vouchsafe my prayers to receive and grant me my request,
And by how much the more the gods have thee advancèd high,
More easily strike the poor estate of wretched misery.[170]
God grant the chaste bed of thy godly wife Penelope
May thee receive, and so again Laerta may thee see,   [700]
And that thy son, Telemachus, may meet thee joyfully,
His grandsire's years and father's wit to pass full happily.
Take pity on the mother's tears, her little child to save.
300   He is my only comfort left and th'only joy I have.

ULYSSES

Bring forth thy son and ask.

The Second Scene[171]

ANDROMACHA

Come hither child out of thy dens to me,
Thy wretched mother's lamentable store.°
This babe, Ulysses, lo, this babe is he
That stay'th your ships and feareth you so sore.

---

[167] prayer] Disyllabic here and often (also 'oar'). See further pp. 289–90.
[168] Let rather die the child] Heywood omits S.'s emphasis: let him die 'ubicumque' (anywhere) other than in the tomb.
[169] father and the son should cause the tone the other's ill] S.'s vivid image is of the corpses of father and son 'crushing' one another.
[170] more easily strike] i.e. crush less heavily. After this line, Heywood omits S. *Tro.* 697, explaining how acting mercifully can keep one in fortune's favour.
[171] Heywood adds a scene break and follows S.'s change in metre which distinguishes Andromache's lament from the dialogue.

Submit thyself my son with humble hand,
And worship flat on ground thy master's feet.
Think it no shame, as now the case doth stand:
The thing that Fortune will'th a wretch is meet.[172]
Forget thy worthy stock of kingly kind;°
10   Think not on Priam's great nobility,
And put thy father, Hector, from thy mind:
Such as thy fortune, let thy stomach be.
Behave thyself as captive; bend thy knee,
And though thy grief pierce not thy tender years,
Yet learn to wail thy wretched state by me,
And take ensample° at thy mother's tears.

Once Troy hath seen the weeping of a child,[173]
When little Priam turned Alcides' threats,
And he to whom all beasts in strength did yield,
20   That made his way from hell and brake their gates,
His little enemy's tears yet overcame.
'Priam,' he said, 'receive thy liberty;
In seat of honour keep thy kingly name,
But yet thy sceptre's rule more faithfully.'[174]
Lo such the conquest was of Hercules.
Of him yet learn your hearts to mollify.
Do only Herc'les' cruel weapons please,
And may no end be of your cruelty?

No less than Priam kneels to thee this boy
30   That lieth and asketh only life of thee.
As for the rule and governance of Troy,
Wherever Fortune will, there let it be.
Take mercy on the mother's ruthful tears[175]
That with their streams my cheeks do overflow,
And spare this guiltless infant's tender years
That humbly falleth at thy feet so low.

---

[172] 8] i.e. 'whatever thing Fortune commands a wretch to do, is proper'.

[173] 17–24] When Alcides (i.e. Hercules) attacked Troy, Priam (still a child) begged for his life and was spared. See also 1.2.72–73.

[174] more faithfully] Priam's father, Laomedon, had broken a promise to give mares to Hercules, which prompted Hercules' attack.

[175] 33–36] Heywood's addition, smoothing the transition back to dialogue.

The Third Scene

ULYSSES ANDROMACHA ASTYANAX

[ULYSSES]

> Of truth the mother's great sorrow doth move my heart full sore,
> But yet the mothers of the Greeks of need must move me more
> To whom this boy may cause in time a great calamity.

ANDROMACHA

> May ever he the burnt ruins of Troy re-edify?°
> And shall these hands in time to come erect the town again?
> If this be th'only help we have, there doth no hope remain
> For Troy. We stand not now in case to cause your fear of
>   mind.
> Doth aught avail his father's force or stock of noble kind?
> His father's heart abated was; he drawn the walls about.[176]
> Thus evil haps; the haughtiest heart at length they bring to
>   nought.
> If ye will needs oppress a wretch, what thing more grievous
>   were
> Than on his noble neck he should the yoke of bondage bear?
> To serve in life: doth any man this to a king deny?

10

ULYSSES

> Not Ulysses willeth his death, but Calchas' prophecy.

ANDROMACHA

> O false inventor of deceit and heinous cruelty,   [750]
> By manhood of whose hand in war no man did ever die,
> But by deceit and crafty train of mind that mischief seeks,
> Before this time full many one dead is, yea of the Greeks.[177]
> The prophet's words and guiltless gods, say'st thou, my son
>   require?
> Nay, mischief of thy breast it is; thou dost his death desire.

20

---

[176] His father's heart abated was] S. has a contrafactual: 'ipse post Troiam pater posuisset animos' (even his father, [if he had lived] after [the fall of] Troy, would have lost heart).

[177] yea] i.e. 'yes, even': Ulysses even caused the deaths of Greeks (Palamedes, Ajax son of Telamon, and Iphigenia, among others).

Thou night soldier and stout of heart,[178] a little child to slay:
This enterprise thou tak'st alone and that by open day.

ULYSSES

Ulysses' manhood well to Greeks, too much to you, is known.
I may not spend the time in words, our Navy will be gone.[179]

ANDROMACHA

A little stay, while I my last farewell give to my child,
And have with oft embracing him my greedy sorrows filled.

ULYSSES

Thy grievous sorrows to redress, would god it lay in me,
But at thy will to take delay of time, I grant it thee.
Now take thy last leave of thy son and fill thyself with tears;
30   Oft times the weeping of the eyes the inward grief outwears.

ANDROMACHA

O dear, O sweet, thy mother's pledge, farewell my only joy,
Farewell the flower of honour left of beaten house of Troy.
O Trojans' last calamity and fear to Grecians' part,
Farewell thy mother's only hope and vain comfort of heart.
Oft wished I thee thy father's strength and half thy grandsire's
    years,
But all for nought, the gods have all disappointed our desires.
Thou never shalt in regal court thy sceptres take in hand,
Nor to thy people give decrees, nor lead with law thy land,
Nor yet thine enemies overcome by might of handy stroke,
40   Nor send the conquered nations all under thy servile yoke.
Thou never shalt beat down in fight and Greeks with sword
    pursue,
Nor at thy chariot Pyrrhus pluck as Achill Hector drew,[180]
And never shall these tender hands thy weapons wield and wrest;
Thou never shalt in woods pursue the wild and mighty beast,
Nor as accustomed is by guise and sacrifice in Troy,
With measure swift between the altars shalt thou dance with
    joy.[181]

---

[178] night soldier] See n. at 1.1.39.

[179] will be gone] i.e. 'wishes to depart'.

[180] as Achill Hector drew] Heywood's addition.

O grievous kind of cruel death that doth remain for thee,[182]
More woeful thing than Hector's death the walls of Troy shall
    see.

ULYSSES

Now break off all thy mother's tears. I may no more time spend.
50   The grievous sorrows of thy heart will never make an end.

ANDROMACHA

Ulysses, spare as yet my tears and grant awhile delay
To close his eyes yet with my hands ere he depart away.
Thou diest but young, yet feared thou art. Thy Troy doth wait
    for thee.[183]
Go noble heart, thou shalt again the noble Trojans see.

ASTYANAX

Help me mother?

ANDROMACHA

              Alas my child, why tak'st thou hold by me?
In vain thou call'st where help none is. I cannot succour thee,
As when the little tender beast that hears the lion cry
Straight for defence he seeks his dam and crouching down doth
    lie;
The cruel beast, when once removèd is the dam away,
60   In greedy jaw with ravening bit° doth snatch the tender prey;
So straight the enemies will thee take and from my side thee
    bear.
Receive my kiss and tears poor child, receive my rented hair.   [800]
Depart thou hence now full of me and to thy father go.
Salute my Hector in my name and tell him of my woe.
Complain thy mother's grief to him, if former cares may move
The sprights, and that in funeral flame they leese not all their
    love.
O cruel Hector sufferest thou thy wife to be oppressed

---

[181] 45–46] Heywood compresses S.'s allusions to Trojan traditions imported to
Rome: (1) the so-called Troy Game, military exercises on horseback, and (2)
celebrations of the goddess Cybele.
[182] Heywood elides S.'s paradox: 'o morte dira tristius leti genus' (o manner of
dying more grievous than dire death).
[183] Thy Troy doth wait] i.e. the walls of Troy, but also 'your destruction'.

With bond of Grecians' heavy yoke, and liest thou still at rest?
Achilles rose. Take here again my tears and rented hair,
70   And, all that I have left to send, this kiss thy father bear.
Thy coat yet for my comfort leave; the tomb hath touchèd it.[184]
If of his ashes aught here lie, I'll seek it every whit.°[185]

ULYSSES

There is no measure of thy tears. I may no longer stay.
Defer no further our return, break off our ships' delay.

CHORUS

Altered by the translator[186]

O Jove that lead'st the lamps of fire,
And deck'st with flaming stars the sky,[187]
Why is it ever thy desire
To care their course so orderly,
That now the frost the leaves hath worn,
And now the spring doth clothe the tree,
Now fiery Leo ripes the corn,
And still the soil should changèd be?[188]
But why art thou, that all dost guide,
10   Between whose hands the poles do sway,
And at whose will the orbs do slide,
Careless of man's estate alway?
Regarding not the good man's case,
Nor caring how to hurt the ill,
Chance beareth rule in every place,
And turneth man's estate at will.

---

[184] the tomb] S. is more elaborate: 'tumulus [...] meus manesque cari' (my tomb and the spirits of the dear deceased).

[185] I will seek it] Heywood omits S.'s 'with my mouth', i.e. by kissing the garment.

[186] In S., the Chorus charts the places in Greece to which the Trojan women will be taken. In 1–20, Heywood substitutes 959–80 from S.'s *Phaedra*, where the Chorus asks why the gods govern the temporal regularity of the world, but do not care about happiness or justice among humans. Heywood freely composes at 21–32.

[187] 1–2] In S., the Chorus addresses Nature along with Jove.

[188] An obscure line. S. 'viresque suas temperet annus' (and the year tempers its strength; *Pha.* 971).

She gives the wrong the upper hand,
The better part she doth oppress.
She makes the highest low to stand.
20   Her kingdom all is orderless.

O perfit proof of her frailty,
The princely towers of Troy beat down,
The flower of Asia here ye see,[189]
With turn of hand quite overthrown.
The ruthful end of Hector's son,
Whom to his death the Greeks have led,
His fatal hour is come and gone,
And by this time the child is dead.[190]
Yet still alas more cares increase,
30   O Trojans' doleful destiny,
Fast doth approach the maid's decease,
And now Polyxena shall die.

THE FOURTH ACT

HELENA ANDROMACHA HECUBA [POLYXENA][191]

[HELENA]

[Aside]

Whatever woeful wedding yet were cause of funeral,
Of wailing, tears, blood, slaughter else, or other mischiefs all,
A worthy match for Helena, and meet for me it were:
My wedding torch hath been the cause of all the Trojans' care.
I am constrained to hurt them yet after their overthrow.
The false and feignèd marriages of Pyrrhus must I show,
And give the maid the Greeks' attire, and by my policy
Shall Paris' sister be betrayed and by deceit shall die.[192]
But let her be beguilèd thus: the less should be her pain

---

[189] 23] Heywood addresses the audience (see also line 1.1.7 and nn. at 1.Cho.53–56 and 2.Cho.65). The line also echoes 1.1.9.

[190] the child is dead] Heywood's addition is inconsistent with Act 5, where the messenger gives the impression that Polyxena and Astyanax die in quick succession.

[191] See n. at 'The Speakers' above.

[192] Paris' sister] As in S., Helen intensifies her own guilt by referring to Polyxena as sister of Paris.

10 If that unware,° without the fear of death,[193] she might be slain.
What, ceasest thou the will of Greeks and message to fulfil?
Of hurt constrained the fault return'th to th'author of the ill.[194]

[To Polyxena]

O noble virgin of the famous house and stock of Troy,
To thee the Grecians have me sent. I bring thee news of joy.[195]
The gods rue on thy afflicted state, more merciful they be.
A great and happy marriage lo, they have prepared for thee.
Thou never should'st if Troy had stood so nobly wedded be,
Nor Priam never could prefer thee to so high degree;
Whom flower of all the Grecian name, the prince of honour
 high,
20 That bears the sceptres over all the land of Thessaly,
Doth in the law of wedlock choose and for his wife require:
To sacred rites of lawful bed doth Pyrrhus thee desire.
Lo, Thetis great with all the rest of gods that guide by sea,[196]
Each one shall thee account as theirs and joy thy wedding day,
And Peleus shall thee daughter call when thou art Pyrrhus' wife,
And Nereus shall account thee his, the space of all thy life.
Put off thy mourning garment now; this regal vesture wear.
Forget henceforth thy captive state and seemly broid° thy hair.
Thy fall hath lift thee higher up and doth thee more advance:
30 Oft to be taken in the war doth bring the better chance.

ANDROMACHA

This ill the Trojans never knew in all their griefs and pain.
Before this time ye never made us to rejoice in vain.[197]
Troy towers give light,[198] O seemly time for marriage to be made.

---

[193] 10] S. is proverbial: 'optanda mors sine metu mortis mori' (Dying without fear of death is a death to be wished for; *Tro.* 869).

[194] 12] i.e. 'the blame for a coerced crime goes back to the one who initiated it' – rather than to Helen, who is merely the messenger.

[195] 14] Heywood's addition.

[196] 23–26] Helen describes Polyxena's future family, but her ambiguous language applies to marrying either Pyrrhus or Achilles (Boyle, *Seneca's 'Troades'*, p. 210).

[197] rejoice in vain] Heywood adds 'in vain', complicating Andromache's more straightforwardly sarcastic use of 'rejoice' in S.: 'hoc derat unum Phrygibus eversis malum, gaudere' (this was the one evil the defeated Trojans had not yet been forced to endure: to have to rejoice).

Who would refuse the wedding day that Helen doth persuade?
The plague and ruin of each part behold.[199] Dost thou not see
These tombs of noble men and how their bones here scattered
   be?
Thy bride bed hath been cause of this. For thee all these be dead,
For thee the blood of Asia both and Europe hath been shed,
When thou in joy and pleasure both the fighting folk from far
40   Hast viewed, in doubt to whom to wish the glory of the war.
Go to, prepare the marriages. What need the torch's light?
Behold the towers of Troy do shine with brands that blaze full   [900]
   bright.
O Trojans all, set to your hands, this wedlock celebrate.
Lament this day with woeful cry and tears in seemly rate.

HELENA

Though care do cause thee want of wit and reason's rule deny,
And heavy hap doth oftimes hate his mates in misery,
Yet I before most hateful judge dare well defend my part,
That I of all your grievous cares sustain the greatest smart.
Andromacha for Hector weeps, for Priam Hecuba,
50   For only Paris privily bewaileth Helena.
A hard and grievous thing it is captivity to bear.[200]
In Troy that yoke I suffered long, a prisoner whole ten year.
Turned are the Fates, Troy beaten down; to Greece I must
   repair.[201]
The native country to have lost is ill, but worse to fear;
For dread thereof you need not care: your evils all be passed.
On me both parts will vengeance take.[202] All lights° to me at
   last.[203]
Whom each man prisoner takes, god wot, she stands in slipper
   stay,[204]

---

[198] Troy towers give light] i.e. 'Troy is on fire'. S. 'flagrant strata passim
Pergama' (Troy is laid low and is here and there in flames), a sarcastic comment
on the untimeliness of a new wedding.

[199] each part] i.e. Trojans and Greeks alike.

[200] 51] In S., probably a rhetorical question.

[201] the Fates] S. 'penates' (the household gods).

[202] both parts] S. 'victor et victus' (victor and vanquished).

[203] All lights to me at last] Heywood's addition.

[204] 57–64] In S. (*Tro.* 915–24), Helen recounts that she has been assigned to one
man (Menelaus) without a lottery (unlike the Trojan captives), that she was

And me not captive made by lot, yet Paris led away.
I have been cause of all these wars, and then your woes were
    wrought,
60   When first your ships the Spartan seas and land of Grecia
    sought.
But if the goddess willed it so that I their prey should be,
And for reward to her beauty's judge, she had appointed me,
Then pardon Paris. Think this thing in wrathful judge doth lie:
The sentence Menelaus gives, and he this case shall try.
Now turn thy plaints, Andromacha, and weep for Polyxene.
Mine eyes for sorrows of my heart their tears may not refrain.

ANDROMACHA

Alas what care makes Helen weep? What grief doth she lament?
Declare what crafts Ulysses casts. What mischief hath he sent?
Shall she from height of Idey hill[205] be headlong tumbled
    down?
70   Or else out of the turret's top in Troy shall she be thrown?
Or will they cast her from the cliffs into Sygeon seas,
In bottom of the surging waves to end her ruthful days?
Show what thy countenance hides and tell the secrets of thy
    breast.
Some woes in Pyrrhus' wedding are far worse than all the
    rest.[206]
Go to, give sentence on the maid, pronounce her destiny.
Delude no longer our mishaps. We are prepared to die.

HELENA

Would god th'expounder of the gods would give his doom° so
    right
That I also on point of sword might leese the loathsome light,
Or at Achilles' tomb with stroke of Pyrrhus' hand be slain,
80   And bear a part of all thy fates, O wretched Polyxene,
Whom yet Achilles woo'th to wed, and where his ashes lie,
Requireth that thy blood be shed and at his tomb to die.[207]

---

abducted by Trojan ships, and that Menelaus will be her judge. Some problems
with the transmitted text may contribute to Heywood's opaque interpretation.
[205] Idey hill] i.e. Mt Ida.
[206] Some woes] In S., the greatest woe is explicitly stated: 'Priami gener
Hecubaeque Pyrrhus' (Pyrrhus becoming son-in-law to Priam and Hecuba).

ANDROMACHA

Behold, lo, how her noble mind of death doth gladly hear.[208]
She decks herself: her regal weed in seemly wise to wear,
And to her head, she sets her hand the broided hair to lay.
To wed she thought it death; to die she thinks a wedding day.
But help, alas, my mother swoons to hear her daughter's death. [950]
Arise, pluck up your heart and take again the panting breath.
Alack, good mother, how slender stay that doth thy life
    sustain.
90   A little thing shall happy° thee. Thou art almost past pain.
Her breath returns, she doth revive, her limbs their life do take.
So see when wretches fain would die, how death doth them
    forsake.

HECUBA

Doth yet Achilles live, alas, to work the Trojans' spite?
Doth he rebel against us yet?[209] O hand of Paris light.[210]
The very tomb and ashes, lo, yet thirsteth for our blood.
A happy heap of children late on every side me stood.
It wearied me to deal the mother's kiss among them all.
The rest are lost and this alone now doth me mother call.
Thou only child of Hecuba, a comfort left to me,
100   A stayer° of my sorry state, and shall I now leese thee?
Depart O wretched soul and from this careful carcas fly,
And ease me of such ruthful fates to see my daughter die.
My weeping wets, alas, my eyes and stains them overall,
And down my cheeks the sudden streams and showers of tears
    do fall.
But thou dear daughter may'st be glad. Cassandra would
    rejoice,
Or Hector's wife thus wed to be, if they might have their
    choice.[211]

---

[207] And at his tomb to die] S. 'campo maritus ut sit Elysio' (so he may be married on the Elysian plains).

[208] Behold, lo, how her noble mind of death doth gladly hear.] Referring to Polyxena's calm reaction.

[209] rebel] S. 'rebellat' (fight back, fight again).

[210] O hand of Paris light] i.e. although Paris killed Achilles, the arrow to his heel was too 'light' to kill his ghost.

ANDROMACHA

We are the wretches, Hecuba, in cursèd case we stand,
Whom straight the ship shall toss by seas into a foreign land.
But as for Helen's griefs be gone and turnèd to the best:[212]

110 She shall again her native country see and live at rest.

HELENA

Ye would the more envy my state if ye might know your own.

ANDROMACHA

And grow'th there yet more grief to me that erst I have not
known?

HELENA

Such masters must ye serve as doth by chance of lots befall.

ANDROMACHA

Whose servant am I then become, whom shall I master call?

HELENA

By lot ye fall to Pyrrhus' hands; you are his prisoner.

ANDROMACHA

Cassandra is happy: Fury saves perhaps and Phoebus her.[213]

HELENA

Chief King of Greeks Cassandra keeps and his captive is she.[214]

HECUBA

Is anyone among them all that prisoner would have me?

---

[211] 105–06] i.e. Polyxena should recognize that her fate is preferable to that faced by Cassandra or Andromache.

[212] 109–11] S. refers to Polyxena (not Helen): 'This one (i.e. Polyxena) the dear earth will cover in her native land'. HELEN: 'You (Hecuba) will envy her all the more if you learn your own fate'.

[213] Fury saves perhaps and Phoebus her] i.e. Andromache speculates that Cassandra's prophetic madness ('Fury'), and possibly her ties to the god Phoebus, will exempt her from being assigned to a Greek master.

[214] King of Greeks] i.e. Agamemnon.

HELENA

You chancèd to Ulysses are; his prey ye are become.

HECUBA

120   Alas what cruel, dire, and ireful dealer of the doom,
    What god unjust doth so divide the captives to their lords?
    What grievous arbiter is he that to such choice accords?
    What cruel hand to wretched folk so evil Fates hath cast?
    Who hath among Achilles' armour Hector's mother placed?[215]
    Now am I captive and beset with all calamity.
    My bondage grieves me not, but him to serve it shameth me.
    He that Achilles' spoils hath won shall Hector's also have,
    Shall barren land enclosed with seas receive my bones in
        grave?[216]
    Lead me, Ulysses, where thou wilt. Lead me. I make no stay.
130   My master, I, and me, my fates shall follow every way.
    Let never calm come to the seas, but let them rage with wind.
    Come fire and sword, mine own mischance and Priam's let me
        find.
    In mean time haps this deep distress, my cares can know no calm.
    I ran the race with Priamus, but he hath won the palm.[217]

    But Pyrrhus comes with swiftened° pace and threatening brows   [1000]
        doth wrest.
    What stay'st thou, Pyrrhus? Strike thy sword now through this
        woeful breast,
    And both at once the parents of thy father's wife now slay.[218]
    Murderer of age, likes thee her blood?[219] He draw'th my
        daughter away.

---

[215] 124] After his death, Achilles' armour was awarded to Ulysses. Heywood omits S.'s clarifying phrase: 'ad Vlixem vocor' (I am summoned to Ulysses).

[216] 128] Negative in S., alluding to the version of the myth in which Hecuba dies in Thrace, i.e. before she can be taken to Ithaca. Heywood simplifies: Hecuba reluctantly confronts Ithaca as her final resting place.

[217] 133–34] Difficult lines in S. (*Tro.* 997–98). Their most likely sense is: 'In the meantime, until these things come about, let the following stand as a punishment: I pre-empted the lottery, and seized your prize from you (Ulysses)'. Heywood makes the reference to Priam.

[218] 137] i.e. unite Hecuba with Priam in the underworld.

[219] Murderer of age, likes thee her blood?] In S., Hecuba invites Pyrrhus to shed her own (not Polyxena's) blood, since he is a 'mactator senum' (murderer of old men, *Tro.* 1002).

Defile the gods and stain the sprights of hell with slaughtered
    blood.
140   To ask your mercy, what avails? Our prayers do no good.
The vengeance ask I on your ships that it the gods may please,
According to this sacrifice to guide you on the seas.
This wish I to your thousand sails: god's wrath light on them all,
Even to the ship that beareth me, whatever may befall.

CHORUS

A comfort is to man's calamity,
A doleful flock of fellows in distress,
And sweet to him that mourns in misery
To hear them wail whom sorrows like oppress.
In deepest care his grief him bites the less
That his estate bewails not all alone,
But see'th with him the tears of many one.

For still it is the chief delight in woe,
And joy of them that sunk in sorrows are,
10   To see like fates befall to many mo°
That may take part of all their woeful fare,
And not alone to be oppressed with care.
There is no wight of woe that doth complain,
When all the rest do like mischance sustain.

In all this world if happy man were none,
None, though he were, would think himself a wretch.
Let once the rich with heaps of gold be gone,
Whose hundred head his pastures overreach,
Then would the poor man's heart begin to stretch.
20   There is no wretch whose life him doth displease,
But in respect of those that live at ease.

Sweet is to him that stands in deep distress,
To see no man in joyful plight to be,
Whose only vessel wind and wave oppress,
Full sore his chance bewails and weepeth he
That with his own none other's wrack doth see,
When he alone mak'th shipwrack on the sand
And naked falls to long desirèd land.

A thousand sail who see'th to drench in seas,
30   With better will the storm hath overpassed,

His heavy hap doth him the less displease,
When broken boards abroad be many cast,
And shipwracked ships to shore they flit full fast,
With doubled waves when stoppèd is the flood,
With heap of them that there have lost their good.

Full sore did Phrixus Hellen's loss complain,[220]
What time the leader of his flock of sheep,
Upon his back alone he bare them twain,
And wet his golden locks amid the deep.
40   In piteous plaint alas he gan to weep,
The death of her it did him deep displease,
That shipwrack made amid the drenching seas.

And piteous was the plaint and heavy mood
Of woeful Pyrrha and eke Deucalion,
That nought beheld about them but the flood,
When they of all mankind were left alone.
Amid the seas full sore they made their moan,
To see themselves thus left alive in woe,
When neither land they saw nor fellows mo.

50   Anon these plaints and Trojans' tears shall quail,°
And here and there the ship them toss by seas,
When trumpets sound shall warn to hoise° up sail,
And through the waves with wind to seek their ways.
Then shall these captives go to end their days,
In land unknown when once with hasty oar,
The drenching deep they take and shun the shore.

What state of mind shall then in wretches be,
When shore shall sink from sight and seas arise,
When Idey hill to lurk aloof they see?[221]
60   Then point with hand from far where Troia lies
Shall child and mother, talking in this wise: [1050]
'Lo yonder Troy, where smoke it fumeth high.'
By this the Trojans shall their country spy.

---

[220] 36–49] Two examples of people grieving in isolation (unlike the Chorus):
Phrixus after Helle's death; and Deucalion and Pyrrha, sole survivors of the
human race.
[221] lurk aloof] i.e. 'disappear from sight', referring to Mt Ida's fading from view.

THE FIFTH ACT

MESSENGER ANDROMACHA HECUBA

[MESSENGER]

O dire, fierce, wretched, horrible, O cruel Fates accursed,
Of Mars his ten years' bloodshed blows the woeful'st and
    the worst.
Alas, which should I first bewail? Thy cares, Andromacha?
Or else lament the wretched age of woeful Hecuba?

HECUBA

Whatever man's calamities ye wail for, mine it is.
I bear the smart of all their woes, each other feels but his.
Whoever he, I am the wretch: all haps° to me at last.[222]

MESSENGER

Slain is the maid and from the walls of Troy the child is cast,
But both, as them became, they took their death with stomach
    stout.

ANDROMACHA

10   Declare the double slaughters then,[223] and tell the whole
    throughout.

MESSENGER

One tower of all the rest ye know doth yet in Troy remain,
Where Priam wonted was to sit and view the armies twain,
His little nephew eke with him to lead, and from afar
His father's fights with fire and sword to show and feats of war.
This tower, sometime well known by fame and Trojans' honour
    most,
Is now with captains of the Greeks beset on every coast,[224]
With swift recourse and from the ships in clustered heaps anon,
Both tag and rag they run to gaze what thing should there be
    done.

---

[222] 7] i.e. Hecuba is the ultimate recipient of all of the violence.

[223] Declare the double slaughters then] Following this phrase, Heywood omits a
significant sentence (S. *Tro.* 1066–67); see Introduction, p. 30.

[224] Captains] S. mentions a crowd of Greek 'leaders and common people' (ducum
plebisque).

Some climb the hills to seek a place where they might see it
    best,
20   Some on the rocks a tiptoe stand to overlook the rest,
Some on their temples wear the pine, some beech, some crowns
    of bay,
For garlands torn is every tree that standeth in their way.
Some from the highest mountain's top aloof beholdeth all,
Some scale the buildings half yburnt, and some the ruinous
    wall.
Yea, some there were, O mischief lo, that for the more despite,
The tomb of Hector sits upon, beholders of the sight.

With princely pace, Ulysses then passed through the pressèd
    band
Of Greeks, King Priam's little nephew leading by the hand.
The child with unrepining gait passed through his enemies'
    hands,
30   Up toward the walls and as anon in turret's top he stands.
From thence adown his lofty looks he cast on every part,
The nearer death, more free from care he seemed and fear of
    heart.
Amid his foes, his stomach swells and fierce he was to sight,
Like Tiger's whelp that threats in vain with toothless chap° to
    bite.[225]
Alas for pity then each one rue on his tender years,
And all the rout that present were for him they shed their tears.
Yea not Ulysses them restrained, but trickling down they fall,
And only he wept not, poor fool, whom they bewailèd all.
But while on gods Ulysses called and Calchas' words expound,   [1100]
40   In midst of Priam's land alas the child leapt down to ground.

ANDROMACHA

What cruel Colchis could or Scyth such slaughter take in
    hand,[226]
Or by the shore of Caspian sea, what barbarous lawless land?
Busirides to th'altars yet no infant's blood hath shed,

---

[225] 34] Heywood compresses S.'s four-line simile into one (*Tro.* 1093–96).

[226] 41–44] Heywood partially renders S.'s catalogue of cruel figures: the Colchian (perhaps suggesting Medea), the Scythian, the Caucasian (omitted), Busiris (an Egyptian tyrant), and Diomedes (Thracian tyrant who fed his horses on human flesh; Heywood elides the horses).

Nor never yet were children slain for feast of Diomed.
Who shall alas in tomb thee lay or hide thy limbs again?

MESSENGER

What limbs from such a headlong fall could in a child remain?
His body's peise thrown down to ground hath battered all his
    bones.
His face, his noble father's marks, are spoiled against the stones.
His neck unjointed is; his head so dashed with flint stone stroke
50   That scattered is the brain about; the skull is all too broke.
Thus lieth he now, dismembered corpse, deformed and all too
    rent.

ANDROMACHA

Lo, herein doth he yet likewise his father represent.°

MESSENGER

What time the child had headlong fallen thus from the walls
    of Troy,
And all the Greeks themselves bewailed the slaughter of the
    boy,
Yet straight return they back and at Achilles' tomb again,
The second mischief go to work: the death of Polyxene.
This tomb the waves of surging seas beset the utter° side,
The other part the fields enclose about and pastures wide.
In vale environèd with hills that round about do rise,
60   A slope on height erected are the banks in theatre-wise.
By all the shore then swarm the Greeks and thick on heaps they
    press.
Some hope that by her death they shall their ships' delay release,
Some other joy their enemies' stock thus beaten down to be.[227]
A great part of the people both the slaughter hate and see.
The Trojans eke no less frequent their own calamities,
And all afraid beheld the last of all their miseries,
When first proceeded torches bright as guise of wedlock is,
And author thereof led the way the lady Tyndaris.[228]
Such wedlock (pray the Trojans then) god send Hermiona,

---

[227] other joy] i.e. 'others rejoice'.
[228] Lady Tyndaris] i.e. Helen, whose father is Tyndareus; her daughter is
Hermione.

70   And would god to her husband so restored were Helena.
     Fear mazed° each part, but Polyxene, her bashful look
        downcast,
     And more than erst her glittering eyes and beauty shined at last,
     As sweetest seems then Phoebus' light, when down his beams
        do sway,
     When stars again with night at hand oppress the doubtful day.
     Astonied much the people were, and all they her commend,
     And now much more than ever erst, they praised her at her
        end.[229]
     Some with her beauty movèd were, some with her tender years,
     Some to behold the turns of chance and how each thing thus
        wears;
     But most them moves her valiant mind and lofty stomach high,
80   So strong, so stout, so ready of heart, and well prepared to die.
     Thus pass they forth, and bold before king Pyrrhus go'th the
        maid;
     They pity her, they marvel her, their hearts were all afraid.

     As soon as then the hard hill top, where die she should, they
        trod,
     And high upon his father's tomb, the youthful Pyrrhus stood,   [1150]
     The manly maid, she never shrunk one foot nor backward drew,
     But boldly turns to meet the stroke with stout, unchangèd hue.
     Her courage moves each one and, lo, a strange thing monstrous-
        like,
     That Pyrrhus even himself stood still for dread and durst not
        strike,
     But as he had his glittering sword in her to hilts up done,
90   The purple blood at mortal wound, then gushing out it spun.
     Ne yet her courage her forsook, when dying in that stound,°
     She fell as th'earth should her revenge, with ireful rage to
        ground.[230]
     Each people wept: the Trojans first with privy, fearful cry;
     The Grecians eke each one bewailed her death apparently.[231]

---

[229] they praised her at her end] Heywood makes specific S.'s general observation: 'et fere cuncti magis peritura laudant' (people generally praise things that are about to perish).

[230] 92] Heywood diverges from S. 'ut Achilli gravem factura terram' (as though to make the earth heavy upon Achilles).

[231] apparently] S. 'clarius' (more discernibly).

This order had the sacrifice. Her blood the tomb up drunk:
No drop remain'th above the ground, but down forthwith it
    sunk.

HECUBA

Now go, now go ye Greeks, and now, repair ye safely home.
With careless ships and hoisèd sails, now cut the salt sea foam.
The child and virgin both be slain, your battles finished are.
100   Alas, where shall I end my age, or whither bear my care?
Shall I my daughter, or my nephew, or my husband moan?[232]
My country else, or all at once, or else myself alone?
My wish is death that children both and virgins fiercely takes.
Wherever cruel death doth haste to strike, it me forsakes.
Amid the enemies' weapons all, amid both sword and fire,
All night sought for, thou flee'st from me that do thee most
    desire.
Not flame of fire, not fall of tower, not cruel enemy's hand,
Hath rid my life: how near, alas, could death to Priam stand?[233]

MESSENGER

Now captives all, with swift recourse repair ye to the seas.
110   Now spread the ships their sails abroad, and forth they seek
    their ways.

FINIS

---

[232] nephew] i.e. Astyanax; S. 'nepotem' (grandson).
[233] how near, alas, could death to Priam stand?] i.e. without also killing Hecuba, who had stood close to Priam when he was killed.

JASPER HEYWOOD
THYESTES (1560)

To the right honourable Sir John Mason, Knight, one of the
Queen's Majesty's Privy Council, his daily orator Jasper Heywood
wisheth health with increase of honour and virtue.[1]

As bounden° breast doth bear the poorest wight°
That duty doth in trifling token send,
As he that doth with plenteous present quit°
Of prouder price and glittering gold his friend;
Whoso repay'th with money's mighty mass
The good that he at others' hands hath found,
Remembrance of the benefit° doth pass:[2]
He thinks himself to him no longer bound.[3]
The poor, whose power may not with price repay
10   The great good gifts that he received before,
With thankful thought yet gudgeon-gift° doth sway
Above the peise° of pearl and gold great store.[4]
If puissant° prince at poor man's hand once took
A radish root and was therewith content,[5]
Your honour, then, I pray this little book
To take in worth that I to you present,
Which though itself a volume be but small,
Yet greater gift it gives than ween° ye might.
Though it a barren book be throughout all
20   Full fruitless, yet not faithless sign in sight
It shows of him that for your honour prays[6]
(as deeds of yours of him deservèd have)
That God above prolong your happy days,
And make the skies your seat soon after grave.

---

[1] Jasper Heywood wisheth health with increase of honour and virtue.] See *Troas* n.
at Dedication. On Mason, see Introduction, p. 34.

[2] benefit] Suggests Heywood's familiarity with S.'s *De Beneficiis*, especially the
ideas that repayment with an object (rather than money) is preferred, that
remembrance of the original gift is an important aspect of gratitude, and that
timing and careful choice enhance the value of a gift.

[3] 1–8] i.e. 'The poor man who repays with a cheap gift is driven by no less a sense
of obligation than one who repays in gold' (1–4), but if someone repays a good
deed with money, he forgets the good deed and then thinks he is no longer
obligated.

[4] 11–12] i.e. 'something of little worth chosen with great care makes more of an
impression than pearl or gold'.

[5] 13–14] In a traditional tale, a poor man gives a radish root to a king.

[6] 20–21] i.e. (the book) is 'a sign of the loyalty of me, who prays for you [...]'

The Translator to the Book

Thou little book my messenger must be[7]
That must from me to wight of honour go.
Behave thee humbly, bend to him thy knee,
And thee to him in lowly manner show.
But do thou not thyself to him present
When with affairs thou shalt him troubled see.
Thou shalt perhaps so worthily be shent°
And with reproof he thus will say to thee:
'So proudly thus presume how darest thou
10   At such a time so rashly to appear?
With things of weight thou see'st me burdened now.
I may not yet to trifles give mine care.'
Spy well thy time when thou him see'st alone,
An idle hour for thee shall be most meet.°
Then step thou forth in sight of him anon,
And as behoves his honour humbly greet.
But now take heed what I to thee shall tell,
And all by rote this lesson take with thee:
In everything thyself to order well,
20   In sight of him give ear and learn of me.
First, what or whence thou art if he would wit,°
Then see that thou thy title to him show.
Tell him thy name is in thy forehead° writ,
By which he shall both thee and me well know.
Then when he hath once looked upon thy name,
If yet he shall neglect to read the rest,
Or if he chide and say thou art to blame,
With trifles such to have him so oppressed:
Beseech him yet thereof to pardon thee,
30   Since thou art but thy master's messenger.
Excuse thyself and lay the fault in me,
At whose commandment thus thou com'st in there.
If my presumption then accuse he do,
If deed so rash of mine he do reprove,
That I thee dare attempt to send him to,[8]
Beware thou speak nothing for my behove,°

---

[7] 1] On the book as messenger, see Introduction, p. 35.
[8] him to] i.e. 'to him'.

138

Nor do thou not excuse my fault in aught,
But rather yet confess to him the same,
And say there may a fault in me be thought,
40   Which to excuse it doubleth but the blame.
Yet with my boldness him beseech to bear,
And pardon give to this my enterprise;
A worthy thing in wight of honour were
A present poor to take in thankful wise.
For tell him though thou slender volume be,
Ungreeing° gift for state of honour guest,
Yet dost thou sign of duty bring with thee,
And pledge thou art of truly bounden breast,
And thou for him art come for to confess,
50   His beadsman° bound to be for his desert,°
And how to him he grants he ow'th no less,
Nor gives no more, but note of thankful heart.
In all the rest that he to thee shall say,
Thy wit shall serve an answer well to make.
Thou hast thine errand. Get thee hence away.
The gods thee speed, to them I thee betake.°

The Preface

It was the four and twentieth day of latest month save one[9]
Of all the year, when flower and fruit from field and tree were
   gone,
And sadder season such ensued as dulls the doleful° sprites,°
And Muse of men that wonted° were to wander in delights.
And weather such there was as well became the pensive pen
With sorry style of woes to write and eke° of mischief, when
Aurora blushed with ruddy cheeks to wail the death again
Of Phoebus' son, whom thunderbolt of mighty Jove had slain,[10]
And clouds from high began to throw their dreary tears adown,
10   And Venus from the skies above on Friday foul to frown.[11]

When (as at book with mazèd° muse I sat and pensive thought,
Deep drowned in dumps° of drowsiness as change of weather
   wrought),
I felt how Morpheus bound my brows and eke my temples struck,
That down I sunk my heavy head and slept upon my book.[12]
Then dreamed I thus that by my side, me thought I saw one stand
That down to ground in scarlet gown was dight,°[13] and in his hand
A book he bare, and on his head of bays, a garland green.[14]
Full grave he was, well stepped° in years and comely to be seen.[15]
His eyes like crystal shined, his breath full sweet, his face full fine.
20   It seemed he had been lodgèd long among the Muses nine.
'Good sir,' quoth I, 'I you beseech (since that ye seem to me
By your attire some worthy wight) it may your pleasure be
To tell me what and whence ye are.' Whereat awhile he stayed,
Beholding me. Anon he spake, and thus, me thought, he said:
'Spain was', quoth he, 'my native soil. A man of worthy fame
Sometime I was in former age, and Seneca my name.'
The name of Senec when I heard, then scantly could I speak.
I was so glad that from mine eyes the tears began to break

---

[9] 1–10] Friday, 24 November 1559. On these lines and line 341, see Introduction,
pp. 35–36; 39; and n. at line 91 below.
[10] Phoebus' son] i.e. Phaethon.
[11] Venus] Friday belongs to Venus (Lat. 'dies Veneris').
[12] On the Preface as dream vision, see Introduction, pp. 35–36.
[13] scarlet gown] A sign of rank or dignity.
[14] of bays, a garland green] i.e. a laurel wreath, identifying S. as a poet.
[15] well stepped in years] i.e. As here, S. is usually presented as a 'senex' (old
man).

For joy, and with what words I should salute him, I ne° wist.°
30 I him embraced. His hands, his feet and face full oft I kissed.
And as at length my trickling tears me thought I might refrain,
'O blissful day', quoth I, 'wherein returnèd is again
So worthy wight. O happy hour that liefer° is to me
Than life, wherein it haps° me so that I should Senec see.
Art thou the same that whilom° did'st thy tragedies indite°
With wondrous wit and regal style? O long desirèd sight.[16]
And liv'st thou yet', quoth I, 'indeed? And art thou come again
To talk and dwell as thou were wont° with men, and to remain
In this our age?' 'I live', quoth he, 'and never shall I die:
40 The works I wrote shall still° preserve my name in memory
From age to age, and now again I will revive the same.
And here I come to seek someone that might renew my name,
And make me speak in stranger speech and set my works to sight,
And scan my verse in other tongue than I was wont to write.
A young man well I wot° there is in th'isle of Brittany
(That from the rest of all the world aloof in seas doth lie)
That once this labour took in hand. Him would I meet full fain,°
To crave that in the rest of all my works he would take pain[17]
To toil, as he in *Troas* did.' 'Is that your will?' quoth I.
50 I blushed and said, 'The same you seek, lo here I stand you by.'
'If thou', quoth he, 'be whom I seek, if glory aught thee move
Of mine to come in after age, if Senec's name thou love
Alive to keep, I thee beseech ˜˜˜ ̇ ̇ ̇ ̇
In metre of thy mother tongu
My other works, whereby the   and me
No little thanks, when they th   shall see
In English verse that never ye   l.[18]
With my renown perhaps thy   ut this land,
And those that yet thee never   'e and praise,
60 And say, "God grant this you   nany days,
And many happy hours to see
Rest, joy, and bliss eternally a

---

[16] wondrous wit and regal style] On sixteenth-century opinions of Seneca's style, see Introduction, p. 10.
[17] my works] Refers (most likely) to the other tragedies.
[18] that never yet could Latin understand] A commonly cited motive for translation in the sixteenth century (see Conley, pp. 82–84 and Wright).
[19] 62] A common expression (see also Dedication, 24, and below at 164).

That so translated hath these books.'" 'To him', quoth I, 'again
(If any be that so with thanks accepts a young man's pain)
I wish great good, but well I wot the hateful cursèd brood,
Far greater is that are long since sprung up of Zoilus'° blood.[20]
That red-haired, black-mouthed, squint-eyed wretch hath couchèd°
    everywhere,
In corner close some imp of his that sits to see and hear
What each man doth, and each man blames. Nor once we may him
    see
70   Come face to face, but we once gone then stoutly steps out he;
And all he carps that there he finds ere half he read to end,
And what he understands not, blames, though nought he can
    amend.
But were it so that such were none, how may these youthful days
Of mine, in thing so hard as this, deserve of other praise?

'A labour long', quoth I, 'it is, that riper age doth crave:
And who shall travail in thy books more judgement ought to have
Than I, whose greener years thereby no thanks may hope to win.
Thou see'st Dame Nature yet hath set no hairs upon my chin.
Crave this therefore of graver age, and men of greater skill.
80   Full many be that better can, and some perhaps that will.
But if thy will be rather bent a young man's wit to prove°
And think'st that elder learnèd men perhaps it shall behove
In works of weight to spend their time, go where Minerva's men,
And finest wits do swarm, whom she hath taught to pass° with pen.
In Lincoln's Inn and Temples twain, Gray's Inn and other mo,°[21]
Thou shalt them find whose painful° pen thy verse shall flourish°
    so,
That Melpomen thou would'st well ween° had taught them for to
    write,
And all their works with stately style and goodly grace t'indite.

---

[20] Heywood echoes complaints of many mid-century translators about malicious detractors. See also Thomas Peend's preface to *Agamemnon* (line 17) and Conley, pp. 86–94.

[21] 85] The four English legal societies, known collectively as the Inns of Court: Lincoln's Inn, the Inner Temple, the Middle Temple, and Gray's Inn. On the literary culture of the Inns, see Introduction, pp. 36–37, Conley, pp. 23–33, and Winston (2011). Below, Heywood mentions texts that were only just or not yet in print.

There shalt thou see the self-same North, whose work his wit
    displays,[22]
90   And Dial doth of Princes paint, and preach abroad his praise.
There Sackville's sonnets sweetly sauced and featly° finèd° be;[23]
There Norton's ditties do delight, there Yelverton's do flee[24]
Well pured° with pen. Such young men three, as ween thou
    might'st again,
To be begot as Pallas was of mighty Jove his brain.
There hear thou shalt a great report of Baldwin's worthy name,[25]
Whose Mirror doth of magistrates proclaim eternal fame.
And there the gentle Blundeville is, by name and eke by kind,[26]
Of whom we learn by Plutarch's lore what fruit by foes to find.
There Bavand bides° that turned his toil a commonwealth to
    frame,°[27]
100   And greater grace in English gives to worthy author's name.
There Googe a grateful gains hath got, report that runneth rife,[28]
Who crooked compass doth describe and Zodiac of Life.
And yet great number more, whose names if I should now recite,

---

[22] Thomas North (1535–1603?; adm. Lincoln's Inn 1556) translated Antonio of Guevara's *Dial of Princes* (1557).

[23] Thomas Sackville (*c* 1536–1608; adm. Inner Temple 1554), praised with Thomas Norton (below) and Christopher Yelverton for shorter poems, is known today for the neo-Senecan play *Gorboduc* (1561–1562, co-authored with Norton) and the 'Induction' and 'Complaint of Buckingham' (pub. 1563, but likely written earlier). The 'Induction's' lines 1–6 may influence or echo lines 1–10 above.

[24] Thomas Norton (1530x32–1584; adm. Inner Temple 1555) is best known now for *Gorboduc* (see n. 23), his translation of Calvin, the *Institution of Christian Religion* (1561), and his version of twenty-four psalms (1562). Christopher Yelverton (1536/7–1612; adm. Gray's Inn 1552) authored an epilogue to Gascoigne and Kinwelmersh's *Jocasta* (1566) and dumb shows in *The Misfortunes of Arthur* (1587–1588).

[25] William Baldwin (d. in or before 1563) is slightly out of place on this list. He is older than the other men, began his literary career earlier (in the reign of Edward VI), and did not attend an inn of court. His appearance perhaps reflects Heywood's admiration for the *Mirror*, and its apparent popularity at the Inns. See Introduction, pp. 23–25.

[26] Thomas Blundeville (1522?–1606?; possibly admitted to Gray's Inn *c*. 1541) authored *Three Moral Treatises* (1561), a translation of selections from Plutarch's *Moralia*, including a verse rendition of 'How to Profit from One's Enemies'.

[27] William Bavand (fl. 1559; adm. Middle Temple 1557) translated Joannes Ferrarius Montanus's *De republica bene instituenda* as *A Work Touching the Good Ordering of a Commonweal* (1559).

[28] 101] Perhaps a reference to the immediate success of Barnabe Googe's translation of Paligenius's *Zodiacus vitae*. See Introduction, pp. 38–39.

A ten times greater work than thine I should be forced to write.[29]
A princely place in Parnass hill for these there is prepared,
Where crown of glittering glory hangs for them a right reward,
Whereas the laps of ladies nine shall duly them defend,[30]
That have prepared the laurel leaf about their heads to bend;
And where their pens shall hang full high, and fame that erst° was
    hid,
110   Abroad in Brutus' realm shall fly as late their volumes did.
These are the wits that can display thy tragedies all ten,[31]
Replete with sugared sentence sweet and practice of the pen.

'Myself, I must confess, I have too much already done
Above my reach, when rashly once with *Troas* I begun.
And more presumed to take in hand than well I brought to end,
And little volume with mo faults than lines abroad to send,[32]
And of that work what men report in faith I never wist.
But well I wot it may be thought so ill, that little list°
I have to do the like. Whereof though mine be all the blame,
120   And all to me imputed is that passeth in my name,
Yet as of some I will confess that I the author was,
And faults too many made myself when I that book let pass
Out of my hands, so must I me excuse of other some.
For when to sign of Hand and Star I chancèd first to come,[33]
To printers' hands I gave the work, by whom I had such wrong
That though myself perused their proofs the first time, yet ere long
When I was gone, they would again the print thereof renew,
Corrupted all in such a sort that scant a sentence true
Now fly'th abroad as I it wrote. Which thing when I had tried,
130   And fourscore greater faults than mine in forty leaves espied,
"Small thanks", quoth I, "for such a work would Senec give to me,
If he were yet alive and should perhaps it chance to see."

---

[29] 103–04] Heywood does not mention the most prolific translator of the time, Arthur Golding (1535/6–1606), who was not a member of an inn, reinforcing the idea that Heywood used the preface to flatter those at the Inns, perhaps in an effort to secure admission or social acceptance (see Introduction, pp. 36–37).

[30] Ladies nine] i.e. the Muses.

[31] On the ten tragedies attributed to Seneca, see Introduction, p. 7.

[32] Heywood further criticizes printers below (287–88, 307–10) and in *Troas* ('Preface to the Readers', line 23). On the printing of *Troas*, see Greg.

[33] sign of Hand and Star] Tottel's printing house.

And to the printer thus I said: "Within these doors of thine,
I make a vow shall never more come any work of mine.'"

'My friend', quoth Senec therewithal, 'no marvel thereof is.
They have myself so wrongèd oft, and many things amiss
Are done by them in all my works, such faults in every book
Of mine they make (as well he may it find that list to look)
That sense and Latin, verse and all, they violate and break,
140   And oft what I yet never meant, they me enforce to speak.
It is the negligence of them, and partly lack of skill,
That doth the works with pains well penned full oft disgrace and
     spill.°
But as for that, be nought abashed: the wise will well it weigh,
And learnèd men shall soon discern thy faults from his and say:
"Lo here the printer doth him wrong, as easy is to try,°
And slander° doth the author's name, and lewdly° him belie."
But where thy years thou say'st lack skill, misdoubt° thou not',
     quoth he,
'I will myself in these affairs a helper be to thee.
Each poet's tale I will expound° and other places hard.[34]
150   Thou shalt, no doubt, find some that will thy labour well regard.'

And therewithal, 'O Lord,'[35] he said, 'now him I think upon,[36]
That here but late too little lived and now from hence is gone.
Whose virtues rare in age so green bewrayed° a worthy wight,
And towardness° tried of tender time, how lovely lamp of light
He would have been, if God had spared his days, till such time
     when
That elder age had abled him by growth to graver man.
How thankful thing think'st thou', quoth he, 'would this to him
     have been,
If given to his name he might a work of thine have seen,
Whom during life he favoured so? But that may never be:
160   For gone he is, alas the while thou shalt him never see,
Where breathing bodies dwell again, nor never shalt thou more,
Eftsoons° with him of learning talk, as thou wert wont before.

---

[34] other places hard] i.e. 'any difficult lines (in them)'.

[35] O Lord] S. appears to refer to a Christian god (see also 155 and 167 below). On the tradition concerning Seneca and Christianity, see Introduction, pp. 8–9.

[36] 151–67] Heywood eulogizes John Mason's recently deceased son.

'Yet wail no more for him,' he said, 'for he far better is.
His seat he hath obtainèd now, among the stars in bliss.
And casting brighter beams about than Phoebus' golden gleed,°
Above the skies he lives with Jove, another Ganymede,
In better place than Aquarie, such grace did God him give.

'But though the son be gone, yet here doth yet the father live,
And long might he this life enjoy in health and great increase
170   Of honour and of virtue both till God his soul release
From corpse to skies, with right reward to recompense him there,
For truth and trusty service done to prince and country here.
His goodness lo thyself hast felt', quoth he, 'and that of late,
When he thee failèd not to help and succour thine estate.[37]
To him it shall beseem° thee well some token for to show,
That of thy duty which thou dost for his deserts him owe
Thou mindful art, and how thou dost thy diligence apply
To thank as power may serve and with thy pen to signify
A grateful mind. And though too light so little trifle be,
180   To give to him that hath so much already done for thee,
Yet since thou can'st none otherwise his honour yet requite,
Nor yet thy years do thee permit more weighty works to write,
This Christmastime thou may'st do well a piece thereof to end,
And many thanks in volume small as thee becomes to send.
And tell him how for his estate thou dost thy prayers make,
And him in daily vows of thine to God above betake.

'But for because the printers all have greatly wrongèd me,
To ease thee of thy pains therein, see what I bring to thee.'
He said, and therewithal began to ope the gilded book,
190   Which erst I told he bare in hand, and thereupon to look.
The leaves within were fine to feel and fair to look upon,
As they with silver had been sleeked,° full clear to see they shone.
Yet far the letters did each one exceed the leaves in sight,
More glorious than the glittering gold and in the eye more bright.
The featly framèd lines throughout in meetest manner stand,
More worthy work it was than might be made by mortal hand.
Therewith me thought a savour sweet I felt, so fresh that was,
That beds of purple violets and roses far did pass,
No princes' perfume like to it in chamber of estate.

---

[37] 174] An unclear reference. Mason (senior) was a fellow of All Soul's and perhaps helped Heywood to move there following his resignation from Merton.

200   I wist it was something divine did me so recreate.°
      I felt myself refreshèd much, well quickened were my wits,
      And oftentimes of pleasure great I had so joyful fits
      That waking now I will confess, you may believe me well,
      Great horde of gold I would refuse in such delights to dwell
      As in that dream I had. Anon me thought I askèd him
      What book it was he bare in hand that showed and smelled so trim.°
      'These are', quoth he, 'the Tragedies indeed of Seneca.
      The Muse herself them truly writ that hight° Melpomena,
      In Parnass' princely palace high she garnishèd this book.[38]
210   The ladies have of Helicon great joy thereon to look,
      When walking in their alleys sweet the flowers so fresh they tread,
      And in the midst of them me place my Tragedies to read.
      These leaves that fine as velvet feel and parchment like in sight,
      Of feat°-fine fawns they are the skins such as no mortal wight
      May come unto, but with the which the Muses wont to play,
      In gardens still with grass full green that garnished are full gay.
      There fostered are these little beasts and fed with Muses' milk,
      Their whitest hands and feet they lick with tongue as soft as silk.
      Their hair not such as have the herd of other common deer,
220   But silken skins of purple hue like velvet fine they wear.
      With proper featly-framèd feet about the arbours green
      They trip and dance before these dames, full seemly° to be seen.
      And then their golden horns adown in ladies' laps they lay,
      A great delight those sisters nine have with these fawns to play.
      Of skins of them this parchment lo that shines so fair they make,
      When aught they would with hand of theirs to written book betake.
      This gorgeous glittering golden ink, so precious thing to see,
      Give ear, and whereof made it is, I shall declare to thee.
      Fair trees amid their paradise there are of every kind,
230   Where every fruit that bough brings forth, a man may ever find.
      And dainties such as princes wont with proudest price to buy,
      Great plenty thereof may be seen hang there on branches high.
      The plum, the pear, the fig, the date, pom'granate wants not there,
      The orange and the olive tree full plenteously do bear.
      Yea, there the golden apples hang, which once a thing much
          worth,
      To joy the wedding day of Jove, the soil itself brought forth.[39]

---

[38] 209–80] On this *locus amoenus*, see Introduction, p. 36.

There Daphne stands, transformed to tree that green is still to sight,
That was sometime the lovèd nymph so fair of Phoebus bright.
Not far from fruit so rich that once did waking dragon keep[40]
240   Doth Myrrha stand with woeful tears that yet doth wail and weep.[41]
Her tears congealèd hard to gum that savour sweet doth cast,
It is that makes to leaf so fine this ink to cleave so fast.[42]

'But with what water is this ink thus made, now learn', quoth he,
'The secrets of the sacred mount I will declare to thee.
Above the rest a cedar high of haughty top there grows,
With bending branches far abroad on soil that shadow shows.
In top whereof do hang full high the pens of poets old,
And posies portured° for their praise in letters all of gold.
In shade whereof a banquet house there stands of great delight,
250   For Muses' joys. The walls are made of marble fair in sight
Four square; an ivory turret stands at every corner high.
The nooks and tops doth beaten gold and amell° overlie.
In fulgent° seat doth fleeing Fame there sit full high from ground,
And praise of Pallas' poets sends to stars with trumpets' sound.
The gate thereof so strong and sure it need no watch nor ward;
A wondrous work it is to see of adamant full hard.
With nine sure locks whereof, of one each lady keeps the key,
That none of them may come therein when other are away.
The floor within with emeralds green is pavèd fair and feat;
260   The board° and benches round about are made of pure black geat.°
The lute, the harp, the citheron,° the shawm,° the sackbut° eke,
The viol° and the virginal,° no music there to seek.[43]
About the walls more worthy work than made by mortal hand,
The poets' painted pictures all in seemly° order stand,
With colours such so lively laid that at that sight I ween,
Apelles' pencil would bear back abashèd to be seen.[44]
There Homer, Ovid, Horace eke full featly portured be,

---

[39] 235–36] Earth gave Hera a tree with golden apples to celebrate her marriage to Zeus.
[40] 239] The dragon Ladon (with the Hesperides, the Daughters of Evening) guarded Hera's apples.
[41] 237–41] Daphne and Myrrha were nymphs transformed into trees.
[42] 242] 'It is this (gum) that makes this ink stick so well to such fine leaf'.
[43] no music there to seek] i.e. 'it is not necessary to look (far) for music'.
[44] would bear back abashèd to be seen] i.e. 'would recoil in shame' being outdone by the pictures' superior artistry.

And there not in the lowest place, they have describèd me.
There Virgil, Lucan, Palingene, and rest of poets all[45]
270   Do stand, and there from this day forth full many other shall.
For now that house by many yards enlargèd out they have,
Whereby they might in wider wall the images engrave,
And paint the pictures more at large of hundreds Englishmen
That give their tongue a greater grace by pure and painful pen.
In midst of all this worthy work there runs a pleasant spring
That is of all the paradise the most delicious thing,
That round about enclosèd is with wall of jasper° stone.[46]
The ladies let no wight therein, but even themselves alone.
The water shines like gold in sight and sweetest is to smell,
280   Full often times they bathe themselves within that blissful well.
With water thereof they this ink have made that writ this book,
And licenced me to bring it down for thee thereon to look.
Thou may'st believe it truly wrote and trust in every whit,°
For here hath never printers' press made fault, nor never yet
Came error here by miss° of man. In sacred seat on high
They have it writ in all whose works their pen can make no lie.[47]
This book shall greatly thee avail to see how printers miss°
In all my works, and all their faults thou may'st correct by this.
And more than that, this golden spring, with which I have thee told
290   This ink so bright, thus made to be, such property doth hold
That who thereof the savour feels, his wit shall quickened be,
And sprites° revived in wondrous wise as now it haps to thee.

'Come on, therefore, while help thou hast', he said, and
    therewithal,
Even at Thyestes chancèd first the leaves abroad to fall.
'Even here,' quoth he, 'if it thee please begin, now take thy pen.
Most dire debates describe of all that ever chanced to men,
And which the gods abhorred to see.[48] The sum of all the strife
Now hearken to: Thyestes keeps° his brother Atreus' wife
And ram with golden fleece, but yet doth Atreus friendship feign

---

[45] Palingene] See n. at line 101 above.

[46] jasper stone] A play on Heywood's name (Vocht, p. 339) and/or the Book of Revelation 21:18–19 (Pincombe, 'Melpomene or Megaera?').

[47] lie] i.e. mistakes.

[48] the gods abhorred to see] In *Thyestes*, the sun reverses its course in response to Atreus's crime, a recurring image (see 1.1.119–20, 4.1.15–16, 4.Cho.1–3, 5.1.8, 5.3.21–25, and 5.4.17).

300 With him, till time for father's food he hath his children slain,
  And dishes dressed', he said, and then begun to read the book.
  I sat attent,° and thereupon I fixèd fast my look.
  First how the Fury drove the spright° of Tantalus from hell
  To stir the strife, I heard him read, and all expound full well.
  Full many pleasant poets' tales that did me please I heard,
  And evermore to book so fair I had a great regard.
  Whereby I saw how often times the printers did him wrong.
  Now Gryphius, Colineus now, and now and then among,
  He Aldus blamed with all the rest that in his works do miss[49]
310 Of sense or verse; and still my book I did correct by his.

  The god of sleep had heard all this when time for him it was
  To dens of slumber whence he came again away to pass.
  The kercher° bound about my brows,[50] dipped all in Limbo lake,[51]
  He straight unknit;° away he flee'th, and I begun to wake.
  When round I rolled mine eyes about and saw myself alone,
  In vain I 'Senec, Senec' cried. The poet now was gone.
  For woe whereof I gan° to weep, 'O gods,' quoth I, 'unkind
  Ye are to blame with shapes so vain our mortal eyes to blind.
  What goodly gain get you thereby, ye should us so beguile,
320 And fancies° feed with joys that last, alas, too little while?'
  I Morpheus cursed a thousand times that he had made me sleep
  At all, or else that he me would in dream no longer keep.
  And never were my joys so great in sleep so sweet before,
  But now as grievous was my woe, alas, and ten times more,
  Myself without the poet there thus left alone to see,
  And all delights of former dream thus vanishèd to be.
  Sometime I cursed, sometime I cried, like wight that waxèd
    wood,°
  Or panther of her prey deprived or tiger of her brood.
  A thousand times my colour goes, and comes as oft again.
330 About I walked; I might nowhere in quiet rest remain.
  In wondrous wise I vexèd was that never man I ween
  So soon might after late delights in such a pang be seen.
  'O thou Megaera,' then I said, 'if might of thine it be[52]

---

[49] 308–10] On these editions, see Appendix on 'The Translators' Latin Sources'.
[50] kercher bound] See line 13 above.
[51] Limbo lake] Common translation of Hades, Styx, Lethe, or Acheron, which may influence Spenser's *Faerie Queene* 1.2.32.5. See Taylor, 'Elizabethan', and below 5.4.6 and 41, and *Agamemnon* 1.1.13, 3.2.19 and 182.

Wherewith thou Tantal draw'st from hell that thus disturbeth me,[53]
Inspire my pen with pensiveness° this tragedy t'indite,°
And as so dreadful thing beseems with doleful style to write.'
This said, I felt the Fury's force enflame me more and more,
And ten times more now chafed° I was than ever yet before.
My hair stood up, I waxèd wood, my sinews all did shake,
340   And as the Fury had me vexed, my teeth began to ache,[54]
And thus enflamed with force of her, I said, 'It should be done',
And down I sat with pen in hand and thus my verse begun.

---

[52] 333–42] As in *Troas* ('Preface', 50–56), Heywood invokes a Fury, here Megaera, a character in Act 1.

[53] Tantal draw'st from hell] Reference to the action of Act 1.

[54] Fury] Avenging spirit; but also connoting 'fury' (i.e. inspired frenzy, poetic rage).

THE SPEAKERS

TANTALUS

MEGAERA

ATREUS

SERVANT

THYESTES

PHYLISTHENES[55]

MESSENGER

CHORUS

---

[55] On this name, see Appendix on 'The Translators' Latin Sources' n. at *Thy.* 3.1.

THE FIRST ACT

TANTALUS MEGAERA

[TANTALUS]

What fury fell° enforceth me to flee th'unhappy seat,[56]
That gape and gasp with greedy jaw the fleeing food to eat?[57]
What god to Tantalus the bowers° where breathing bodies dwell
Doth show again? Is aught found worse than burning thirst of hell
In lakes alow?° Or yet worse plague than hunger is there one,
In vain that ever gapes for food? Shall Sisyphus his stone,
That slipper° restless rolling peise,° upon my back be borne?
Or shall my limbs with swifter swinge° of whirling wheel be
    torn?[58]
Or shall my pains be Tityus' pangs, th'increasing liver still,
10   Whose growing guts the gnawing gripes° and filthy fowls do fill,
That still by night repairs the paunch that was devoured by day,
And wondrous womb unwasted lieth a new preparèd prey?
What ill° am I appointed for? O cruel judge of sprights,[59]
Whoso thou be that torments new among the souls delights
Still to dispose, add what thou can'st to all my deadly woe,
That keeper even of dungeon dark would sore° abhor to know,[60]
Or hell itself it quake to see, for dread whereof likewise
I tremble would – that plague seek out. Lo now there doth arise
My brood, that shall in mischief far the grandsire's guilt outgo
20   And guiltless make, that first shall dare unventured ills to do.
Whatever place remaineth yet of all this wicked land,
I will fill up, and never once, while Pelops' house doth stand,
Shall Minos idle be.

MEGAERA

                Go forth thou detestable spright,
And vex the gods of wicked house with rage of fury's might.
Let them contend with all offence by turns, and one by one

---

[56] 1–6] On the translation style in these lines, see Introduction, pp. 40–41.

[57] 2–6] Tantalus refers to his 'tantalizing' punishment in the underworld: food and drink that flee his grasp.

[58] 8] i.e. like Ixion.

[59] judge of sprights] King Minos, who passes judgement in Hades, named at 23.

[60] keeper even of dungeon dark] Cerberus, guardian of the entrance to Hades.

Let swords be drawn, and mean of ire procure° there may be
    none,[61]
Nor shame. Let fury blind enflame their minds and wrathful will.
Let yet the parents' rage endure and longer lasting ill
Through children's children spread. Nor yet let any leisure be
30   The former fault to hate, but still more mischief new to see,
Nor one in one.[62] But ere the guilt with vengeance be acquit,
Increase the crime. From brethren° proud let rule of kingdom
    flit
To runagates.° And swerving state of all unstable things,
Let it by doubtful° doom° be tossed between th'uncertain
    kings.[63]
Let mighty fall to misery, and miser° climb to might.
Let chance turn th'empire up-so-down,° both give and take the
    right.[64]
The banishèd for guilt, when god restore their country shall,
Let them to mischief fall afresh, as hateful then to all
As to themselves. Let ire think nought unlawful to be done.
40   Let brother dread the brother's wrath, and father fear the son,[65]
And eke the son his parent's power. Let babes be murdered ill,°
But worse begot:[66] her spouse betrapped in treason's train to kill,
Let hateful wife await.° And let them bear through seas their
    war.
Let bloodshed lie the lands about and every field afar,
And over conquering captains great of countries far to see,
Let lust triumph: in wicked house, let whoredom counted be
The light'st offence. Let trust that in the breasts of brethren
    breeds,
And truth, be gone. Let not from sight of your so heinous deeds
The heavens be hid, about the pole when shine the stars on high

---

[61] mean of ire procure there may be none] i.e. 'make sure' (= procure) 'that there may be no moderation of anger'.

[62] Nor one in one] i.e. 'not one crime against one victim, but many crimes against many victims'.

[63] by doubtful doom] Omits S. 'violentae domus' (of violent house).

[64] both give and take the right] A surprising shift in sense from S. 'fluctu [...] assiduo' ([buffeted] by frequent waves).

[65] 40–45] Megaera prefigures events of *Thyestes* and *Agamemnon*, as well as the Trojan War.

[66] But worse begot] A reference to Aegisthus, incestuous son of Thyestes who collaborates with Clytemnestra to kill her husband Agamemnon.

50 And flames with wonted beams of light do deck the painted [50]
    sky.⁶⁷
    Let darkest night be made, and let the day the heavens
        forsake.
    Disturb the gods of wicked house: hate, slaughter, murder make.
    Fill up the house of Tantalus with mischiefs and debates.
    Adornèd be the pillars high with bay, and let the gates
    Be garnished green, and worthy there for thy return to sight,
    Be kindled fire. Let mischief done in Thracia once, there light
    More manifold.⁶⁸ Wherefore doth yet the uncle's hand delay?
    Doth yet Thyestes not bewail° his children's fatal day?
    Shall he not find them where with heat of fires that under glow
60 The cauldron boils? Their limbs each one apieces let them go
    Dispersed. Let father's fires with blood of children filèd° be.
    Let dainties° such be dressed. It is no mischief new to thee
    To banquet so.⁶⁹ Behold this day we have to thee released,
    And hunger-starvèd womb of thine we send to such a feast.
    With foulest food thy famine fill; let blood in wine be drowned,
    And drunk in sight of thee. Lo now such dishes have I found
    As thou would'st shun. Stay! Wither dost thou headlong way
        now take?

TANTALUS

    To pools and floods of hell again and still-declining° lake,
    And flight of tree full fraught° with fruit that from the lips doth
        flee;
70 To dungeon dark of hateful hell let leeful° be for me
    To go, or if too light be thought the pains that there I have,
    Remove me from those lakes again, in midst of worser wave
    Of Phlegethon to stand, in seas of fire beset to be.
    Whoso beneath thy pointed pains by Destiny's decree
    Dost still endure, whoso thou be that underliest alow
    The hollow den, or ruin who that fears and overthrow

---

⁶⁷ 49–50 about the pole [...] the painted sky] Heywood is opaque. See n. in
Appendix on 'The Translators' Latin Sources'.
⁶⁸ mischief done in Thracia once] Allusion to the cannibalistic revenge of Procne
on her husband Tereus, king of Thrace, after he raped her sister Philomela: she
tricked him into eating their son Itys. 'Once' contrasts the single Itys with the
'manifold' sons whom Thyestes will eat.
⁶⁹ It is no mischief new to thee / To banquet so] Tantalus attempted to serve the
flesh of his son, Pelops, at a banquet of the gods.

Of falling hill, or cruel cries that sound in caves of hell[70]
Of greedy roaring lions' throats, or flock of furies fell
Who quakes to know, or who the brands of fire, in direst pain,
80   Half-burnt throws off, hark to the voice of Tantalus again
That hastes to hell, and, whom the truth hath taught, believe
    well me:
Love well your pains; they are but small. When shall my hap so
    be
To flee the light?

MEGAERA

                  Disturb thou first this house with dire discord.
Debates and battles bring with thee and of th'unhappy sword
Ill love to kings.[71] The cruel breast strike through and hateful
    heart,
With tumult mad.

TANTALUS

                To suffer pains it seemeth well my part,
Not woes to work.[72] I am sent forth like vapour dire to rise
That breaks the ground, or poison like the plague in wondrous
    wise
That slaughter makes. Shall I to such detested crimes apply
90   My nephews'° hearts? O parents great of gods above the sky,[73]
And mine (though shamed I be to grant), although with greater
    pain
My tongue be vexed, yet this to speak I may no whit refrain
Nor hold my peace: I warn you this, lest sacred hand with blood
Of slaughter dire, or frenzy fell of frantic fury wood,[74]
The altars stain, I will resist and guard° such guilt away.
With stripes° why dost thou me afright? Why threat'st thou me
    to fray°

---

[70] or cruel cries that sound in caves of hell] Heywood's addition.

[71] bring […] of th'unhappy sword / Ill love to kings] i.e. 'and bring to kings the evil love of the unhappy sword'; 'unhappy' is Heywood's addition.

[72] Not woes to work] i.e. 'not to contrive woes'. Heywood misses S.'s point in 'non esse poenam' (not to be the punishment [myself]).

[73] O parents] S. has singular 'parens' (parent).

[74] or frenzy fell of frantic fury wood] For S. 'furiali malo' (fury-like evil); Heywood's typical alliterative expansion.

Those cralling° snakes?[75] Or famine fixed in empty womb,
  wherefore
Dost thou revive? Now fries within with thirst enkindled sore
My heart, and in the bowels burnt the boiling flames do glow.   [100]

MEGAERA

100   I follow thee. Through all this house now rage and fury throw.
    Let them be driven so, and so let either thirst to see
    Each other's blood. Full well hath felt the coming in of thee[76]
    This house, and all with wicked touch of thee begun to quake.
    Enough it is. Repair again to dens and loathsome lake
    Of flood well known. The sadder soil with heavy foot of thine
    Aggrievèd is. See'st thou from springs how waters do decline
    And inward sink? Or how the banks lie void by droughty° heat,
    And hotter blast of fiery wind the fewer clouds doth beat,
    The trees be spoiled and naked stand to sight in withered woods,
110   The barren boughs whose fruits are fled? The land between the
      floods,
    With surge of seas on either side that wonted to resound,
    And nearer fords° to separate sometime with lesser ground,
    Now broader spread, it heareth how aloof the waters rise.[77]
    Now Lerna turns against the stream; Phoronides likewise
    His pores be stopped. With customed course Alpheus drives not
      still[78]
    His holy waves. The trembling tops of high Cithaeron hill
    They stand not sure. From height adown they shake their silver
      snow,
    And noble fields of Argos fear their former drought to know.[79]
    Yea, Titan doubts, himself, to roll the world his wonted way,
120   And drive by force to former course the backward drawing
      day.[80]

---

[75] 96–97 'Why threat'st thou me to fray / Those cralling snakes] Perhaps 'Why do
you brandish those twisted snakes to frighten me?'
[76] 102–20] 'The reaction of the house to Tantalus' presence [...] is now enacted on
a larger scale, reproducing on earth a version of Tantalus' customary punishment'
(Tarrant, p. 104).
[77] 110–13] Heywood partially conveys S.'s point: the Isthmus of Corinth, which
gets thinner or broader as the seas on either side rise or recede, now broadens to
such an extent that the two seas can only be heard distantly.
[78] 114–15 Lerna [...] Phoronides [...] Alpheus] Three rivers.
[79] 118] Argos suffered a drought early in its history.

CHORUS

This Argos town if any god be found,[81]
And Pisey bowers that famous yet remain,[82]
Or kingdoms else to love of Corinth's ground,
The double havens or sundered seas in twain;[83]
If any love Taygetus his snows[84]
(by winter which when they on hills be cast
By Boreas' blasts that from Sarmartia blows,
With yearly breath the summer melts as fast),
Where clear Alpheus runs with flood so cold
10 By plays well known that there Olympics hight:°[85]
Let pleasant power of his from hence withhold
Such turns of strife that here they may not light,
Nor nephew worse than grandsire spring from us,
Or direr deeds delight the younger age.
Let wicked stock of thirsty Tantalus
At length leave off and weary be of rage.

Enough is done, and nought prevailed the just[86]
Or wrong.[87] Betrayed is Myrtilus and drowned,
That did betray his dame, and with like trust
20 Borne as he bare himself hath made renowned
With changèd name the sea, and better known
To mariners thereof no fable is.[88]
On wicked sword the little infant thrown,[89]

---

[80] 119–20] Heywood imaginatively adapts S.'s description of the sun ('Titan'), 'dubitat an iubeat sequi cogatque habenis ire periturum diem' (doubts whether he should command [the daylight] to follow, and should with his reins compel the day, soon to meet its end, to advance); an allusion to the sun's later horror at Thyestes' banquet (see n. at 'Preface', line 297).

[81] 1–10] The Chorus invokes 'any' (i.e. all) deities who 'love' (i.e. favour) Argos and its vicinity.

[82] Pisey bowers] i.e. the district of Pisa, famously associated with the Olympic games (cf. line 10 below).

[83] double havens or sundered seas] i.e. the waters on either side of the Isthmus of Corinth (named explicitly in S.).

[84] Taygetus] Quadrisyllabic 'Ta-y-ge-tus'.

[85] plays] i.e. games.

[86] Enough is done] Less specific than S. 'satis peccatum est' (enough wrong-doing has been done).

[87] Or wrong] S. 'aut commune nefas' (or shared wickedness), apparently referring to the complicity of both parties (Tarrant, pp. 109–10).

[88] 18–22] On Myrtilus, see Introduction, p. 33.

As ran the child to take his father's kiss,
Unripe for th'altars offering, fell down dead
And with thy hand, O Tantalus, was rent,°
With such a meat for gods thy boards to spread.

Eternal famine for such food is sent,
And thirst; nor for those dainty meats unmild°   [150]
30   Might meeter pain appointed ever be.
With empty throat stands Tantalus beguiled;
Above thy wicked head there leans to thee,
Than Phiney's fowls in flight a swifter prey,[90]
With burdened boughs declined on every side;
And of his fruits all bent to bear the sway,
The tree deludes° the gapes of hunger wide.[91]
Though he full greedy feed thereon would fain,
So oft deceived neglects to touch them yet:
He turns his eyes; his jaws he doth refrain,
40   And famine fixed in closèd gums doth shet.°
But then each branch, his plenteous riches all,
Lets lower down, and apples from on high
With lither° leaves they flatter like to fall[92]
And famine stir, in vain that bids to try[93]
His hands, which when he hath rought forth anon[94]
To be beguiled, in higher air again
The harvest hangs and fickle fruit is gone.
Then thirst him grieves no less than hunger's pain,
Wherewith when kindled is his boiling blood
50   Like fire, the wretch the waves to him doth call
That meet his mouth, which straight the fleeing flood
Withdraws, and from the drièd ford doth fall
And him forsakes that follows them. He drinks
The dust so deep of gulf that from him shrinks.

---

[89] little infant] Pelops (see n. at 1.1.62–63).

[90] Phiney's fowls] i.e. legendary Harpies, sent to punish Phineus.

[91] deludes] S. 'alludit' (mocks). Perhaps influences the Tantalus-like punishment of Satan and the fallen angels: 'Yet parched with scalding thirst and hunger fierce / Though to delude them sent, could not abstain' (*Paradise Lost* 10.557–60) (cf. Byville, p. 256).

[92] flatter like to fall] S. 'insultant' (bob around mockingly).

[93] that bids to try] i.e. (the famine) 'which tempts (him)'.

[94] rought] reached.

THE SECOND ACT

ATREUS   SERVANT[95]

[ATREUS]

[Aside]

O dastard,° coward, O wretch and (which the greatest yet of all[96]
To tyrant's check° I count that may in weighty things befall)
O unrevengèd! After guilts so great, and brother's guile,
And truth trod down, dost thou provoke with vain complaints
    the while
Thy wrath? Already now to rage all Argos town throughout
In armour ought of thine, and all the double seas about
Thy fleet to ride.[97] Now all the fields with fervent flames of
    thine
And towns to flash it well beseemed, and everywhere to shine
The bright drawn sword. All underfoot of horse let every side
Of Argos land resound, and let the woods not serve to hide
Our foes, nor yet in haughty top of hills and mountains high
The builded towers. The people all, let them to battle cry
And clear forsake Mycenas town. Whoso his hateful head[98]
Hides and defends with slaughter dire, let blood of him be shed.
This princely Pelops' palace proud and bowers of high renown,
On me, so on my brother too, let them be beaten down.

Go to;[99] do that which never shall no after age allow,°
Nor none it whist.° Some mischief great there must be ventured
    now,
Both fierce and bloody, such as would my brother rather long

10

---

[95] 2.1] A Senecan 'passion-restraint' scene: a lesser character seeks unsuccessfully to deter the protagonist from a course of action (cf. *Agamemnon* 2.1).

[96] O dastard, coward, O wretch] To make the line parallel with the Latin (S. 176), we punctuate 'dastard' as a noun, though it is possibly adjectival. Heywood's diction may influence Studley's distribution of this same series of terms over two lines of *Hercules Oetaeus* (S. 1720–21): 'Dost dastard thou forslow, / for fear to this wicked deed? O coward, peasant slave' (Newton, fol. 214ʳ). Those lines by Studley perhaps influence *Hamlet* (see Taylor, 'Shakespeare').

[97] 5–7] i.e. 'all Argos town ought to be raging throughout in your armour, and your fleet ought to be riding around the double seas (of the Isthmus)'.

[98] his] i.e. Thyestes'.

[99] Go to] Atreus addresses himself; in S., he exhorts his mind (animus).

20 To have been his. Thou never dost enough revenge the wrong,
Except thou pass;[100] and fiercer fact° what may be done so dire
That his exceeds? Doth ever he lay down his hateful ire?
Doth ever he the modest mean in time of wealth regard?
Or quiet in adversity? I know his nature hard,
Intractable that broke may be, but never will it bend.   [200]
For which, ere he prepare himself, or force to fight intend,
Set first on him, lest while I rest, he should on me arise.
He will destroy or be destroyed. In midst the mischief lies[101]
Prepared to him that takes it first.

SERVANT

          Doth fame° of people nought
30 Adverse thee fear?[102]

ATREUS

      The greatest good of kingdom may be thought
That still the people are constrained their prince's deeds as well
To praise as them to suffer all.

SERVANT

        Whom fear doth so compel
To praise, the same his foes to be doth fear enforce again;
But who indeed the glory seeks of favour true t'obtain,[103]
He rather would with hearts of each be praised than tongues of
  all.

ATREUS

The truer praise full oft hath happed to meaner men to fall;
The false but unto mighty man. What nill° they, let them will.[104]

---

[100] 20–21] The idea is a central theme in Renaissance tragedy (Miola, p. 16). Except thou pass] i.e. 'unless you surpass (it)'.

[101] In midst] Between us.

[102] 29–30] i.e. 'does contrary public opinion not frighten you at all?'

[103] 34–37] Vocht (pp. xxxvii–xxxviii) suggests these lines may influence a similar passage in *The Misfortunes of Arthur*: CONAN: 'But whoso seeks true praise and just renown, / Would rather seek their praising hearts than tongues. / MORDRED: True praise may happen to the basest groom. / A forcèd praise to none but to a prince' (2.2.82–85).

[104] What nill they, let them will] i.e. 'what they refuse, let them [be made to] want'.

SERVANT

Let first the king will honest things, and none the same dare nill.

ATREUS

40　　Where leeful are to him that rules but honest things alone,
There reigns the king by others' leave.

SERVANT

And where that shame is none,
Nor care of right, faith, piety, nor holiness none stay'th,°
That kingdom swerves.

ATREUS

Such holiness, such piety and faith[105]
Are private goods. Let kings run on in that that likes their will.

SERVANT

The brother's hurt a mischief count, though he be ne'er so ill.[106]

ATREUS

It is but right to do to him that wrong to brother were.
What heinous hurt hath his offence let pass to prove, or where
Refrained the guilt? My spouse he stale away for lechery[107]
And reign by stealth. The ancient note and sign of empery
By fraud he got. My house by fraud to vex he never ceased.
50　　In Pelops' house there fostered is a noble worthy beast,
The close-kept ram, the goodly guide of rich and fairest flocks,
By whom throughout on every side depend° adown the locks
Of glittering gold with fleece of which the new kings wonted
　　were[108]
Of Tantal's flock their sceptres gilt and mace of might to bear.
Of this the owner reigneth he, with him of house so great
The fortune flee'th.[109] This sacred ram, aloof in safety shet,

---

[105] 42–45] On the translation style of these lines, see Introduction pp. 41–42.

[106] ne'er so ill] i.e. 'as evil as can be'.

[107] stale] stole.

[108] glittering gold with fleece] Different from the Golden Fleece pursued by Jason and the Argonauts.

[109] with him of house so great / The fortune flee'th] i.e. 'the fortune of so great a house flees with the ram'.

In secret mead° is wont to graze, which stone on every side
With rocky wall encloseth round the fatal beast to hide.
This beast (adventuring mischief great), adjoining yet for prey
60   My spousèd mate, the traitor false hath hence conveyed away.
From hence the wrongs of mutual hate and mischief all up
    sprung.
In exile wandered he throughout my kingdoms all along.
No part of mine remaineth safe to me from trains° of his.[110]
My fere° deflowered and loyalty of empire broken is,
My house all vexed, my blood in doubt, and nought that trust is
    in
But brother foe.

[Aside]

              What stayest thou yet? At length, lo now begin.
Take heart of Tantalus to thee; to Pelops cast thine eye:
To such examples well beseems I should my hands apply.

[To Servant]

Tell thou which way were best to bring that cruel head to death.

SERVANT

70   Through pierced with sword let him be slain and yield his
    hateful breath.

ATREUS

Thou speak'st of th'end, but I him would oppress with greater
    pain.
Let tyrants vex with torment more. Should ever in my reign
    Be gentle death?

SERVANT

              Doth piety° in thee prevail no whit?

ATREUS

Depart thou hence all piety, if in this house as yet
Thou ever wert, and now let all the flock of furies dire,   [250]
And full of strife Erinnys come, and double brands of fire

---

[110] of mine] of my family.

Megaera shaking, for not yet enough with fury great
And rage doth burn my boiling breast. It ought to be replete
With monster more.

SERVANT

What mischief new dost thou in rage provide?

ATREUS

80   Not such a one as may the mean of wonted grief abide.
No guilt will I forbear, nor none may be enough despite.

SERVANT

What, sword?

ATREUS

Too little that.

SERVANT

What, fire?

ATREUS

And that is yet too light.

SERVANT

What weapon then shall sorrow such find fit to work thy will?

ATREUS

Thyestes' self.

SERVANT

Than ire itself yet that's a greater ill.

ATREUS

I grant. A tumbling tumult quakes within my bosoms, lo,
And round it rolls. I movèd am and wot not whereunto,
But drawn I am. From bottom deep the roaring soil doth cry,
The day so fair with thunder sounds, and house, as all from high
Were rent from roof and rafters, cracks, and lares° turned about
90   Have wried° their sight. So be't, so be't; let mischief such be sought
As ye, O gods, would fear.

SERVANT

What thing seek'st thou to bring to pass?

[ATREUS]

I note° what greater thing my mind, and more than wont it was
Above the reach that men are wont to work, begins to swell
And stay'th with slothful hands. What thing it is I cannot tell,[111]
But great it is. Be't so, my mind now in this feat proceed.
For Atreus and Thyestes both, it were a worthy deed.
Let each of us the crime commit. The Thracian house did see
Such wicked tables once.[112] I grant the mischief great to be,
But done ere this: some greater guilt and mischief more, let ire
100   Find out. The stomach of thy son,[113] a father thou inspire;
And sister eke, like is the cause, assist me with your power,
And drive my hand.[114] Let greedy parents all his babes
    devour,
And glad to rent his children be, and on their limbs to feed.
Enough, and well it is devised: this pleaseth me indeed.
In meantime,[115] where is he? So long and innocent wherefore
Doth Atreus walk? Before mine eyes already more and more
The shade of such a slaughter walks. The want of children
    cast[116]
In father's jaws.

[Aside]

But why, my mind, yet dread'st thou so at last

And faint'st before thou enterprise? It must be done, let be.
110   That which in all this mischief is the greatest guilt to see,
Let him commit.

---

[111] And stay'th with slothful hands] An inversion of the sense of S. 'instatque
pigris manibus' (and *urges on* my slothful hands).

[112] See n. at 1.1.56–57.

[113] stomach] Heywood's translation of 'animus' (mind), perhaps with a deliberate
play on the cannibalism to come.

[114] 100–02 The stomach of thy son [...] drive my hand] Heywood presents Atreus
as calling on his father Pelops and Pelops's sister Niobe (cf. O'Keefe, 'Analysis',
p. 156). In S., Atreus invokes the Thracian Procne and Philomela to inspire him as
he plans a similar meal to that which they prepared for Tereus.

[115] In meantime] S. 'tantisper', usually taken with the previous line: 'this pleases
me for the meantime'.

[116] want of children] S. 'orbitas' (deprivation of children).

SERVANT

> But what deceit may we for him prepare,
> Whereby betrapped he may be drawn to fall into the snare?
> He wots full well we are his foes.

ATREUS

> He could not taken be,
> Except himself would take. But now my kingdoms hopeth he.
> For hope of this he would not fear to meet the mighty Jove,
> Though him he threatened to destroy, with lightning from
>   above.
> For hope of this to pass the threats of waves he will not fail,
> Nor dread no whit by doubtful shelves of Lybic seas to sail.
> For hope of this (which thing he doth the worst of all believe)
120 He will his brother see.

SERVANT

> Who shall of peace the promise give?
> Whom will he trust?

ATREUS

> His evil hope will soon believe it well.
> Yet to my sons the charge which they shall to their uncle tell
> We will commit: That home he would from exile come again,
> And miseries for kingdom change and over Argos reign
> A king of half. And though too hard of heart our prayers all
> Himself despise, his children yet nought woting what may fall,   [300]
> With travails tired and apt to be enticed from misery,[117]
> Requests will move.[118] On th'one side his desire of empery,
> On th'other side his poverty and labour hard to see,
130 Will him subdue and make to yield, although full stout he be.

SERVANT

His travails now the time hath made to seem to him but small.

---

[117] travails] S. 'malis' (evils). Pronounced like and connotes 'tra'-vels', since Thyestes' sufferings included wandering in exile.
[118] Requests will move] i.e. '(the children's) requests will move Thyestes to return'.

166

ATREUS

Not so. For day by day the grief of ill increaseth all.
'Tis light to suffer miseries, but heavy them t'endure.

SERVANT

Yet other messengers to send in such affairs procure.

ATREUS

The younger sort the worse precepts do easily hearken to.

SERVANT

What thing against their uncle now you them instruct to do,
Perhaps with you to work the like, they will not be adread.
Such mischief wrought hath oft returned upon the worker's
    head.

ATREUS

Though never man to them the ways of guile and guilt have
    taught,
140   Yet kingdom will. Fear'st thou they should be made by counsel
    naught?[119]
They are so born. That which thou call'st a cruel enterprise,
And direly deemest done to be and wickedly likewise,
Perhaps is wrought against me there.

SERVANT

                                    And shall your sons of this
Deceit be 'ware that work you will?[120] No secretness there is
In their so green and tender years; they will your trains° disclose.

ATREUS

A privy counsel close to keep is learned with many woes.

SERVANT

And will ye them, by whom ye would he should beguilèd be,
Themselves beguiled?[121]

---

[119] naught] S. 'mali' (evil).
[120] 143–44] i.e. 'And shall your sons know of your deception?'

ATREUS

                    Nay let them both from fault and blame be free.
For what shall need in mischiefs such as I to work intend
150   To mingle them? Let all my hate by me alone take end.

Thou leav'st thy purpose, ill my mind. If thou thine own forbear,
Thou sparest him. Wherefore of this let Agamemnon here
Be minister, and client eke of mine for such a deed.
Let Menelaus present be. Truth of th'uncertain seed,
By such a practice° may be tried. If it refuse they shall,
Nor of debate will bearers be, if they him uncle call,[122]
He is their father.[123] Let them go.

                    But much the fearful face
Bewrays itself. Even him that feigns the secret, weighty case
Doth oft betray. Let them therefore not know how great a guile
160   They go about. And thou these things in secret keep the while.

SERVANT

I need not warnèd be, for these within my bosom deep
Both faith and fear, but chiefly faith doth shut and closely keep.

CHORUS

The noble house at length of high renown,
The famous stock of ancient Inachus,
Appeased and laid the threats of brethren down.
But now what fury stirs and drives you thus,
Each one to thirst the other's blood again,
Or get by guilt the golden mace in hand?
Ye little wot that so desire to reign
In what estate or place doth kingdom stand.

---

[121] Themselves beguiled] i.e. 'to be deceived themselves?' 'Beguiled' also connotes 'to be guiled' (cf. 139).

[122] 155–56] Heywood's terms 'practice', 'it' and 'debates' are softer than those of S.: 'scelere' (crime), 'bella' (wars), 'odia' (hatreds).

[123] 154–57 Truth of th'uncertain seed [...] He is their father] Atreus imagines that the mission of his sons will test their legitimacy. If they hesitate to trick Thyestes (for example, by affectionately calling Thyestes 'uncle'), this will be proof that they are not evil enough to be Atreus's own children, but must be Thyestes' (fathered during his adultery with Atreus's wife Aerope).

Not riches make a king or high renown,[124]
10 Not garnished weed° with purple Tyrian dye,
Not lofty looks, or head enclosed with crown,
Not glittering beams with gold and turrets high.[125]
A king he is that fear hath laid aside,
And all affects° that in the breast are bred;
Whom impotent ambition doth not guide,[126]   [350]
Nor fickle favour hath of people led,
Nor all that west in metals' mines hath found,
Or channel clear of golden Tagus shows,
Nor all the grain that threshèd is on ground,
20 That with the heat of Lybic harvest glows;
Nor whom the flash of lightning flame shall beat,
Nor eastern wind that smites upon the seas,
Nor swelling surge with rage of wind replete,
Or greedy gulf of Adria displease;
Whom not the prick of soldier's sharpest spear,
Or pointed pike in hand hath made to rue,°
Nor whom the glimpse of sword might cause to fear,
Or bright drawn blade of glittering steel subdue;
Who in the seat of safety sets his feet,
30 Beholds all haps how under him they lie,
And gladly runs his fatal day to meet,
Nor aught complains or grudgeth for to die.

Though present were the princes everychone°[127]
The scattered Dakes to chase that wonted be,[128]
That shining seas beset with precious stone
And red sea coasts do hold, like blood to see;[129]
Or they which else the Caspian mountains high[130]

---

[124] 9–12] On the translation style of these lines, see Introduction pp. 42–43.

[125] glittering beams with gold] i.e. 'beams glittering with gold', a metonym for ornate ceilings.

[126] impotent] S. 'impotens' (lacking in self-control).

[127] 33] S. 'reges conveniant licet' (even if [all] kings should congregate), introducing a catalogue of kings from diverse regions.

[128] chase] S. 'agitant' (rouse), describing the actions of the Dacians' leaders.

[129] 35–36] In S., one and the same sea: the Indian Ocean, or 'mare rubrum' (red sea), famous for its gems (cf. Tarrant, p. 144).

[130] they] Refers to the Armenians, who were protected from the Sarmatians by the Caspian (Caucasus) mountains.

From Sarmats strong with all their power withhold;
Or he that on the flood of Danubye
40   In frost a foot to travel dare be bold;
Or Seres in whatever place they lie
Renowned with fleece that there of silk doth spring;
They never might the truth hereof deny:
It is the mind that only makes a king.[131]

There is no need of sturdy steeds in war,
No need with arms or arrows else to fight,
That Parthus wonts with bow to fling from far,
While from the field he falsely feigneth flight.
Nor yet to siege no need it is to bring
50   Great guns in carts to overthrow the wall,
That from far off their battering pellets sling.
A king he is that feareth nought at all.
Each man himself this kingdom gives at hand.

Let whoso list with mighty mace to reign,[132]
In tickle° top of court delight to stand.
Let me the sweet and quiet rest obtain,
So set in place obscure and low degree,[133]
Of pleasant rest I shall the sweetness know.
My life, unknown to them that noble be,[134]
60   Shall in the step of secret silence go.
Thus when my days at length are overpassed,
And time without all troublous tumult spent,
An agèd man I shall depart at last,
In mean estate to die full well content.   [400]
But grievous is to him the death that when
So far abroad the bruit° of him is blown
That known he is too much to other men,
Departeth yet unto himself unknown.[135]

---

[131] 43–44] Heywood adds 43 to introduce the *sententia* in 44: S. 'mens regnum bona possidet' (a good mind possesses a kingdom).

[132] 54–68] A Senecan passage often imitated in English poetry. See Daalder, p. 45. Hunter in *Seneca*, ed. by Costa, pp. 197–201, collects multiple versions

[133] and low degree] Heywood adds this modernizing phrase.

[134] to them that noble be] Heywood's adaptation of S. 'Quiritibus' (Romans) – itself a striking anachronism in this tragedy on a Greek subject.

[135] Departeth] S. 'moritur' (dies).

THE THIRD ACT

THYESTES   PHYLISTHENES

[THYESTES]

[Aside]

My country bowers so long wished for and Argos' riches all,
Chief good that unto banished men and misers may befall,
The touch of soil where born I was, and gods of native land
(If gods they be), and sacred towers I see of Cyclops' hand
That represent than all man's work a greater majesty;
Renownèd stadies° to my youth,[136] where noble sometime I
Have not so seld as once the palm in father's chariot won.[137]
All Argos now to meet with me and people fast will run –
But Atreus too.

          Yet rather lead in woods again thy flight,
10   And bushes thick, and hid among the brutish beasts from sight,
Like life to theirs: where splendent pomp of court and princely
    pride
May not with flattering fulgent face allure thine eyes aside.
With whom the kingdom given is, behold and well regard.
Beset but late with such mishaps as all men count full hard,
I stout and joyful was, but now again thus into fear
I am returned: my mind misdoubts and backward seeks to bear
My body hence, and forth I draw my pace against my will.[138]

PHYLISTHENES

[Aside]

With slothful step (what meaneth this?) my father standeth still,
And turns his face and holds himself in doubt what thing to do.

---

[136] Renowned stadies to my youth] An awkwardly literal rendering of S. 'celebrata iuveni stadia' (racecourses frequented *by* me as a young man).

[137] 7] i.e. have won victory more than once, using the chariot of Pelops (on which see Introduction, p. 33).

[138] 1–17] Thyestes' uneasy feelings about returning from exile are echoed in other plays: e.g. Seneca in the Roman play *Octavia* (377–84) and Shakespeare's *Richard II* (3.2.4–26).

THYESTES

[Aside]

20   What thing, my mind, consider'st thou? Or else so long whereto
Dost thou so easy counsel wrest? Wilt thou to things unsure
Thy brother and the kingdom trust? Fear'st thou those ills
    t'endure
Now overcome, and milder made? And travails dost thou flee
That well were placed? It thee avails a miser now to be.
Turn hence thy pace while leeful is and keep thee from his hand.

PHYLISTHENES

What cause thee drives, O father dear, thus from thy native land
Now seen to shrink? What makes thee thus from things so good
    at last
Withdraw thyself? Thy brother comes, whose ires be overpassed,
And half the kingdom gives, and of the house dilacerate°
30   Repairs the parts,[139] and thee restores again to former state.

THYESTES

The cause of fear that I know not, thou dost require to hear.
I see nothing that makes me dread and yet I greatly fear.
I would go on, but yet my limbs with weary legs do slack,
And other way than I would pass, I am witholden back.[140]
So oft the ship that driven is with wind and eke with ore,
The swelling surge resisting both beats back upon the shore.

PHYLISTHENES

Yet overcome whatever stays° and thus doth let° your mind,
And see what are at your return prepared for you to find.
You may, O father, reign.

THYESTES

                I may, but then when die I mought.°[141]

---

[139] the parts] S. 'artus' (the limbs), an image of dismemberment.

[140] 34] S. 'alioque quam quo nitor abductus feror' (I am carried off in another direction than I try to move in).

[141] but then when die I mought] S. 'cum possim mori' ([yes,] since I have the ability to die; Tarrant, p. 154), possibly echoing the moralizing approach to kingship in the preceding choral ode (13–32).

PHYLISTHENES

40   Chief thing is power.

THYESTES

                        Nought worth at all if thou desire it nought.

PHYLISTHENES

        You shall it to your children leave.

THYESTES

                                The kingdom takes not twain.

PHYLISTHENES

        Who may be happy, rather would he miser yet remain?

THYESTES

        Believe me well, with titles false the great things us delight,
        And heavy haps in vain are feared. While high I stood in sight,
        I never stinted then to quake, and self-same sword to fear
        That hangèd by mine own side was. Oh how great good it were
        With none to strive, but careless° food to eat and rest to know.   [450]
        The greater guilts, they enter not in cottage set alow.
        And safer food is fed upon at narrow board alway,
50   While drunk in gold the poison is. By proof well taught I say:
        That evil haps before the good to love it likes my will.[142]

        Of haughty house that stands aloft in tickle top of hill,
        And sways aside, the city low need never be affright.
        Nor in the top of roof above there shines no ivory bright,
        Nor watchman none defends my sleeps by night, or guards my
            rest.
        With fleet I fish not; nor the seas I have not backward pressed,
        Nor turned to flight with builded wall; nor wicked belly I
        With taxes of the people fed; nor parcel none doth lie
        Of ground of mine beyond the Getes and Parthians far about;
60   Nor worshippèd with frankincense I am, nor (Jove shut out)
        My altars deckèd are; nor none in top of house doth stand
        In-garden trees; nor kindled yet with help of each man's hand,

---

[142] 51] i.e. 'that I prefer bad fortune over good fortune' (S. malam bonae praeferre
fortunam).

The baths do smoke; nor yet are days in slothful slumbers led,
Nor nights passed forth in watch° and wine, without the rest of
  bed.
We nothing fear; the house is safe without the hidden knife,
And poor estate the sweetness feels of rest and quiet life.
Great kingdom is to be content without the same to live.[143]

PHYLISTHENES

Yet should it not refusèd be, if god the kingdom give.

THYESTES

Not yet desired it ought to be.[144]

PHYLISTHENES

                              Your brother bids you reign.

THYESTES

70   Bids he? The more is to be feared; there lurketh there some
        train.

PHYLISTHENES

From whence it fell, yet piety is wont to turn at length,
And love unfeigned repairs again his erst omitted strength.

THYESTES

Doth Atreus then his brother love? Each Ursa first on high
The seas shall wash, and swelling surge of seas of Sicily
Shall rest and all assuagèd be, and corn to ripeness grow
In bottom of Ionian Seas, and darkest night shall show,
And spread the light about the soil.[145] The waters with the fire,
The life with death, the wind with seas, shall friendship first
        require
And be at league.[146]

---

[143] 67] S. 'immane regnum est posse sine regno pati' (it is a great kingdom to be able to endure without a kingdom), a characteristic Senecan paradox.

[144] Not yet] i.e. 'not even' or 'no longer'. On the attribution of this half-line to Thyestes, see n. in Appendix on 'The Translators' Latin Sources'.

[145] spread the light about the soil] i.e. 'give the earth daylight'.

[146] 73–79] Before Atreus loves his brother, the seas will wash the constellations of Ursa Major and Ursa Minor – and other unimaginable events. In ancient Greek poetics these are termed 'adunata' (impossibles).

PHYLISTHENES

>Of what deceit are you so dreadful° here?

THYESTES

80   Of everychone. What end at length might I provide of fear?
In all he can he hateth me.

PHYLISTHENES

>To you what hurt can he?

THYESTES

As for myself, I nothing dread; you little babes make me[147]
Afraid of him.

PHYLISTHENES

>Dread ye to be beguiled when caught ye are?
Too late it is to shun the train in middle of the snare.
But go we on. This, father, is to you my last request.

THYESTES

I follow you. I lead you not.

PHYLISTHENES

>God turn it to the best
That well-devisèd is for good. Pass forth with cheerful pace.[148]

The Second Scene

ATREUS   THYESTES

[ATREUS]

[Aside]

Entrapped in train the beast is caught and in the snare doth fall;
Both him and eke of hated stock with him the offspring all
About the father's side I see. And now in safety stands
And surest ground my wrathful hate. Now comes into my hands

---

[147] little babes] Heywood's addition.
[148] with cheerful pace] Heywood adds a positive note to S.'s more neutral 'non dubio gradu' (with unhesitating step).

At length Thyestes. Yea, he comes and all at once to me.[149]
I scant refrain myself, and scant may anger bridled be.
So, when the bloodhound seeks the beast by step, and quick of
    scent
Draws in the lyme,° and pace by pace to wind° the ways he
    went,
With nose to soil doth hunt, while he the boar aloof hath found
10   Far off by scent, he yet refrains and wanders through the ground   [500]
With silent mouth; but when at hand he once perceives the prey,
With all the strength he hath he strives with voice and calls
    away
His lingering master, and from him by force outbreaketh he:
When ire doth hope the present blood, it may not hidden be.
Yet let it hidden be. Behold, with ugly hair to sight
How irksomely° deformed with filth his foulest face is dight;
How loathsome lies his beard unkempt. But let us friendship
    feign.

[To Thyestes]

To see my brother me delights. Give now to me again
Embracing long desirèd for. Whatever strife there was
20   Before this time between us twain, forget and let it pass.
Fro this day forth let brother's love, let blood and law of kind,°
Regarded be; let all debate be slaked in either's mind.

THYESTES

I could excuse myself, except thou wert as now thou art.
But (Atreus) now I grant the fault was mine in every part,
And I offended have in all. My cause the worse to be,
Your this day's kindness makes.[150] Indeed a guilty wight is he
That would so good a brother hurt as you in any whit.
But now with tears I must entreat, and first I me submit.[151]

[Thyestes supplicates]

---

[149] And all at once] S. 'et totus quidem' (and whole, indeed), alluding to the
presence of the sons and looking ahead to the killings and cannibalism.
[150] 25–26 My cause […] day's kindness makes] i.e. 'your kindness today makes
my guilt seem all that much worse'.
[151] First I me submit] S. 'supplicem primus vides' (you are the first to see me as a
suppliant).

These hands that at thy feet do lie, do thee beseech and pray,
30   That ire and hate be laid aside and from thy bosom may
Be scrapèd out and clear forgot. For pledges take thou these,
O brother dear, these guiltless babes.

ATREUS

Thy hands yet from my knees
Remove and rather me to take in arms upon me fall.
And ye, O aids of elder's age, ye little infants all,
Me clip° and coll° about the neck. This foul attire forsake,
And spare mine eyes that pity it, and fresher vesture° take,
Like mine to see. And you with joy, the half of empery,
Dear brother take. The greater praise shall come to me thereby,
Our father's seat to yield to you, and brother to relieve.
40   To have a kingdom is but chance, but virtue it to give.

THYESTES

A just reward for such deserts, the gods, O brother dear,
Repay to thee. But on my head a regal crown to wear,
My loathsome life denies, and far doth from the sceptre flee
My hand unhappy. In the midst let leeful be for me
Of men to lurk.[152]

ATREUS

This kingdom can with twain full well agree.

THYESTES

Whatever is, O brother, yours, I count it mine to be.

ATREUS

Who would Dame Fortune's gifts refuse, if she him raise to
reign?

THYESTES

The gifts of her, each man it wots, how soon they pass again.

ATREUS

Ye me deprive of glory great, except ye th'empire take.

---

[152] 44–45 In the midst [...] / Of men to lurk] S. 'in media [...] latere turba' (to lie
hidden amid the [common] crowd).

THYESTES

50   You have your praise in offering it, and I it to forsake.
       And full persuaded to refuse the kingdom, am I still.

ATREUS

      Except your part ye will sustain, mine own forsake I will.

THYESTES

      I take it then, and bear I will the name thereof alone.
      The rights and arms, as well as mine, they shall be yours each
         one.

ATREUS

      The regal crown as you beseems upon your head then take.
      And I th'appointed sacrifice for gods will now go make.

CHORUS

Would any man it ween?° That cruel wight,
Atreus, of mind so impotent to see,[153]
Was soon astonied with his brother's sight.
No greater force than piety may be.
Where kindred is not, lasteth every threat;   [550]
Whom true love holds, it holds eternally.

The wrath but late with causes kindled great
All favour brake, and did 'To battle' cry,
When horsemen did resound on every side;
10   The swords each where then glistered more and more,[154]
Which raging Mars with often stroke did guide,
The fresher blood to shed yet thirsting sore.
But love the sword against their wills doth swage,°
And them to peace persuades with hand in hand.
So sudden rest, amid so great a rage,
What god hath made? Throughout Mycenas land
The harness clinked but late of civil strife,
And for their babes did fearful mothers quake;
Her armèd spouse to leese° much feared the wife,

---

[153] impotent] See n. at 2.Cho.15.
[154] each where] S. 'hinc illinc' (now from this side, now from that).

20   When sword was made the scabbard° to forsake
That now by rest with rust was overgrown.
Some to repair the walls that did decay,
And some to strength the towers half overthrown,
And some the gates with gins° of iron to stay
Full busy were, and dreadful watch by night
From turret high did overlook the town.
Worse is than war itself the fear of fight.

Now are the threats of cruel sword laid down,
And now the rumour whists of battles sown;
30   The noise of crooked trumpet silent lies,
And quiet peace returns to joyful town.

So, when the waves of swelling surge arise,[155]
While Corus wind the Bruttian seas doth smite,
And Scylla sounds from hollow caves within,
And shipmen are with wafting waves affright,
Charybdis casts that erst it had drunk in;
And Cyclops fierce his father yet doth dread[156]
In Etna bank that fervent is with heats,
Lest quenchèd be with waves that overshed°
40   The fire that from eternal furnace beats;
And poor Laertes thinks his kingdoms all
May drownèd be, and Ithaca doth quake.
If once the force of winds begin to fall,
The sea lieth down more mild than standing lake;
The deep, where ships so wide full dreadful were
To pass, with sails on either side outspread,
Now fallen adown, the lesser boat doth bear;
And leisure is to view the fishes dead[157]
Even there, where late with tempest beat upon
50   The shaken Cyclades were with seas aghast.[158]

---

[155] 32–44] The idea is that when the north-west wind, Corus, stirs up the Bruttian Sea off southern Italy, the sea becomes so violent that even Laertes (king of Ithaca) and the Cyclops (on Sicily) become fearful; but their fears are abated as soon as the sea grows calm.

[156] his father] i.e. the sea-god Poseidon.

[157] dead] S. 'mersos' (probably 'immersed').

[158] 45–50] Heywood slightly obscures S.'s image: the seas which were recently stirred up are now clear and calm, and covered in boats, including light craft.

No state endures; the pain and pleasure one
To other yields, and joys be soonest passed.
One hour sets up the things that lowest be;
He that the crowns to princes doth divide,
Whom people please with bending of the knee,   [600]
And at whose beck their battles lay aside
The Medes, and Indians eke to Phoebus nigh,
And Dakes that Parthians do with horsemen threat,
Himself yet holds his sceptres doubtfully,
60   And men of might he fears and chances great
(That each estate may turn) and doubtful hour.

O ye, whom lord of land and waters wide,
Of life and death grants here to have the power,
Lay ye your proud and lofty looks aside.
What your inferior fears of you amiss,
That your superior threats to you again.
To greater king, each king a subject is.
Whom dawn of day hath seen in pride to reign,
Him overthrown hath seen the evening late.
70   Let none rejoice too much that good hath got;
Let none despair of best in worst estate.
For Klotho mingles all, and suffereth not
Fortune to stand, but fates about doth drive.[159]
Such friendship find with gods yet no man might
That he the morrow might be sure to live.
The god our things all tossed and turnèd quite
Rolls with a whirlwind.

THE FOURTH ACT

MESSENGER CHORUS

[MESSENGER]

What whirlwind may me headlong drive and up in air me fling,
And wrap in darkest cloud, whereby it might so heinous thing
Take from mine eyes? O wicked house that even of Pelops ought
And Tantalus abhorrèd be.[160]

---

[159] fates about doth drive] S. 'rotat omne fatum' (turns every fate [as if on a wheel]).

CHORUS

What new thing hast thou brought?

MESSENGER

What land is this?[161] Lieth Sparta here and Argos that hath bred
So wicked brethren, and the ground of Corinth lying spread
Between the seas? Or Ister else, where wont to take their flight[162]
Are people wild? Or that which wonts with snow to shine so
  bright,
Hyrcana land? Or else do here the wandering Scythians dwell?

CHORUS

10   What monstrous mischief is this place then guilty of?[163] That
  tell,
And this declare to us at large, whatever be the ill.

MESSENGER

If once my mind may stay itself, and quaking limbs, I will.
But yet of such a cruel deed before mine eyes the fear
And image walks. Ye raging storms now far from hence me bear
And to that place me drive to which now driven is the day
Thus drawn from hence.[164]

CHORUS

Our minds ye hold yet still in doubtful stay.
Tell what it is ye so abhor, the author thereof show.
I ask not who, but which of them. That quickly let us know.

---

[160] of Pelops ought / And Tantalus abhorrèd be] S. 'Pelopi [...] et Tantalo pudenda' (ought to abhorred by Pelops and Tantalus): Atreus will dare what even his wicked ancestors did not.

[161] 5–7] In S., the Chorus wonders whether this is a civilized part of the world, such as Argos, Sparta (home of the harmonious pair of semi-divine brothers Castor and Pollux), or Corinth – or, alternatively, one of the barbarous places mentioned in 7–9.

[162] wont to take their flight] In S., the idea is that the river Hister, being frozen, gives the wild Alans (a nomadic tribe whose name Heywood omits) a means of escape.

[163] guilty of] A strong rendering of S. 'conscius', which can mean simply 'witness to'.

[164] 15–16] The first explicit mention in the play of the sun's reversal in response to Atreus's crime, prefigured earlier (see n. at 'Preface', line 297).

181

MESSENGER

	In Pelops' turret high, a part there is of palace wide	
20	That toward the south erected leans, of which the utter° side	
	With equal top to mountain stands, and on the city lies,	

And people proud against their prince,[165] if once the traitors
    rise,[166]
Hath underneath his battering stroke. There shines the place in
    sight
Where wont the people to frequent, whose golden beams so
    bright
The noble spotted pillars grey of marble do support.
Within this place well known to men, where they so oft
    resort,
To many other rooms about the noble court° doth go.[167]
The privy palace underlieth in secret place alow,   [650]
With ditch full deep that doth enclose the wood of privity,°
30   And hidden parts of kingdom old, where never grew no tree
That cheerful boughs is wont to bear, with knife or loppèd be,
But tax,° and cypress, and with tree of holm° full black to see,[168]
Doth beck° and bend the wood so dark. Aloft above all these
The higher oak doth overlook surmounting all the trees.

From hence with luck the reign to take, accustomed are the
    kings,[169]
From hence in danger aid to ask, and doom in doubtful things.
To this affixèd are the gifts, the sounding trumpets bright,
The chariots broke, and spoils of sea that now Myrtoan hight;
There hang the wheels once won by craft of falser axel-tree,[170]
40   And every other conquest's note;[171] here leeful is to see[172]
The Phrygian tire° of Pelops' head, the spoil of enemies here,
And of Barbarian triumph left the painted gorgeous gear.[173]

---

[165] prince] S. 'regibus' (kings).

[166] if once the traitors rise] Heywood's addition.

[167] court] i.e. palace.

[168] 32] The yew (Lat. 'taxus'), cypress, and holm-oak are all associated with poison, mourning, and dense shade (Tarrant, p. 185).

[169] the kings] S. 'Tantalidae' (the descendants of Tantalus).

[170] 38–39] See n. at 1.Cho.18–22.

[171] every other conquest's note] A shift in sense from S. 'omne gentis facinus' (the family's every deed).

[172] here leeful is to see] Heywood's addition.

A loathsome spring stands under shade, and slothful course doth
    take,
With water black, even such as is of irksome° Stygian Lake
The ugly wave, whereby are wont to swear the gods on high.[174]
Here all the night the grisly ghosts and gods of death to cry
The fame reports;[175] with clinking chains resounds the wood
    eachwhere
The sprights cry out; and everything that dreadful is to hear
May there be seen: of ugly shapes from old sepulchres sent
A fearful flock doth wander there, and in that place frequent
Worse things than ever yet were known. Yea, all the wood full
    oft
With flame is wont to flash, and all the higher trees aloft
Without a fire do burn; and oft the wood beside all this
With triple-barking roars at once;[176] full oft the palace is
Affright with shapes, nor light of day may once the terror quell.
Eternal night doth hold the place, and darkness there of hell
In midday reigns. From hence to them that pray out of the
    ground
The certain answers given are, what time with dreadful sound
From secret place the fates be told, and dungeon roars within,
While of the god breaks out the voice.

                             Whereto when entered in
Fierce Atreus was that did with him his brother's children trail,
Decked are the altars. Who, alas, may it enough bewail?
Behind the infants' backs, anon, he knit their noble hands,[177]
And eke their heavy heads about, he bound with purple bands.
There wanted there no frankincense, nor yet the holy wine,
Nor knife to cut the sacrifice besprinked° with leavens° fine.
Kept is in all the order due, lest such a mischief great
Should not be ordered well.

CHORUS

                       Who doth his hand on sword then set?

---

[173] 42] A reference to the embroidered toga worn by the (Roman) triumphator
during celebrations of foreign conquest.
[174] 44–45] A reference to the gods' habit of swearing oaths upon the river Styx.
[175] 46–47] i.e. 'Rumour reports that here all the night...'
[176] triple-barking] Likely a reference to Cerberus.
[177] knit] i.e. 'knotted back'.

MESSENGER

70

He is himself the priest, and he himself the deadly verse
With prayer dire from fervent mouth doth sing and oft
    rehearse.[178]
And he at th'altars stands himself; he them, assigned to die,
Doth handle and in order set and to the knife apply.
He lights the fires; no rites were left of sacrifice undone.
The wood then quaked and all at once from trembling ground
    anon
The palace becked in doubt which way the peise thereof would
    fall,
And shaking as in waves it stood. From th'air and therewithal[179]
A blazing star, that foulest train drew after him, doth go.
The wines that in the fires were cast with changèd liquor° flow,   [700]
And turn to blood. And twice or thrice th'attire fell from his
    head,

80

The ivory bright in temples seemed to weep and tears to shed.

The sights amazed all other men, but steadfast yet alway
Of mind unmovèd Atreus stands and even the gods doth fray
That threaten him, and all delay forsaken by and by
To th'altars turns, and therewithal aside he looks awry.
As hungry tiger wonts that doth in Gangey° woods remain
With doubtful pace to range and roam between the bullocks
    twain,
Of either prey full covetous, and yet uncertain where
She first may bite, and roaring throat now turns the tone° to
    tear,
And then to th'other straight returns, and doubtful famine
    holds:[180]

90

So Atreus dire, between the babes doth stand and them beholds
On whom he points° to slake his ire. First slaughter where to
    make,
He doubts; or whom he should again for second offering take.

---

[178] oft rehearse] Heywood's addition, perhaps with a funeral pun ('re-hearse')
(Daalder, p. 61).
[179] From th'air and therewithal] S. 'e laevo aethere' (from the left portion of the
sky), the unlucky side in poetic depictions of augury.
[180] and doubtful famine holds] S. 'et famem dubiam tenet' (and keeps her hunger
in doubt).

Yet skills it nought,[181] but yet he doubts and such a cruelty
It him delights to order well.

CHORUS

Whom take he first to die?

MESSENGER

First place, lest in him think ye might no piety to remain,
To grandsire dedicated is: first Tantalus is slain.

CHORUS

With what a mind and countenance could the boy his death
   sustain?

MESSENGER

All careless of himself he stood, nor once he would in vain
His prayers leese. But Atreus fierce the sword in him at last
100   In deep and deadly wound doth hide to hilts, and gripping fast
His throat in hand, he thrust him through. The sword then
   drawn away
When long the body had upheld itself in doubtful stay,
Which way to fall, at length upon the uncle down it falls.
And then to th'altars cruelly, Phylisthenes he trawls,°
And on his brother throws, and straight his neck off cutteth he.
The carcass headlong falls to ground – a piteous thing to see.[182]
The mourning head with murmur yet uncertain doth complain.

CHORUS

What after double death doth he and slaughter then of twain?
Spares he the child? Or guilt on guilt again yet heapeth he?[183]

MESSENGER

110   As long-mained lion fierce amid the wood of Armenie,
The drove pursues and conquest makes of slaughter many one,
Though now defilèd be his jaws with blood, and hunger gone,

---

[181] Yet skills it nought] S. 'nec interest' (and it makes no difference).

[182] a piteous thing to see] Heywood's addition, making the Messenger a less neutral reporter of the crimes. On the Messenger's reaction to Atreus's crimes, see Pincombe, 'Tragic Inspiration', pp. 541–42.

[183] Spares he the child?] i.e. the third child, after Tantalus and Phylisthenes.

Yet slaketh not his ireful rage, with blood of bulls so great,
But slothful now, with weary tooth, the lesser calves doth threat,
None otherwise doth Atreus rage, and swells with anger
    strained,
And holding now the sword in hand with double slaughter
    stained,
Regarding not where fell his rage, with cursèd hand unmild,
He strake° it through his body quite. At bosom of the child
The blade go'th in, and at the back again out went the same.
120   He falls, and quenching with his blood the altar's sacred flame,
Of either wound at length he dieth.

CHORUS

                        O heinous hateful act.

MESSENGER

Abhor ye this? Ye hear not yet the end of all the fact:
There follows more.

CHORUS

               A fiercer thing, or worse than this to see,
Could nature bear?

MESSENGER

             Why think ye this of guilt the end to be?
It is but part.

CHORUS

           What could he more? To cruel beasts he cast
Perhaps their bodies to be torn, and kept from fires at last.

MESSENGER

Would god he had.[184] That never tomb the dead might over-hide,
Nor flames dissolve, though them for food to fowls in pastures   [750]
    wide
He had out-thrown, or them for prey to cruel beasts would fling.
130   That which the worst was wont to be were here a wishèd
    thing,[185]

---

[184] Would god he had] Heywood adds 'god'; S. 'utinam arcuisset' (would that he had kept [him way from fires]).

186

That them their father saw untombed.° But oh more cursèd
    crime
Uncredible, the which deny will men of after time.
From bosoms yet alive out drawn the trembling bowels shake,
The veins yet breathe, the fearful heart doth yet both pant and
    quake.
But he the strings° doth turn in hand, and destinies behold,
And of the guts the signs each one doth view not fully cold.[186]
When him the sacrifice had pleased, his diligence he puts
To dress his brother's banquet now, and straight asunder cuts
The bodies into quarters all, and by the stumps anon,
140   The shoulders wide, and brawns of arms, he strikes off
    everychone.
He lays abroad their naked limbs, and cuts away the bones.
The only heads he keeps,[187] and hands, to him committed once.
Some of the guts are broached,° and in the fires that burn full
    slow
They drop.[188] The boiling liquor some doth tumble to and fro
In mourning cauldron. From the flesh that overstands° aloft,
The fire doth fly and scatter out, and into chimney oft
Up heaped again, and there constrained by force to tarry yet
Unwilling burns. The liver makes great noise upon the spit,
Nor easily wot I if the flesh or flames they be that cry,
150   But cry they do. The fire like pitch, it fumeth by and by.
Nor yet the smoke itself so sad like filthy mist in sight
Ascendeth up as wont it is, nor takes his way upright.
But even the gods and house it doth with filthy fume defile.[189]

O patient Phoebus though from hence thou backward flee the
    while,
And in the midst of heaven above dost drown the broken day,
Thou flee'st too late. The father eats his children well away,

---

[185] 127–30] Heywood does not fully articulate S.'s sense: these lines are a series of wishes (that the dead should not be buried or cremated, and that they should be thrown to birds or flung to animals) – normally punishments, but in the present circumstances a 'wished thing'.

[186] 135–36] An allusion to extispicy, inspecting entrails to divine the future.

[187] The only heads] i.e. 'only the heads' (S. 'ora', faces).

[188] drop] S. 'stillant' (drip).

[189] the gods and house] The phrase divides the Lat. term 'penates' (household gods).

And limbs to which he once gave life with cursèd jaw doth
   tear.[190]
He shines with ointment shed full sweet all round about his hair,
Replete with wine; and often times so cursèd kind of food

160   His mouth hath held that would not down, but yet this one thing
   good
In all thy ills, Thyestes, is that them thou dost not know.
And yet shall that not long endure, though Titan backward go
And chariots turn against himself to meet the ways he went,
And heavy night so heinous deed to keep from sight be sent,
And out of time from east arise so foul a fact to hide,[191]
Yet shall the whole at length be seen: thy ills shall all be spied.

CHORUS

Which way, O prince of lands and gods on high,
At whose uprise eftsoons of shadowed night
All beauty flee'th – which way turn'st thou awry?[192]
And draw'st the day in midst of heaven to flight?
Why dost thou, Phoebus, hide from us thy sight?
Not yet the watch that later hour brings in[193]
Doth Vesper warn the stars to kindle light.
Not yet doth turn of Hesper's wheel begin
To loose thy chare° his well-deservèd way.[194]

10   The trumpet third not yet hath blown his blast[195]
While toward the night begins to yield the day.
Great wonder hath of sudden supper's haste   [800]
The plowman yet whose oxen are untired.
From wonted course of heaven what draws thee back?

---

[190] limbs to which he once gave life] In S., a simpler, more menacing phrase: 'artus [...] suos' (his own limbs).

[191] out of time] S. 'tempore alieno' (at a time not its own), since night arrives during the day.

[192] 1–3] The Chorus is unaware of why the sun is reversing its course, suggesting that it is a different group from the Chorus who spoke with the Messenger in Act 4.

[193] the watch] S. 'nuntius' (the messenger): Vesper signals the evening.

[194] 8–9] i.e. the sun has not yet reached the western (Hesperian) turning point of its course, where its chariot can be unharnessed.

[195] the trumpet third] A signal at the end of the ninth daylight hour, ushering in dinner time and the last quarter of the day; a Roman custom.

What causes have from certain race conspired
To turn thy horse?[196]

          Do yet from dungeon black[197]
Of hollow hell the conquered giants prove
A fresh assault? Doth Tityus yet assay
With trenchèd heart and wounded womb to move
20   The former ires? Or from the hill away
Hath now Typhoeus wound his side by might?[198]
Is up to heaven the way erected high
Of Phlegrey foes by mountains set upright?
And now doth Ossa Pelion overlie?

The wonted turns are gone of day and night.
The rise of sun, nor fall shall be no more.
Aurora, dewish mother of the light,
That wonts to send the horses out before,
Doth wonder much again returned to see
30   Her dawning light.[199] She wots not how to ease
The weary wheels, nor manes that smoking be
Of horse with sweat to bathe amid the seas.[200]
Himself unwonted there to lodge likewise
Doth setting sun again the morning see,
And now commands the darkness up to rise,
Before the night to come preparèd be.
About the pole yet glow'th no fire in sight,
Nor light of moon the shades doth comfort yet.

Whatso it be, god grant it be the night.
40   Our hearts do quake with fear oppressèd great,
And dreadful are lest heaven and earth and all[201]
With fatal ruin shaken shall decay;

---

[196] horse] Probably plural (cf. S. 'equos', horses).

[197] 16–24] An allusion to the Gigantomachy, the attack by the Giants on the gods on Mt Olympus by piling up Mts Pelion and Ossa (24). This event was often conflated, as by S., with the Titanomachy, the battle between the Titans and the Olympian gods on the Phlegraean fields (hence 'Phlegrey foes' at 23). The Giants were punished by imprisonment in the underworld.

[198] 20–21] i.e. 'has Typhoeus shaken off the mountain under which he was buried as a punishment?'.

[199] 27–30] i.e. Dawn is surprised to see the sun's chariot return to the east.

[200] 30–32] Normal tasks of Tethys, the sea-goddess, when the sun sets into the sea.

[201] heaven and earth] Heywood's addition.

And lest on gods again, and men, shall fall
Disfigured Chaos;[202] and the land away,
The seas, and fires, and of the glorious skies
The wandering lamps, lest nature yet shall hide.

Now shall no more with blaze of his uprise
The lord of stars that leads the world so wide[203]
Of summer both and winter give the marks.
50   Nor yet the moon with Phoebus' flames that burns,[204]
Shall take from us by night the dreadful carks,°
With swifter course o'erpass her brother's turns,
While compassless° she fets° in crooked race.[205]
The gods on heaps shall out of order fall
And each with other mingled be in place.

The wrièd° way of holy planets all,
With path aslope that doth divide the zones,
That bears the signs and years in course doth bring,
Shall see the stars with him fall down at once.[206]
60   And he that first not yet with gentle spring
The temperate gale doth give to sails, the Ram,
Shall headlong fall adown to seas again,   [850]
Through which he once with fearful Hellen swam.[207]
Next him the Bull that doth with horn sustain
The Sisters Seven, with him shall overturn
The Twins, and arms of crooked Cancer all.[208]

---

[202] Disfigured] S. 'deforme' (formless), a standard characterization of Chaos.

[203] The lord of stars] i.e. the sun.

[204] that burns] In S., the moon only faces the sun (obvia) and reflects it.

[205] 52–53] Heywood's translation (esp. 'in crooked race') is imprecise. In S., in the newly disordered universe the moon will no longer 'run a shorter course in curving orbit' (curvo brevius limite currens). In ancient thought, the sun and moon both orbit the earth, but the moon is closer to earth and moves more quickly.

[206] 56–59] i.e. the zodiac, which cuts across the zones of the heavens; these wrap around the earth parallel to the equator at an oblique angle ('obliquo tramite', here 'with path aslope'). At 60, the Chorus begins to describe the ruin of the zodiac's twelve constellations.

[207] 60–63] A reference to Helle's escape from danger on the back of the Ram with the Golden Fleece, before she fell into the sea from the back of the Ram, which then became the constellation Aries.

[208] 64–66] Taurus (the Bull) contains the cluster of stars known as the Hyades (S.'s term, translated by Heywood as 'the Sisters Seven', though there were usually only five). When Taurus falls, he will bring down Gemini (the Twins) and Cancer (the Crab).

190

The Lion hot that wonts the soil to burn
Of Hercules again from heaven shall fall.[209]
To lands once left the Virgin shall be thrown,
70   And levelled peise of Balance sway alow,
And draw with them the stinging Scorpion down.[210]
So likewise he that holds in Thessale bows
His swift well-feathered arrows, Chiron old
Shall break the same and eke shall leese his shot.[211]
And Capricorn that brings the winter cold
Shall overturn and break thy Water Pot,
Whoso thou be, and down with thee to ground
The last of all the signs shall Pisces fall,[212]
And monsters eke in seas yet never drowned,[213]
80   The water gulf shall overwhelm them all.
And he which doth between each Ursa glide,
Like crooked flood, the slipper Serpent twined;
And Lesser Bear by greater Dragon's side,
Full cold with frost congealèd hard by kind,
And carter dull that slowly guides his Wain,°
Unstable shall Boötes fall from high.[214]

We are thought meet of all men whom again
Should hugie heap of Chaos overlie,
And world oppress with overturnèd mass.

---

[209] 67–68] Leo (the Lion), associated with the Nemean Lion slain by Hercules, is in some legends said to have fallen from the moon.

[210] 69–71] Virgo (the Virgin), associated with Astraea (Roman goddess of justice), who lived on earth during the golden age, but left because of the impieties of humankind. She will 'be thrown' back to earth, drawing down with her Libra (the Balance, i.e. set of scales) and Scorpio (the Scorpion).

[211] 73–74] Chiron, a Centaur (half-man, half-horse) from Thessaly, associated with Sagittarius (the Archer), will lose his arrows when he also falls.

[212] 75–78] Capricorn, associated with the onset of winter (since the sun enters Capricorn on the winter solstice), will bring down Aquarius (the Water-Bearer or 'Water Pot') and Pisces (the Fish). 'Whoso thou be' alludes to an ancient difference of opinion regarding the identity of the Water-Bearer.

[213] and monsters eke] A reference to the fixed stars that never set below the horizon, with 'monsters' (Lat. monstra) referring to the Bear and the Serpent/Dragon in the following lines.

[214] 81–86] The constellation Draco (i.e. the 'Serpent' and 'Dragon') lies between Ursa Major (the greater bear or Big Dipper) and Ursa Minor (the 'Lesser Bear' or Little Dipper). Ursa Minor will fall with Draco, and the constellation Boötes (the Wagoner) will pull down his wagon ('Wain'), which is Ursa Major.

90   The latest° age now falleth us upon.[215]
With evil hap we are begot alas,
If, wretches, we have lost the sight of sun,
Or him by fault enforcèd have to fly.[216]
Let our complaints yet go, and fear be passed.
He greedy is of life that will not die[217]
When all the world shall end with him at last.

THE FIFTH ACT

ATREUS ALONE[218]

Now equal with the stars I go, beyond each other wight,
With haughty head the heavens above and highest pole I smite.°
The kingdom now and seat I hold where once my father reigned.
I now let go the gods, for all my will I have obtained.
Enough and well, yea even enough for me I am acquit.°
But why enough? I will proceed and fill the father yet
With blood of his. Lest any shame should me restrain at all,
The day is gone. Go to, therefore, while thee the heaven doth call.
Would god[219] I could against their wills yet hold the gods that flee,
10   And of revenging dish constrain them witnesses to be.

But yet (which well enough is wrought), let it the father see.
In spite of all the drownèd day, I will remove from thee
The darkness all, in shade whereof do lurk thy miseries.
And guest at such a banquet now too long he careless lies
With merry face. Now eat and drunk enough he hath. At last   [900]
'Tis best himself should know his ills. Ye servants all, in haste,
Undo the temple doors, and let the house be open all.
Fain would I see, when look upon his children's heads he shall,
What countenance he then would make, or in what words break out
20   Would first his grief, or how would quake his body round about
With sprite amazèd sore. Of all my work the fruit were this.
I would him not a miser see, but while so made he is.[220]

---

[215] 87–90] These lines are usually understood as questions. Line 89 is Heywood's addition, and the other lines are translated imprecisely.

[216] by fault] Heywood's addition, perhaps building on Ascensius's comment 'per culpam nostram' (by our fault) (cf. O'Keefe, 'Analysis', p. 171).

[217] will not] S. 'non vult' (is unwilling to).

[218] Alone] Heywood translates a rare stage direction in his source, 'Atreus solus'.

[219] god] Heywood's addition.

Behold the temple opened now doth shine with many a light.
In glittering gold and purple seat he sits himself upright,[221]
And, staying up his heavy head with wine upon his hand,[222]
He belcheth out. Now chief of gods in highest place I stand,
And king of kings. I have my wish and more than I could think.
He fillèd is; he now the wine in silver bowl doth drink.
And spare it not, there yet remains a worser draught for thee
30   That sprung out of the bodies late of sacrifices three,
Which wine shall hide. Let therewithal the boards be taken up.[223]
The father, mingled with the wine his children's blood, shall sup
That would have drunk of mine. Behold, he now begins to strain
His voice and sings, nor yet for joy his mind he may refrain.

The Second Scene

THYESTES ALONE[224]

O beaten bosoms dulled so long with woe,[225]
Lay down your cares, at length your griefs relent.
Let sorrow pass, and all your dread let go,
And fellow eke of fearful banishment,
Sad poverty and ill in misery,
The shame of cares. More whence thy fall thou hast,
Than whither, skills.° Great hap to him from high
That falls it is in surety to be placed
Beneath.[226] And great it is to him again
10   That pressed with storm of evils feels the smart,
Of kingdom lost the peises to sustain

---

[220] 22] S. 'miserum videre nolo, sed dum fit miser' (I do not want to see him a wretch, but rather [I want to see him] as he becomes a wretch).

[221] he sits himself upright] S. 'resupinus [...] incubat' (reclines on his back), a traditional dining posture.

[222] heavy head] i.e. 'head heavy'.

[223] Let therewithal the boards be taken up] S. 'hoc, hoc mensa cludatur scypho' (let this be the goblet that concludes the table [i.e. meal]).

[224] Alone] Heywood's addition on analogy with the previous scene. The previous scene, however, invites us to imagine Atreus eavesdropping now.

[225] Heywood's shift from fourteeners to iambic pentametre mirrors S.'s shift to lyric metre, unusual in a character speech but expressive of Thyestes' festivity and his singing (described at 5.1.33–34). Compare the speech of Andromache at *Troas* 3.2.

[226] 7–9 Great hap to him [...] be placed / Beneath] i.e. 'It is a great thing for someone who falls from on high to be placed in security beneath'.

With neck unbowed; nor yet deject of heart,
Nor overcome, his heavy haps always
To bear upright. But now of careful carks
Shake off the showers, and of thy wretched days
Away with all the miserable marks.
To joyful state return thy cheerful face.
Put fro thy mind the old Thyestes hence.

It is the wont of wight in woeful case,
20   In state of joy to have no confidence.
Though better haps to them returnèd be,
Th'afflicted yet to joy it irketh sore.
Why call'st thou me aback, and hinderest me
This happy day to celebrate? Wherefore
Bid'st thou me, Sorrow, weep without a cause?
Who doth me let° with flowers so fresh and gay
To deck my hairs? It lets, and me withdraws.
Down from my head the roses fall way;
My moistèd hair with ointment overall,
30   With sudden maze° stands up in wondrous wise;
From face that would not weep, the streams do fall,   [950]
And howling cries amid my words arise;
My sorrow yet th'accustomed tears doth love,
And wretches still delight to weep and cry;
Unpleasant plaints it pleaseth them to move,
And flourished fair it likes with Tyrian dye
Their robes to rent:[227] to wail it likes them still.[228]
For sorrow sends (in sign that woes draw nigh)
The mind that wots before of after ill.[229]
40   The sturdy storms the shipmen overlie,
When void of wind th'assuagèd seas do rest.[230]

What tumult yet or countenance to see
Mak'st thou, mad man?[231] At length a trustful breast

---

[227] 36–37 And flourished fair [...] robes to rent] i.e. 'and they like to tear their robes, which are beautified with purple Tyrian dye'.
[228] 35–37] Thyestes generalizes about wretches ('them'). In S. the repeated phrase 'libet' probably describes Thyestes' own feelings (i.e. 'it pleases me', 'I like to').
[229] 38–39] i.e. the mind, which knows in advance of suffering to come ('after ill'), sends sorrow as an indication of impending trouble.
[230] 40–41] An imprecise rendering of S.: sailors can tell from the billowing of the water that a storm is coming, even though the sea is still calm.

To brother give, whatever now it be,
Causeless or else too late thou art adread.
I, wretch, would not so fear, but yet me draws[232]
A trembling terror. Down mine eyes do shed
Their sudden tears, and yet I know no cause.
Is it a grief or fear? Or else hath tears
50   Great joy itself?

The Third Scene

ATREUS   THYESTES

[ATREUS]

> Let us this day with one consent, O Brother, celebrate.
> This day my sceptres may confirm and 'stablish my estate,
> And faithful bond of peace and love between us ratify.[233]

THYESTES

> Enough with meat and eke with wine, now satisfied am I.
> But yet of all my joys it were a great increase to me,
> If now about my side I might my little children see.

ATREUS

> Believe that here, even in thine arms, thy children present be.
> For here they are, and shall be here, no part of them fro thee
> Shall be withheld. Their lovèd looks, now give to thee I will,
10   And with the heap of all his babes, the father fully fill.
> Thou shalt be glutted, fear thou not; they with my boys as yet
> The joyful sacrifices make at board where children sit.
> They shall be called. The friendly cup now take of courtesy[234]
> With wine upfilled.

THYESTES

> Of brother's feast, I take full willingly
> The final gift. Shed some to gods of this our father's land,[235]

---

[231] 42–43] i.e. 'what [...] do you imagine (S. fingis) you see?'
[232] 46–50] On the translation style of these lines, see Introduction, p. 43.
[233] and love] Heywood's addition.
[234] friendly] In S., 'gentile' (belonging to the family) is more perverse: the cup contains the blood of kin.
[235] Shed some to gods] i.e. 'let a libation be made' (S. libentur).

Then let the rest be drunk. What's this? In no wise will my hand
Obey. The peise increaseth sore, and down mine arm doth sway,
And from my lips the wafting° wine itself doth fly away,
And in deceivèd mouth about my jaws it runneth round.
20   The table too itself doth shake and leap from trembling ground.
Scant burns the fire. The air itself, with heavy cheer to sight,
Forsook of sun amazèd is between the day and night.
What meaneth this? Yet more and more of backward beaten sky
The compass° falls, and thicker mist the world doth overlie
Than blackest darkness, and the night in night itself doth hide.
All stars be fled. Whatso it be, my brother god provide
And sons to spare. The gods so grant that all this tempest fall
On this vile head. But now restore to me my children all.

ATREUS

I will, and never day again shall them from thee withdraw.

THYESTES

30   What tumult tumbleth so my guts, and doth my bowels gnaw?
What quakes within? With heavy peise I feel myself oppressed,   [1000]
And with another voice than mine bewails my doleful breast.
Come near, my sons, for you now doth th'unhappy father call;
Come near, for you once seen this grief would soon assuage and
    fall.[236]
Whence murmur they?

ATREUS

                With father's arms embrace them quickly now.

[Atreus displays the heads]

For here they are, lo come to thee. Dost thou thy children know?

THYESTES

I know my brother. Such a guilt yet can'st thou suffer well,
O earth, to bear? Nor yet from hence to Stygian Lake of hell
Dost thou both drown thyself and us? Nor yet with broken
    ground
40   Dost thou these kingdoms and their king with Chaos rude
    confound?°

---

[236] you once seen] S. 'visis [...] vobis' (once I see you).

Nor yet uprenting° from the soil the bowers of wicked land
Dost thou Mycenas overturn? With Tantalus to stand,
And ancestors of ours, if there in hell be any one,
Now ought we both. Now from the frames on either side anon
Of ground, all here and there rent up, out of thy bosom deep,
Thy dens and dungeons set abroad, and us enclosèd keep
In bottom low of Acheront. Above our heads aloft
Let wander all the guilty ghosts; with burning fret° full oft,[237]
Let fiery Phlegethon, that drives his sands both to and fro,
50   To our confusion overrun and violently flow.
O slothful soil, unshaken peise, unmovèd yet art thou?
The gods are fled.

ATREUS

                    But take to thee with joy thy children now,
And rather them embrace. At length, thy children all, of thee
So long wished for (for no delay there standeth now in me),
Enjoy and kiss; embracing arms divide thou unto three.

THYESTES

Is this thy league?[238] May this thy love and faith of brother be?
And dost thou so repose thy hate? The father doth not crave
His sons alive (which might have been without the guilt) to have,
And eke without thy hate; but this doth brother brother pray:
60   That them he may entomb, restore, whom see thou shalt
            straightway
Be burnt. The father nought requires of thee that have he shall,
But soon forgo.

ATREUS

                    Whatever part yet of thy children all
Remains, here shalt thou have; and what remaineth not, thou
            hast.

THYESTES

Lie they in fields, a food out flung for fleeing fowls to waste?
Or are they kept a prey for wild and brutish beasts to eat?

---

[237] fret] S. 'freto' (waters).
[238] Is this thy league?] S. 'hoc foedus?' (Is this [what you call] a truce?).

ATREUS

> Thou hast devoured thy sons, and filled thyself with wicked
> meat.

THYESTES

> Oh this is it that shamed the gods, and day from hence did drive
> Turned back to east? Alas, I wretch, what wailings may I give?
> Or what complaints? What woeful words may be enough for me?
> 70 Their heads cut off, and hands off torn, I from their bodies see,
> And wrenchèd feet from broken thighs, I here behold again.
> 'Tis this that greedy father could not suffer to sustain.
> In belly roll my bowels round, and closèd crime so great
> Without a passage strives within, and seeks a way to get.
> Thy sword, O brother, lend to me. Much of my blood, alas,
> It hath. Let us therewith make way for all my sons to pass.
> Is yet the sword fro me withheld? Thyself thy bosoms tear.
> And let thy breasts resound with strokes.²³⁹ Yet, wretch, thy
> hand forbear,
> And spare the dead. Whoever saw such mischief put in proof?
> 80 What rude Heniochus that dwells by ragged coast aloof
> Of Caucasus unapt° for men? Or, fear to Athens, who
> Procrustes wild? The father I oppress my children do,   [1050]
> And am oppressed.²⁴⁰ Is any mean of guilt or mischief yet?²⁴¹

ATREUS

> A mean in mischief ought to be when guilt thou dost commit,
> Not when thou quit'st.²⁴² For yet even this too little seems to
> me.
> The blood yet warm even from the wound, I should in sight of
> thee

---

²³⁹ 77–78 bosoms [...] breasts] Heywood follows S.'s poetic plural 'pectora'.

²⁴⁰ 82–83 The father I oppress [...] am oppressed] Heywood conveys the physical pressure and mental vexation implied by S. 'premo premorque' (I press upon and am pressed by).

²⁴¹ Is any mean of guilt or mischief yet?] Different from the standard interpretation of S. 'sceleris est aliquis modus': 'There is (after all) a measure (balance) of crime!'

²⁴² 84–85 when guilt thou dost commit, / Not when thou quit'st] i.e. 'when committing a crime to begin with (as Thyestes did to him), not when one is requiting a prior crime (as Atreus is justifiably doing now)'. For Atreus, revenge should exceed the original crime.

Even in thy jaws have shed, that thou the blood of them might'st
    drink
That livèd yet. But while too much to haste my hate I think,
My wrath beguilèd is. Myself with sword the wounds them gave;
90   I strake them down.[243] The sacred fires with slaughter vowed I
    have
Well pleased; the carcass cutting then and liveless limbs on
    ground
I have in little parcels chopped, and some of them I drowned
In boiling cauldrons; some to fires that burnt full slow I put,
And made to drop. Their sinews all and limbs atwo I cut
Even yet alive, and on the spit that thrust was through the same,
I heard the liver wail and cry, and with my hand the flame
I oft kept in. But every whit the father might of this
Have better done. But now my wrath too lightly ended is.
He rent his sons with wicked gum, himself yet woting nought,
100   Nor they thereof.

THYESTES

               O ye enclosed with bending banks about,
All seas me hear, and to this guilt ye gods now hearken well,
Whatever place ye fled are to. Hear all ye sprights of hell,
And hear ye lands, and night so dark, that them dost overlie
With cloud so black, to my complaints do thou thyself apply.
To thee now left I am, thou dost alone me miser see,
And thou art left without thy stars. I will not make for me
Petitions yet, nor aught for me require; may aught yet be
That me should vail?° For you shall all my wishes now
    foresee.[244]
Thou guider great of skies above, and prince of highest might
110   Of heavenly place, now all with clouds full horrible to sight
Enwrap the world, and let the winds on every side break out,
And send the dreadful thunderclap through all the world about.
Not with what hand thou guiltless house and undeservèd wall
With lesser bolt art wont to beat, but with the which did fall

---

[243] I strake them down] Heywood omits S. 'ad aras' (at the altars).

[244] For you shall all my wishes now foresee] S. 'vobis vota prospicient mea' (all my prayers will look out for your interests), addressing sea, gods, etc., listed in 100–03.

The thrice upheapèd mountains once, and which to hills in
    height
Stood equal up the Giants huge.[245] Throw out such weapons
    straight,
And fling thy fires, and therewithal revenge the drownèd day.
Let flee thy flames, the light thus lost and hid from heaven away,
With flashes fill; the cause (lest long thou should'st doubt whom
    to hit)
120   Of each of us is ill. If not, at least let mine be it,[246]
Me strike. With triple-edgèd tool,[247] thy brand of flaming fire,
Beat through this breast. If father I my children do desire
To lay in tomb, or corpses cast to fire as doth behove,
I must be burnt. If nothing now the gods to wrath may move,
Nor power from skies with thunderbolt none strikes the wicked
    men,
Let yet eternal night remain, and hide with darkness then
The world about. I, Titan, nought complain, as now it stands,
If still thou hide thee thus away.

ATREUS

                      Now praise I well my hands.
Now got I have the palm;[248] I had been overcome of thee,
130   Except thou sorrowed'st so.[249] But now even children born to
    me
I count, and now of bride-bed chaste the faith I do repair.[250]

THYESTES

In what offended have my sons?   [1100]

---

[245] 109–16] Thyestes asks Jove ('guider of great skies above', 109) to strike with the same thunderbolt with which he overthrew the Giants. (See n. at 4.Cho.16–24.)

[246] let mine be it] S. 'mala sit mea' (let my cause [i.e. my part in the crime] be [considered] ill).

[247] tool] S. 'telo' (weapon); Heywood echoes the sound (Daalder, p. 78).

[248] the palm] i.e. victory.

[249] 129–30 I had been overcome [...] thou sorrowed'st so] S. 'perdideram scelus, nisi sic doleres' (I would have squandered my crime, if you were not grieving thus).

[250] 130–31 But now even children [...] I do repair] Atreus returns to the idea that his plot will assure him of the legitimacy of his own children (see 2.1.154–57), now expressing confidence that they are his and irrationally implying that he has undone Thyestes' earlier adultery (Tarrant, p. 241).

ATREUS

In that, that thine they were.

THYESTES

Set'st thou the sons for father's food?

ATREUS

I do, and, which is best,
The certain sons.[251]

THYESTES

The gods that guide all infants,[252] I protest.

ATREUS

What, wedlock gods?[253]

THYESTES

Who would the guilt with guilt so quit again?

ATREUS

I know thy grief; prevented now with wrong, thou dost
   complain.
Nor this thee irks, that fed thou art with food of cursèd kind,
But that thou had'st not it prepared. For so it was thy mind,
Such meats as these to set before thy brother woting nought,
140   And by the mother's help to have likewise my children caught,
And them with such like death to slay. This one thing letted°
   thee:
Thou thought'st them thine.

THYESTES

The gods shall all of this revengers be,
And unto them for vengeance due, my vows thee render shall.

---

[251] The certain sons] Atreus expresses confidence that Thyestes' sons are really Thyestes'.
[252] infants] S. 'piorum' (dutiful persons). Heywood builds on a gloss in Ascensius 'natorum innocentium' (innocent children) (Daalder, p. 79).
[253] What, wedlock gods] S. 'coniugales' ([gods] of marriage) – a dig at Thyestes' adultery.

ATREUS

But vexed to be I thee the while give to thy children all.

The Fourth Scene

Added to the tragedy by the translator[254]

THYESTES ALONE

O King of Ditis' dungeon dark, and grisly ghosts of hell,[255]
That in the deep and dreadful dens of blackest Tartar dwell,
Where lean and pale diseases lie, where fear and famine are,
Where discord stands with bleeding brows, where every kind of
    care,
Where furies fight in beds of steel, and heres° of crawling snakes,
Where Gorgon grim, where Harpies are, and loathsome Limbo
    lakes,
Where most prodigious ugly things, the hollow hell doth hide,
If yet a monster more misshaped than all that there do bide,
That makes his brood his cursèd food, ye all abhor to see,
10   Nor yet the deep Avern itself may bide to cover me,
Nor grisly gates of Pluto's place yet dare themselves to spread,
Nor gaping ground to swallow him, whom gods and day have fled,
Yet break ye out from cursèd seats, and here remain with me:
Ye need not now to be afraid, the air and heaven to see.
Nor triple-headed Cerberus, thou need'st not be affright,
The day unknown to thee to see or else the loathsome light.
They both be fled, and now doth dwell none other countenance
    here,
Than doth beneath the foulest face of hateful hell appear.
Come see a meetest match for thee, a more than monstrous womb,
20   That is of his unhappy brood become a cursèd tomb.

---

[254] In this added speech, Thyestes does not entertain revenge against Atreus until lines 53–62 (see next n.), or foreshadow the specific vengeance of Aegisthus against Agamemnon: instead, he emphasises the horror of what he has done, and summons appropriate witnesses.

[255] 1–17] Thyestes' summoning of the underworld partly develops his wish at 5.3.42–52. The lines also build on earlier themes, specifically the darkening of the sky (see n. at 'Preface', line 297), adduced as a reason for the underworld forces to be less afraid to ascend (14).

Flock here ye foulest fiends of hell, and thou, O grandsire great,
Come see the glutted guts of mine, with such a kind of meat,
As thou did'st once for gods prepare.[256] Let torments all of hell
Now fall upon this hateful head, that hath deserved them well.
Ye all be plaguèd wrongfully; your guilts be small in sight
Of mine, and meet it were your pangs on me alone should light.
Now thou, O grandsire, guiltless art, and meeter were for me,
With fleeing flood to be beguiled, and fruit of fickle tree.
Thou slew'st thy son, but I my sons, alas, have made my meat.
30   I could thy famine better bear; my paunch is now replete
With food, and with my children three my belly is extent.
O filthy fowls and gnawing gripes that Tityus' bosom rent,

Behold a fitter prey for you to fill yourselves upon,
Than are the growing guts of him: four wombs enwrapped in one.
This paunch at once shall fill you all; if ye abhor the food,
Nor may yourselves abide to bathe in such accursèd blood,
Yet lend to me your clinching claws, your prey awhile forbear,
And with your talons suffer me, this monstrous maw° to tear.
Or whirling wheels, with swinge of which, Ixion still is rolled,
40   Your hooks upon this glutted gorge would catch a surer hold.
Thou filthy flood of Limbo lake, and Stygian pool so dire,
From chokèd channel belch abroad. Thou fearful fret of fire,
Spew out thy flames, O Phlegethon, and overshed the ground;
With vomit of thy fiery stream let me and earth be drowned.
Break up thou soil from bottom deep, and give thou room to hell,
That night where day, that ghosts where gods were wont to reign
    may dwell.
Why gap'st thou not? Why do you not, O gates of hell, unfold?[257]
Why do ye thus th'infernal fiends so long from hence withhold?
Are you likewise afraid to see and know so wretchèd wight,
50   From whom the gods have wried their looks, and turnèd are to
    flight?
O hateful head, whom heaven and hell have shunned and left alone,
The sun, the stars, the light, the day, the gods, the ghosts be gone.

---

[256] 21–23 O grandsire great [...] for gods prepare] Thyestes invokes Tantalus as a witness, alluding to earlier comparisons with Tantalus's cannibalistic crime (e.g. 1.1.62–63).

[257] 47] Thyestes' frustration is typical of S.'s characters who invoke punishment against themselves, but complain that it is too slow in coming (compare the words of Hippolytus at *Phaedra* 671–86).

Yet turn again ye skies awhile, ere quite ye go fro me.
Take vengeance first on him whose fault enforceth you to flee.[258]
If needs ye must your flight prepare, and may no longer bide,
But roll ye must with you forthwith the gods and sun aside,
Yet slowly flee, that I, at length, may you yet overtake,
While wandering ways I after you and speedy journey make.
By seas, by lands, by woods, by rocks, in dark I wander shall;
60 And on your wrath for right reward to due deserts will call.
Ye scape not fro me so ye gods; still after you I go,
And vengeance ask on wicked wight your thunderbolt to throw.

FINIS

---

[258] 53–62] The target of revenge seems deliberately double: Thyestes is primarily concerned with punishing himself (cf. Daalder, p. 82), but 'him whose fault enforceth you to flee' (53) and 'wicked wight' (62) suggest Atreus.

JOHN STUDLEY
AGAMEMNON (1566)

In Agamemnona Senecae
Thomae Newcei[1]

Non secus ac rostro crudelis vultur obunco
Caucasei rodit iecur immortale Promethei,
Invida mens stolidi, vitio contorta perenni,
Derogat assidue famam nomenque merentis.
Cum legis hanc igitur, si quicquam versio ridet,
Non quid verba velint, sed quid res ipsa, videto.
Sanguine spumantes pateras cum mente revolvit,
Saevit in Atridem mens impia saevit adultri.
Et Deus Atream, patris de crimine, prolem
10   Perdit; et iniustae tollunt Agamemnona parcae.
Debuit exemplum quosvis terrere superbos;
Et, cuivis, opus hoc iuvenis laudare molestum.
Sed si turba ruant in quaevis aequora praeceps,
Flumine poenarum iusto Deus obruet illos.

[(Verses) of Thomas Nuce
on the Agamemnon of Seneca

Just as the cruel vulture with its curving beak
gnaws the undying liver of Prometheus on the Caucasus,
(so) the envious mind of the fool, twisted into perennial vice,
continually maligns the name and reputation of one deserving.
If, then, this translation appeals at all when you read it,
see not what the words, but what the thing itself, intends.
When the adulterer considers in his mind the sacrificial dishes
    foaming with blood,
his wicked mind rages against the son of Atreus.[2]
And God destroys Atreus' progeny on account of the father's crime
10   and unjust fates elevate Agamemnon.[3]

---

[1] Thomas Nuce (c.1545–1617) translated *Octavia* (pub. 1566?). For this and the other prefatory poem in Latin below, we add our own translations in brackets. Nuce's Latin poem is in dactylic hexametres.

[2] 7–8] Strange wording, and the printed Latin may contain an error. But the sense is clear: the adulterer Aegisthus is motivated for revenge against Agamemnon by the memory of the cannibalistic feast served to his father Thyestes by Agamemnon's father Atreus.

The example ought to terrify any men of excessive pride;
and it is troubling for anyone to praise this young man's work.[4]
But if the crowd should rush headlong into open waters, no matter
    which,
God will obliterate them in a righteous torrent of punishments.]

Upon the Same, To the Same,
the Verses of the Same

Sith° friends to friends do friendly grant in friendly cases much,
And I perceivèd that his cause and his request was such,[5]
How that to painful° laboured stuff my mind I would annex,°
And do but as his watchèd° work, which he doth here contex,°
Deserves; when as the poet's crabbèd° style I weighed aright,[6]
And saw how well and saw how apt and featly° he did write,[7]
How hidden stories° oft he shows to make his poet plain[8]
(So as in double office he might seem for to remain),
As sometime barely to expound,° to comment sometime eke,°[9]
10   So that to understand this book, ye need no farther seek;
This well-deservèd work of his, when as I weighèd well,
And partly knew his filèd° frame,° as other men can tell,[10]
And wholly knew his springing youth and years for age yet green,
So that dame Nature's grave array on face was scarcely seen;[11]
I could not choose, but when I saw his labour to be sore,°
And eke his weary° web° than this for to deserve much more;

---

[3] 9–10] i.e. God's justice punishes the crimes of Atreus, correcting the aberration seen in Agamemnon's temporary success.

[4] young man's work] Probably referring to Studley's translation as well as to Aegisthus' deed. For emphasis on Studley's youth in the later prefaces, see e.g. 'Upon the Same', 14–15.

[5] his] i.e. Studley's.

[6] crabbèd] Heywood also notes the difficulty of translating S. (See *Troas*, 'Preface to the Readers', lines 21–27).

[7] he did write] i.e. 'Studley did translate'.

[8] hidden stories [...] he shows] i.e. 'he illuminates obscure allusions'.

[9] to expound, to comment] On the explicative aspect of Studley's translation, see Introduction, pp. 51 and 55–56.

[10] partly knew his filèd frame] i.e. 'already knew some of his verse'.

[11] 13–14] One of several direct references to Studley's youth in the prefatory poems.

Forthwith at his request, both to refresh his watching° eyes
And praisèd pains to others' praise this little work devise,[12]
Lest haply he should meet with such as would scarce speak the best,
20   Nor half that it deserves, but unto nipping° words be pressed;
And though I know this painful wight° cannot his carpers° want,
Which oftentimes discourage men and make such studies scant;
Yet be not thou dismayed, go on and bolden° well thyself:
The worthiest wight that ever wrote did never want his elf.°[13]

Such emules,° and such friendly freaks, if 'e' thou take away,
Plain mules they be that mump° and mow,° and nothing else can
      say;
Who if in rancours poisoned sink, they lurk and wallow still,[14]
Nor yet with cankered venom bolne° do leave their waspish will,
But slothful sluggards still upbraid that painful heads devise,[15]
30   And with their triple-forkèd tongues annoy this enterprise,
Discourage him from other work and further fruits of wit,
And other toward° pains disgrace, if they such poison spit.
Take heed: if tongues far worse do bite than double-edgèd sword,
If biting tongues be stinging ills, why maugre° then thy beard,[16]
Thou can'st not shun° Jove's ruddy wrath that such deservers have,
Which willingly, though woefully, themselves they do it crave,
In whom it is, if that they will, much better to deserve,
And cease their witless appetite for any more to serve.

This woeful work that Senec here depaints° before thy face,
40   The bloody ire of mighty Jove propounds in ruthful° case
To such as by their devilish deeds and hearts with rancour mixed
Already be, although they live, in snakish dungeon fixed.[17]

---

[12] 17–18 both to refresh [...] little work devise] i.e. 'to allow Studley to sleep and to celebrate his commendable labours to others'.

[13] worthiest wight that ever wrote] i.e. Homer, who never lacked someone to spite him, specifically the critic Zoilus, whose name appears below in 'Idem in Zoilum' (at 11) and in the 'Preface' to *Thyestes* (at 66).

[14] 27] i.e. 'if they (the 'carpers' of 21) do fall into a pit of poison, they only wallow there', and do not try to get out.

[15] that] i.e. 'that which'.

[16] why maugre then thy beard] i.e. 'why in spite of your best effort'

[17] 39–42] Nuce links the play with punishments that Studley's detractors will receive, since S. shows what Jove does to those who commit devilish deeds. Lines 41–42 are a 'Calvinist explanation for [the carpers'] angry envy': 'Their "rancour" is both symptom and cause of their predestined damnation' (See Pincombe, '*Agamemnon*', 'Notes on Preliminary Materials', entry 2).

The crumpled brows of lofty lord in cloudy throne that sits,[18]
His sore displeasèd mind portend to evil usèd wits,[19]
Who in his foaming wrath can turn the world's well-settled seat,
And make an indigested thing and mingle-mangle° great.
Beware, therefore, of Tantalus, that stem and lineage vile
May cause thee well, with virtue's tool, thy vicious life to file.[20]

For deadly deed which Atreus did unto Thyestes' child
50   (Although Thyest his brother then his spousal bed defiled),
His grisly ghost comes back again from deep infernal pit,
To make revenge in Aegist's heart, his only son, to sit.
That filthy great adulter,[21] straight to strife and blood ypressed,
Thyestal° tables to revenge, doth scarcely take his rest:
First Atreus' life he seeks, then while that Agamemnon lay[22]
In castral° camp by Trojan town for country's cause, straight way
This drowsy swinehead filthy be in brutish pleasures wrapped,
Hath Agamemnon's loving wife in Cupid's snares entrapped,
Whereby of sacred Hymeneus the bonds he makes her fly,
60   And Agamemnon's private bed through pleasure to deny,
And which is greater grief than this and villainy most vile,
With deadly thought he makes the wife upon her husband smile,
When as triumphantly he came a conqueror from Troy,
To th'end he should suspect the less and have the greater joy,
And thinking naught, but meaning well, might take a cursèd coat,
Which doing on they easily might the sooner cut his throat.

This deed was done by Talion law.[23] Here blood did blood require:
And now Thyest hath that revenge that he did long desire,

---

[18] lofty lord] i.e. Jove.

[19] 44] Continued emphasis on predestination: Jove foresees who will develop an 'evil [i.e. overly critical] wit'.

[20] 47–48] Perhaps read: 'Watch out in case, as in [the house of] Tantalus, your wicked ancestry may require you to polish away the evil in your life using the tool of virtue'. The idea that a 'carper's' criticisms will haunt the carper himself and his descendants is elaborated at 69–78.

[21] That filthy, great adulter] i.e. Aegisthus.

[22] 55–66] Catalogues Aegithus's acts of revenge: killing Atreus (55); seducing Clytemnestra (55–60); and convincing Clytemnestra to welcome her husband, only to cut his throat (61–66).

[23] Talion law] i.e. 'lex Talionis', the principle of exacting compensation for a crime (as in 'an eye for an eye' or 'blood for blood').

Whereby thou chiefly may'st be taught the providence of God,
70   That so long after Atreus' fact° Thyest's revenge abod,°
And to thyself take better heed lest loitering still in sin,
In pinching slanders, touching° talk (where greater griefs begin),
Thyself alone thou do not plague, which of itself is much,
But also make thine after stock to smart – and for thy touch.°[24]
For be thou sure, though God doth spare thee for a season here,
And suffer thee with poisoned tongue to frump° and carp this gere,°
That either thou thyself shalt feel some bitter biting grief,
Or else shall thy posterity with pain have their relief.
Unlucky children reap that wicked parents' hands have sown;
80   A wary wight by others' woes that knows t'avoid his own.
Learn here to live aright and know how that there is a God,
That well-deservers well rewards, and ill doth scourge with rod.
For to this end is this compiled this play thou hast in hand,
In virtue's race to make thee run and vice for to withstand;
Which well-deserving work of his, if thou can well digest,
There shalt thou have his budding pen to greater matters pressed.

W.R. to the Reader

If troublous toils most tragical,
Or bloody broils of envious ire,
Described with art poetical
Can move thy heart or set on fire
    Thy wavering mind, then still proceed
    With good advice this book to read.

For herein is set forth at large,
With sugared sops° of lettered tongue,
Th'unstable state of glorious barge,
10   Which envious heart hath freshly stung.
    For when that hate increaseth ire,
    Nought else but death can quench that fire.

---

[24] 69–74] A potential detractor should learn from Agamemnon: his 'touching (i.e. reproachful) talk' (line 72) and his 'touch' (i.e. reproachful stroke of wit) (line 74) will hurt him and his children ('after stock') (see also 75–78).

What did avail the martial deeds,
Which Agamemnon's valiant hand
Did bring to pass? They sow[ed] the seeds
Of envious hate in Mycene land.
  For Aegist and his cruel wife,
  At length do rid him of his life.

Of fickle Fortune's wavering wiles
20 This book ensample° doth declare,
For when most pleasantly she smiles,
She doth nought else but plant a snare,
    To catch at length with woeful chance
    The same, whom she aloft did 'vance.

I need not praise this golden book,
So fully freight with learning's lore:
The work enough, if thou dost look,
Doth praise itself and needs no more.
    For words availeth not a rush,°
30   And good wine needs no tavern bush.[25]

Therefore ere that thou hast it read,
With timorous rancour judge none ill.
For oft the churlish curious head
Condemneth youth as wanting skill.
    Yet Daniel young sent Judith rest,[26]
    When hoary° heads had her oppressed.[27]

Idem in Zoilum

Zoile quid frendes? quid mandis spumea labra?[28]
    Quid volat horrisono fulmen ab ore tuo?
Evome corrupto tabescens gutture virus;
    Eructa bullas, O furibunde, vafras
Faucibus ignivomis minitans et dente lupino:

---

[25] tavern bush] i.e. 'no advertisement'.
[26] Judith] i.e. Susanna, who was wrongly accused of adultery by two old men, until the young judge Daniel exposed the lie.
[27] hoary] i.e. grey, with pun on 'horry', i.e. 'slanderous'.
[28] The poem is in elegiac couplets.

Praeda tuo denti non opus istud erit.
Non potes istius calami corrumpere fructus:
    Conservat famulos magna Minerva suos.
Insulsus nitidum reprehendit sutor Apellem.
10   Invidiam virtus clara praeire solet.
Zoile tuque furis: iuvenis quum musa triumphet,
    Iratus turges; verbula vana vomis.
Ipse tamen rigidi peries Acherontis in urna,
    Et Phlegethonteas ante natabis aquas,
Quam tu Studlei dimittes carmen in umbras,
    Quam possis nomen dilacerare suum.
Perpetuo vivet res invictissima virtus:
    Non abolent enses, unda, nec ignis eam.

[The same against Zoilus.[29]

Zoilus, why do you snarl? Why do you gnash your foamy lips?
    Why does a thunderbolt fly from your cacophonous mouth?
Spew out your corrosive venom from your rotten gullet;
    belch forth your clever bubbles, in your madness,
hurling your threats from fire-breathing throat and wolfish tooth:
    this work will not be your tooth's prey.
You cannot corrupt the fruits of this one's pen:
    great Minerva protects her servants.[30]
The dull-witted cobbler rebukes the shining Apelles.[31]
10   Splendid virtue always outdoes resentment.
And you, Zoilus, rage; though the young man's muse triumphs,
    you swell with anger; you sputter futile little words.
But you yourself will perish in the urn of unyielding Acheron
    and will sooner swim the waters of Phlegethon,
than you can confine the poem of Studley to the shadows
    – than you can tear apart his name.
Virtue will live on forever, a thing unconquered,
    abolished not by sword, nor wave, nor fire.]

---

[29] The same] W. R.

[30] Minerva] Possible allusion to inns-of-court writers as 'Minerva's men' (see 'Preface' to *Thyestes*, line 83). On Studley's inn, see Introduction, p. 46.

[31] 9] A cobbler noticed a mistake made by the famed Greek painter in painting a shoe. When the cobbler then took this as licence to criticize the painting further, Apelles commented that he should 'stick to his last', i.e. what he knows best.

H. C. to the Reader

Be not too rash in judging aught, but weigh well in thy mind
The pleasure and commodity° that thou herein shall find,
And deem him not presumptuous, whom muses movèd right,
The stately style of Senec sage in vulgar° verse to write.
For though the work of graver age the cunning seem to crave,
Sometime we see yet younger years a riper wit to have.
Accept it, therefore, as it is of greener years indeed,
And as his pains deserveth praise, so pay him for his meed.°

To the Reader
Thomas de la Peend in the Translator's Behalf[32]

In volume small, a present great, a worthy gift to thee,
Good reader here is offerèd, if thou so thankful be,
According to the value full, the same for to receive,
Vouchsafing for the writer's pains, deservèd praise to give.
He boldly hath presented here unto thy gazing eyes
The wisdom great, and worthy things, which erst by tragedies,
Sage Senec showing so sometime in Latin verse did write.
The same in perfect English rhyme this author doth indite,°
Which, though thy skilful judgement may discern of praise to be
10   Well worthy, yet by this, I do commend the same to thee,
Because that virtue praisèd still increaseth everywhere,
And that each reader's rigour hard the learnèd should not fear.
Sith fame and virtue evermore pale envy doth pursue,
Nor Homer great himself could sting of slanderous words eschew.
Contented better men may take the lot, which unto all
That ever wrote 'till this time doth alike in common fall.
Though curious carping Zoili breed rancour black within,[33]
Their poisoned breasts of infamy the spiteful thread to spin,
Let folly feed their frenzy still, unto their own despite,
20   For men discrete and learnèd will read things with judgement right.

---

[32] Thomas Peend (*fl.* 1565–66) translated *Pleasant Fable of Hermaphroditus and Salmacis* (1565) from Ovid's *Metamorphoses* and Matteo Bandello's *Moste Notable Historie of John Lord Mandosse* (1565).
[33] Zoili] Trisyllabic: Zo-i-li.

W. Parker to the Reader

To beat the brain about such trifling toys,[34]
Whose vain delights, by fickle fancy fed,
Enforce the mind t'embrace such fading joys,
Doth argue plain a fond, unsteadfast head;

As to inveigh, enraged with rancour's bile,
And rail on them whose works deserveth praise;
Or else to gloze° and paint with coloured style
Their cloakèd craft, when reason's ground decays;

Or as the proud, enflamèd with desire
10   Of praise, and gape for glorious renown,
Have utter shame (their due reward and hire),
Whereas they hoped of an immortal crown;

And some there be that pining pangs of love
Describe at large, and show their frantic fits,
Cupido's thralls, whom fond affections move,
Plain to bewray° their wanton wavering wits.

But Studley, pricked with fervent, hearty zeal,
And virtue's force prevailing in his mind,
Regarding laud and honour never-a-deal,[35]
20   Not ranging wide like hair-brained rovers blind,

Attempted hath to publish this his book,
This tragedy of worthy Seneca,
Whose saws profound, whoso thereon do look,
To virtue's race° do show a ready way.

Persist, therefore, thy happy years to train
In science lore, that fame thy bruit° may blaze,°
And sound thy praise that ever shall remain:
No term of time thy doings may deface.

---

[34] 1–16] Some people write inappropriate works ('trifling toys') or for the wrong reasons (envy, flattery, ambition, or love [5–16]), and thus have 'unsteadfast head[s]' and 'wavering wits', in contrast with Studley at 17.

[35] never a deal] i.e. not at all.

T. B. to the Reader[36]

When Heywood did in perfect verse and doleful tune set out,[37]
And by his smooth and filèd style declarèd had about,
What rough reproach the Trojans of the hardy Greeks received,
When they of town, of goods, and lives together were deprived,
How well did then his friends requite his travail and his pain,
When unto him they have as due ten thousand thanks again?
What greater praise might Virgil get, what more renown than this,
Could have been given unto him for writing verse of his?
Did Virgil aught request but this, in labouring to excel?
10   Or what did fame give to him more than praise to bear the bell?[38]
May Heywood this alone get praise, and Phaer be clean° forgot,[39]
Whose verse and style doth far surmount and gotten hath the lot?
Or may not Googe have part with him, whose travail and whose
    pain,[40]
Whose verse also is full as good or better of the twain?
A Neville also one there is in verse that gives no place[41]
To Heywood, though he be full good, in using of his grace.
Nor Golding can have less renown, which Ovid did translate,[42]
And by the thundering of his verse hath set in chair of state.
With him also, as seemeth me, our Edwards may compare,[43]
20   Who nothing giving place to him doth sit in egal° chair.
A great sort more I reckon might with Heywood to compare,[44]
And this our author one of them to compte° I will not spare.
Whose pains is egal with the rest in this he hath begun,
And lesser praise deserveth not than Heywood's work hath done.

---

[36] T.B.] Thomas Blundeville? (cf. O'Keefe, 'Innovative', p. 93). See n. at *Thyestes*, 'Preface', 97.

[37] 1–4] On Heywood and *Troas*, see Introduction, pp. 16–17; 18–32.

[38] bear the bell] i.e. take first place.

[39] Phaer] Thomas Phaer (1510?–1560) translated Virgil's *Aeneid* (1558 and 1562).

[40] Googe] See Introduction, pp. 37–39 and 49.

[41] Neville] Alexander Neville (1544–1614), Googe's cousin, translator of S.'s *Oedipus* (1563), and author of occasional poems, including several in Googe's *Eglogs, Epytaphes, and Sonnettes* (1563).

[42] Golding] See *Thyestes*, n. at 'Preface', 103–04

[43] Edwards] Richard Edwards (1525–1566) author of *Damon and Pithias* (1564–1565) and the play *Palamon and Arcite* (1566), and poetry (published posthumously in *Paradise of Dainty Devices* (1576)).

[44] a great sort more] Echoes Heywood's *Thyestes*, 'Preface', line 13.

Give, therefore, Studley part of praise to recompense his pain.[45]
For egal labour evermore deserveth egal gain.

> Read ere thou judge, then judge thy fill,
> But judge the best and mend the ill.

Vale.[46]

To the Right Honourable Sir William Cecil, Knight,[47] one of the most honourable Privy Council, Master of the Wards and Liveries, Secretary to the Queen's Highness and Chancellor of the University of Cambridge, John Studley wisheth long life with increase of honour.[48]

When as I had, Right Honourable Sir, at the request of my friends both performed and minded to publish this my simple translation of so notable a tragedy, written by the prudent and sage Seneca, I thought it good for diverse considerations to bestow this, the first fruits of my good will and travail, rather upon your Honour than upon any other person: first, in that I considered your Honour's authority, wisdom, and learning (taking the tuition° of it upon you) might be a terror and abashment to such slanderous tongues who by my simple and slender skill either in this or any other like faculty

10   might take courage rather of maliciousness than of right to reprehend my doings; furthermore, having understanding partly by the report of men, and partly perceiving when I was sometime scholar in the Queen's Majesty's grammar school at Westminster, the hearty goodwill and friendly affection that your Honour bare towards all students, I conceived this hope, that you would accept my good will and doings the better, in that I profess myself to be a student and that in the University of Cambridge, wherein sometime your Honour were trained up in learning, and now being most worthily Chancellor thereof, do greatly tender the commodity° of

20   the students in the same, with the advancement and increase of learning, furtherance of virtue, and abolishment of vice. Thus, therefore, trusting your Honour's courtesy will have me excused for my rude boldness and accept my goodwill herein signified, I leave you to the tuition of almighty God, who increase you with honour, grant you long life with eternal felicity.

Your Honour's to Command,
John Studley

---

[47] Sir William Cecil (1520/21–1598), later Baron Burghley, Elizabeth's Secretary of State, 1558–1571. He became Chancellor of the University of Cambridge in 1559 and Master of Wards and Liveries in January 1560.

[48] wisheth long life with increase of honour] See n. at *Troas*, Dedication.

The Preface to the Reader

Behold, gentle reader, how Seneca in this present tragedy hath most lively painted out unto thee the unstability of Fortune, who when she hath advanced to the highest him with whom (as the cat with the mouse) it liketh her to dally, suddenly she turning her wheel doth let him fall to greater misery than was his former felicity, whereof Agamemnon may be a perfect pattern as is at large showed in the tragedy itself; which although it be but grossly and after a rude manner translated, condemn it not for the baseness of the phrase, but embrace it for the excellency of the matter therein
10   contained. And although that the other tragedies which are set forth by Jasper Heywood and Alexander Neville[49] are so excellently well done (that in reading of them it seemeth to me no translation, but even Seneca himself to speak in English), take no offence that I (being one of the most that can do least) have thus rashly attempted so great an enterprise to mingle my barbarousness with others' eloquency. For when I had at the earnest request of certain my familiar friends thus rudely performed the same, they yet not satisfied herewith willed me not to hide and keep to myself that small talent which God hath lent unto me to serve my country
20   withal,[50] but rather to apply it to the use of such young students as thereby might take some commodity,°[51] therewith I, considering that keeping it close it could profit nothing, and again being published it could do no hurt, trusting of thy gentleness that thou wilt esteem this my good will, I have presumed to set it forth thus simply and rudely, submitting it to the friendly correction of the learnèd.

Thus desiring thee to bear with my boldness and pardon my ignorance, I leave thee to God.

Farewell.

---

[49] On Heywood, see pp. 16–17; on Neville, see 'T.B.' above (n. at 15).

[50] small talent] An allusion to the parable of the talents (Matthew 25: 14–30), common in mid-Tudor translations, for instance, in Heywood's *Hercules Furens*, sig. A2ᵛ and one I.A.'s translation of Pliny (1566), sig. A2ʳ.

[51] to apply it [...] might take some commodity] Echoes Heywood's preface to *Hercules Furens*, which provides 'some means to further understanding the unripened scholars of this realm' (sig. A2ᵛ).

THE SPEAKERS[52]

THYESTES

CHORUS

CLYTEMNESTRA

NUTRIX[53]

AEGISTHUS

EURYBATES

A COMPANY OF GREEKS[54]

CASSANDRA

AGAMEMNON

ELECTRA

STROPHILUS[55]

---

[52] Soldiers appear as non-speaking characters in 4.1.; also Orestes in 5.2 and 5.3.

[53] Nutrix] 'Nurse', confidante to the heroine (as also in S.'s *Medea* and *Phaedra*).

[54] A Company of Greeks] In S., there are two choral groups: the main Chorus of Greek (Argive) men and the separate Chorus of Trojan women who speak in 3.2. It is unclear whether Studley understands this 'Company' and the 'Chorus' listed above as registering these two groups.

[55] On the spelling 'Strophilus', see n. in Appendix, 'The Translators' Latin Sources'.

THE FIRST ACT

THYESTES

Departing from the darkened dens, which Ditis low doth keep,[56]
Lo, here I am sent out again from Tartar dungeon deep.
Thyestes, I, that whither coast to shun do stand in doubt,[57]
Th'infernal fiends I fly, the folk of earth I chase about.
My conscience, lo, abhors that I should hither passage make;
Appallèd sore with fear and dread, my trembling sinews shake.

My father's house or rather yet my brother's I espy.[58]
This is the old and antique porch of Pelops' progeny.
Here first the Greeks on princes' heads do place the royal crown,
10   And here in throne aloft they lie that jetteth° up and down
With stately sceptre in their hand; eke° here their courts do lie.
This is their place of banqueting,[59] return therefore will I.[60]
Nay, better were it not[61] to haunt the loathsome Limbo lakes,[62]
Whereas° the Stygian porter doth advance with lusty crakes,°[63]
His triple gorge behung with mane, shag hairy, rusty, black;
Where Ixion's carcass linkèd fast, the whirling wheel doth rack,[64]
And rolleth still upon himself, whereas full oft in vain,
Much toil is lost (the tottering stone down tumbling back again);
Where growing guts the greedy gripe° do gnaw with ravening bits;
20   Where parchèd up with burning thirst amid the waves he sits,
And gapes to catch the fleeting flood with hungry chaps° beguiled,
That pays his painful punishment, whose feast the gods defiled.[65]

---

[56] 1–7] On Studley's translation style in these lines, see Introduction, pp. 52–53.

[57] whither coast to shun do stand in doubt] S. 'incertus utras oderim sedes magis' (in doubt as to which region I should hate more), referring to the underworld and the world of the living.

[58] or rather yet my brother's] i.e. the palace and kingdom inherited by Thyestes and Atreus from their father Pelops, but stolen by Atreus.

[59] their place of banqueting] i.e. where Atreus served the cannibalistic feast to Thyestes.

[60] will I] S. 'libet' (I wish to).

[61] Nay, better were it not] In S., a rhetorical question: the ghost thinks it far preferable to return to the underworld than to look upon Argos. Studley's ghost seems more ambivalent.

[62] Limbo] Studley's addition. See n. at *Thyestes*, 'Preface', 313.

[63] Stygian porter] S. 'custodem Stygis' (guardian of the Styx), i.e. Cerberus.

[64] 16–22] A list of those who endure the most severe punishments in Hades: Ixion (16), Sisyphus (17–18), Tityus (19), and Tantalus (20–22). A similar catalogue appears in S.'s *Thyestes* (6–12).

Yet that old man so stepped° in years at length by tract of time,
How great a part belongs to me and portion of his crime.[66]
Account we all the grisly ghosts, whom guilty found of ill,
The Cnossian judge in Pluto's pits doth toss in torments still.[67]
Thyestes, I, in dreary° deeds will far surmount the rest,
Yet to my brother yield I, though I gorged my bloody breast,
And stuffèd have my pampered paunch even with my children
    three,
30   That crammèd lie within my ribs and have their tomb in me.
The bowels of my swallowed babes devourèd up I have,
Nor fickle Fortune me alone the father doth deprave,
But enterprising greater guilt than that is put in ure,°
To file° my daughter's baudy bed; my lust she doth allure.[68]
To speak these words I do not spare.[69] I wrought the heinous deed
That, therefore, I through all my stock might parent still proceed.
My daughter driven by force of Fates and Destinies divine
Doth breed young bones and lades° her womb with sinful seed of
    mine.
Lo, nature changèd upside down, and out of order turned.[70]
40   This mingle-mangle° hath she made[71] (O fact° to be forlorned)!°[72]
A father and a grandsire, lo, confusedly I am,
My daughter's husband both become and father to the same.
Those babes that should my nephews be, when nature rightly runs,
She being jumbled° doth confound and mingle with my sons.
The crystal clearness of the day, and Phoebus' beams so bright,
Are mixèd with the foggy clouds and darkness dim of night.

---

[65] 22] Studley misses S.'s allusion to the feast where Tantalus tried to serve his son Pelops's flesh to the gods.

[66] 23–24] The 'old man' is Tantalus: Thyestes owns a greater 'portion of his crime', since he participated in a worse cannibalistic feast, described at 29–31 below.

[67] Cnossian judge] i.e. Minos, judge of the dead.

[68] 32–34] A reference to Thyestes' incest with his daughter, Pelopia, resulting in the birth of Aegisthus.

[69] To speak these words I do not spare] A change from S. 'non pavidus hausi dicta' (undaunted I took up [Fortune's] instructions).

[70] 39–46] A typical expansion by Studley, rendering S.'s three lines (*Aga.* 34–36) in eight, lingering over the incest and its cosmic resonances.

[71] mingle-mangle] 'Studley delights in these jingling compounds'; cf. 'flym flam' and 'slybber slabbar' in *Medea* (Spearing, *Studley's Translations*, p. 231).

[72] O fact to be forlorned] S. 'pro nefas' (unspeakable outrage!).

When wickedness had wearied us, too late truce taken was,
Even when our detestable deeds were done and brought to pass.[73]
But valiant Agamemnon he, grand captain of the host
50   – Who bare the sway among the kings and rulèd all the roost,
Whose slanting flag and banner brave displayed in royal sort
A thousand sail of sousing° ships did guard to Phrygian port,[74]
And with their swelling shatling sails, the surging seas did hide,[75]
That beateth on the banks of Troy and floweth by her side –
When Phoebus' cart the zodiac ten times had overrun,[76]
And waste the battered walls do lie of Troy destroyed and won,
Returned he is to yield his throat unto his traitorous wife,
That shall with force of bloody blade bereave him of his life.

The glittering sword, the hewing axe, and wounding weapons mo,°
60   With blood for blood new set abroach° shall make the floor to flow.
With sturdy stroke and boisterous blow of pithy pole-axe given,
His beaten brains are pashed° abroad, his crackèd skull is riven.[77]
Now mischief marcheth on apace; now falsehood doth appear;
Now butchers' slaughter doth approach, and murther draweth near.
In honour of thy native day, Aegisthus, they prepare[78]
The solemn feast with junketing° and dainty toothsome° fare.
Fie, what doth shame abash thee so and cause thy courage quail?
Why doubts thy right hand what to do? To smite why doth it fail?   [50]
What he forecasting might suspect, why should'st thou take
    advice?
70   Why frettest thou, demanding if thou may it enterprise?
Nay, if another it beseem° thou rather may'st surmise.[79]

What now? How happeneth it that thus the smiling summer's night,
When Phoebus from th'antipodes should render soon the light,

---

[73] 47–48] In S., these lines have a more positive sense as Thyestes thinks things have taken a turn for the better.

[74] to Phrygian port] a typical added detail by Studley.

[75] Shatling] Unclear. Perhaps 'shackling', i.e. 'shaking, rattling' (Spearing, *Studley's Translations*, p. 233).

[76] 55] i.e. 'when ten years had passed'.

[77] 61–62] In S., these events are the object of a verb 'video' (I see), suggesting that Thyestes' ghost can see ahead to the play's later action.

[78] native day] i.e. birthday. In S., Agamemnon's murder is 'causa natalis tui' (the reason for your [Aegisthus's] being born).

[79] 71] Obscure. In S., the ghost insists that it is seemly for Aegisthus, as the child of Thyestes, to kill Agamemnon.

On sudden change their turns with nights that last and linger long,
When winter's Boreas bitter blasts doth puff the trees among?[80]
Or what doth cause the gliding stars to stay still in the sky?
We wait for Phoebus: to the world bring day now by and by.

CHORUS

O Fortune that dost fail the great estate of kings,[81]
On slippery sliding seat thou placest lofty things,
And set'st on tottering sort where perils do abound,
Yet never kingdom calm, nor quiet could be found.
No day to sceptres sure doth shine that they might say,
'Tomorrow shall we rule as we have done today.'[82]
One clod of crooked care another bringeth in;
One hurly-burly° done, another doth begin.[83]

Not so the raging sea doth boil upon the sand,[84]
10   Whereas the southern wind that blows in Affric land
One wave upon another doth heap with sturdy blast;[85]
Not so doth Euxine sea his swelling waves upcast,
Nor so his belching stream from shallow bottom roll,
That borders hard upon the icy frozen pole,
Whereas Boötes bright doth twine° his wain° about
And of the marble seas doth nothing stand in doubt.[86]

---

[80] 72–75] The sun (Phoebus) lingers on the other side of the world, making the night more winter-like. Thyestes impatiently awaits day. The scene recalls the sun's reversal in *Thyestes* (See n. at *Thyestes*, 'Preface', 297).

[81] fail] Studley preserves the sound of S. 'fallax' (deceptive, deceitful). 1–6] On Studley's translation style in these lines, see Introduction, p. 54.

[82] 6] Studley's expansive rendering of S. 'certum sui [...] diem' (a day certain of itself). In *Macbeth*, Shakespeare may echo this and numerous other lines from this Chorus. Compare line 6 with *Macbeth* 5.5.18: 'tomorrow, and tomorrow, and tomorrow', and also 'One hurly-burly done' (8) with 'when the hurlyburly's done' (*Macbeth* 1.1.3). Compare also: 'light and vain conceit' (32) with 'self and vain conceit' (*Richard II* 3.2.162). (For a complete list, see Muir, 'A borrowing'.) See also nn. at 2.2.99 and 5.1.7–24.

[83] 8] S. 'vexatque animos nova tempestas' (and a new storm assails their minds), introducing the storm metaphor.

[84] upon the sand] S. refers explicitly to Syrtes, the shallows off the coast of Libya that caused many shipwrecks.

[85] another] Disyllabic here and often ('anoth'r', like 'weath'r') (see pp. 289–90).

[86] 15–16] The constellation Boötes (the Wagoner) drives his wagon (the Wain, Ursa Major); by contrast with those on earth, Boötes is 'caeruleis immunis aquis' (untouched by the green-blue waters).

O how doth Fortune toss and tumble in her wheel[87]
The staggering states of kings that ready be to reel.
Fain would they dreaded be, and yet not settled so;
20   When as they fearèd are, they fear and live in woe.
The silent lady Night, so sweet to man and beast,
Cannot bestow on them her safe and quiet rest.
Sleep that doth overcome and break the bonds of grief,
It cannot ease their hearts, nor minister relief.

What castle strongly built, what bulwark, tower, or town,
Is not by mischief's means brought topsy turvy down?
What rampart walls are not made weak by wicked war?
From stately courts of kings doth justice fly afar.
In princely palaces of honesty the lore
30   And wedlock vow devout is set by little store.
The bloody Bellon those doth haunt with gory hand
Whose light and vain conceit in painted pomp doth stand,
And those Erinys wood turmoils with frenzy's fits,[88]
That evermore in proud and haughty houses sits,
Which fickle Fortune's hand, in twinkling of an eye,
From high and proud degree drives down in dust to lie.
Although that skirmish cease, no banners be displayed,
And though no wiles be wrought and policy be stayed,
Down peisèd° with their weight the massy things do sink,
40   And from her burden doth unstable Fortune shrink.[89]

The swelling sails puffed up with gale of western wind[90]
Do yet mistrust thereof a tempest in their mind.[91]
The threatening tops that touch the clouds of lofty towers
Be soonest [peised°] and beat with south wind rainy showers.
The darksome wood doth see his tough and sturdy oak
Well waynd° in years to be clean° overthrown and broke.

---

[87] O how doth Fortune toss and tumble] S. more explicitly compares the storm and Fortune: the sea does not boil 'ut [...] Fortuna rotat' (as much as Fortune turns).

[88] Erinys wood] i.e. a raging Fury.

[89] 37–40] i.e. Even if kings avoid war and treachery, greatness and good fortune collapse from their own weight.

[90] western wind] In S. 'Notus', the south wind.

[91] 42] S. 'vela [...] ventos nimium timuere suos' (the sails are very afraid of their winds). This and the following examples (sails, towers, trees, bodies) illustrate that the most conspicuous are the most vulnerable.

The lightning's flashing flame out breaking in the sky,
First lighteth on the mounts and hills that are most high.
The bodies corpulent and of the largest size
50 Are rifest still to catch diseases when they rise.
When as the stock to graze in pasture fat is put,
Whose neck is larded best his throat shall first be cut. [100]

What Fortune doth advance and hoiseth° up on high,
She sets it up to fall again more grievously.
The things of middle sort and of a mean degree
Endure above the rest and longest days do see.
The man of mean estate most happy is of all,
Who pleasèd with the lot that doth to him befall,
Doth sail on silent shore, with calm and quiet tide,
60 And dreads with bruisèd barge on swelling seas to ride,
Nor lancing° to the deep, where bottom none is found,
May with his rudder search and reach the shallow ground.

THE SECOND ACT

CLYTEMNESTRA NUTRIX[92]

[CLYTEMNESTRA]

[Aside]

O drowsy, dreaming, doting soul, what commeth in thy brain,
To seek about for thy defence what way thou may'st attain?
What ails thy skittish, wayward wits to waver up and down?
The fittest shift° prevented is, the best path overgrown.
Thou mightest once maintainèd have thy wedlock chamber
     chaste,
And eke have ruled with majesty by faith conjoinèd fast.
Now nurture's° lore neglected is, all right doth clean decay,
Religion and dignity with faith are worn away,
And ruddy shame with blushing cheeks so far, god wot,° is
     passed
10 That when it would it cannot now come home again at last.
O let me now at random run with bridle at my will.
The safest path to mischief is by mischief open still.[93]

---

[92] A Senecan passion-restraint scene. See n. at *Thyestes* 2.1.

Now put in practise, seek about, search out and learn to find
The wily trains° and crafty guiles of wicked womankind.
What any devilish traitorous dame durst do in working woe,
Or any wounded in her wits by shot of Cupid's bow,
Whatever rigorous stepdame could commit with desperate hand,
Or as the wench, who flaming fast by Venus' poisoning brand,[94]
Was driven by lewd, uncourteous love in ship of Thessale land
To flit away from Colchis isle, where Phasis channel deep,
With silver stream down from the hills of Armenie doth sweep.
Get weapons good, get bilbo° blades, or temper poison strong,
Or with some younker° trudge from Greece by theft the seas
    along.[95]
Why dost thou faint to talk of theft, exile or privy flight?
These came by hap.°[96] Thou, therefore, must on greater
    mischief light.

NUTRIX

O worthy queen among the Greeks that bears the swinging sway,
And born of Leda's royal blood, what muttering dost thou say?
What fury fell enforceth thee, bereavèd of thy wits,
To rage and rave with bedlam° brains, to fret with frantic fits?
Though, madam, thou do counsel keep and not complain° thy
    case,
Thine anguish plain appeareth in thy pale and wanny° face.
Reveal, therefore, what is thy grief; take leisure good and stay.
What reason could not remedy oft curèd hath delay.

CLYTEMNESTRA

So grievous is my careful case, which plungeth° me so sore,[97]
That deal I cannot with delay, nor linger anymore.

20 (left margin)
30 (left margin)

---

[93] 12] Lat. 'per scelera semper sceleribus tutum est iter'. The saying appears often in Renaissance drama. (Cunliffe, pp. 24–25; Dent, *Shakespeare's Proverbial*, C825 and *Proverbial Language*, C826; and Miola, p. 16).

[94] 18–21 the wench [...] doth sweep] Medea, who fled from her homeland (Colchis) aboard the Argo ('ship of Thessale land') with Jason; 'uncourteous' corresponds to S. 'impia' (disloyal), indicating her betrayal of her father. Studley adds the references to Venus, Phasis, and Armenia.

[95] 22–23] i.e. 'Copy Medea', who used violence and sorcery, and escaped by boat with her lover and ally.

[96] These came by hap] i.e. Medea's crimes were determined by fortune, whereas you can choose yours.

[97] 34–41] On Studley's translation style in these lines, see Introduction, pp. 54–55.

The flashing flames and furious force of fiery fervent heat,
Outraging in my boiling breast, my burning bones doth beat.
It sucks the sappy marrow out, the juice° it doth convey,°
It frets, it tears, it rents,° it gnaws my guts and gall away.
40   Now feeble fear still eggs me on, with dolour being pressed,
And cankered hate with thwacking thumps doth bounce upon
    my breast.
The blinded boy that lovers' hearts doth reave° with deadly
    stroke,
Entangled hath my linkèd° mind with lewd and wanton yoke,
Refusing still to take assoil° or clean to be confound,°
Among these broils and agonies, my mind besieging round.
Lo, feeble, weary, battered down, and undertrodden° shame,
That wrestleth, striveth, struggleth hard, and fighteth with the
    same.
Thus am I driven to diverse shores, and beat from bank to bank,
And tossèd in the foamy floods that strive with courage crank.°
50   As when here wind, and there the stream, when both their force
    will try,
From sands alow° doth hoist and rear the seas with surges high,
The waltering° wave doth staggering stand, not witting what to
    do,
But, hovering, doubts whose furious force he best may yield
    him to.

My kingdom, therefore, I cast off, my sceptre I forsake,
As anger, sorrow, hope, me lead that way I mean to take.
At all adventure to the seas I yield my beaten barge,
At random, careless will I run, now will I rove at large.
Whereas my mind to fancy fond doth gad° and run astray,
It is the best to choose that chance and follow on that way.

NUTRIX

60   This desperate dotage doth declare, and rashness rude and blind,
To choose out chance to be the guide and ruler of thy mind.

CLYTEMNESTRA

He that is driven to utter pinch,° and furthest shift° of all,
What need he doubt his doubtful lot, or how his luck befall?

228

[NUTRIX]

> In silent shore thou sailest yet, thy trespass we may hide,[98]
> If thou thyself detect it not, nor cause it be descried.°

CLYTEMNESTRA

> Alas it is more blazed° abroad, and further is it blown,
> Than any crime that ever in this princely court was sown.

NUTRIX

> Thy former fault with pensive heart and sorrow thou dost rue,
> And fondly yet thou go'st about to set abroach anew.[99]

CLYTEMNESTRA

70   It is a very foolishness to keep a mean therein.   [150]

NUTRIX

> The thing he fears he doth augment, who heapeth sin to sin.

CLYTEMNESTRA

> But fire and sword, to cure the same, the place of salve
>   supply.[100]

NUTRIX

> There is no man who, at the first, extremity will try.[101]

CLYTEMNESTRA

> In working mischief men do take the readiest way they find.

NUTRIX

> The sacred name of wedlock once revoke° and have in mind.

---

[98] 64–67] On Studley's translation style in these lines and in 71–72 below, see Introduction, p. 53.

[99] to set abroach] An archaic expression meaning 'to tap a cask (of liquor) and set it running'; Studley's figurative translation of S. 'novum crimen struis' (you prepare a new crime).

[100] 72] i.e. 'fire and sword [...] serve as a salve'.

[101] who, at the first, extremity will try] i.e. 'who will try the most extreme measures first'.

CLYTEMNESTRA

Ten years have I been desolate, and led a widow's life.
Yet shall I entertain anew my husband as his wife?

NUTRIX

Consider yet thy son and heir, whom he of thee begot.

CLYTEMNESTRA

And eke my daughter's wedding blaze as yet forget I not.[102]
80   Achilles eke my son-in-law to mind I do not spare,
How well he kept his vow that he to me his mother swear.

NUTRIX

When as our navy might not pass by wind, nor yet by stream,
Thy daughter's blood in sacrifice their passage did redeem.
She stirred and brake the sluggish seas, whose water still did
    stand,
Whose feeble force might not hoise up the vessels from the
    land.

CLYTEMNESTRA

I am ashamèd here withal; it maketh me repine
That Tyndaris, who from the gods doth fetch her noble line,[103]
Should give the ghost t'assuage the wrath of gods and them
    appease,
Whereby the Greekish navy might have passage free by seas.
90   My grudging mind still harps upon my daughter's wedding day,
Whom he hath made for Pelops' stock the bloody ransom
    pay,[104]
When as with cruel countenance imbrued° with gory blood,
As at a wedding altar side th'unpitiful parent stood.

---

[102] 79–81] A reference to Iphigenia, whom Clytemnestra was deceived into
sending as a bride for Achilles, but who was sacrificed by Agamemnon so that the
Greeks could sail to the Trojan War (see also 82–85). At 81, Studley takes 'he' to
be Achilles, whom Clytemnestra sarcastically says 'kept the vow' to 'his
(prospective) mother(-in-law)'; in modern translations 'he' is Agamemnon.

[103] Tyndaris] In most translations, Clytemnestra first refers to herself ('daughter of
Tyndareus') and then laments that her daughter Iphigenia was sacrificed.

[104] 91] A change in sense from S. 'thalamos [...] quos ille dignos Pelopia fecit
domo' (wedding [...] which he [Agamemnon] made worthy of the house of
Pelops).

It irkèd Calchas' woeful heart, who did abhor the same,
His oracle he rued and eke the back reflecting flame.[105]
O wicked and ungracious stock that winnest ill with ill,
Triumphing in thy filthy feats, increasing lewdness still,
By blood we win the wavering winds, by death we purchase war.

NUTRIX

But by this means a thousand ships at once releasèd are.

CLYTEMNESTRA

100   With lucky fate attempt the seas did not the loosèd° rout?[106]
For Aulis isle th'ungracious° fleet from port did tumble out.
As with a lewd, unlucky hand, the war he did begin,
So Fortune favoured his success to thrive no more therein.
Her love as captive holdeth him, whom captive he did take,[107]
Not movèd with the earnest suit that could Achilles make;
Of Phoebus' prelate Sminthical he did retain the spoil,[108]
When for the sacred virgin's love his furious breast doth boil.
Achilles' rough and thundering threats could not him qualify,°
Nor he that doth direct the fates above the starry sky.[109]
110   To us he is an augur just, and keeps his promise due,
But while he threats his captive trulls° of word he is not true.[110]
The savage people fierce in wrath once might not move his
    sprite,°
Who did purloin the kindled tents with fire blazing bright.
When slaughter great on Greeks was made in most extremest
    fight,
Without a foe he, conquerèd, with leanness pines away,
In lewd and wanton chamber tricks he spends the idle day,

---

[105] back reflecting flame] i.e. the altars that recoiled from Iphigenia's sacrifice.
[106] 100–01] In S., Clytemnestra sets the story straight: the fleet was not released by the favour of a deity, but was expelled by Aulis in disgust.
[107] captive] i.e. Achilles' war-prize, Chryseis, whom Agamemnon took as his own.
[108] Phoebus' prelate Sminthical] i.e. Chryses, priest of Apollo Smintheus and father of Chryseis (who is 'the spoil' at 106 and the 'sacred virgin' at 107).
[109] he] i.e. Calchas, though Studley may mean Jove, translating S. 'videt' (sees) as 'doth direct'.
[110] 110–11] Agamemnon believed that Calchas was a trustworthy prophet regarding Iphigenia and Clytemnestra, but he did not believe Calchas when he 'threatened' Agamemnon's captive, Chryseis, commanding that she be returned to her father. Agamemnon refused, until Apollo sent a plague against the Greeks.

And freshly still he feeds his lust lest that some other while,
His chamber chaste should want a stews° that might the same
    defile.
On lady Briseis' love again his fancy fond doth stand,
120   Whom he hath got that wrested was out of Achilles' hand.
And carnal copulation to have he doth not shame,[111]
Though from her husband's bosom he hath snatched the wicked
    dame.
Tush,° he that doth at Paris grudge with wound but newly
    stroke,
Enflamed with Phrygian prophet's love, his boiling breast doth
    smoke.[112]
Now after Trojan booties brave, and Troy overwhelmed he saw,
Returned he is a prisoner's spouse and Priam's son-in-law.

Now, heart be bold, take courage good, of stomach° now be
    stout,
A field that easily is not fought to pitch thou go'st about.[113]
In practice mischief thou must put. Why hop'st thou for a day,
130   While Priam's daughter come from Troy in Greece do bear the
    sway?[114]
But as for thee, poor silly wretch, awaiteth at thy place –
Thy widow virgins, and Orest, his father like in face.[115]
Consider their calamities to come and eke their cares,
Whom all the peril of the broil doth threat in thy affairs.
O cursèd captive, woeful wretch, why dost thou loiter so?
Thy little brats a stepdame have whose wrath will work their
    woe,[116]
With gashing sword, and if thou can none other way provide,
Nor thrust it through another's ribs, then launch thy gory side.[117] [200]

---

[111] copulation] Five syllables. The suffix '-ion' is disyllabic here and in other words such as 'region', 'fornication', etc. See further pp. 289–90.

[112] Phrygian prophet's love] i.e. love for Cassandra.

[113] 128] S. 'bella non levia apparas' (you are initiating heavy battles).

[114] Why hop'st thou for a day, / While] i.e. 'What day are you waiting for? Until'.

[115] 131–32] Clytemnestra mocks her remaining family: her unmarried daughters and Orestes.

[116] a stepdame] i.e. Cassandra.

[117] 137–38] Clytemnestra urges herself toward self-sacrifice, if that is the only way to get to Agamemnon.

So murther° twain with brewèd blood, let blood immirèd° be,
140   And by destroying of thyself destroy thy spouse with thee.
       Death is not sauced with sops° of sorrow, if some man else I
          have,
       Whose breathless corse° I wish to pass with me to deadly grave.

NUTRIX

       Queen, bridle thine affections, and wisely rule thy rage,
       Thy swelling mood now mitigate, thy choler eke assuage.
       Weigh well the weighty enterprise that thou dost take in hand:
       Triumphant victor he returns of mighty Asia land,
       Avenging Europe's injury, with him he brings away
       The spoils of sackèd Pargamie, a huge and mighty prey.[118]

       In bondage eke he leads the folk of long assaulted Troy,
150   Yet darest thou by policy attempt him to annoy?
       Whom with the dint of glittering sword Achilles durst not
          harm,[119]
       Although his rash and desperate dicks° the froward knight did
          arm;
       Nor Ajax yet more hardy man up yielding vital breath,
       Whom frantic fury fell enforced to wound himself to death;[120]
       Nor Hector, he, whose only life procured the Greeks' delay,
       And long in war for victory enforcèd them to stay;
       Nor Paris' shaft, whose cunning hand with shot so sure did
          aim;
       Nor mighty Memnon, swart and black, had power to hurt the
          same;
       Nor Xanthus flood, where to and fro, dead carcases did swim,
160   With armour hewed and therewithal some maimèd broken limb;
       Nor Simois that purple walms° with slaughter dyed doth
          stir;[121]
       Nor Cygnus, lily-white, the son of fenny° god so dear;[122]

---

[118] Pargamie] i.e. Pergamum, the citadel of Troy, but here meaning 'Troy'.

[119] 151–66] A catalogue of those who tried and failed to kill Agamemnon: Greeks (Achilles and Ajax, son of Telamon), Trojans (Hector, Paris), and Trojan allies (Memnon, Cygnus, Rhesus, king of Thrace, and Amazons).

[120] 153–54] Ajax, son of Telamon, committed suicide after Achilles' arms were posthumously awarded to Ulysses instead of to him.

[121] 159–61 Xanthus […] Simois] Rivers in Troy.

[122] fenny god] i.e. Neptune.

Nor yet the mustering Thracian host, nor warlike Rhesus king;
Nor Amazons, who to the wars, did painted quivers bring,
And bare their hatchets in their hands, with target and with
    shield,
Yet had no power with ghastly wound to foil him in the field.
Sith he such scourings hath escaped, and plunge° of perils
    passed,
Intendest thou to murther him, returning home at last,
And sacred altars to profane with slaughter so unpure?

170   Shall Greece th'avenger let this wrong long unrevenged endure?
The grim and fierce courageous horse, the battle's shouts and
    cries,
The swelling seas, which bruisèd barks do dread when storms
    arise –[123]
Behold the fields with streams of blood overflown and deeply
    drowned,[124]
And all the chivalry of Troy in servile bondage bound,
Which Greeks have writ in registers.[125] Thy stubborn stomach
    bind,
Subdue thy fond affections and pacify thy mind.

The Second Scene

AEGISTHUS CLYTEMNESTRA

[AEGISTHUS]

The cursèd time that evermore my mind did most detest,
The days that I abhorrèd have and hated in my breast
Are come, are come, that mine estate will bring to utter wrack.
Alas, my heart, why dost thou fail and fainting fliest back?
What dost thou mean at first assaults from armour thus to fly?
Trust this, the cruel gods intend thy doleful destiny,

---

[123] 172] S. 'classibusque horrens fretum' (the sea bristling with ships); Studley takes 'horrens' in the sense of 'terrifying' ('do dread') and characteristically expands the line, adding storms.

[124] Behold] S. 'propone' (summon in your mind): the Nurse prompts Clytemnestra to learn from pondering the Trojan War.

[125] Which Greeks have writ in registers] An interesting translation of 'regesta Danais' (rebounding on the Greeks): with 'registers', Studley invites an association with history writing (Lat. 'res gestae').

To wrap thee in with perils round, and catch thee in a band.
Endeavour, drudge, with all thy power their plagues for to
    withstand;
With stomach stout, rebellious, to fire and sword appeal.[126]

CLYTEMNESTRA

10   It is no plague, if such a death thy native destinies deal.

AEGISTHUS

O [partner] of my perils all, begot of Leda thou,
Direct thy doings after mine, and unto thee I vow:
This drossel,° sluggish ringleader, this stout, strong-hearted sire,
Shall pay thee so much blood again as shed he hath in fire.[127]
How haps it that his trembling cheeks to be so pale and white,[128]
Lying aghast as in a trance with fainting face upright?

CLYTEMNESTRA

His conscience wedlock vow doth prick and brings him home
    again.[129]
Let us return the self-same trade° anew for to retain,
To which at first we should have stuck and ought not to forsake.
20   To covenant continent anew let us ourselves betake.[130]
To take the trade of honesty at no time is too late:
He purgèd is from punishment whose heart the crime doth hate.

AEGISTHUS

Why whither wilt thou gad, O rash and unadvisèd dame?
What, dost thou earnestly believe and firmly trust the same,

---

[126] 8–9] Aegisthus resists the perils sent by the gods. In S., he complies: 'oppone cunctis vile suppliciis caput' (subject your worthless head to all their punishments).

[127] as shed he hath in fire] Studley's addition, evidently referring to Agamemnon's former acts of violence against enemies and kin.

[128] his] i.e. 'Agamemnon's'. Studley apparently misreads S. here: Aegisthus refers to Clytemnestra.

[129] 'his' and 'him'] Studley's continued misreading. S. still refers to Clytemnestra. In S., here and in the following lines Clytemnestra does an about face, suggesting: 'I am having second thoughts about betraying my marriage, and it is not too late to mend my ways'.

[130] covenant continent] S. 'casta [...] fides' (chaste fidelity).

That Agamemnon's spousal bed will loyal be to thee,
That nought doth underprop° thy mind, which might thy terror
    be?
His proud success puffed up too high with lucky blast of wind
Might make so crank° and set aloft his haughty swelling mind.
Among his peers he stately was ere Trojan turrets torn:

30   How think ye then his stomach stout, by nature given to scorn,   [250]
In haughtiness augmented is, more in himself to joy,
Through this triumphant victory and conquest got of Troy?
Before his voyage Mycene king most mildly did he reign,
But now a tyrant truculent returned he is again.[131]
Good luck and proud prosperity do make his heart so rise.

With what great preparation preparèd solemnwise
A rabblement of strumpets come that clung about him all?
But yet the prophetess of Phoebe, whom god of truth we call,[132]
Appears above the rest. She keeps the king, she doth him guide.

40   Wilt thou in wedlock have a mate and not for it provide?[133]
So would not she: the greatest grief this is unto a wife,
Her husband's minion in her house to lead an open life.
A queen's estate cannot abide her peer with her to reign,
And jealous wedlock will not her companion sustain.

CLYTEMNESTRA

Aegist in desperate mode again why set'st thou me afloat?
Why kindlest thou the sparks of ire in embers covered hot?
If that the victor's own free will release his captive's care,
Why may not I his lady spouse have hope as well to fare?[134]
One law doth rule in royal throne and pompous princely towers;

50   Among the vulgar sort another, in private simple bowers.
What though my grudging fancy force that at my husband's
    hand
Sharp execution of the law I stubbornly withstand?[135]

---

[131] returned he is] S. 'veniet' (will he come).

[132] prophetess of Phoebe] i.e. Cassandra. 'Phoebe' is monosyllabic (for Phoebus Apollo, god of prophecy).

[133] 40] S. 'feresne thalami victa consortem tui?' (will you admit defeat and tolerate sharing the marriage bed with a consort?).

[134] 47–48] Clytemnestra aspires to be treated well, as Cassandra has been. In S., it is different: Clytemnestra insists that it is indecorous for a wife to complain about her husband taking a captive bride.

Recording this that heinously offended him I have,
He gently will me pardon grant who need the same to crave?

AEGISTHUS

Even so, on this condition thou may'st with him compound:°
To pardon him, if he again to pardon thee be bound.
The subtle science of the law, the statutes of our land
That long ago decreèd were, thou dost not understand.[136]
The judges be malicious men, they spite and envy us,
But he shall have them partial his causes to discuss.[137]
This is the chiefest privilege that doth to kings belong:[138]
What laws forbiddeth other men, they do and do no wrong.

CLYTEMNESTRA

He pardoned Helen: she is wed to Menela again,[139]
Which Europe all with Asia did plunge alike in pain.

AEGISTHUS

No lady's lust hath ravished yet Atrides in his life,[140]
Nor privily purloined his heart betrothèd to his wife.
To pick a quarrel he begins, and matter thee to blame,[141]
Suppose thou nothing hast commit that worthy is of shame?
What booteth° him whom princes hate an honest life to frame?°
He never doth complain his wrong, but ever bears the blame.
Wilt thou repair to Spart and to thy country trudge aright?[142]
Wilt thou become a runagate° from such a worthy wight?°

60

70

---

[135] 51–52] Clytemnestra apparently refers to her own punishment for adultery.
'Withstand' misreads S. 'ferre' (impose): Clytemnestra sees that, given her own guilt, she cannot 'impose' severe laws on Agamemnon.

[136] 57] An expansion (and softening) of S.'s phrase 'iura regnorum' (the laws of kingdoms, i.e. the way kings behave). The criticism of kings becomes more explicit at 61–62.

[137] 59–60] Studley obscures a reference to kings' self-serving judgements: S. 'nobis maligni iudices, aequi sibi' ([kings are] spiteful judges to us, but fair to themselves).

[138] that doth to kings belong] Omits a significant detail in S.: kings merely 'think' (putant) they are above the law.

[139] Menela] i.e. Menelaus.

[140] Atrides] Studley may not see that S. 'Atrides' (i.e. son of Atreus) refers here to Atreus's other son, Menelaus, who remained devoted to Helen.

[141] 67] i.e. Agamemnon actively seeks reasons to blame you.

[142] Spart] i.e. Sparta, Clytemnestra's homeland.

Divorcement made from kings will not so let the matter scape:
Thou easest fear by fickle hope that falsely thou dost shape.

CLYTEMNESTRA

My trespass is disclosed to none but to a trusty wight.

AEGISTHUS

At princes' gates fidelity yet never enter might.

CLYTEMNESTRA

I will corrupt and feed him so with silver and with gold
That I by bribing bind him shall no secrets to unfold.

AEGISTHUS

The trust that hirèd is and bought by bribes and money's fee,
80   Thy counsel to bewray° again with bribes enticed will be.

CLYTEMNESTRA

The remnant left of shamefastness of those ungracious tricks,
Wherein of late I did delight, my conscience freshly pricks.
Why keep'st thou such a busy stir° and with thy flattering
    speech
Instructing me with lewd advice dost wicked counsel preach?
Shall I forsooth of royal blood, with all the speed I can,
Refuse the king of kings and wed an outcast banished man?

AEGISTHUS

Why should you think in that Thyest was father unto me,
And Agamemnon Atreus' son, he should my better be?

CLYTEMNESTRA

If that be but a trifle small, add nephew° to the same.[143]

AEGISTHUS

90   I am of Phoebus' lineage born, whereof I do not shame.[144]

---

[143] add nephew] i.e. Aegisthus is Thyestes' son *and* grandson (nepos).

[144] I am of Phoebus' lineage born] S. 'auctore Phoebo gignor' (Phoebus is author of my begetting). Aegisthus perversely claims divine parentage, since Thyestes' incest occurred on the advice of Phoebus Apollo's oracle.

[CLYTEMNESTRA]

Why mak'st thou Phoebus author of thy wicked pedigree,
Whom out of heaven ye forced to fly when bridle back he
    drew,[145]
When lady Night with mantle black did spread her sudden
    shade?
Why makest thou the gods in such reproachfulness to wade,
Whose father hath thee cunning made by slight and subtle guile,
To make thy kinsman cuckold while his wife thou do defile?[146]
What man is he whom we do know to be thy father's mate,
Abusing lust of lechery in such unlawful rate?[147]   [300]
Avaunt,° go pack thee hence in haste, dispatch out of my
    sight[148]
100   This infamy, whose blemish stains this blood of worthy
    wight.[149]

AEGISTHUS

This is no new exile to me that wickedness do haunt,
But if that thou, O worthy queen, command me to avaunt,
I will not only straight avoid the house, the town, and field:
My life on sword at thy request I ready am to yield.

CLYTEMNESTRA

This heinous deed permit shall I, most churlish cruel drab.°
Against my will though I offend, the fault I should not blab.[150]
Nay, rather come apart with me, and let us join our wits,
To wrap ourselves out of this woe and parlous° threatening fits.°

---

[145] 92] A reference to the reversal of the sun (Phoebus) after Thyestes' feast; 'ye'
refers generally, not to Aegisthus alone.

[146] 95–96] An allusion to the adultery between Aegisthus's father Thyestes and
Aerope, Atreus' wife. In 95–98, Clytemnestra characterizes Aegisthus as his
father's pupil in adultery, an idea absent in S.

[147] 97–98] S. has a different point: Clytemnestra says that adultery is the only
piece of (perverse) evidence Aegisthus gives of being a man.

[148] Possibly echoed in Macbeth's 'Avaunt, and quit my sight!' (*Macbeth* 3.4.94).
See also n. at 1.Cho.6.

[149] this blood] S. 'nostrae domus' (our house). Studley also omits Clytemnestra's
following declaration in S.: 'This house lies open for its king and husband'.

[150] 106] Different in S.: 'She who does wrong in collaboration with another owes
some loyalty to guilt'.

CHORUS

Now chant it lusty lads; Apollo's praise suborn.°[151]

[To Apollo]

To thee the frolic flock their crownèd heads adorn.
To thee, King Inachus' stock of wedlock chamber void[152]
Braid out their virgins' locks and thereon have employed
Their favourite garlands green – it [wift]° of laurel bough.
Draw near with us O Thebes, our dancing follow thou.[153]
Come also ye that drink of Ismen bubbling flood,[154]
Whereas the laurel tree full thick on banks doth bide;°
Eke ye whom Mando mild,[155] the prophetess divine,
10 Foreseeing fate and born of high Teiresias' line,
Hath stirred to celebrate with sacred use and rite
Apollo and Diane, born of Latona bright.

O victor Phoebe, unbend thy nockèd° bow again,[156]
Sith quietness and peace anew we do retain.[157]
And let thy twangling° harp make melody so shrill,
While that thy nimble hand strike quavers° with thy quill.°
No curious descant I nor lusty music crave,
No jolly rumbling note, nor trolling° tune to have.
But on thy treble Lute (according to thy use)
20 Strike up a plainsong note, as when thy learnèd muse
Thy lessons do record, though yet on baser string
It liketh thee to play the song that thou did sing[158]

---

[151] The Chorus anticipates the news of the Greek victory over Troy with a hymn to Apollo, then Juno, Pallas Athena, Diana, and Jupiter.

[152] King Inachus' stock of wedlock chamber void] i.e. 'unmarried women of Argos'.

[153] Thebes] Editors question the reading, since Thebes is invoked separately below (7–10); Fitch (in *Seneca: Tragedies*) corrects to 'Parrhasians' (residents of Arcadia). Studley also omits two following phrases summoning residents of southern Greece and Sparta (S. *Aga.* 316).

[154] that drink of Ismen bubbling flood] i.e. who drink from the river Ismenos in Thebes.

[155] Mando] i.e. Manto, daughter of the Theban prophet Teiresias; she warned Thebes to honour the children of Latona.

[156] Phoebe] i.e. Phoebus Apollo, god of prophecy, archery, music; see also n. on 1.2.38.

[157] Studley omits two further lines urging Apollo to put aside his quiver and arrows.

As when from fiery heaven the dint of lightning flew,[159]
Sent down by wrath of gods, the Titans overthrew;
Or else when mountains were on mountains heapèd high
That raise for giants fell their steps into the sky,
The mountain Ossa stood on top of Pelion laid,
Olymp (whereon the pines their budding branches braid)
Down peisèd both.

                Draw near, O Juno, noble dame,
30   Both spouse of mighty Jove and sister to the same,
Thou that dost rule with him, made jointer° of his mace;
Thy people we of Greece give honour to thy grace.
Thou only dost protect from perils Argos land
That ever careful was to have thine honour stand
(Most suppliant thereunto). Thou also with thy might
Dost order joyful peace and battles fierce of fight.
Accept, O conquering queen, these branches of the bays
That Agamemnon here doth yield unto thy praise.
The hollow boxen° pipe (that doth with holes abound)
40   In singing unto thee doth give a solemn sound.
To thee the damsels eke that play upon the strings
With cunning harmony melodious music sings.   [350]
The matrons eke of Greece by riper years more grave
To thee the taper pay that vowèd oft they have.[160]
The heifer young and white, companion of the bull,
Unskilful yet by proof° the painful plow to pull,
Whose neck was never worn, nor galled with print of yoke,
Is in thy temple slain, receiving deadly stroke.

O lady Pallas, thou of most renownèd hap,
50   Bred of the brain of Jove that smites with thunder clap,[161]
Thou lofty Trojan towers of craggy, knotty flint,
Hast beat with battering blade, and stroke with javelin dint.[162]

---

[158] 19–22] Unclear. In S., the Chorus invites Apollo to play as he chooses, whether on a lighter note or a heavier, plaintive note.

[159] 23–29] Apollo is invited to celebrate the epic stories of the Olympian gods' victories against the Titans (in the Titanomachy) and the Giants (the Gigantomachy).

[160] To thee the taper pay] A reference to the practice of throwing small lamps as votives to a deity.

[161] Bred of the brain of Jove] Pallas Athena was born from Zeus's head; a characteristic learned addition by Studley.

The elder matrons with the dames that younger be
Together in mingled heaps do honour due to thee.
When thou approaching nigh, thy coming is espied,
The priest unbars the gate and opes° the temple wide.
By clustering throngs the flocks thine altars haunt apace,
Bedecked with twisted crowns so trim with comely grace.
The old and ancient men, well stepped and grown in years,
60   Whose feeble, trembling age procureth hoary hairs,
Obtaining their request craved of thy grace divine,
Do offer up to thee their sacrificèd wine.

O bright Diane,[163] whose blaze sheds light three sundry ways,
We mindful are of thee and render thankful praise.
Delon, thy native soil, thou didest firmly bind
That to and fro was wont° to wander with the wind,[164]
Which with foundation sure main ground forbids to pass:
For navies (after which to swim it wonted was),
It is become a road,[165] defying force of wind.
70   The mother's funerals of Tantalus his kind,[166]
The daughters seven by death, thou victress dost accompt,°
Whose mother Niobe abides on Sipyl mount,
A lamentable rock, and yet unto this hour,
Her tears new gushing out the marble old doth pour.
The godhead of the twins in sumptuous solemnwise,[167]
Both man and wife adore with savoury sacrifice.

---

[162] 51–52 Thou lofty Trojan towers [...] hast beat] Pallas Athena was instrumental in the Greek victory at Troy.

[163] Diane] A simplification: in S., the Chorus invokes 'Trivia', the three-natured goddess (cf. 'three sundry ways') manifested in the sky (moon), on earth (Diana), and in the underworld (Hecate), and also as 'Lucina'.

[164] 65–66] 'Delon' is Delos, the island where Latona gave birth to Diana and Apollo, twins fathered by Zeus. In order to protect Latona from the wrath of Zeus's wife, Hera, the sea-god Poseidon raised the island out of the sea, where it was 'wont to wander' until Diana (or Apollo) made it stand still.

[165] It is become a road] Obscure. S. 'religatque rates' ([the island] fastens ships), whereas previously it drifted around.

[166] 70–74] Niobe, daughter of Tantalus, boasted to Latona about her many children; Latona appealed to the gods for revenge. All of Niobe's children were killed, and Niobe was turned into a rock on Mt Sipylus. S. includes the detail that Diana counts ('numeras', Studley 'accompt') Niobe's children's deaths ('funera', Studley 'funerals'). Studley adds Niobe's name and the number of the daughters.

[167] the twins] i.e. Apollo and Diana.

But thee above the rest, O father great and guide,
Whose mighty force is by the burning lightning tried,
Who when thou gav'st a beck and did'st thy head but shake,
80   At once th'extremest poles of heaven and earth did quake.
O Jupiter, the root that of our lineage art,[168]
Accept these offered gifts and take them in good part.
And thou, O grandsire great, to thy posterity
Have some remorse, that do not swerve in chivalry.[169]

But yonder lo, with striving steps the soldier comes amain°
In all post-haste, with token that good news declareth plain.
A laurel branch that hangeth on his spearhead he doth bring.
Eurybates is come, who hath been trusty to the king.

THE THIRD ACT

EURYBATES CLYTEMNESTRA

[EURYBATES]

Sore tired after many years with travail and with toil,
Scant crediting myself the gods of this my native soil,
The temple and the altars of the saints that rule the sky,[170]
In humble sort with reverence devoutly worship I.
Now pay your vows unto the gods. Returnèd is again[171]
Unto his country court, where wont he was to rule and reign,
Prince Agamemnon, victor he, of Greece the great renown.

CLYTEMNESTRA

The tidings of a message good unto mine ears is blown.
Where stays my spouse, whom longing for ten years I have out
scanned?°
10   What doth he yet sail on the seas, or is he come aland?
Yet hath he fixed and set his foot back stepping home again   [400]
Upon the sandy shore that long he wishèd to attain?

---

[168] root that of our lineage art] Jupiter is Agamemnon's great-great-grandfather.

[169] 83–84] i.e. 'be mindful of your posterity that maintains its nobility'.

[170] the saints that rule the sky] A Christian-sounding expansion of 'caelitum' (the celestial gods).

[171] pay your vows] i.e. make good on the sacrifices you promised for their safe return.

And doth he still enjoy his health, enhanced in glory great,
And painted out in pomp of praise whose fame the sky doth
    beat?[172]

EURYBATES

Bless we with burning sacrifice at length this lucky day.

CLYTEMNESTRA

And eke the gods, though gracious, yet dealing long delay.
Declare if that my brother's wife enjoy the vital air,[173]
And tell me to what kind of coast my sister doth repair.[174]

EURYBATES

God grant and give us better news than this that thou dost crave.
20   The heavy hap of fighting floods forbids the truth to have.
Our scattered fleet the swelling seas attempts in such a plight,
That ship from ship was taken clean out of each other's sight.
Atrides in the waters wide turmoiled and straying far,
More violence by seas sustained than by the bloody war,
And as it were a conquered man escaping home all wet,
Now bringeth in his company of such a mighty fleet,
A sort of bruisèd, broken barks° beshaken,° torn, and rent.

CLYTEMNESTRA

Show what unlucky chance it is that hath our navy spent:
What storm of seas dispersèd hath our captains here and there?

EURYBATES

30   Thou willest me to make report of heavy, woeful gear.°
Thou biddest me most grievous news with tidings good to part,°
For uttering of this woeful hap, my feeble mind doth start,
And horribly appallèd is with this so monstrous ill.

CLYTEMNESTRA

Speak out and utter it. Himself with terror he doth fill,

---

[172] whose fame the sky doth beat] i.e. whose fame is so great it bumps the sky.
[173] my brother's wife] A mistranslation of S. 'coniugis frater mei' (my husband's brother), i.e. Menelaus.
[174] my sister] i.e. Helen.

Whose heart his own calamity and cark° doth loathe to know.
The heart whom doubted damage dulls with greater grief doth
    glow.[175]

EURYBATES

When Trojan buildings blazing bright did burn away and broil,
Enkindled first by Greekish brand, they fall to part the spoil.
Repairing fast unto the seas, again we come aboard,[176]
40   And now the soldier's weary loins were easèd of his sword.
Their bucklers cast aside upon the hatches lie above,
Their warlike hands in practice put and oars learn to move.[177]
Each little hindrance seems too much to them in hasty plight.
When of recourse the admiral gave watchword by his light,[178]
And trumpet blast began to call our army from delay,
The painted poop with gilded snout did first guide on the way,
And cut the course, which following on a thousand ships did
    rive.°

Then first a wind with pipling° puffs our lancing ships did drive,
Which glided down upon our sails, the water being calm,
50   With breath of western wind so mild scant movèd any walm.
The shining seas bespread about with ships doth glister° bright,
And also covered with the same lay hid fro Phoebus' light.
It doth us good to gaze upon the naked shore of Troy,
The desert Phrygian plots so bare to view we hop for joy.
The youth each one bestirs themselves and striking altogether
They tough their oars, and with their toil, they help the wind and
    weather.
They tug and cheerly row by course; the spurting seas updash
Against the rattling ribs of ships, the flapping floods do flash;
The hoary froth of wrestling waves, which oars aloft doth raise,
60   Do draw and trace a furrow through the marble-facèd seas.

When stronger blast with belly swollen our hoisted sails did fill,
They row no more but let the poop to go with wind at will.

---

[175] 36] S. 'dubia plus torquent mala' (doubtful evils torture more).

[176] we] S. 'they' (petunt); Studley may seek to convey Eurybates' point of view.

[177] oars] Disyllabic here and often (like 'prayer'). See further pp. 289–90.

[178] of recourse [...] watchword] S. 'signum recursus' (the signal for the return voyage).

Their shearing oars laid aside, our pilot doth espy
How far from any land aloof our sails recoiling fly,
Or bloody battles doth display, the threats of Hector stout;
Or of his rattling wagons tells, wherein he rode about;
Or how his gashèd carcass slain and trained about the field
To funeral flames and obit° rites for coin again was yield;
How Jupiter embathèd was all in his royal blood.[179]
70   The frolic fish disposèd was to mirth in Tyrrhene flood,[180]
And fetching frisks both in and out, plays on the water's brim,   [450]
And on his broad and finny back about the seas doth swim,
With gambols° quick in rings around and side to side inclined.
Erewhile he sports afront the poop and whips again behind,
Now sidling on the snout before the dallying, wanton rout,
With jocundary,° jolly tricks doth skip the fleet about.
Sometime he standeth gazing on and eyes the vessels bright.

Now every shore is covered clean and land is out of sight.[181]
The parlous point of Ida rock in sight doth open lie,
80   And that alone espy we could with firmly fixèd eye.
A dusky cloud of stifling smoke from Troy did smoulder black,
When Titan from the weary necks the heavy yokes did slack.[182]
The fading light did grovelling bend and down the day did
    shroud.
Against the stars amounting up a little misty cloud
Came belching out in irksome lump, and Phoebus' gallant
    beams
He spewed upon, bestaining them ducked down in western
    streams.
The sunset swerving in such sort with diverse change of face
Did give us cause to have mistrust of Neptune's doubted grace.
The evening first did burnish bright and paint with stars the sky,
90   The winds were laid and clean forsook our sails that quiet lie,

---

[179] his royal blood] i.e. the blood of Priam, killed at Jupiter's altar.

[180] frolic fish] i.e. dolphins. Studley perhaps imitates Golding's Ovid 3.864–65 (cf. Taylor, 'Echoes', p. 187). See also n. at 120 below. Tyrrhene flood] Refers to the sea west of Italy; but in S., 'Tyrrhenian' is simply a traditional epithet for the dolphins (alluding to a mythological origin in the Tyrrhenian sea), rather than a reference to the fleet's location.

[181] is covered clean] i.e. is concealed by the rising horizon of the water as they move farther away.

[182] Titan] i.e. the sun.

When cracking, rattling, rumbling noise rushed down with
    thundering sway
From top of hills, which greater stir doth threaten and bewray.
With bellowings and yellings loud, the shores do grunt and
    groan.
The craggy cliffs and roaring rocks do howl in hollow stone.
The bubbling [water] swells upreared before the wrestling wind,
When suddenly the lowering light of moon is hid and blind.
The glimpsing stars do go to glade, the surging seas are tossed[183]
Even to the skies; among the clouds the light of heaven is lost.
More nights in one compacted are, with shadow dim and black,
100   One shade upon another doth more darkness heap and pack,
And every spark of light consumed, the waves and skies do
    meet.

The ruffling winds range on the seas, through every coast they
    flit.
They heave it up with violence, overturned from bottom low.
The western wind flat in the face of eastern wind doth blow;
With hurly-burly Boreas set ope his blasting mouth,[184]
And girdeth° out his boisterous breath against the stormy south.
Each wind with all his might doth blow, and worketh dangers
    deep.
They shake the floods; a sturdy blast along the seas doth sweep,
That rolls and tumbles wave on wave; a northern tempest strong,
110   Abundance great of flaky snow, doth hurl our ships among.
The south wind out of Lybia doth rage upon a shoal,
And with the puissant force thereof, the quick sands up be rolled.
Nor bideth in the south, which doth with tempest lump and lour,°
And force the flowing floods to rise by pouring out a shower;
The stubborn Eurus earthquakes made and shook the country's
    east,
And Eos' coast, where Phoebus first ariseth from his rest.
How violent Corus stretched and tore his yawning mouth full
    wide?[185]
A man would sure have thought the world did from his center
    slide,

---

[183] go to glade] i.e. set.

[184] With hurly burly] i.e. in a confused commotion.

[185] How violent Corus [...] tore] i.e. '(Why mention) how violent Corus [...] tore?'.

And that, the frames of heaven broke up, the gods adown would fall,

120 And Chaos' dark, confusèd heap would shade and cover all.[186]

The stream strove with the wind, the wind did beat it back again;
The springing sea within his banks cannot itself contain.
The raging shower his trilling° drops doth mingle with the seas,
And yet in all this misery, they find not so much ease,
To see and know what ill it is that worketh their decay.
The darkness dim oppresseth still and keeps the light away.
The black-faced night with hellish hue was clad of Stygian lake,
And yet full oft with glimpsing beams the sparkling fire outbreak.
The cloud doth crack, and being rent, the lightning leapeth out.
130 The wretches like the same, so well it shining them about,
That still they wish such light to have (although god wot but ill).[187]
The navy swaying down itself doth cast away and spill.
One side with other side is cracked and helm is rent with helm,
The ship itself the gulping seas do headlong overwhelm.[188]
Erewhile a greedy, gaping gulf doth sup it up amain,
Then by and by tossed up aloft, it spews it out again.   [500]
She with her swagging° full of sea to bottom low doth sink,
And drencheth deep aside in floods her tottering broken brink,
That underneath a dozen waves lay drownèd out of sight;[189]
140 Her broken planks swim up and down, spoiled is her tackle quite.
Both sail and oars clean are lost, the main mast eke is gone
That wonted was to bear upright the sailyard thereupon;
The timber and the broken boards lie on the water's brim.
When cold and shivering fear in us doth strike through every limb,
The wisest wits intoxicate° dare nothing enterprise,
And cunning practice nought avails when fearful storms arise.

---

[186] dark, confusèd heap] Golding may influence this phrase (cf. Taylor, 'Echoes', p. 187).

[187] although god wot but ill] i.e. even though the light comes from a destructive source (the lightning).

[188] 134–43] Studley describes a single ship; S. moves from one ship to another.

[189] a dozen waves] In S. 'tenth wave' (fluctus [...] decimus) refers to a rogue wave.

The mariners letting duty slip stand staring all aghast.
Their scooping oars suddenly out of their hands are wrast.[190]
To prayer then apace we fall, when other hope is none;
150   The Greeks and Trojans to the gods alike do make their
        moan:[191]
'Alack what succour of the fates may we poor wretches find?'
Against his father Pyrrhus bears a spiteful, cankered mind,
At Ajax grudge Ulysses doth, king Menela doth hate
Great Hector; Agamemnon is with Priam at debate.[192]
'O happy man is he that doth lie slain in Trojan ground,
And hath deserved by handy stroke to take his fatal wound,
Whom fame preserveth, taking up his tomb in conquered land.
Those momes,° whose melting, coward's heart durst never take
        in hand,[193]
Or enterprise no noble act, those force of floods shall drown,
160   But fate forbearing long will take stout brutes of high renown.
Full well we may ashamèd be in such a sort to die.
If any man his spiteful mind yet cannot satisfy,
With these outrageous plunging plagues that down from gods
        are sent,
Appease at length thy wrathful god again and eke relent.
Even Troy for pity would have wept to see our woeful case.
But if that in thy boiling breast black rancour still have place,
And that the Greeks to ruin run, it be thy purpose bent,
Why do these Trojans go to wrack? For whom thus are we
        spent?
Assuage the rigor of the sea that threatening hills uprears.
170   This drenchèd fleet the Trojan folk and Greeks together bears.'

---

[190] wrast] i.e. 'wrested', as at 3.2.33 and 4.Cho.36.

[191] Greeks and Trojans [...] alike] A reminder that the ships contain Greek warriors and Trojan captives.

[192] 152–54] Studley portrays Pyrrhus and others with surprising negativity. In S. the idea is that Pyrrhus, Ulysses, Menelaus, and Agamemnon envy those who have died at Troy (Achilles, Ajax [son of Telamon], Hector, and Priam), which leads to the generalization about the 'happy man' who is 'slain in Trojan ground' at 155–57.

[193] 158–70] In S., the sailors bitterly contrast two types of seafarer (traders, who do nothing noble yet are spared, and the returning Greek warriors, who are about to be drowned); they then appeal to 'whoever you are of the gods' to stop harassing them with storms. Studley makes a different (and obscure) point, in which cowards deservingly drown, and 'spiteful' people (162) are criticized for watching and for imagining that the storm is a fitting punishment of the Greeks.

Then from their prayers are they put, their faltering tongues do
    stay,
The roaring seas doth drown their voice and carries their cries
    away.[194]

Then mighty Pallas, armèd with the leaping lightning fire
That testy Jove doth use to hurl provoked to swelling ire,
With threatening javelin in her hand her prowess means to try,
And eke her force, whose boiling breast with gorgon fits doth
    fry,[195]
Or what with target she can do and with her father's fire.
Then from the skies another storm begins abroad to spire.
But Ajax nothing yet dismayed all force withstandeth stout,[196]

180   Whom when he spread his swelling sails with cable stretchèd out,
She lighting down did wring him hard and wrapped him in her
    flame,
And flung another flashing dint of lightning on the same;
With all her force and violence, her hand brought back again,
She tossed him out as late that feat her father taught her plain.
Both over Ajax and his poop she flyeth overthwart,°
And renting man and ship of both, she bears away a part.
His courage nought abated yet he all too singed doth seem,
Even like a stubborn, ragged rock amid the striving stream.
He trains along the roaring seas and eke the waltering wave,

190   By shoving on his burly breast, in sunder quite he drave.[197]
The bark with hand he caught and on itself did tip it over,
Yet Ajax shineth in the flood, which darkness blind doth cover.
At length attaining to a rock, his thundering crakes° were these:
'I conquered have the force of fire and rage of fighting seas.
It doth me good to master thus the anger of the sky,
With Pallas' wrath, the lightning flames and floods tumulting
    high.
The terror of the warlike god once could not make me fly,
The force of Mars and Hector both at once sustained have I,
Nor Phoebus' darts could me constrain from him one foot to
    shun:

---

[194] carries] monosyllabic.
[195] 176] Studley partly conveys a reference to Pallas Athena's aegis, i.e. her
goatskin cape (or, in some accounts, shield) with a Medusa's head in the centre.
[196] Ajax] i.e. Ajax the Lesser, son of Oileus.
[197] drave] Archaic inflection of 'drove'.

200   All these beside the Phrygians subdued we have and won.   [550]
When other meacocks° flings his darts, shall I not them
    withstand?
Yea, what if Phoebus came himself to pitch them with his
    hand?'[198]
When in his melancholy mood he boasted without mean,
Then father Neptune lift his head above the waters clean.
The beaten rock with forkèd mace he undermining plucked
From bottom loose and sunk it down, when down himself he
    ducked.
There Ajax lay by land, by fire, and storm of seas destroyed.

But we by suffering shipwreck are with greater plagues annoyed.
A subtle, shallow flood there is, flown on a stony shoal,
210   Where crafty Caphar out of sight the lurking rocks doth hold,[199]
Upon whose sharp and ragged tops the swelling tide doth flow;
The boiling waves do beat thereon still swaying to and fro.
A turret nodding over it doth hang with falling sway,
From whence on either side from height prospect espy we may
Two seas, and on this hand the coast where Pelops once did
    reign,[200]
And Isthmus flood in narrow creek, recoiling back again,
Doth stop Ionian Sea, lest in to Hellespont it run,[201]
On th'other part is Lemnon flood that fame by bloodshed won.[202]
On th'other side Calcedon town doth stand against this fort,
220   And Aulis isle that stayed our ships that thither did resort.[203]
This castle here inhabit doth our Palamedes' sire,
Whose cursèd hand held in the top a brand of flaming fire

---

[198] if Phoebus came himself] In S., the allusion is to Jupiter, 'the owner himself'
(ipse) of the lightning bolts.

[199] Caphar] i.e. Caphereus, the cape at the south-east tip of the Greek island of
Euboea. Here Nauplius, in revenge for the death of his son Palamedes, hangs a
light, luring the Greek fleet to its destruction (recounted at 221–30).

[200] Pelops] Son of Tantalus; he gave his name to the Peloponnese, which is joined
to the Greek mainland by the Isthmus.

[201] Hellespont] Studley's adaptation of 'Phrixeis' (Phrixean: the Aegean sea).

[202] the same by bloodshed won] Women on the island of Lemnos murdered their
husbands.

[203] 219–20] For 'Calcedon' Studley follows his Latin source, but editors now read
a reference to Chalcis on the island of Euboea. Aulis is the port (not an 'isle')
facing Euboea from which the Greek fleet launched their ships for Troy.

That did allure our fleet to turn on lurking rocks aright,
Enticing them with wily blaze to come unto the light.
All into fitters° shaken are the vessels on the shoal,
But other some do swim and some upon the rocks are rolled.
And other slipping back again so to eschew the rocks,
His bruisèd ribs and rattling sides against each other knocks,
Whereby the other he doth break and broken is himself,
230   Then would they lance into the deep, for now they dread the
            shelf.
This peck of troubles chanced to hap in dawning of the day,
But when the gods besought of us began the rage to stay,
And Phoebus' golden beams began afresh to render light,
The doleful day descrièd all the damage done by night.

CLYTEMNESTRA

O whither may I now lament and weep with wailing sad,
Or shall I else in that my spouse returnèd is be glad?
I do rejoice and yet I am compellèd to bewail°
My country's great calamity that doth the same assail.
O father great, whose majesty doth thundering sceptres shake,
240   The louring gods unto the Greeks now favourable make,
With garlands green let every head rejoicing now be crowned.
To thee the pipe in sacrifice melodiously doth sound,
And on thine altar lieth slain an heifer lily white.
Before the same do present stand, with hanging locks undight,°
A careful Trojan company in heavy, woeful plight,[204]
On whom from high the laurel tree with spreading branch doth
            shine,
Whose virtue hath inspirèd them with Phoebus' grace divine.[205]

---

[204] Trojan company] Elides the gender of S. 'Iliades' (Trojan women).
[205] 246–47] Studley misses a reference to Cassandra, inspired by Phoebus Apollo
and waving laurel branches.

[The Second Scene][206]

CHORUS[207] CASSANDRA

[CHORUS]

Alas the cruel sting of love, how sweetly doth it taste,[208]
A misery to mortal man annexed while life doth last.
The path of mischief for to fly now sith there is a gap,[209]
And wretched souls be frankly called from every woeful hap[210]
By death, a pleasant port, for aye in rest themselves to shroud,
Where dreadful tumults never dwell nor storms of Fortune
    proud;
Nor yet the burning, fiery flakes of Jove the same doth doubt,
When wrongfully with thwacking thumps he raps his thunder
    out.

Here lady Peace th'inhabitors doth never put in flight,[211]
10   Nor yet the victor's threatening wrath approaching nigh to fight;
No whirling western wind doth urge the ramping seas to prance,
No dusty cloud that raisèd is by savage demi-lance,°
On horseback riding rank by rank, no fierce and cruel host,   [600]
No people slaughtered with their towns clean topsy turvy
    tossed,
While that the foe with flaming fire doth spoil and waste the
    wall:
Untamèd and unbridled Mars destroys and batters all.

---

[206] In S., a choral ode begins here, with Act 4 starting at 3.2.69 below. Studley combines the ode and the interaction into its own scene, likely because the Chorus of the ode remains in dialogue with Cassandra. S. uses lyric metre for the Chorus and Cassandra at the lines corresponding to 3.2.1–68, 74–106, 185–94 (= S. *Aga.* 589–659, 665–92, 761–74). Studley renders it all in fourteeners. He delays Act 4 until the entrance of Agamemnon (making for a very brief fourth act). See also Introduction pp. 14–15 and 53–54, and compare Heywood's view of *Troas* Act 1 as lacking a chorus, 'Preface to the Readers', lines 35–37.

[207] Chorus] Captive Trojan women. See n. at 'Company of Greeks' in 'The Speakers' above.

[208] the cruel sting of love] Likely a misinterpretation of S. 'vitae dirus amor' (cruel love of life): the Chorus will praise death as preferable to life's troubles.

[209] 3] S. 'cum pateat malis effugium' (since a way to flee from evils is open).

[210] frankly] Dilutes S. 'libera' (free), describing death as a liberator.

[211] 9] Obscure. S. 'pax alta nullos civium coetus timet' (the deep peace [of death] does not fear crowds of citizens), followed by the other threats listed in 10–16.

That man alone – who forceth° not the fickle fates a straw,
The visage grim of Acheront whose eyes yet never saw,
Who never viewed with heavy cheer the ugsome° Limbo
    lake,[212]
20   And putting life in hazard dare to death himself betake –
That person is a prince's peer and like the gods in might.
Who knoweth not what death doth mean is in a piteous plight.

The ruthful ruin of our native country we beheld
That woeful night in which the roofs of houses overquelled°
In Dardan's city blazing bright with flashing fiery flames,
When as the Greeks with burning brands enkindle did the
    frames,[213]
That Troy – whom war and deeds of arms might not subdue
    and take,[214]
As once did mighty Hercules, whose quiver caused it quake;
Which neither he that Peleus' son and son to Thetis was,[215]
30   Nor whom Achilles loved too well could ever bring to pass,[216]
When glittering bright in field he were, false armour on his
    back,
And counterfeiting fierce Achill the Trojans drove to wrack;
Nor when Achilles he himself his mind from sorrow wrast,
And Trojan women to the walls did scudding° leap in haste.[217]
In misery she lost her proud estate and last renown,
By being stoutly overcome and hardly pullèd down.[218]
Years five and five did Troy resist that yet hereafter must
In one night's space by destiny be layèd in the dust.

Their feignèd gifts well have we tried, that huge and fatal gin.°[219]
40   We light of credit with our own right hand have halèd in[220]

---

[212] 18–19] In S., the point is not that the man has never seen death, but that he looks on it 'non tristis' (without sadness).

[213] the Greeks] In S., 'you Greeks': the Chorus of Trojan women partly address their captors.

[214] might not subdue] i.e. were unable to, even after ten years of war.

[215] Peleus's son and son to Thetis] i.e. Achilles.

[216] Nor whom]: i.e. 'nor he whom'; refers to Patroclus, who wore Achilles' armour into battle (cf. 31–32) and was killed, causing Achilles' 'sorrow' (at 33).

[217] to the walls did scudding leap in haste] S. has a different meaning: 'the Trojan women on the high walls feared [Achilles] swift in leaping'.

[218] 35–36] In S., the point is that Troy was not 'stoutly overcome' (thereby earning renown), but was defeated by the deceit of the Trojan Horse, described below.

[219] that huge and fatal gin] The Trojan Horse.

That fatal gift of Greeks, what time at entry of the gap
The hugie horse did shivering stand, wherein themselves did
    wrap
The captains close in hollow vaults with bloody war yfreight.°
When lawfully we might have tried and searchèd their deceit,
So by their own contrivèd snares the Greeks had been confound,
The brazen bucklers being shook did give a clattering sound.
A privy whispering oftentimes came tickling in our ear,
And Pyrrhus (in a murrain's° name so ready for to hear[221]
The crafty counsel pickèd out of false Ulysses' brain)
50   Did jangle° in the hollow vaults that rang thereof again.
But fearing and suspecting nought, the heady youth of Troy
Laid hands upon the sacred ropes to hale° and pull with joy.
On this side young Astyanax came guarded with his train;[222]
On th'other part Polyxena despousèd° to be slain
Upon Achilles' tomb. She comes with maids and he with men,
A jolly flock with equal years as young as they were then.
Their vowed oblations to the gods in holiday attire
The matrons bring, and so to church repaireth every sire,[223]
And all the city did alike, yea Hecuba our queen
60   (That since the woeful Hector's death or now was never seen)
She merry is.

        O grief accursed of all thy sorrows deep,
For which that first, or last befell, intendest thou to weep?   [650]
Our battered walls, which heavenly hands erected have and
    framed?
Or else the burning temples which upon their idols flamed?
Lamenting these calamities we have not time and space,
O mighty parent Priam we poor Trojans wail thy case.
The old man's throttling° throat I saw, alas, I saw ybored
With cruel Pyrrhus' blade that scant with any blood was
    gored.[224]

---

[220] light of credit] S. 'creduli' (quick to trust).

[221] in a murrain's name] An exclamation, perhaps equivalent to 'a plague upon him' – Studley's translation of S. 'male' (badly). But in S., 'male' more likely characterizes Pyrrhus's reluctance in obeying Ulysses' commands.

[222] 53–54] An ironic description of Astyanax and Polyxena working to pull the Trojan Horse into Troy. Act 5 of *Troas* describes their unhappy fate.

[223] to church] S. 'ad aras' (to the altars).

[224] scant with any blood] i.e. due to Priam's old age.

255

CASSANDRA

> Refrain your tears that down your cheeks should trickle
>   evermore,[225]
> 70   With woeful wailings piteously your private friends deplore.[226]
> My miseries refuse a mate so much accursed as I.
> To rue my careful case refrain your lamentable cry,
> As for mine own distress to mourn I shall suffice alone.

CHORUS

> To mingle tears with other tears, it doth us good to moan.
> In those the burning teary streams more ardently do boil,
> Whom secret thoughts of lurking cares in privy breast
>   turmoil.[227]
> Though that thou were a gossip stout that brook much sorrow
>   may,[228]
> I warrant thee, thou mightest well lament this sore decay.[229]
>
> Not sad and solemn Aedon that in the woods doth sing[230]
> 80   Her sugared ditties finely tuned on sweet and pleasant string,
> Recording Itys' woeful hap in diverse kind of note,
> Whom Procne though he were her child and of her womb begot,
> For to revenge his father's fault, she did not spare to kill,
> And gave his flesh and blood for food the father's maw to fill;
> Nor Procne who in swallow's shape upon the ridges high
> Of houses sits in Biston town bewailing piteously,
> With chattering throat of Tereus her spouse the cruel act,
> Who did by strength and force of arms a shameful, brutish fact,

---

[225] See n. at 3.2 above.

[226] your private friends deplore] Obscure for S. 'ipsae vestra [...] lugete [...] funera' (mourn your own [imminent] deaths), i.e. 'as opposed to mine and the other Trojans'.

[227] After 76, Studley omits: 'It is helpful to weep publicly for one's own' (S. *Aga.* 666).

[228] a gossip stout] S. 'dura virago' (tough heroic woman).

[229] 78] A shift from S. 'nec tu [...] poteris tantas flere ruinas' (nor will you be able to mourn [i.e. sufficiently] such great ruin).

[230] 78–83] In S., 'aedon' is the common noun (nightingale), referring to the bird into which Philomela was transformed. In Thrace ('Biston town' at 86), Philomela had been raped by Tereus, the husband of her sister Procne, and in her nightingale form Philomela mourns Itys, Tereus and Procne's son, whom Procne had killed and served to Tereus to eat. Procne was turned into a swallow. Studley freely composes at 80, 82–84, and 88–90 to clarify the myth.

90 Defile the sister of his wife, fair Philomel by name,
And eke cut out her tongue, lest she should blab it to his shame;
Though Procne this her husband's rape lamenting very sore
Do wail and weep with piteous plaint, yet can she not deplore
Sufficiently, though that she would, our country's piteous
    plight.[231]

Though he himself among the swans sir Cygnus lily white,[232]
Who dwells in stream of Ister flood and Tanais channel could,
His weeping voice most earnestly though utter out he would;[233]
Although the mourning halcyons with doleful sighs do wail,
At such time as the fighting floods their Ceyx did assail,
Or rashly waxing bold attempt the seas now laid at rest,
100 Or being very fearful feed their brood in tottering nest;
Although as squeamish hearted men those priests in bedlam
    rage,[234]
Whom mother Cybele being born on high in lofty stage[235]
Doth move to play on shawms,° Attis the Phrygian to lament;
Yet cannot they this lot bewail though brawn from arms they
    rent.

Cassandra, in our tears there is no measure to refrain
Those miseries, all measure passed, that plungèd us in pain.[236]
The sacred fillets° from thy head, why dost thou hale and pull?
They chiefly ought to worship god, whose hearts with grief be
    dull.

CASSANDRA

My fear by this affliction is clean abated all,
110 Nor praying to the heavenly ghosts for mercy will I call.

---

[231] our country's piteous plight] S. 'tuam [...] domum' (your [i.e. Cassandra's] house).

[232] sir Cygnus] S. 'cycnus' (the swan); Studley elucidates the bird's connection with Cygnus, son of Sthenelus, whose grief for Phaethon changed him into a swan.

[233] his weeping voice] S. 'extrema' (his final voice), i.e. his 'swan song'.

[234] 101–03] The 'squeamish-hearted men' are the 'Galli', self-castrated followers of the goddess Cybele, whose lover is the Phrygian Attis; ostentatious music and self-mutilation in mourning for Attis were a regular part of their ritual.

[235] being born on high in lofty stage] Studley may misunderstand 'turritae [...] parenti' (turreted mother): Cybele wore a crown shaped like crenelated towers.

[236] 105–06] Perhaps echoed by Mary Sidney's *Antonius* (1592): 'In measure let them plain / Who measured griefs sustain' (2.Cho.390–91).

Although they were disposed to chafe and fret in fustian° fumes,
They nothing have me to displease.[237] Fortune her force
   consumes,
Her spite is worn unto the stumps. What country have I left?
Where is my sire? Am I of all my sisters quite bereft?
The sacred tombs and altar stones our blood have drunk and   [700]
   swilled.
Where are my brethren blessed knot? Destroyèd in the field.[238]

All widow wives of Priam's sons may easily now behold
The palace void and caste° of court of silly° Priam old.
And by so many marriages so many widows are,
120   But only Helen coming from the coast of Lacon far.
That Hecuba, the mother of so many a princely wight,
Whose fruitful womb did breed the brand of fire blazing
   bright,[239]
Who also bare the swinge° in Troy, by practice now doth learn
New laws and guise of destiny in bondage to discern.
On her she taketh heart of grace with looks so stern and wild,
And barketh as a bedlam bitch about her strangled child,
Dear Polydor, the remnant left, and only hope of Troy,
Hector and Priam to revenge and to restore her joy.[240]

CHORUS

The sacred Phoebus prophet is with sudden silence hushed,
130   A quaking, trembling, shivering fear throughout her limbs hath
   rushed.
Her face as pale as ashes is, her fillets stand upright,
The soft and gentle goldilocks start up of her affright.
Her panting, breathing breast stuffed up within doth grunt and
   groan,
Her glaring, bright, and steaming eyes are hither and thither
   thrown:

---

[237] They nothing have me to displease] S. 'nec [...] quo noceant habent' (they have no way they can harm me).

[238] my brethren blessed knot] S. 'illa felix turba fraterni gregis' (that fortunate crowd, my herd of brothers).

[239] the brand of fire] i.e. Paris. See n. at *Troas* 1.1.37–44.

[240] 126–28] A reference to Polydorus, the youngest child of Hecuba and Priam, sent for safekeeping to Thrace, where he was murdered. Studley clarifies, adding Polydor's name and his role as 'hope' and avenger who will 'restore [...] joy'.

Now glancing up and down they roll, now standing stiff they
    stare;
She stretcheth up her head more straight than commonly she
    bare.
Bolt up she goes, her wrestling jaws that fast together cling,
She doth attempt by diverse means asunder [now] to wring.
Her mumbling words in gabbling° mouth shut up she doth
    assuage,
140   As Maenads mad that Bacchus' airs doth serve in furious rage.

CASSANDRA

How doth it hap, O sacred tops of high Parnassus hill,
That me berapt° of sense with pricks of fury fresh ye fill?
Why do you me with ghost inspire that am beside my wits?
O Phoebus, none of thine I am. Release me from the fits.
Infixèd° in my burning breasts the flames extinguish out.
Who forceth me with fury fell to gad and trot about?
Or for whose sake inspired with sprite° mad mumbling make
    must I?
Why play I now the prophet cold, sith Troy in dust doth lie?²⁴¹
The day doth shrink for dread of war, the night doth dim mine
    eyes,
150   With mantle black of darkness deep clean covered is the skies.

But, lo two shining suns at once in heaven appeareth bright,
Two Grecian houses muster do their armies twain to fight.
Among the mighty goddesses in Ida woods I see
The fatal shepherd in his throne as umpire placed to be.²⁴²
I do advise you to beware, beware, I say, of kings,²⁴³
A kindred in whose cankered hearts old privy grudges springs:
That country clown, Aegisthus he, this stock shall overthrow.
What doth this foolish, desperate dame her naked weapons
    show?²⁴⁴

---

²⁴¹ the prophet cold] Bold translation of 'falsa vates' (false prophet). In 148,
Studley omits Cassandra's rhetorical 'Where am I?' (S. *Aga.* 726).
²⁴² fatal shepherd] Cassandra speaks with the ambiguity of prophecy, referring to
Aegisthus and Paris (the latter the 'umpire' in the Judgement of Paris). Both were
raised among herdsmen, both were adulterers, and both brought ruin on their
households.
²⁴³ Beware, I say, of kings] A striking reinterpretation or misconstrual: in S.,
Cassandra says *to* kings to beware *of* Aegisthus and his kindred.

160

Whose crown entendeth she to crack in weed° of Lacon land,
With hatchet by the Amazons invented first in hand?
What face of mighty majesty bewitchèd hath mine eyes?
The conqueror of savage beasts, Marmarick lion, lies,[245]
Whose noble neck is worrièd with currish fang and tooth;
The churlish snaps of eager lioness abide he doth.

[Seeing a vision of Hades]

170

180

Alack ye ghosts of all my friends, why should ye say that I
Among the rest am only safe from perils far to lie?[246]
Fain father follow thee I would, Troy being laid in dust.
O brother terror of the Greeks, O Trojan's aid and trust,[247]
Our ancient pomp I do not see, nor yet thy warmèd hands
That fierce on Greekish flaming fleet did fling the fiery
    brands,
But mangled members, scorchèd corpse and eke thy valiant
    arms,
Hard pinionèd and bound in bands, sustaining grievous harms.
O Troilus, a match unfit, encountering with Achill,
That mighty man of arms too soon, come unto thee I will.[248]
I do delight to sail with them on stinking Stygian flood.   [750]
To view the churlish mastiff cur of hell, it doth me good,[249]
And gaping-mouthèd kingdom dark of greedy Ditis' reign.
The barge of filthy Phlegethon this day shall entertain
Me conquering, and conquerèd, and princes' souls withal.
You flittering shades, I you beseech and eke on thee I call,
O Stygian pool (whereon the gods their solemn oaths do take)
Unbolt awhile the brazen bars of darksome Limbo lake,

---

[244] this foolish, desperate dame] i.e. Clytemnestra from Sparta ('Lacon land' in 159).
[245] Marmarick lion] i.e. hyena. Recent editors amend the Lat. to say that the lion ('conqueror of savage beasts': Agamemnon) is being bitten by the hyena (an ignoble, bi-sexual, scavenger, i.e. Aegisthus) and by the lioness (i.e. Clytemnestra) (cf. Hendry).
[246] 165–66 say that I [...] am only safe] S. 'me vocatis sospitem solam' (summon me [...] the sole survivor).
[247] 168 O brother] i.e. Hector.
[248] too soon] Troilus did not live to be twenty; it was prophesied that if he did, Troy would not fall. Studley omits the following lines in which Cassandra also addresses her deceased brother Deiphobus (S. *Aga.* 749–50).
[249] churlish mastiff] i.e. Cerberus.

Whereby the Phrygian folk in hell may Mycene state behold.
Look up ye silly, wretched souls, the fates are backward
    rolled.[250]

The squally° sisters do approach and deal their bloody
    strokes.[251]
Their smouldering faggots in their hands half burned to ashes
    smokes.
Their visages so pale do burn with fiery, flaming eyes.
A garment black their gnawèd guts doth gird in mourning
    guise.
Dire dread of night begins to howl, the bones of body vast,
190   With laying long do rot corrupt in miry puddle cast.
Behold, the weary agèd man, his burning thirst forgot,[252]
The waters dallying at his lips to catch endeavours not,
But mourneth for the funeral that shall ensue anon.
The Trojan prince his royal robes triumphant putteth on.[253]

CHORUS

The furious rage clean overpassed begins itself to slake,
And slips away, even as a bull that deadly wound doth take
On gashèd neck affront the ears.[254] Come let us ease at last
Her limbs that of the sprite of god hath felt the mighty blast.

Returning home again at length and crowned with laurel bough
200   (A sign of worthy victory) is Agamemnon now.
The wife to meet her husband doth her speedy passage ply,
Returning hand in hand, and foot by foot, most lovingly.

---

[250] the fates are backward rolled] i.e. the Trojans will get to see Greeks suffering a fate like their own.

[251] 185–94] In S., these lines are in lyric metre, as Cassandra sees the Furies ('squally sisters').

[252] the weary, agèd man] i.e. Tantalus, now in the underworld, who loses his characteristic thirst as he grieves for his grandson's imminent death.

[253] The Trojan prince] S. gives his name: Dardanus, ancestor of the Trojan royal household and counterpart to Tantalus.

[254] affront the ears] i.e. 'in front of the ears'.

THE FOURTH ACT[255]

AGAMEMNON   CASSANDRA   [SOLDIERS]

[AGAMEMNON]

[Aside]

At length I do arrive again upon my native soil.
God save thee, O dear lovèd land: to thee so huge a spoil
So many barbarous people yield. The flower of Asia, Troy,[256]
To bear thy yoke submits herself that long did live in joy.

Why doth this prophet on the ground her sprawling body laid
Thus reel and stagger on her neck, all trembling and dismayed?

[To soldiers]

Sirs,[257] take her up, with liquor warm let her be cherishèd.
Now peeps she up again, with drooping eyes sunk in her head.

[To Cassandra]

Pluck up thy sprite, here is the port, wished for in misery.
10   This day is festival.

CASSANDRA

                  At Troy so was it wont to be.

AGAMEMNON

Let us to th'altars worship give.

CASSANDRA

                  At th'altars died my sire.[258]

AGAMEMNON

Pray we to Jove.

CASSANDRA

                  To Jove whose grace divine doth me inspire?[259]

---

[255] See n. at 3.2 above.
[256] The flower of Asia] Echoes Heywood's *Troas* 1.1.9 and 4.Cho.3.
[257] Sirs] S. 'famuli' (servants).
[258] See n. at 3.1.65–69.

AGAMEMNON

Dost thou suppose that Troy you see'st?

CASSANDRA

And Priam eke I see.

AGAMEMNON

Troy is not here.

CASSANDRA

Where Helen is, there take I Troy to be.[260]

AGAMEMNON

Fear not as maid to serve thy dame.[261]

CASSANDRA

Nay, freedom draweth nigh.

AGAMEMNON

Take thou no thought how you shalt live.

CASSANDRA

All cares for to defy,
Death gives a courage unto me.

AGAMEMNON

Yet say I once again:
There is no danger left, whereby thou mightest hurt sustain.

CASSANDRA

But yet much troublous danger doth hang over thy head I wot.

AGAMEMNON

20   What mischief may a victor dread?

---

[259] 12] S. 'Herceum Iovem' (Jove of the Household), alluding to the god at whose altar Priam was slain; Studley instead makes Jove the god who inspires Cassandra's prophecies (usually Apollo).
[260] Helen] i.e. Clytemnestra, a 'Helen', being Helen's sister and also an adulteress.
[261] thy dame] i.e. Clytemnestra, to whom Cassandra is now to be a servant.

CASSANDRA

Even that he dreadeth not.

AGAMEMNON

Ye trusty many of my men, come carry her away   [800]
Till of the sprite she rid herself, lest fury force her say
That may be prejudicial. Her tongue she cannot frame.

[Praying]

To thee, O Father, flinging forth the lightning's flashing flame
That dost disperse the clouds and rule the course of every star,
And guide the globe of earth, to whom the booties won by war
With triumph victors dedicate. To thee, O Juno hight,
The sister dear of doughty Jove (thy husband full of might),
Both I and Greece with flesh and blood and eke our vowèd
    beast
30   And gorgeous gifts of Araby give worship to thy hest.[262]

CHORUS

O Greece by noble gentlemen in honour shining clear,[263]
O Greece to wrathful Juno thou that art the darling dear,
Some jolly, worthy, lusty blood thou fosters evermore,
Thou hast made even the gods that were a number odd before.[264]
That puissant, mighty Hercules, a noble imp of thine,[265]
Deservèd by his travails twelve rapt° up in heaven to shine,
For whom the heavens did alter course and Jupiter withal
Did iterate the hours of night when dampish dew doth fall,
And chargèd Phoebus' chariot swift to trot with slower pace,
10   And leisurely bright lady moon thy homeward wain° to trace.
Bright Lucifer, that year by year his name anew doth change,
Came back again to whom the name of Hesper seemèd strange.[266]

---

[262] gorgeous gifts of Araby] i.e. incense.

[263] Greece] S. 'Argos', the city ruled by the Tantalids.

[264] Thou has made even] i.e. by making Hercules into a god.

[265] imp of thine] Hercules was an Argive through his mother Alcmene. His father was Jupiter, and he was conceived during a night that was twice its normal length (7–10).

[266] 11–12] The Latin text is missing some words, but as Studley conveys, Jupiter's deferral of the morning meant that the planet (Venus) known alternatingly as Lucifer ('morning star') and Hesper ('evening star') was surprised to find itself

Aurora to her common course her rearèd head addressed,
And couching backward down again the same she did arrest,
Upon the shoulder of her spouse, whose years with age are worn.[267]
The east did feel, so felt the west, that Hercules was born.
Dame Nature could not clean dispatch to utter° in one night
That boisterous lad. The whirling world did wait for such a wight.

O babe, whose shoulders underprop the ample, spacious sky,[268]
20   In claspèd arms thy prowess did the crushèd lion try,
Who from his fiery, yawning throat spews out his broiling brand.
The nimble hind in Maenal mount hath known thy heavy hand.[269]
The bore hath felt thy fist, which did Arcadia destroy.
The monstrous conquered bull hath roared that Creta did annoy.[270]
The dragon dire, that breeding beast, in Lerna pool he slew,
And chopping off one head forbad thereof to rise anew.
With clubbèd, bruising, battering bat, he cranckly did subdue
The brethren twins that tewd° on teat, whereof three monsters
         grew;[271]
Of triple-formèd Geryon, the spoil into the east,
30   A drove of cattle Hercules did fetch out of the west.
Away from tyrant Diomed the Thracian horse he led,
Which neither with the grass that grew by Strymon flood he fed,
Nor yet on Heber banks, but them the villain did refresh[272]
His greedy, munching, cramming jades° with aliens' blood and
         flesh;[273]

---

greeted as Hesper, at the time when it would normally have been morning.
Studley's 'year to year' is misleading: the name alternated daily .

[267] her spouse] i.e. Tithonus, for whom Aurora had secured eternal life but had
forgotten to request eternal youth.

[268] 19–52] A list of Hercules' labours: the Nemean lion (20–21), the Arcadian
hind (22), the Erymanthian boar (23), the Cretan Bull (24), the Lernaean hydra
(25–26), the cattle of Geryon (27–30), the man-eating horses of Diomedes (31–
35), the girdle of the Amazon, Hippolyte (36), the Stymphalian birds (37–38), the
apples of the Hesperides (39–45), and Cerberus (46–48). The list concludes with
Hercules' expedition against Troy (49–52; see n. at 49 below) and excludes
another labour, the Augean Stables.

[269] nimble hind in Maenal mount] i.e. the Aracadian hind; Studley adds 'Maenal',
from Maenalus, an Arcadian mountain range.

[270] Creta] i.e. Crete.

[271] 28] S. 'geminosque fratres pectore ex uno tria monstra natos' (the twin [i.e.
triplet] brothers born as three monsters [projecting] from a single breast); Studley
imagines a maternal breast (cf. 'tewd on teat'); S. likely refers to Geryon (cf. 29).

[272] Heber] i.e. the river Hebrus.

Their raw-fed jaws imbrued were with the carman's° blood at
    last.
The spoils and shafts Hippolyte saw from her bosom wrast.
As soon as he with clattering shaft the dusky cloud did smite,   [850]
The Stymphal bird that shadowèd the sun did take her flight.
The fertile tree that apples bears of gold did fear him sore,
40   Which never yet acquaintance had with taster's tooth before,
But whipping up with lively twigs into the air she flies;
And while the chinking plate doth sound,[274] then Argos full of
    eyes,[275]
The watchman shrinking close for cold that sleep yet never knew,
Doth hear the noise while Hercules with metal of yellow hue
Well-laden packs away, and left the grove befilchèd clean.
The hound of hell did hold his tongue, drawn up in triple chain,
Nor barked with any boughing° throat, nor could abide the hue,
Or colour of the heavenly light, whose beams he never knew.
– When thou wert captain general and did'st conduct our host,[276]
50   They that of Dardan's line to come their stock do falsely boast,
Were vanquishèd by force of arms, and since they felt again
Thy grey goose wing, whose bitterness to fear might them
    constrain.[277]

THE FIFTH ACT

CASSANDRA

Within a revel-rex° is kept as sore as ever was
Even at the ten years' siege of Troy. What thing is this? Alas,[278]

---

[273] aliens'] i.e. guests'.

[274] while the chinking plate doth sound] i.e. when the golden apples jangled.

[275] Argos full of eyes] A misidentification: S. mentions only a 'custos nescius somni' (unsleeping guardian), an allusion to the serpent Ladon who guarded the apples; Studley inserts Argos, the hundred-eyed guardian of the cow-nymph Io.

[276] 49–52] When Laomedon, a descendant 'of Dardan's line', was king of Troy, he asked Hercules for aid in killing a sea monster. Laomedon 'falsely boast[ed]', since he refused to give Hercules his promised reward for killing the monster, whereupon Hercules gathered an army and attacked Troy (which was thus 'vanquishèd by force of arms'). Troy 'felt again' the arrows of Hercules when his bow was wielded by Philoctetes against Troy.

[277] grey goose wing] i.e. the arrows of Hercules. Studley omits the ode's final two lines: 'Once you were in charge, Troy fell in as many days as the years (for which it had held out against the Greek siege)' (S. *Aga.* 865–66).

266

Get up, my soul, and of the rage avengement worthy crave;
Though Phrygians we be vanquishèd, the victory we have.
The matter well is brought about. Up Troy, thou risest now,
Thou flat on floor hast pulled down Greece to lie as low as thou.
Thy conqueror doth turn his face. My prophesying sprite
Did never yet disclose to me so notable a sight.
I see the same and am thereat, and busied in the broil,
No vision fond fantastical my senses doth beguile:
Such fare as Phrygians feasted with on last unhappy night,[279]
At Agamemnon's royal court full daintily they dight.°
With purple hangings all adorned, the broided° beds do shine.
In old Assarac's goblets gilt, they swinck and swill the wine.[280]
The King in gorgeous royal robes on chair of state doth sit,
And pranked° with pride of Priam's pomp of whom he conquered
   it.

'Put off this hostile weed', to him the Queen his wife gan say,[281]
'And of thy loving lady wrought wear rather this array,
This garment knit.' It makes me loath that shivering here I stand.
O shall a king be murthered by a banished wretch's hand?
Out!° Shall th'adulterer destroy the husband of the wife?
The dreadful destinies approached; the food that last in life
He tasted of before his death, their master's blood shall see;
The gobs of blood down dropping on the wind shall pourèd be.[282]
By traitorous trick of trapping weed, his death is brought about,
Which being put upon his head, his hands could not get out.
The stoppèd poke° with mouth set ope, his muffled head doth
   hide,[283]
The mankind dame with trembling hand the sword drew from her
   side;[284]

10

20

---

[278] 1–2 Within a revel-rex [...] of Troy] S. 'res agitur intus magna, par annis decem' (a major thing is taking place inside, equal to the ten years).

[279] 11] Studley omits S. 'spectemus' ('let us watch!').

[280] Assarac] i.e. Assaracus, great-grandfather of the Trojan Aeneas.

[281] 17–19] In S., indirect speech (not a quotation).

[282] 7–24 My prophesying sprite [...] shall pourèd be] Perhaps influences Macbeth's trance-like vision of murder (1.3.139–42 and 2.1.36–47) (cf. Muir 'Seneca and Shakespeare', 243–44). See also n. at 1.Cho.6.

[283] The stoppèd poke with mouth set ope] S. 'laxi et invii [...] sinus' (the capacious and constraining folds).

[284] mankind dame] S. 'semivir' (half-man). In S., this refers to Aegisthus; in Studley, to Clytemnestra (cf. 'her side', 'she', etc.).

Nor to the utmost of her might, it in his flesh she thrast,°
30 But in the giving of the stroke, she stayèd all aghast.
He as it were a bristled bore entangled in the net
Among the briars in bushy woods yet tryeth out to get.
With struggling much, the shrinking bands more straightly he doth
      bind.
He strives in vain and would slip off the snare that doth him blind,
Which catcheth hold on every side, but yet th'entangled wretch
Doth grope about, his subtle foes with gripping hand to catch.
But furious Tyndaris prepared the pole-axe° in her hand,[285]
And as the priest to sacrifice at th'altar-side doth stand,[286]
And views with eye the bullock's neck, ere that with axe he smite,
40 So to and fro she heaves her hand to strike and level right.   [900]
He hath the stroke. Dispatched it is, not quite chopped off the head;
It hangeth by a little crop. Here from the carcass dead,
The spouting blood came gushing out, and there the head doth lie,
With wallowing, bobbling, mumbling tongue. Nor they do by and
      by[287]
Forsake him so. The breathless corpse Aegist doth all to coil,°
And mangled hath the gashèd corpse, while thus he doth him spoil.
She putteth too her helping hand by detestable deed;
They both accord unto the kind, whereof they do proceed.

Dame Helen's sister, right she is, and he Thyestes' son.
50 Lo, doubtful Titan standeth still, the day now being done,
Not knowing whether best to keep still on his wonted way,
Or turn his wheels unto the path of dire Thyestes' day.[288]

The Second Scene

ELECTRA [ORESTES]

[ELECTRA]

O thou whom of our father's death the only help we have,
Fly, fly from force of furious foes, make haste thyself to save.

---

[285] Tyndaris] i.e. Clytemnestra.

[286] the priest] Studley follows a conjecture of Ascensius: 'pius' (sacred, dutiful) as referring to a sacrificer; the manuscripts read 'prius' (first) (cf. Billerbeck and Somazzi, p. 258).

[287] they] i.e. Clytemnestra and Aegisthus.

[288] 52] i.e. or reverse his course as on the day of Thyestes' cannibalistic feast.

Our house is topsy turvy tossed, our stock is cast away,
Our ruthful realms to ruin run, our kingdoms do decay.
Who cometh here in chariot swift, thus galloping amain?[289]
Brother, disguisèd in thy weed, let me thy person feign.[290]

[Aside]

O buzzard blind, what dost thou mean from foreign folk to
    fly?[291]
Whom dost thou shun? It doth behove to fear this family.[292]

[To Orestes]

Orestes, now be bold and set all shivering fear aside:
10   The certain succour of a trusty friend I have espied.

The Third Scene

STROPHILUS   ELECTRA   [ORESTES]

[STROPHILUS]

With solemn pomp, I, Strophilus, forsaking Phocis land,[293]
Bearing a branch of palm that grows at Elis in my hand,
Returnèd back I am; the cause that willed me hither wend,
Is with these gifts to gratify and welcome home my friend,
Whose valiant army scald and shook the tattered Trojan walls,
Who wearied with the ten years' war now flat on floor she falls.

What woeful wight is this that stains her mourning face with
    tears,
And drownèd deep in drowsy dumps oppressèd is with fears?
I know full well this damsel is of princes' lineage born.
10   What cause, Electra, hath this joyful family to mourn?

---

[289] Who cometh here] Electra spies a stranger approaching, and does not recognize him as the friend, Strophilus, until 9–10.

[290] let me thy person fain] In S. 'furabor' (I will steal). Studley understands Electra to be taking Orestes' clothing and identity; a more likely reading of S. is that she wants to steal him away in the folds of her own clothes, concealing him from the stranger.

[291] O buzzard blind] S. 'anime demens' (crazy mind of mine), a self-address.

[292] It doth behove to fear this family] S. 'domus timenda est' (the household [i.e. her mother's household] is what we need to be afraid of).

[293] Strophilus] Friend of Agamemnon, on his way home to Phocis after winning a victory at the Elean Games.

ELECTRA

By treason that my mother wrought, my father lieth slain,
And drinking of their father's cup, the children do complain.[294]
Aegist engrosseth castles got by fornication.

STROPHILUS

Alack that of so long a time, felicity is none.

ELECTRA

I thee request even for the love my father thou dost owe,
And for the honour of the crown, whose bruit° abroad doth grow
In every coast, and by the gods that diversely do deal,
Take into thy tuition, convey away, and steal
This poor Orest. Such kind of theft is piety indeed.

STROPHILUS

20   Although that Agamemnon's death doth teach me to take heed,
Yet will I undertake the same, and with all diligence,
Orestes, shall I go about, with strength to have thee hence.
Prosperity requireth faith, but trouble exacts the same;
Have here a price for those that do contend and wage in game,[295]
An ornament with comely grace ordained to deck the brow,
And let thy head be covered with this green and pleasant bough,
And carry this victorious, triumphant branch in hand.
God grant this palm that planted was in fertile Pisa land
(Where solemn games were celebrate, Jove's honour to express)
30   May both a safeguard be to thee and bring thee good success.
Thou that bestrides thy father's steeds, as he before hath done,
Go strike a league of amity with Pylades, my son.[296]

Now, nimble nags – let Greece hereof recording testify –
With headlong scouring course amain this traitorous country fly.

[Exit Strophilus and Orestes]

---

[294] 12] A substantial shift in sense from S. 'comes paternae quaeritur natus neci' (the child is sought as partner to the father's death): Studley likely reads 'queritur' (complains, laments).

[295] Have here a price] i.e. Strophilus confers on Orestes the palm of victory mentioned at 2.

[296] Studley simplifies S., where Pylades (present as a non-speaking character) is directly addressed: 'and you, Pylades, learn loyalty by your father's example'.

ELECTRA

He is escaped and gone and with unmeasurable might
The chariot horse, with rein at will, do scud° out of my sight.
Now free from peril, on my foes attendance will I make,
And offer willingly my head the deadly wound to take.

The cruel conqueress of her spouse is come, whose spotted
    weed
40   With sprinkles (sign of slaughter) do bear record of her deed.
Her gory hands new bathed in blood as yet they be not dry,
Her rough and churlish, rigorous looks the fact do notify.   [950]
Unto the temple will I trudge. Cassandra, suffer me,
Oppressed with egal° grief, take part of sacrifice with thee.

The Fourth Scene

CLYTEMNESTRA ELECTRA AEGISTHUS CASSANDRA
[SOLDIERS]

[CLYTEMNESTRA]

O thou, thy mother's enemy, ungracious, saucy face,
After what sort dost thou, a maid, appear in public place?

ELECTRA

I have with my virginity the bowers of bawds forsook.

CLYTEMNESTRA

What man is he that ever thee to be a virgin took?

ELECTRA

What, your own daughter?

CLYTEMNESTRA

                With thy mother, more modest should you be.

ELECTRA

Do you at length begin to preach such godliness to me?

CLYTEMNESTRA

A manly stomach stout thou hast, with swelling, haughty heart;
Subdued with sorrow, learn thou shall to play a woman's part.

271

ELECTRA

> A sword and buckler very well a woman doth beseem.
10   (Except I dote.)[297]

CLYTEMNESTRA

>   Thyself dost thou hail-fellow° with us esteem?[298]

ELECTRA

> What Agamemnon new is this, whom thou hast got of late?

CLYTEMNESTRA

> Hereafter shall I tame and teach thy girlish tongue to prate,
> And make thee know how to a queen thy taunting to forbear.

ELECTRA

> The whilst (thou widow) answer me directly to this gear.
> Thy husband is bereavèd quite of breath. His life is done.

CLYTEMNESTRA

> Inquire where thy brother is, so seek about my son.[299]

ELECTRA

> He is departed out of Greece.

CLYTEMNESTRA

>   Go fetch him out of hand.

ELECTRA

> Fetch thou my father unto me.

CLYTEMNESTRA

>   Give me to understand
> Where doth he lurking hide his head? Where is he shrunk away?

ELECTRA

20   All plunge of perils passed he is and at a quiet stay,

---

[297] Except I dote] i.e. 'unless I am mistaken'.
[298] Thyself dost thou hail-fellow with us esteem] i.e. do you think you are our equal?
[299] Inquire] S. 'edissere' (explain).

And in another kingdom where no harm he doth mistrust.
This answer were sufficient to please a parent just,
But one whose breast doth boil in wrath, it cannot satisfy.

CLYTEMNESTRA

Today by death thou shalt receive thy fatal destiny.

ELECTRA

On this condition am I pleased the altar to forsake:

[Indicating Clytemnestra's hand]

If that this hand shall do the deed, my death when I shall take,
Or else if in my throat to bathe thy blade thou do delight,
Most willingly I yield my throat and give the leave to smite.
Or if thou will chop off my head in brutish, beastly guise,
30   My neck awaiting for the wound outstretchèd ready lies.
Thou hast committed sinfully a great and grievous guilt.
Go purge thy hardened hands the which thy husband's blood
    have spilt.

CLYTEMNESTRA

O thou that of my perils all dost suffer part with me,
And in my realm dost also rule with egal dignity,
Aegisthus, art thou glad at this? As doth her not behove,
With checks and taunts the daughter doth her mother's malice
    move.
She keeps her brother's counsel close, conveyed out of the way.

AEGISTHUS

Thou malapert and witless wench, thine elvish prating stay,
Refrain those words unfit thy mother's glowing ears to vex.

ELECTRA

40   What, shall the breeder of this broil control me with his checks,
Whose father's guilt hath causèd him to have a doubtful name,
Who both is to his sister son, and nephew° to the same?[300]

---

[300] See n. at 1.1.32–34 and text at 2.2.89.

CLYTEMNESTRA

To snap her head off with thy sword, Aegist, does thou refrain?
Let her give up the ghost or bring her brother straight again.
Let her be locked in dungeon dark, and let her spend her days
In caves and rocks; with painful pangs torment her everyways.
I hope him whom she hidden hath, she will again descry,
Through being clapped in prison strong and suffering poverty
With irksome and unsavoury smells on every side annoyed,
50   Enforced to wear a widow's weed, ere wedding day enjoyed.
Put in exile and banishment when each man doth her hate,
So shall she be by misery compelled to yield too late,
Prohibited of wholesome air fruition to have.

ELECTRA

Grant me my doom by means of death to pass unto my grave.

CLYTEMNESTRA

I would have granted it to thee, if thou should it deny.
Unskilful is the tyrant who, by suffering wretches die,
Doth end their pains.

ELECTRA

                    What after death, doth anything remain?

CLYTEMNESTRA

And if thou do desire to die, the same see you refrain.[301]
Lay hands, sirs, on this wondrous wretch, whom being carried
      on,
60   Even to the farthest corner of my jurisdiction,
Far out beyond Mycenas land in bonds let her be bound,
With darkness dim in hideous hold, let her be closèd round.   [1000]

[Indicating Cassandra]

This captive spouse and wicked queen, the trull of prince's bed,
Shall pay her pains and suffer death by losing of her head.

---

[301] the same see you refrain] Obscure for S. 'vita, si cupias mori' (if you desire to
die, [your punishment will be] life).

274

Come hale her on that she may follow that way my spouse is
    gone,
Whose love from me enticèd was.

CASSANDRA

                              Do not thus hale me on.
I will before you take the way, these tidings first to tell
Unto my countrymen of Troy, beneath in lowest hell,
How overwhelmèd ships each where are spread the seas upon,
And Mycene country conquered is brought in subjection.
He that of thousand captains was grand captain general,
Come to as great calamity as Troy itself did fall,
Entrappèd was by traitorous train and whoredom of his wife,
And by a gift received of her, deprivèd of his life.
Let us not linger. On with me, and thanks I do you give.
I joy that it might be my hap thus after Troy to live.

70

CLYTEMNESTRA

Go to, prepare thyself to die, thou frantic, raging wight.

CASSANDRA

The frenzy fits of fury fell on you shall also light.

[The Fifth Scene]

EURYBATES

Added to the tragedy by the translator

Alas, ye hateful, hellish hags, ye Furies foul and fell,°
Why cause ye rusty rancour's rage in noble hearts to dwell,
And cankered hate in boiling breasts to grow from age to age?
Could not the grandsire's painful pangs the children's wrath
    assuage,[302]
Nor famine faint of pining paunch with burning thirst of hell,
Amid the blackest stream of Styx, where poisoning breaths do
    dwell,
Where vapours vile parbreaking° out from dampish, miry mud
Increase the pains of Tantalus, deserved by guiltless blood?

---

[302] the grandsire] i.e. Tantalus.

Could not thine own offence suffice, Thyestes, in thy life,
10   To file thy brother's spousal bed and to abuse his wife?
But after breath from body fled and life thy limbs hath left,
Cannot remembrance of revenge out of thy breast be wrest?
What, yet hast thou not laid thy lips to taste of Lethe's flood?[303]
Now after death why dost thou come to move thy son to blood?
Could cruel Ditis grant to thee thy passport back again
To work this woe upon the world and make such rigor reign
That Clytemnestra is become the fifty sister dire
Of Danaus' daughters that did once their husbands' death
    conspire?[304]

Lo here, how fickle Fortune gives but brittle, fading joy.
20   Lo, he who late a conqueror triumphèd over Troy,[305]
Enduring many sturdy storms with mighty toil and pain
To sow the seed of fame hath reaped small fruit thereof again.
When as his honour budding forth with flower began to bloom,
Alas, the stock was hewèd down and sent to deadly doom,
And they that of his victory and coming home were glad,
To sudden mourning change their mirth with heaviness bestad.°
The lusty pomp of royal court is dead, O doleful day,
The people moan their prince's death with woe and weal° away,
With howling, crying, wringing hands, with sobs, with sighs, and
    tears,
30   And with their fists they beat their breasts, they pull and hale their
    hairs,
And as the sheep amazèd run and ramp° about the field,
When as their shepherd to the wolf, his gory throat doth yield,
Even so as mad they rage and rave throughout Mycenas land,
Deprivèd of their prince, they fear the bloody tyrant's hand.
While thus were woeful wailings heard in every place about,
The good Cassandra (come from Troy) to death is halèd out.[306]

---

[303] laid thy lips to taste of Lethe's flood] i.e. 'erased all memories of your life'.

[304] Danaus had fifty daughters who married his brother's fifty sons. Forty-nine of the daughters killed their husbands; one, Hypermnestra, spared Lynceus (and their descendants became rulers of Argos). Studley adds Clytemnestra as a fiftieth murderous wife.

[305] 19–20 Lo here […] Lo, he] Echoes Chaucer's anaphoric conclusion to *Troilus and Criseyde*: 'Lo here, of payens […] Lo here, the forme of olde clerkis speche' (V.1849–54). See also the Epilogue to George Gascoigne's and Francis Kinwelmersh's *Jocasta* (1566): 'Lo here the fruit of high aspiring mind / […] / Lo here the trap that titles proud do find' (1–3).

Like as the swan, who when the time of death approacheth nigh,
By nature warnèd is thereof and pleasèd well to die,
Doth celebrate her funeral with dirge and solemn song,
40   Even so the noble virgin who in woe hath livèd long,
Most joyful goes she to her death with mild and pleasant face,
Stout bolstering out her burly breast with princely port and grace.
Nothing dismayed, with courage bold and cheerful countenance,
On stage ordainèd for her death, she gan herself advance,
As though she had not thither come to leave her loathsome life,
As though she had not come to taste the stroke of fatal knife,
But even as if in bridal bed her journey were to meet
Corebus dear, not having mind of death, nor winding sheet;[307]
When looking round on every side, she took her leave of all,
50   From vapoured eyes of young and old, the trickling tears do fall.
The Greeks themselves to grief are moved to see this heavy sight:
So pity pierced the headman's heart that thrice, about to smite,
He stayed the smot,° with shivering hand; yet once again he tried,
And from her shoulders stroke her head, and thus the virgin died.

But now the Greeks another cause of mourning have in hand:
Orestes, Agamemnon's son, is forced to fly the land.
Among old, rotten, ragged rocks, there lies an ugly place,[308]
A dungeon deep, as dark as hell, unknown to Phoebus' face,
An hollow, huge, wide-gaping hole, with way still bending down,
60   Whose mouth with venomous withered weeds is hid and
        overgrown,
Where stinking smells come belching out from filthy, dirty dike,
Where vermin vile do creep and crawl – in hell is not the like.
Ill-favoured, foul, misshapen bugs do lurk about this cave,
With dreadful sounds and roaring noise within the pit they rave.
Even hither is Electra sent in darkness deep to lie,
In poverty and comfortless, without the light of sky,

---

[306] Studley models Cassandra's death on the account of the death of Polyxena (also a young Trojan woman) in *Troas*: e.g. the emphasis on her face (lines 41, 43 below; cf. *Troas* 5.1.71–74, 86) and on the pity felt by the Greeks looking on (line 51; *Troas* 5.1.94).

[307] Corebus] i.e. Coroebus, the Phrygian prince who joined the Trojan War out of love for Cassandra and died defending her from rape by Ajax the Lesser (son of Oileus).

[308] 57–64] Borrows details from other 'loci horridi' in Seneca, especially *Oed.* 530–47, *Thy.* 641–64.

Fast clogged with iron bolts and chains, thus by her mother laid
In torments till by her to death Orestes be betrayed,
Who, as Cassandra telleth, shall revenge his father's death,
70   Deprive with sword th'adulterer and mother both of breath.

So after all these bloody broils, Greece never shall be free.
But blood for blood and death by turns the after age shall see.

FINIS

THE TRANSLATORS' LATIN SOURCES

WITH SOME NOTES ON INSTANCES WHERE THE TRANSLATIONS DIFFER FROM MODERN VERSIONS

The translators knew Senecan tragedy both in *florilegia* and in Latin printed editions. Specific traditions of textual transmission, commentary, and translation shaped their understanding of Seneca and his writings. They may have been familiar with the recent Italian translations by Lodovico Dolce (*c*. 1550).[1] The tragedies had already been subject to critical attention in fourteenth-century Italy, with commentaries by the Paduan Alberto Mussato (d. 1315), who also wrote his own 'Senecan' tragedy, *Ecerinis*, and by the Oxford scholar Nicholas Trevet (*c*. 1315). The most recent commentary was by Jodocus Badius Ascensius (Paris, 1514), and there are some signs that Heywood made use of it.[2]

Sixteenth-century printed editions of the tragedies drew almost exclusively on one branch of the manuscript tradition known as A, which differs in some significant ways from the other main branch now known as E. But E tends to be the more trusted authority in modern editions of Seneca, such as the Oxford Classical Text (Zwierlein 1986) and the Loeb Classical Library bilingual edition (Fitch 2002 and 2004); E is therefore hugely influential on present-day translations.[3] Although the A and E branches ultimately go back to a single archetype in late antiquity, they diverge on numerous individual readings of words and phrases as well as in the attribution of lines to speakers (see below). They also differ in the titles given to plays: the works known in the sixteenth century as *Hercules Furens, Troas, Thebais,* and *Hippolytus* are now conventionally referred to by their titles in E: *Hercules, Troades, Phoenissae,* and *Phaedra*. The numerical order ascribed to them by the translators (e.g. *Troas* as 'The Sixt Tragedie of Seneca' in

---

[1] On this and other vernacular translations, see Gilbert Highet, *The Classical Tradition: Greek and Roman Influences on Western Literature* (New York and London: Oxford University Press, 1949), p. 122.

[2] For evidence of use of Ascensius's commentary, see the notes on e.g. *Troas* 5.1.22, *Thyestes* 4.Cho.19. On Mussato and Trevet, see Mayer, pp. 153–56.

[3] On the manuscript tradition, see R. J. Tarrant, 'The Younger Seneca: Tragedies', in *Texts and Transmission: A Survey of the Latin Classics*, ed. by L. D. Reynolds and N. G. Wilson (New York: Oxford University Press, 1984), pp. 378–81.

Heywood's translation) derives from the order in which they are organized in A. It may also be significant that only A includes *Octavia*, which gives a decidedly historical and political slant to the Senecan tragic corpus as a whole.

Heywood raises the choice of an appropriate source text in the preface to *Thyestes* (lines 308–09), where he complains about the many errors found in the editions by 'Gryphius' (1541), 'Aldus' (i.e. the 1517 Aldine edition by Jerome Avantius), and 'Colineus' (reference uncertain).[4] Heywood there claims to have solved this problem by resorting to a manuscript of Seneca – something he could in theory have done, perhaps using manuscripts possessed by some Oxford colleges – but it appears that in practice he, and Studley too, followed Gryphius's text in almost every instance.[5] Robinson's London edition of the Latin in 1589 (the first such edition in England) was based on Gryphius. Although Gryphius incorporated many of the conjectures and emendations made in the editions by Ascensius (1514) and Avantius (1517), all of these editions, as noted above, were equally dominated by the A manuscripts.

Below we provide a representative (but not exhaustive) comparison of what Heywood or Studley evidently read in his 'source' (i.e. Gryphius) with readings that are found in E and are more influential in present-day editions and translations. Readers who might wish to conduct a more comprehensive comparison of Heywood's and Studley's translations against different textual variants should consult the Oxford or Loeb edition (listed in the 'Further Reading').

---

[4] It is possible that Heywood is thinking of the printer Rudolphus Collinus (aka Dorotheus Camillus). Although no publication of Seneca by Collinus is attested, his Latin translation of Euripides' *Tragoediae XVIII* appeared in Basel in 1541. This, or a possible identification with the sixteenth-century French printer Simon de Colines (H. de Vocht, *Jasper Heywood and His Translations of Seneca's 'Troas', 'Thyestes', and 'Hercules Furens'* [Louvain: A. Uystpruyst, 1913], p. 339), is more likely than the suggestion that Heywood invented 'Colineus' to obscure his exclusive debt to Gryphius (Joost Daalder, ed., *'Thyestes': Translated by Jasper Heywood (1560)* [London: Ernest Benn, 1982], p. 86).
[5] On Gryphius as Heywood's primary Latin source for *Thyestes*, see Daalder, pp. 83–88; also John O'Keefe, 'An Analysis of Jasper Heywood's Translations of *Troas*, *Thyestes*, and *Hercules Furens*' (unpublished doctoral thesis, Loyola University, Chicago, 1974), pp. 43–53. For the older view, that Heywood used several Latin editions, see e.g. Vocht, pp. xxiv–xxvii.

TROAS

1.2.32–68] Heywood follows the speech assignments in his source; E assigns 32–52 to the Chorus and 53–68 to Hecuba (S. *Tro.* 98–116 and 117–32).

2.3.6] E places this line after line 30 (S. *Tro.* 226).

2.Cho.39–40] In E these lines appear at the ode's conclusion (after 70 below; S. *Tro.* 407–8). Heywood follows his source.

3.1.79–90] Modern editions reorder these lines and make different divisions between the speakers (S. *Tro.* 488–99).

3.1.127 And saith your augur Calchas so?] In E this is a statement and part of Ulysses' speech (S. *Tro.* 533).

3.1.186] In E this line is Andromache's (S. *Tro.* 588).

3.1.278 Break up the deep Avern] Heywood translates 'repelle Avernum' (S. *Tro.* 581), an emendation by Avantius (1517) for the obscure reading in A 'repelle animum' (beat back my mind [?]). Compare E 'repellor heu me' (alas, I am beaten back).

3.3.68] With bond of Grecians' heavy yoke] Heywood's source has 'iugo' (yoke), whereas the consensus of the manuscripts is 'viro' ([servitude to a] man or husband; *Tro.* 804).

4.Cho.50 plaints] Heywood's source unusually follows E 'questum' (lament) rather than A 'coetum' (group; S. *Tro.* 1042). Both variants emphasize the imminent scattering of the women's community of suffering.

5.1.22] Heywood seems familiar with the interpretation by Ascensius (1514), who sees this as referring to garlands worn by individuals (O'Keefe, 'Analysis', p. 85). The line in S. (*Tro.* 1082) is usually understood as distinguishing the kinds of trees the spectators climbed.

THYESTES[6]

The Speakers

Megaera] Heywood follows his source; E identifies the speakers as 'Tantali umbra' (ghost of Tantalus) and 'Furia' (Fury).

1.1.1 What fury fell] Heywood translates 'quis me furor' in his source and treats 'furor' (rage, madness) as 'furia' (Fury). E has 'quis inferorum' (who of those below; S. *Thy.* 1).

1.1.49–50 about the pole [...] the painted sky] Heywood follows 'cum' in his source rather than 'cur' found in E. In E, Megaera says that she expects even the starry sky will not go unscathed (S. *Thy.* 49).

1.1.51 darkest] Heywood follows his source, 'atra' (black). Other manuscript readings include: 'alia' (another [in E]) and 'alta' (deep; S. *Thy.* 51).

1.1.53 Fill up the house of Tantalus] Heywood follows his source; but E has 'imple Tantalo totam domum' (fill the whole house *with* Tantalus; S. *Thy.* 53).

1.1.60 The cauldron boils] Heywood follows his source, 'spumante aheno' (the cauldron boiling). Editions following E have 'spument aena' (let the cauldrons boil) and punctuate differently to make this the subject of the following sentence (S. *Thy.* 60).

1.1.93–94] lest sacred hand with blood / Of slaughter dire] Heywood follows his source. Most modern editions make this a command: 'Do not stain …'. Heywood mistakenly takes 'sacra' to describe the (sacred) hand, rather than (sacrilegious) slaughter (S. *Thy.* 93–94).

1.1.100 I follow thee] Spoken by Tantalus in E (S. *Thy.* 100).

1.1.118 fields of Argos] Heywood fuses 'agri' (field) and a marginal correction 'Argi' (of Argos) in his source (Vocht, p. 34) (S. *Thy.* 119).

---

[6] A greater number of examples are given from *Thyestes* than from the other two plays because the influence of A is easier to trace and to illustrate, given Heywood's more direct translation of the play; we also benefit from the painstaking observations on Heywood's sources by Daalder throughout his edition.

1.Cho.2 Pisey bowers] 'bowers' corresponds to 'turribus' (towers) in Heywood's source. E has 'curribus' (chariots; S. *Thy.* 123).

1.Cho.18–22 Betrayed is Myrtilus [...] no fable is] Heywood's source has 'dominae' (mistress, dame; perhaps alluding to Hippodamia?), but E has 'domini' (master, lord; i.e. Oenomaus). 'Mariners' translates 'navitis', a marginal reading in Heywood's source (E has 'navibus', ships; S. *Thy.* 139–43).

1.Cho.31 beguiled] Translates 'lusus' in Heywood's source; E has 'lassus' (exhausted; S. *Thy.* 152).

2.1 SERVANT] Corresponds to 'servus' in Heywood's source. E has 'satelles' (attendant; S. *Thy.* 176).

2.1.5] Heywood follows his source in referring to Argos (iras et Argos [...] totum). E has a reference to Atreus (iratus Atreus) and makes it part of the preceding question (S. *Thy.* 180).

2.1.58 beast] Heywood translates 'pecus' in his source; the manuscripts read 'pascuum' (pasture; S. *Thy.* 233).

2.1.62 wandered he] E has 'erravi' (I wandered). Heywood follows 'erravit' in his source, thus making Atreus seem to have suffered less than Thyestes, and his cruelty less justified (Daalder, p. 37) (S. *Thy.* 237).

2.1.72–73] Heywood follows his source 'perimat tyrannus: lenis in regno meo [...]?'; editions following E punctuate differently: 'perimat tyrannus lenis: in regno meo [...]' (let a *gentle* tyrant *kill*: in *my* kingdom let death be received as a *favour* [i.e. as respite from torture]; S. *Thy.* 247–48).

2.1.128 Requests will move] Heywood follows his source. E has 'prece commovebo' (I will bring around by my request; S. *Thy.* 302).

2.1.135] E attributes this line to the Servant (S. *Thy.* 309).

2.1.147] E attributes this line to the Servant (S. *Thy.* 319).

2.1.152 Thou sparest him] Heywood translates 'illi' (him) in his source; E has 'illis' (those ones), referring to Thyestes and his sons (S. *Thy.* 325).

2.1.153 and client eke of mine] Heywood translates 'patris cliens' in his source; most editions (following A and a scholar's emendation) read 'fratri sciens' ([let Menelaus be present as] knowing [accomplice] to his brother; S. *Thy.* 326).

2.Cho.52] Heywood's source omits a following line, 'rex est qui cupiet nihil' (a king he is that will desire nothing at all) in E (S. *Thy.* 389).

3.1 Phylisthenes] Heywood adopts a variant in his source (Philisthenes). E names him 'Tantalus', with a second, silent son named 'Plisthenes' (= Pleisthenes; S. *Thy.* 404).

3.1.13] Heywood follows his source, where the sense is obscure; E has 'cum quod datur spectabis, et dantem aspice' (when you look at what is being given, inspect also the giver; S. *Thy.* 416).

3.1.58 doth lie] Heywood follows 'metitur' (extends) in his source, but the manuscripts read 'metatur' (is harvested; S. *Thy.* 462).

3.1.65 We nothing fear] Heywood follows his source, which has 'timemus', an emendation by Avantius (1517) (cf. Billerbeck and Somazzi, p. 288). The manuscripts all read 'sed non timemur' (but we are not feared, i.e. we do not provoke threats against us; S. *Thy.* 468).

3.1.69 Not yet desired it ought to be.] Most editions give this half-line to the son. Heywood follows his source (S. *Thy.* 472).

3.1.84–85] Most editions (following some manuscripts) ascribe these lines to Thyestes, along with a different text (following E) in 85: 'testor tamen' (but I your father] testify [this one thing]) – introducing the following line. Heywood follows his source (S. *Thy.* 487–88).

3.2.14 hope] Heywood translates 'sperat', the reading in most editions (and the manuscripts) – a rare deviation from Gryphius's 'spirat' (breathes) (cf. Daalder, p. 52) (S. *Thy.* 504).

3.2.29 that at thy feet do lie] Heywood apparently follows a marginal reading in Gryphius, 'iniunctae' ([hands] joined to [feet]); Gryphius and the manuscripts read 'intactae' ([hands] untouched [by feet]) (cf. Daalder, p. 52) (S. *Thy.* 518).

3.2.32 hands] Heywood translates his source. E has 'manum' (hand; S. *Thy.* 521).

3.Cho.45 so wide] Heywood follows his source 'spatiosa'; the manuscripts have 'speciosa' (resplendent, dotted), describing the sea (S. *Thy.* 591).

3.Cho.60 men of might] Heywood translates his source 'dynastas'; E has 'divinat' (i.e. the king 'divines' as well as 'fears' the changes brought by 'chances great'; S. *Thy.* 605).

4.1.6 So wicked brethren] Heywood follows his source 'impios' (wicked); E has 'pios' (dutiful; S. *Thy.* 627).

4.1.10] Assigned to the Messenger in E (S. *Thy.* 632).

4.1.56 the place] Heywood apparently reads 'loco' for 'luco' (grove; S. *Thy.* 662).

4.1.63 knit] S. follows his source 'renodat' (in Gryphius) rather than the manuscripts (A 'revocat', calls back; E 'religat', ties back; S. *Thy.* 685).

4.1.66 fine] Heywood follows his source 'fusa'; E has 'salsa' (salted; S. *Thy.* 688).

4.1.122–23] Heywood translates his source 'hactenus non stat nefas, plus est'; E has 'hactenus si stat nefas, pius est' (if the crime stops here, he is kind; S. *Thy.* 744).

4.1.145 mourning] Heywood follows his source 'querente'; E has 'candente' (white hot; S. *Thy.* 767).

4.1.149 wot I] Heywood follows his source (and the manuscripts) 'dicam'. Recent editions usually follow a scholar's emendation, 'dicas' (could you say; S. *Thy.* 771).

4.Cho.19 trenchèd] Heywood appears to translate Ascensius (1514) 'fosso' (dug up) rather than 'fesso' (tired) in Gryphius (and the manuscripts) (cf. Daalder, 66) (S. *Thy.* 807).

4.Cho.30 light] Heywood translates his source 'lumina'; E has 'limina' (threshold; S. *Thy.* 818).

5.1.8 doth call] Heywood translates his source 'vocat'; E has 'vacat' (is empty), referring to the absence of the sun, which would normally serve as a witness and thereby arouse a sense of shame in the evildoer (alluded to at 7–8; S. *Thy.* 892).

5.2.26 so fresh and gay] Heywood captures the sense of his source 'recenti' (fresh) and a marginal variant in Gryphius 'decenti' (fitting, fine, 'gay') (Daalder, p. 71) (S. *Thy.* 945).

5.2.42 countenance] Heywood translates his source 'vultus'; E has 'luctus' (griefs; S. *Thy.* 961).

5.3.43 if there in hell be any one] Heywood translates his source 'intra Tartara' (in the underworld); E has 'infra' (below): i.e. 'if there is anything below the underworld and our (dead) ancestors' (S. *Thy.* 1013).

5.3.50 confusion] Heywood follows his source 'exitia' (ruin, destruction); E has 'exilia' (exile; S. *Thy.* 1019).

5.3.63 shalt thou have] Heywood follows the future tense of his source 'habebis'; E has 'habes' (thou hast), intensifying the paradox (S. *Thy.* 1031).

5.3.127 The world] Heywood follows his source 'immensa [...] secla' (our age [or world] without measure); most editions (following the manuscripts) read 'immensa [...] scelera' (measureless crimes; S. *Thy.* 1095).

AGAMEMNON

The Speakers

Thyestes] Studley follows his source; E has 'Thyestis umbra' (ghost of Thyestes).

A Company of Greeks] Studley translates 'chorus Graecorum' in his source.

Strophilus] S. 'Strophius': the change (or error) may be Studley's own.

1.1.48 detestable] Translates 'inceste' in A; E has 'incertae' (uncertain), and 47–48 have a more positive sense as Thyestes thinks things have taken a turn for the better (S. *Aga.* 38).

1.Cho.42 in their mind] May translate an erroneous reading in Studley's source (perhaps 'animi' for 'nimium', S. *Aga.* 91).

2.1.6 conjoinèd] Studley follows his source 'iuncta' (joined); E has 'vidua' (abandoned) and involves different syntax: 'and have guarded the abandoned sceptre with fidelity' (S. *Aga.* 111).

2.1.25 hap] Studley translates his source 'sors' (chance), but E has 'soror' (sister), i.e. Clytemnestra's sister Helen of Troy (S. *Aga.* 124).

2.1.87 Tyndaris] Studley, influenced by his source (reading 'peperit' for 'peperi' at S. *Aga.*163), makes 'Tyndaris' refer to Iphigenia.

2.1.99] Attributed to Clytemnestra in most editions (S. *Aga.* 171).

2.1.112–13] Studley follows his source in referring to a hostile attack; E refers to the plague: Agamemnon was unmoved by sick people and funeral pyres (S. *Aga.* 181).

2.2.10] In E, assigned to Aegisthus (S. *Aga.* 234).

2.2.70 He never doth complain] Studley apparently sees 'queritur'; E and A read: 'fit nocens, non quaeritur' (he is held guilty without trial; S. *Aga.* 280).

3.1.13–15] In most editions, Eurybates is given 11–14 (S. *Aga.* 400–1), with line 15 (S. *Aga.* 402) assigned to Clytemnestra.

3.1.79–81] Studley follows his source, but in modern editions and translations the sense is that Mount Ida was now out of view, with only smoke still visible (S. *Aga.* 457–60).

3.1.219 Calcedon town] Studley follows his source. Editors now read a reference to Chalcis (S. *Aga.* 567).

3.2.197 affront the ears] In S. 'ante aras' (before the altars); Studley perhaps reads 'ante auris' (S. *Aga.* 585).

3.2.198 that of the sprite [...] the mighty blast] Editors now connect the reference to the divine ('sprite') to the following line: i.e. Agamemnon 'returns [...] to his [household] gods' (S. *Aga.* 778).

4.1.7 warm] Contrasts with S. 'gelido' (ice-cold); Studley perhaps reads 'calido' (hot; S. *Aga.* 788).

5.4.14–15] In E, these lines (S. *Aga.* 795–96) are spoken after 11 above (S. *Aga.* 792).

5.4.23] In E, assigned to Clytemnestra, who asserts righteous anger (S. *Aga.* 971).

5.4.35 art thou glad] Studley follows his source 'gaudes'; E has 'gradere' (walk [with me]; S. *Aga.* 980).

5.4.45–53, 55–57, 58–66] E assigns these lines to Aegisthus. In Studley's source, after 39 (S. *Aga.* 984), Aegisthus has no speaking role.

EDITORIAL POLICIES AND TEXTUAL NOTES

For each of the plays, the copy-text is the first printed octavo. There is some question about the first printed edition of *Troas* (discussed below).

We have silently expanded and regularized speech tags and punctuation. The spelling in the texts (and all quotations throughout) has been modernized. The modernized text has the effect of obscuring an interesting feature of the early editions, the printing of many rhyme words with similar orthography, something that is especially noticeable when the rhyme seems (to a modern ear) to be only approximate. For example, in *Troas*, 'display' at 2.2.19 appears as 'disploye' to rhyme with Troy at 2.2.20 (spelled 'Troye'), while at 1.Cho.45 it appears as 'displaye' to rhyme with 'day' (1.Cho.46). Indeed, 'day' always appears as 'day' except in its appearance twice (at 1.1.14 and 4.1.24) in a rhyme with 'sea'. In these cases, it is printed 'dea'. In the textual notes below, we record examples of several of these orthographic rhymes when they occur in what now appear to be 'approximate' rhyme pairs. The majority of examples are in *Troas*, where the tendency is most noticeable, but we also include some instances from the other two plays.

Also for the purposes of versification, the translators add or subtract syllables in a few characteristic contexts. We mark the suffix 'ed' when it is stressed (e.g. 'learnèd'). Where relevant, we also indicate elided syllables of verbs ending in 'eth' or 'est', such as 'driveth' as 'driv'th' or 'standest' as 'stand'st'. For consistency, we also indicate second person singular inflections of verbs like 'mayst' as 'may'st'. An exception to this standard are the words 'liest', 'fliest', and 'diest', as well as 'lieth' and 'dieth', which are difficult to read in their contracted form (e.g. 'di'th). Heywood often contracts sequences of vowels, and we also indicate these, for instance the two-word contractions of 'see it' or 'be it' as 'see't' or 'be't', or the contraction of 'to' and 'the' with a word beginning with a vowel, such as 'to obtain' as 't'obtain' or 'the estate' as 'th'estate'. Except in a couple of other incidental cases ('Hercules' as disyllabic 'Herc'les'), we have not sought to indicate syllabification in other instances (e.g. 'easily' and 'enemy' are spelled out in full, although they usually have a two-syllable pronunciation, 'eas'ly' and 'en'my').

A few basic principles will help the reader to navigate some of the most common (and sometimes surprising) patterns of syllabification. In both Heywood and Studley, words ending in 'er', 'en', 'on' – 'flower', 'power', 'tower', 'happen', 'heaven', 'fallen', and 'poison' – are monosyllabic. Words ending in 'dering' and 'tering' – e.g. 'wandering', 'glittering' – usually elide the middle 'er' syllable, and thus should be read 'wand'ring' or 'glitt'ring'. Likewise, a word like 'wandereth' or 'glittereth' should usually be read 'wand'reth' or 'glitt'reth'. Words with intervocalic 'v' are frequently monosyllabic (e.g. 'driven', 'even', 'heaven', 'over', 'seven'). In Studley especially, words frequently have an extra syllable in certain easily recognizable contexts (e.g. disyllabic: 'cruel', 'oar', 'prayer'; trisyllabic: 'Asia', 'gracious', 'partial', 'region'; 'violence'; and extra syllables are also added to 'affections', 'condition', 'religion', 'subjection', 'sufficient'; 'copulation', 'fornication', 'prejudicial', etc.); and in Studley, the vowel in '-ther' is occasionally elided (monosyllabic: 'weath'r'; disyllabic: 'anoth'r').

In the texts presented here, we sometimes have silently adopted variants from sixteenth-century editions other than the copy-text, recording these instances in the notes below. Other editorial additions and emendations appear in the texts in brackets, with the specific changes indicated in the notes below. The most notable editorial addition is the inclusion of stage directions, which are virtually absent in the Latin texts as well as the early English translations. (For exceptions, see the notes at *Thyestes* 5.1 and 5.2.)

Unless otherwise indicated, the English glosses of Seneca's Latin are ours. Readers of the present volume seeking to conduct a line-by-line comparison with a modern standard translation should refer to the Loeb edition. To this end, in our text we have given line numbers corresponding to the standard numbering in modern editions of Seneca. These appear in square brackets in 50-line increments in the right-hand margin. Some notes on important differences between the modern translations and the translators' Latin sources appear above in 'The Translators' Latin Sources'.

In early modern editions of the translations of Seneca, long speeches appear as a single, continuous block of text. To assist readers, we have added line spaces to these to indicate where a new stage of thought begins.

A special issue concerns the capitalization of the words 'gods' and 'God' as well as other metaphysical terms such as 'fates', 'parcae', 'fortune', and 'fury', all of which are inconsistently capitalized. In the main text of the translations, for 'god' and 'gods' we have followed the most common form in the copy-text. So, for example, in the first three editions of *Troas* 'god' and 'gods' are almost always lower case, and for this reason, in this edition, the words appear in lower case all of the time, even though the two words are always capitalized in Newton's 1581 *Tenne Tragedies*. For 'fates', etc., we have consistently used lower case, unless a figure is an actual character or strongly personified.

Seneca's pervasive impact on Renaissance drama has been thoroughly discussed (see 'Further Reading'). In our notes, we indicate only those passages where the language of the translations themselves appears to have informed later writings.

In an effort to keep the notes manageable, we left some mythological details unexplained. Readers should consult the *'Mythological Background'* sections for each play in the Introduction and the background information included on places and names in the Index.

In the textual notes, the MHRA series standard is to refer to early editions by STC numbers or dates. Because the six texts referred to below have STC numbers that vary by only their last digit, making it difficult to differentiate the texts by number alone, we have referred to texts by date. A range of dates (e.g. 1559–1562) indicates all of the editions published within and including those dates.

TROAS

Troas exists in three sixteenth-century octavos. It also appears, without the dedication, but with 'The Preface to the Reader' and the 'Preface to the Tragedy' (retitled 'The Argument') in Newton's compilation of the *Tenne Tragedies* of 1581.

1559]	STC 22227
1559a]	STC 22227a
1562]	STC 22228
1581]	STC 22221, *Tenne Tragedies*

There is some question about which 1559 edition was published first. Copies of these are preserved as BL Grenville Library G.9440 (STC 22227) and BL King's Library 238. l. 27 (STC 22227a). Vocht contends that BL King's (STC 22227a) precedes Grenville

(STC 22227), arguing that there are more errors in King's and that any printer would correct these in printing (hence the reason that Grenville has fewer turned letters and obvious mistakes, such as the printing of 'be' for 'he'). W. W. Greg counters that Grenville precedes King's, contending that errors in King's are the result of resetting loose type that fell out during the printing process, although he acknowledges that no proof 'can be held to be conclusive' as to which one came first (p. 169).

The text of this edition is based upon STC 22227, designated here as '1559'. This is our copy text because it is a more readable text than STC 22227a (designated here '1559a') and, as Vocht and Greg agree, contains fewer obvious errors. Where there are differences between '1559' and '1559a', '1559' is also more consistent with the later editions, designated '1562' and '1581'.

Printed by Richard Tottel, '1559' is an octavo in five quires of eight leaves and one of four leaves: [A^8], B^8, C^8, D^8, E^8, F^4. The dedicatory epistle to Elizabeth, the running titles, and the act and scene headers are in Roman italic type. The text is in black letter. The title-page and sig. F3^v contain the licence 'cum privilegio ad imprimendum solum' (with privilege for printing only).

The Epistle
    The Epistle] running header on A2^v–A3^r
THE PREFACE to the Readers
    THE PREFACE] running header (sigs. A4^r–^{v}) 1559–1562; [...]
        1581
    42 Quae] Que 1559–1581
    45 the English] thinglishe 1559; the englishe 1559a; the
        english 1562; the Englishe 1581
Preface to the Tragedy
    Preface to the Tragedy] The preface to the tragedie 1559; The
        Argument 1581
    33 gods] gods 1559–1559a; god 1562; God 1581
    51 could'st] couldest 1559–1562; couldst 1581
The Speakers
    The Speakers] The speakers in this tragedie 1559–1562; The
        Speakers names 1581
    Senex] an Old[e] Man Troian 1559–1581
1.1.13 day] dea 1559–1581
1.1.26 And] An 1559–1562; And 1581
1.1.32–33 overtrod…stood] overtrode [...] stode 1559–1562;
    Overtrode [...] stood 1581

1.2.85 Atrids] Atrides 1559–1562; Atrids 1581

2.1.13 post] paste 1559; post 1559a–1581

2.1.16 Troy provèd hath what Achill's] Troy hath proude what Achilles 1559–1559a; Troy hath proved what Achilles 1562; Troy proved hath what Achills 1581

2.1.26 Yea] Ye 1559–1581

2.1.44 thirst] thrust 1559–1581

2.1.61 spirits'] sprites 1559–1562; spirites 1581

2.1.62 me] me 1559; we 1559a–1581

2.1.67 vengeance] ungeans 1559; vengeans 1559a; vengeance 1562–1581

2.2.10 [Me]] My 1559–1581

2.2.19–20 display […] Troy] disploye […] Troye 1559–1562; disploy…Troy 1581

2.3.5–6 delay […] sea] deleae […] seae 1559; delaye […] sea 1559a; delay […] sea 1562–1581

2.3.8 haste] hast 1559–1581

2.3.10 else] less 1559; else 1559a–1581

2.3.23 When] Then 1559; When 1559a–1581

2.3.25 fell] fill 1559–1581

2.3.32 Caycus] Cayicus 1559; Caicus 1559a–1581

2.3.42 son] soon 1559–1559a; sonne 1562–1581

2.Cho.61 stain] strayne 1559; staine 1559a–1562; stayne 1581

3.1.44 to] of 1559; to 1559a–1581

3.1.71 guile] [?]uyle 1559; guyle 1559a; guile 1562–1581

3.1.104 to] of 1559; to 1559a–1581

3.1.131–32 beast […] rest] beste […] reste 1559; beste […] rest 1559a–1581

3.1.221 been] be 1559; been 1559a–1562; bene 1581

3.1.227 sirs] sears 1559–1559a; sirs 1562–1581

3.1.270 Maenad] Menas 1559–1581

3.1.276 pluck] dlucke 1559; plucke 1559a–1581

3.3.14 willeth] wylth 1559–1559a; with 1562–1581

3.3.25–26 child […] filled] chylde […] fylde 1559; chyld […] filed 1559a; childe […] filde 1562; child […] fild 1581

3.3.42 Achill] Achylles 1559–1559a; Achilles 1562; Achill 1581

3.3.72 I'll] I will 1599–1562; Ile 1581

4.1.3–4 were […] care] ware […] care 1559–1581

4.1.17 shouldst] shouldst 1559; should 1559a–1581

4.1.23–24 sea […] day] sea […] dea 1559–1562; sea […] day 1581

4.1.34 Helen] Helayne 1559–1581

4.1.90 past pain] past thy payne 1559–1559a; past thy paine 1562; past payne 1581

4.Cho.16–19 wretch […] overreach […] stretch] wretche […] overretche […] stretche 1559–1562; wretch […] overretch […] stretch 1581

5.1.7 he] be 1559; he 1559a–1581

5.1.107 not cruel] nor cruel 1559–1562; not cruel 1581

THYESTES

Thyestes exists in two sixteenth-century editions. The first is an octavo, dated March 26, 1560. *Thyestes* also appears, without the dedication and other 'Prefaces', but with an 'argument' providing some mythological context, in Newton's *Tenne Tragedies* of 1581. The editions are referred to below as:

1560] STC 22226
1581] STC 22221, *Tenne Tragedies*

The text of this edition is based on '1560', which, according to the title page, was printed 'in the house late Thomas Berthelet's'. Berthelet had passed away by this date, so the likely printer was his nephew Thomas Powell. The octavo consists of seven quires of eight leaves, with signatures $*^8$, $\clubsuit^8$, A^8, B^8, C^8, D^8, E^8. It is printed in black letter, with the act and scene divisions and the running headers in the play itself in Roman type. The final printed page (E7v) contains the phrase 'cum privilegio ad imprimendum solum'. On the title page, the title is framed by a woodcut print, with the date 1534 placed predominantly at the bottom. This is a reprint of a woodcut used for other Berthelet imprints, including Thomas Lupset's *An Exhortation to Yonge Men* (1535; STC 16936) and his *Treatise of Charitie* (1535; STC 16940), a reprint Thomas Elyot's 1531 *Boke Named the Governour* (1537; STC 7636); Gentian Hervet's translation of Xenophon's *Oecenomicus* (1537); STC 26071), Littleton's *Tenures* (1538; STC 15761), John Fitzherbert's *Boke of Husbandry* (1540; STC 10996), among others (See Vocht, p. xlv).

Heywood complains about the printing of *Troas* in the 'Preface' to *Thyestes*, and compared with either of the first octavos of *Troas*, *Thyestes* appears to be printed more carefully, with few obvious errors, although there are some, such as the printing of 'feerce' instead of 'feere', i.e. 'fere'. The text is also more readable than either of the first two quartos of *Troas*, with little bleeding between the letters.

Preface

13–14 struck [...] book] strooke [...] booke 1560 (Dalder
has 'stroke [...] book', p. 7, ll. 13–14)
The Speakers] The Speakers 1560; The names of the Speakers
1581
2.1.64 fere] feerce 1560; feere 1581
2.1.144 be 'ware] beware 1560–1581
3.1.69 Not] Nor 1560–1581
4.1.139–40 anon [...] everychone] anone [...] every chone 1560;
Anone [...] everychone 1581
4.Cho.38, 40 yet [...] great] yet [...] gret 1560–1581
4.Cho.50 flames] f ames 1560; flames 1581
5.1.9 Would] Wo de 1560; would 1581
5.3.134 all] A l 1560; all 1581

AGAMEMNON

Agamemnon appears in two sixteenth-century editions, an octavo of 1566 and, without the numerous prefaces and dedication but with an 'Argument' in quarto in Newton's *Tenne Tragedies* in 1581. These are referred to below as:

1566] STC 22222
1581] STC 22221, *Tenne Tragedies*

This edition is based on the octavo of 1566, which was printed by Thomas Colwell, who also printed Studley's next translation, *Medea*, as well as Alexander Neville's translation of *Oedipus* (1563). The octavo of *Agamemnon* is in eight quires, with signatures ¶^{8}, A^4, B^8, C^8, D^8, E^8, F^8, G^8. The text is primarily in black letter, although some text appears in Roman type, including the Latin prefaces, Latin titles and parts of the English titles of the prefatory poems, the names of the speakers at the beginning of the play and heading each scene, the running header 'Agamemnon', and proper names within the text.

'Upon the same'
83 end] and 1566
'W.R. to the Reader'
15 sow[ed]] sows 1566

'To the Reader. Thomas de la Peend'

 4 Praise] Paynes 1566 [correction noted in 'Faults Escaped in the Verses']

[Fault Escaped in the Verses]

 Appears in '1566' between 'T.B. to the Reader' and the dedicatory epistle to William Cecil. Omitted in present edition; the corrections have been incorporated into the present text.

THE SPEAKERS] The names of the speakers of this tragedie 1566; The speakers names 1581

1.1.4 earth] yearth 1566; earth 1581

1.1.26 Cnossian] Gnosian 1566–1581

1.1.27 dreary] dryrye 1566; driery 1581

1.1.44 jumbled] jumbled 1566; tumbled 1581

1.1.49 host] oste 1566; Hoste 1581

1.1.49–50 host [...] roost] oste [...] roste 1566; hoste [...] roste 1581

1.1.53 shatling] sha[?]ling 1566; shatling 1581

1.Cho.3 set'st] sytst 1566; setst 1581

1.Cho.24 It] I 1566; It 1581

1.Cho.30 vow] now 1566; vowe 1581

1.Cho.44 [peised]] payd 1566; payde 1581 (Spearing, 1913, suggests 'paysd' or 'peised' [234])

1.Cho.61 lancing] lawncyng 1566; launcing 1581

2.1.38 juice] joyce 1566; juice 1581

2.1.47 wrestleth] wresteth 1566; wrestleth 1581

2.1.64 [NUTRIX]] [...] 1566; Nut. 1581

2.1.124 enflamed] Eflamd 1566–1581

2.1.146 he] be 1566; he 1581

2.1.161 walms] wawmes 1566–1581

2.1.161–62 stir [...] dear] steare [...] deare 1566–1581

2.2.11 [partner]] partners 1566–1581

2.2.38   Phoebe] Phoebe 1566; Thebe 1581

2.2.91 [CLYTEMNESTRA]] [...] 1566; Cl. 1581

2.2.91–92 pedigree [...] drew] pedagrew [...] drew 1566–1581

2.Cho.5 [wift]] wy(s/f?)t 1566; wist 1588

2.Cho.7–8 flood [...] bide] flood [...] bood 1566–1581

2.Cho.45 heifer] heyferd 1566–1581

2.Cho.48 stroke] strook 1566; stroke 1581

2.Cho.73–74 hour [...] pour] howre [...] power 1566–1581

3.1.25–26 wet [...] fleet] weete [...] fleete 1566–1581

3.1.75 sidling] fydlyng 1566; sidling 1581

3.1.81 smoulder] smolter 1566–1581

3.1.95 [water]] waters 1566–1581

3.1.111–12 shoal […] rolled] shold […] rould 1566; shold […] rold 1581

3.1.136 and] an 1566; and 1581

3.1.149 other] others 1566; other 1581

3.1.172 carries] cares 1566; caryes 1581

3.1.209–10 shoal […] hold] shold […] hould 1566; shold […] hold 1581

3.1.225–26 shoal […] rolled] shold […] roulde 1566; sholde […] roulde 1581

3.1.242 To thee] To to thee 1566; To thee 1581

3.2.13–14 host […] tossed] host […] tost 1566–1581

3.2.45 contrivèd] contryned 1566; contryued 1581

3.2.54 despoused] desponsed 1566–1581

3.2.107 head] heds 1566–1581

3.2.138 [now]] how 1566–1581 (S. 'nunc')

5.2.2 thyself] myself 1566; thyself 1581

5.2.5 thus] this 1566; thus 1581

5.5.6 dwell] well 1566; dwel 1581

5.5.73 FINIS] […] 1566; FINIS 1581

GLOSSARY

The glossary contains archaic, obsolete, or less common words and/or meanings in the three plays. For some words, we record only less common meanings. For instance, the word 'gird' appears in the text in the sense of 'encircle' and 'girdle', but we mark it and include the definition here when it is used in the less common sense of 'move suddenly'. In cases where a word has two (or more) grammatical functions with distinct meanings (e.g. 'plunge'), the word appears twice with the part of speech noted with abbreviations for noun (*n*), verb (*v*), adjective (*a*), and adverb (*adv*). Definitions are based on those in *The Oxford English Dictionary* (*OED*). Entries marked with * designate words or usages that precede or do not appear in *OED*.

A

A	to, in
abod	abided, delayed
abroach	open, flowing freely (commonly 'set abroach')
accompt	account
acquit	satisfied
affect	passion, lust, desire
affiance	trust, faith
allow	praise, commend
alow	below (opposite of aloft)
amain	violently, with full force
amel	enamel
annex	append, add to a composition or book
apparently	manifestly, clearly
assoil	absolution
astonied	stunned, stupefied
attent	earnestly, eagerly attentive
avaunt	depart
await	watch stealthily with hostile purpose; plot harm

B

bands	confinement at childbirth
bark	small ship; a sailing vessel
beadsman	beggar
beck	nod or bow

bedlam	mad, foolish
behove	benefit, advantage
benefit	kindness, favor
berapt	bereft?
bereave	deprive, rob, strip, dispossess
beseem	seems, appears
beshake*	to shake about
besprink	sprinkle all over
bestad	beset
betake	hand over, entrust, commit
betrapped	trapped
bewail	lament loudly, cry over
bewray	expose, divulge, disclose
bide	reside; also endure, suffer
bilbo*	a kind of sword
bit	act of biting or eating
blaze	proclaim
board	table
bolden	embolden, encourage
bolne	swell
boot	help, aid, avail
boughing	barking
bounden	obliged, indebted
bower	dwelling-place, abode
boxen	made of box-wood
brethren	brothers
broach	roast; put on a spit
broid	plait, intertwine
bruit (*n*)	report, rumor, celebrity, reputation
bruit (*v*)	noise, rumor (often with abroad)

C

careless	free from worry; also carelessly
carman*	driver of a cart or car
carper	fault-finder, a captious critic
cark	burden, distress (often coupled with 'care')
caste	people, stock, breed (usually of men)
casteth	throw
castral*	military
chafed	angered, irritated, vexed
chap	a bone that makes the mouth; jaw(s)

char or chare	chariot
check	reproach, taunt
citheron	plucked, guitar-like musical instrument
clean	completely
clip	clasp, embrace
coil	beat, thrash
coll	embrace about the neck
comely	fair, beautiful, nice looking
commodity	convenience, advantage, benefit, interest
compass	circumference or bounds (of space, the heavens)
compassless*	without a compass
complain	lament
complaint	lament, utterance of grief
compound	come to a mutual agreement, compromise
compte	count
confound(ed)	destroy(ed), overthrow(n); mix up or mingle
contex	compose as by interweaving of parts
convey	take away, to remove
corse	corpse
corved	carved, cut
couch	hide, lurk
crabbed	perversely intricate, difficult to understand
crake*	harsh, grating cry
cralling*	twisted, curled
crank	bold, cocky
crank(ly)	boldly, lustily, briskly

D

dainty	delicacy
dandle(d)	(of a child) move(d) up and down in arms or on knee
danky*	dank, dampish
dastard	dullard, sot, despicable coward
declining*	receding
delude	mock hopes, expectations; cheat or disappoint
demi-lance	short shaft
depaint	depict, paint
depend	hand down, be suspended
decry*	condemnation
descry	announce, proclaim; disclose, reveal
desert	worthiness for recompense, reward

despouse	betroth
detect	uncover, expose
dick*	lad, fellow, man
dight	dress, clothe, make up
dilacerate*	rent apart, torn asunder
doleful	sorrowful, sad, dismal
dolour	sorrow, grief
doom	judgement, decision, condemnation; fate
doubtful	uncertain
drab	harlot, prostitute
dreadful	fearful, terrified
dreary	bloody, gory, horrid
drossel*	a sloven, a slut
droughty	dry, arid
dugs	breasts
dumps	melancholy, depression (often plural)
durst	dared

E

eftsoons	again, repeatedly
egal	equal
eke	also, too, moreover
elf	spiteful and malicious creature
emule*	rival, emulator
endued	invested, endowed (with power or a quality)
ensample	example
erst	at first, first
everychone	everyone; contracts 'ever each' and 'each one'
except	unless
expound	explain; translate

F

fact	deed; evil deed, crime
fain	glad, well-pleased; common in 'full fain'
fainest	gladly, willingly
fame	public report, common talk; report, rumour
fancy	imagination or apparition; illusory appearance
feat	elegant; common in phrases 'feat-fine', 'fair and feat'
featly	graceful, elegant
fell	fierce, ruthless, savage

fenny	boggy, swampy, damp
fere	wife
fet	fetch
fined	refined
file	dirty, pollute, defile
filed	polished smooth; also form of 'defiled'
fillet	headband
fit	position of hardship
fitter*	small fragment
fool	term of endearment or pity, i.e. 'poor fool'
force	attach importance to, care for
ford	tract of shallow water; sea
foredo	render powerless, neutralize
forehead	front part, forefront
forlorned	put to shame; depraved
flyte	strive, contend
flourish	adorn, set off with fine words or phrases
frame (*n*)	form or arrangement of words, such as a verse
frame (*v*)	to shape, fashion, form
fraught	laden
fray(ed)	be afraid; frightened
freight	laden
fret*	strait, a passage made by the sea; gust, squall
fruition	enjoyment; pleasure arising from possession
frump	mock, insult
fulgent	brilliant, glittering
fustian	inflated; 'fustian fumes', display of anger

G

gabbling*	chattering, jabbering
gad	wander, rove idly
gambol	capering movement
gan	shortened form of 'began'
Gangey*	related to the Ganges river
gate	begat
gear	business, affair, goings on
geat	jet or black marble
gere*	sudden fit of passion; (nonsensical) talk
gin	mechanical device, machine, engine
gird	move suddenly; also phrase 'to gird out'
gleed*	beam of light

glister	sparkle, glitter
gloze	flatter
gripe	vulture
guard	defend from or against
gudgeon-gift	trifling or small gift; something of little value

H

hail-fellow*	intimate, familiar associate
hale	pull, tug
happy*	to make happy
hap	occurrence, accident
hap	come about by chance, happen
heaviness	sadness, grief
helm	helmet
heres	multitudes, armies
hight	called
hoary	grey or white with age
hoise	raise aloft with rope, pulley, or tackle
holden	maintained, preserved; also loyal?
holm	holm-oak (evergreen oak with leaves like holly)
hurly-burly	commotion, tumult

I

ill	wickedly, sinfully
ill	evil, mischief, crime
imbrue(d)	stain(ed) with blood; also defile(d)
immire*	immerse in mire
indite	write, narrate, tell
infix	fix, fasten firmly
intoxicate*	inebriated
irksome(ly)	disgusting(ly), loathsome(ly)

J

jade	horse
jangle	talk excessively, angrily, harshly; grumble
jasper	precious stone
jetteth	strut, swagger (often with 'up and down')
jocundary*	mirthful, jocular
jointer	joint possessor
jot	smallest part
juice	life-blood; bodily humours

jumble*	know carnally
junketing	feating, banqueting

K

keep	snatch, use for enjoyment (as a mistress)
kercher	cloth to cover the head, a kerchief
kind	nature, descent, kindred
knapped	broken by a sharp blow

L

lade	burden, load oppressively
lancing	launching (of boats), push out (from land)
lares*	household gods
latest	last
lawful*	permissible
leam	light, rays, beams of light; also eyes, eyesight
leavens*	finely ground grain, i.e. meal
leeful	lawful, just, right
leese	lose
let(ted)	hinder(ed), prevent(ed), obstruct(ed)
lewdly	ignorantly, vilely
liefer	dearer
liking	pleasing, agreeable, attractive
limit	limited
linked	joined, coupled (i.e. in married)
liquor	liquid, fluid
list (*n, v*)	desire, care
lither	pliant, supple
loosed	freed, released
lour	frown, scowl
lyme	leash

M

maugre	notwithstanding, in spite of
maugre thy beard	in spite of your resistance or efforts
maw	stomach
maze (*n*)	amazement, bewilderment
maze (*v*)	stupefy, bewilder, confuse
mazed	stupefied, bewildered, confused
meacock	coward, weakling
mead	meadow

meed	recompense, reward, deserts; merit, worth
meet	suitable, fit for a purpose or occasion
mingle-mangle	mishmash; jumble
misdoubt (*n*, *v*)	fear, worry
miser	miserable or wretched person
miss* (*n*)	error or mistake
miss (*v*)	make a mistake, go wrong
mo	a greater number (of persons)
mome or momus	carping critic
mought	past tense of 'may'; 'might'
mow	grimace, make a face
mump*	grimace (often in phrase 'mump and mow')
murrain	pestilence, disease, plague
murther	murder

N

ne	not, nor
naught (*a*)	wicked, evil
naught* (*n*)	bad or wicked person
nephew	descendent, successor; grandson
nill	refuse (often in phrases with 'will')
nocked*	of an arrow, fitted into a bowstring
nones	a particular purpose (version of 'nonce')
nipping	stinging, sarcastic
note	do not know
nurture	moral training or discipline

O

obit	deceased
ope	to open
ought	possessed or owed
out	exclamation of reproach (similar to 'alas')
overquell	overcome, subdue
overshed*	overflow (of a river)
overstain*	stain completely
overstand	stand over, above, higher than
overthwart	from side to side

P

painful	careful, diligent
parbreak	spew out

parlous	perilous, desperate, dire
pashed*	crushed, smashed
pass	excel, surpass
part*	mix
peise (*n*)	weight, heaviness
peise (*v*)	burden, add weight to
peised	weighed, driven down by force
pensiveness	thoughtfulness, melancholy; also apprehension
perfit	perfect
piety	loyalty, respect, dutifulness
pile	(funeral) pyre
pinch	crisis, emergency
pipling	ently blowing
plain (*a*)	simple, easily intelligible, readily understood
plain (*adv*)	absolutely, unequivocally
plaint	lament (see complaint)
plunge (*n*)	critical situation; moment of difficulty
plunge (*v*)	cast into difficulty, misfortune, confusion
point	fix, determine
pole	the skies, heavens
pole-ax	a kind of weapon
poke*	pocket in a person's clothing
portured	depicted, portrayed
practice	deed, undertaking
pranked	dressed up, decked out
privy	secret, private
privity	secret
procure	use means, take measures
proof	striving, effort
prove	test; attempt
puissant	mighty, potent, powerful
pured	refined

Q

qualify	appease
quail	fade away, wither
quaver	eighth note
quill	pluck for stringed instrument
quit	repay, avenge, requite

R

race	path
ramp	run wildly
rapt	transported into heaven
reave	split, cleave
recreate	restore, revive, refresh
re-edify	rebuild, reconstruct
refuge*	shortened form of 'refugee'?
rent (*a*)	torn apart
rent (*v*)	rend, tear in pieces
reprehension	censure, rebuke
represent	resemble
revoke	recall to a right belief, way of life
revel-rex	antics, capers (associated with revelry)
rive	split, tear, plow
roges	pyre
rue	affect with pity, remorse; to feel contrite
runagate	vagabond, wanderer; runaway, fugitive
rush	something of little value
ruthful	pitiable, lamentable

S

sackbut	bass-trumpet with a trombone-like slide
scabbard	sheath (for sword)
scan*	look searchingly
scanned*	metrical (i.e. capable of being scanned)
scud(ding)	run(ning) briskly; dart(ing) nimbly
seemly (*a*)	pleasing, handsome, proper
seemly (*adv*)	handsomely, in a pleasing way
shawm	double-reeded oboe-like instrument
shent	disgraced, ruined
shet	variant form of 'shut'; closed
shift	stratagem, subterfuge
shore	prop, stake
shun	prevent the occurrence of
shut	close, come at the end of
silly*	helpless, defenseless; week, feeble
sith	seeing that
skill	separate, part from; in negative clauses: matter
slacker	literally 'more slack', i.e. loose
slander	disgrace, discredit

sleek	make smooth and glossy
slipper	slippery; difficult to stand upon
smite	strike or hit (sense of injure, pollute, infect)
smot	stroke, blow
sop	bread dipped in water or wine
sore (*a*)	painful, distressing
sore (*adv*)	with great hardship, painful exertion, dearly
sousing*	drenching, soaking
spill	destroy or ruin
spinet	portable, keyed instrument
spright	disembodied spirit, ghost
sprite	spirit; liveliness; energy; vigour of mind, readiness
squally*	loathsome, repulsive
stadie	stadium; place for athletic games
stay	halt; settle in a strong position; delay; hesitate
stayer*	one who stays or supports
stave	verse or stanza of a poem, song
stepped*	advanced
stews	prostitute(s) or bawd(s)
still	constantly, always
stir	commotion, disturbance, tumult
stomach	spirit, courage, valour, bravery
store	reserves, possession; treasure
story	purport, meaning conveyed
stound	short time, a moment
stout	brave; proud; menacing; determined; stubborn
strake	struck; archaic past-tense of 'strike'
string	ligament, tendon, nerve, muscle fiber
stripe	lash with whips, scourge
suborn	procure (esp. by underhanded means); bribe
swage	appease, pacify, abate
swagging	action of swaying to and fro
swiftened*	swift
swinge*	power, authority; forcible whirling motion
swink	labour; drink deeply

T

targe	light shield
tax	yew-tree
tenebrous	dark

tew*	tug, pull
thirst	desire or long for vehemently
thrast	pierce, stab
throttling	strangled
Thyestal*	Thyestean, belonging to Thyestes
tickle	unreliable; changeable, capricious, fickle
tire	tiara (crown)
tone	the one (of two) (as opposed to 'tother')
toothsome	tasty, palatable
touch	stroke of wit; reproach or taint
touching*	reproachful or overly critical
toward(ly)	promising, apt to learn
towardness	readiness, willingness
train	treachery, deceit, guile, trick
trade	way, path
trawl*	drag
trilling	falling down in a flowing manner
trim	vague term of approval; beautiful, elegant
trolling*	warbling, merrily chanting
trull	prostitute, concubine
trump	trumpet-like sound
try	ascertain
tuition	safe-keeping, protection
tush	expression of contempt or disparagement
twangling*	twanging; lightly or continuously played
twine	proceed in a winding manner
twink	wink of the eye

U

ugsome	horrid, loathsome
unapt	unfit, unsuitable
underprop	support, maintain, sustain
undertrodden*	downtrodden
undight	not adorned or put in order
ungracious	wicked, unfortunate, rude
ungreeing	unfitting
unknit	untie
unmild	harsh, rough, unkind
unperfect	unfinished, incomplete, or defective
unrepining*	uncomplaining, without fretting or discontent
untombed	not provided with a place of burial

unware	unwary, incautious; without knowledge
upshet	shut up, enclosed
up-so-down	upside down
ure	i.e. in ure; in(to) practice or performance
utter	outermost, furthermost
utter	issue or produce

V

vail	profit, benefit
vesture	clothing, garment
viol	stringed instrument played with a bow
virginal	keyed instrument
vulgar	vernacular, common

W

wafting*	move to and fro, wave
wain	wagon, cart
walm (*n*)	wave, billow
walm (*v*)	gush, swirl
waltering	rolling to and fro
wanny	pallid, wan
watch	wakefulness; the state of being awake
watched	kept under close observation
watching	unsleeping (i.e.wakeful)
waynd*	mature, advanced (in years)
weal	prosperity, public good (as opposed to 'woe')
weary	fatiguing, toilsome, exhausting
web*	complicated structure or workmanship
weed	garment, apparel
ween	think; expect; anticipate
whereas	where
whilom	in a former time
whist	become or be silent (about); silence; hush
whit	least amount, a particle
wift	to move lightly to and fro
wight	person (man or woman)
wind	get a wind of; perceive the scent of
wist	knew
wit	know, become cognizant of
wont (*v*)	be accustomed or in the habit of doing
wont(ed) (*a*)	accustomed, used to, familiar with, customary

wood (*a*)	out of one's mind, lunatic, mad
wood (*n*)	madness
wot	know
wreak	avenge
wried*	twisting, contorted
wry	turn away

Y

y	prefix, i.e. 'ycorved', 'yburnt', 'yfreight'
younker	young gentleman, youth of high rank

Z

Zoilus*	a malicious or envious critic

BIBLIOGRAPHY

The following bibliography is divided into two sections, (1) pre-1660 print sources, and (2) post-1660 editions and secondary works.

PRE-1660 PRINT SOURCES

Following the practice in the *Short Title Catalogue* (STC), we use square brackets to indicate printers or dates that do not appear directly on title-pages. Here and throughout the text, the names of the printers appear in the standard spelling by which they are indexed in the STC. Unless otherwise noted, the place of publication is London.

A[ggas], E[dward], trans., *Defence of Death Contayning a Moste Excellent Discourse of Life and Death* (John Allde for Edward Aggas, 1576)

Ascensius (Jodocus Badius), ed., *L. Annei Senecae Tragoediae* (Paris, 1514)

Avantius, Hieronymus, ed., *Scenecae* [sic] *Tragoediae* (Venice: Aldus Manutius, 1517)

Baldwin, William, *Treatise of Morall Phylosophie* ([Edward Whitchurch, 1547])

Collinus, Rudolphus, *Euripidis* [...] *tragœdiæ XVIII* (Basel: Robert Winter, 1541)

Drout, John, *The Pityfull Histori[e] of Two Louing Italians* (Henry Bynneman, 1570)

Elyot, Thomas, *The Boke Named the Governour* (Thomas Berthelet, [1531])

Erasmus, Desiderius, ed., *L. Annei Senecae Opera* (Brussels: Officina Frobeniana, 1529)

Golding, Arthur, trans. *The Woorke of the Excellent Philosopher Lucius Annaeus Seneca Concerning Benefyting* ([John Kingston for] John Day, 1578)

Googe, Barnabe, trans., *Firste Three Bokes of the Most Christia[n] Poet Marcellus Palingenius, Called the Zodyake of Lyfe* (John Tisdale for Ralph Newbery, 1560)

Gryphius, S., ed., *L. Annei Senecae Cordubensis Tragoediae* (Lyon, 1541)

Hall, Arthur, trans., *Ten Books of Homers Iliades* ([Henry Bynneman for?] Ralph Newbery, 1581)

Haward, Nicholas, *The Line of Liberalitie: Dulie Directing the Wel Bestowing of Benefites and Reprehending the Comonly Used Vice of Ingratitude* (Thomas Marsh, [1569])

Heywood, Jasper, trans., *The Sixt Tragedie of the Most Graue and Prudent Author Lucius, Anneus, Seneca, Entituled Troas with Diuers and Sundrye Addicions to the Same* ([Richard Tottell, [1559]])

—, *The Seconde tragedie of Seneca Entituled Thyestes* ([in the house of late] Thomas Berthelet, 1560)

—, *The First Tragedie of Lucius Anneus Seneca, intituled Hercules Furens* ([Henry Sutton, [1561]])

Humphrey, Lawrence, *The Nobles or Of Nobilitye* (Thomas Marsh, [1563])

I.A. [John Alday?], trans., *A Summarie of the Antiquities, and Wonders of the Worlde, Abstracted out of the Sixtene First Bookes of the Excellente Historiographer Plinie* (Henry Denham for Thomas Hacket, [1566])

Lodge, Thomas, 'Protogenes Can Know Apelles' [Reply to *School of Abuse*] ([H[ugh] Singleton?, 1579])

—, trans. *Workes of Lucius Annaeus Seneca, both Morrall and Naturall* (William Stansby, 1614)

Lydgate, John, *The Fall of Prynces* (John Wayland, [1554?])

Neville, Alexander, trans., *Lamentable Tragedie of Oedipus* (Thomas Colwell, 1563)

Newton, Thomas, ed., *Seneca: His Tenne Tragedies Translated into English* (Thomas Marsh, 1581)

N[uce], T[homas], trans., *The Ninth Tragedie of Lucius Anneus Seneca called Octauia* (Henry Denham, [1566[?]])

Partridge, John, *The Notable Hystorie of Two Famous Princes of the Worlde, Astianax and Polixena* (Henry Denham for Thomas Hacket, [1566])

Preston, Thomas, *A Lamentable Tragedy...Conteyning the Life of Cambises King of Percia* ([John Allde, [1570?]])

Puttenham, George, *Arte of English Poesie* (Richard Field, 1589)

Robinson, Richard, *Rewarde of Wickednesse* ([William Williamson, [1574]])

Robinson, R., ed. *L. Annaei Senecae Cordubensis Tragoediae* (R. R[obinson] *impensis* Thomas Man and Thomas Gubbin, 1589)

S.P., trans., *Troades Englished* (W.G. for Henry Marsh, 1660)

Studley, John, trans., *The Eyght tragedie of Seneca. Entituled Agamemnon* (Thomas Colwell, [1566])

—, *The Seuenth Tragedie of Seneca, Entituled Medea* (Thomas Colwell, [1566])

Webbe, William, *A Discourse of English Poetrie* (John Charlewood for Robert Walley, 1586)

Wood, Anthony, *Athenae Oxonienses* (London: Thomas Bennet, 1691)

POST-1660 EDITIONS AND STUDIES

Armstrong, W. A., 'Elizabethan Conception of the Tyrant', *Review of English Studies*, 22 (1946), 161–81

—, 'Influence of Seneca and Machiavelli on the Elizabethan Tyrant', *Review of English Studies*, 24 (1948), 19–35

Ayres, Harry Morgan, 'Chaucer and Seneca', *Romanic Review*, 10 (1919), 1–15

Bartsch, S. and D. Wray, eds, *Seneca and the Self* (Cambridge: Cambridge University Press, 2009)

Bennett, H. S., *English Books and Readers, 1558–1603* (Cambridge: Cambridge University Press, 1965)

Billerbeck, Margarethe, and Somazzi, Mario, *Repertorium der Konjekturen in den Seneca-Tragödien* (Leiden: Brill, 2009)

Binns, J. W., *Intellectual Culture in Elizabethan and Jacobean England* (Leeds: Francis Cairns, 1990)

Boyle, A. J., *Seneca Tragicus: Ramus Essays on Senecan Drama* (Berwick: Aureal Publications, 1983)

——, ed., *Seneca's 'Troades': Introduction, Text, Translation and Commentary* (Leeds: Francis Cairns, 1994).

——, *Tragic Seneca: An Essay in the Tragic Tradition* (New York: Routledge, 1997)

Braden, Gordon, *Renaissance Tragedy and the Senecan Tradition: Anger's Privilege* (New Haven: Yale University Press, 1985)

——, 'Tragedy' in *Oxford History of Literary Translation in English*, ed. by Gordon Braden, Robert Cummings, and Stuart Gillespie (New York: Oxford University Press, 2010), pp. 262–79

Bushnell, Rebecca, *Tragedies of Tyrants: Political Thought and Theater in the English Renaissance* (Ithaca: Cornell University Press, 1990)

Byville, Eric, '"This More Delusive": Tantalus and Seneca in *Paradise Lost*', *Modern Language Quarterly*, 69 (2008), 245–68

Charlton, H. B., *The Senecan Tradition in Renaissance Tragedy: A Re-Issue of an Essay Published in 1921* (Manchester: Manchester University Press, 1946)

Chaucer, Geoffrey, *The Riverside Chaucer*, 3rd edn, ed. by Larry D. Benson (Boston: Houghton Mifflin, 1987)

Cohon, Jerome Bertram, 'Seneca's Tragedies in *Florilegia* and Elizabethan Drama' (unpublished doctoral thesis, Columbia University, 1960)

Collection and Catalogue of Tudor and Early Stuart Books Lists, ed. by Joseph Black and E. S. Leedham-Green, 7 vols (Tempe: Arizona Center of Medieval and Renaissance Studies, 1992–2009)

Conley, C. H., *The First English Translators of the Classics* (New Haven: Yale University Press, 1927)

Cunliffe, J. W., *The Influence of Seneca on Elizabethan Tragedy* (London: Macmillan, 1893; repr. Hamden, CT.: Archon Books, 1965)

Daalder, Joost, ed., *'Thyestes': Translated by Jasper Heywood (1560)* (London: Ernest Benn, 1982)

Davis, P. J., *Seneca: 'Thyestes'*, Duckworth Companions to Greek and Roman Tragedy (London: Duckworth, 2003)

——, *Shifting Song: The Chorus in Seneca's Tragedies* (Hildesheim: Olms-Weidmann, 1993)

Dent, J. W., *Proverbial Language in English Drama, Exclusive of Shakespeare, 1495–1616: An Index* (Berkeley: University of California Press, 1984)

——, *Shakespeare's Proverbial Language: An Index* (Berkeley: University of California Press, 1981)

Dominik, William J., 'The Style is the Man: Seneca, Tacitus and Quintilian's Canon', in *Roman Eloquence: Rhetoric and Society in Literature*, ed. by William J. Dominik (London: Routledge, 1997), pp. 50–68

Douglas, Gavin, trans., *The Aeneid* (1513), ed. by Gordon Kendal, MHRA Tudor and Stuart Translations (London: Modern Humanities Research Association, 2011)

Eliot, T. S. 'Introduction', in *Seneca: His Tenne Tragedies*, ed. by Thomas Newton, 2 vols, Tudor Translations series (London: Constable and Co., 1927), I, v–liv

Fantham, E., *Seneca's 'Troades': A Literary Introduction with Text, Translation, and Commentary* (Princeton: Princeton University Press, 1982)

Fitch, J. G., ed., *Seneca*, Oxford Readings in Classical Studies (Oxford: Oxford University Press, 2008)

——, *Seneca: Tragedies*, 2 vols, Loeb Classical Library (Cambridge, MA: Harvard University Press, 2002)

Flynn, Dennis, 'The English Mission of Jasper Heywood, S. J'. *Archivum historicum societatis Jesu*, 54 (1985), 45–76

——, *John Donne and the Ancient Catholic Nobility* (Bloomington: Indiana University Press, 1995)

Greg, W. W., 'Notes on Early Plays: Seneca's *Troas* Translated by Jasper Heywood, 1559', *The Library*, 4th ser., 11 (1930), 162–72

Griffin, Miriam T., *Seneca: A Philosopher in Politics*, 2nd edn (Oxford: Oxford University Press, 1992)

Griffin, N. H., *Jesuit School Drama: A Checklist of Critical Literature*, Supplement 1, Research Bibliographies and Checklists (London: Grant & Cutler, 1985)

Habinek, Thomas N., 'Seneca's Renown: *Gloria, Claritudo*, and the Replication of the Roman Elite', *Classical Antiquity*, 19 (2000), 264–303

Hackel, Heidi Brayman, *Reading Material in Early Modern England: Print, Gender, and Literacy* (Cambridge: Cambridge University Press, 2005)

Hardison, O. B. *Prosody and Purpose in the English Renaissance* (Baltimore: Johns Hopkins University Press, 1989).

Hendry, Michael, 'A Beastly Love Triangle? Seneca, *Agamemnon* 737–40', *Classical Quarterly*, 50 (2000), 317–20

Herington, C. J., 'Senecan Tragedy', *Arion*, 5 (1966), 422–71

Highet, Gilbert, *The Classical Tradition: Greek and Roman Influences on Western Literature* (New York and London: Oxford University Press, 1949)

Hine, Harry M., '*Interpretatio Stoica* of Senecan Tragedy', in *Sénèque le tragique*, ed. by Margarethe Billerbeck and Ernst A. Schmidt (Geneva: Fondation Hardt, 2004), pp. 173–220

Hunter, G. K. 'Seneca and the Elizabethans: A Case-Study in 'Influence', *Shakespeare Survey*, 20 (1967), 17–26

—, 'Drab and Golden Lyrics of the Renaissance', in *Forms of Lyric: Selected Papers from the English Institute*, ed. by Reuben A. Brower (New York: Columbia University Press, 1970), pp. 1–18

Jockers, Ernst, 'Die englischen Seneca-Uebersetzer des 16. Jahrhunderts' (Doctoral thesis, Strassburg, Druckerei der Strassburger Neuesten Nachrichten A.-G., 1909)

Ker, James, *The Deaths of Seneca* (New York: Oxford University Press, 2009)

—, 'Seneca, Man of Many Genres', in *Seeing Seneca Whole: Perspectives on Philosophy, Poetry and Politics*, ed. by Katharina Volk and Gareth D. Williams (Leiden: Brill, 2006), pp. 19–41

Kiefer, Frederick, 'Seneca Speaks in English: What the Elizabethan Translators Wrought', *Comparative Literature Studies*, 15 (1978), 372–87

Life and Letters of Sir Thomas Wyatt, ed. by Kenneth Muir (Liverpool: Liverpool University Press, 1963)

Littlewood, Cedric J., *Self-Representation and Illusion in Senecan Tragedy* (Oxford: Oxford University Press, 2004)

Lyons, Tara, 'English Printed Drama in Collection Before Jonson and Shakespeare' (unpublished doctoral thesis, University of Illinois, Urbana-Champagne, 2011)

Mayer, Roland, 'Personata Stoa: Neostoicism and Senecan Tragedy', *Journal of the Warburg and Courtauld Institutes*, 57 (1994), 151–74

Maxwell, J. C., 'Seneca in *The Misfortunes of Arthur*', *Notes and Queries*, n.s., 7 (1960), 171

Miola, Robert S., *Shakespeare and Classical Tragedy: The Influence of Seneca* (Oxford: Clarendon Press, 1992)

Miller, Edwin Haviland, 'New Year's Day Gift Books in the Sixteenth Century', *Studies in Bibliography*, 15 (1962), 233-41

Milton, John, *Complete Poetry*, rev. edn, ed. by John T. Shawcross (New York: Anchor Books, 1963)

Mirror for Magistrates, ed. by Lily B. Campbell (New York: Barnes and Noble, 1938)

More, Thomas, *Utopia*, 3rd edn, ed. and trans. by George M. Logan (New York: W. W. Norton, 2011)

Mueller, Janel, and Joshua Scodel, eds., *Elizabeth I: Translations, 1544–1589* (Chicago: University of Chicago Press, 2009)

Muir, Kenneth, 'A Borrowing from Seneca', *Notes and Queries*, 194 (1949), 214–16

—, 'Seneca and Shakespeare', *Notes and Queries*, n.s., 3 (1956), 243–44

O'Keefe, John, 'An Analysis of Jasper Heywood's Translations of *Troas*, *Thyestes*, and *Hercules Furens*' (unpublished doctoral thesis, Loyola University, Chicago, 1974)

—, 'Innovative Diction in the First English Translations of Seneca: Jasper Heywood's Contribution to the English Language', *English Language Notes*, 18 (1980), 90–98

Oxford Dictionary of National Biography, ed. by H. C. G. Matthew and Brian Harrison, 60 vols (Oxford: Oxford University Press, 2004)

Panizza, Lutezia A., 'Biography in Italy from the Middle Ages to the Renaissance: Seneca, Pagan or Christian?', *Nouvelles de la république des lettres*, 2 (1984), 47–98.

Paradise of Dainty Devises, 1576–1606, ed. by Hyder Edward Rollins (Cambridge, MA: Harvard University press, 1927)

Perry, Curtis, 'British Empire on the Eve of the Armada: Revisiting *The Misfortunes of Arthur*', *Studies in Philology*, 108 (2011), 508–37

—, '*Gismond of Salern* and the Elizabethan Politics of Senecan Drama', in *Gender Matters*, ed. by Mara R. Wade (Amsterdam: Rodopi) (forthcoming)

—, and Melissa Walter, 'Staging Secret Interiors: *The Duchess of Malfi* as Inns of Court and Anticourt Drama', in *The Duchess of Malfi: A Critical Guide*, ed. by Christina Luckyj (London: Continuum, 2011), pp. 85–105

Pincombe, Mike, '*Agamemnon*', in *Origins of Early Modern Literature: Recovering Mid-Tudor Writing for a Modern Readership*, ed. by Cathy Shrank et al. (Sheffield: University of Sheffield and HRI Online, 2007) <http://www.hrionline.ac.uk/origins/frame.html> [Accsessed 30 November 2011]

—, 'Tragic Inspiration in Jasper Heywood's Translation of Seneca's *Thyestes*: Melpomene or Megaera?' in *The Oxford*

Handbook of Tudor Drama, ed. by Tom Betteridge and Greg Walker (Oxford: Oxford University Press, 2012), pp. 531–46

Pugh, Beverly Jane, 'Jasper Heywood's Translation of Seneca's *Thyestes,* with Particular Reference to the Latter's Sixteenth and Seventeenth-Century Reception of the Themes of Tyranny, Kingship and Revenge', 2 vols (unpublished doctoral thesis, University of Warwick, 1997)

Rees, B. R., 'English Seneca: A Preamble', *Greece and Rome*, 2nd ser., 16 (1969), 119–33

Regenbogen, Otto, 'Schmerz und Tod in den Tragödien Senecas', in *Kleine Schriften* (Munich: Beck, 1961), pp. 409–62

Rosenmeyer, Thomas G., *Senecan Drama and Stoic Cosmology* (Berkeley: University of California Press, 1989)

Schiesaro, A., *The Passions in Play: 'Thyestes' and the Dynamics of Senecan Drama* (Cambridge: Cambridge University Press, 2003)

Seneca, ed. by C. D. N Costa (London: Routledge, 1974)

Seneca in Performance, ed. by George W. M. Harrison (London: Duckworth, 2000)

Seneca: Six Tragedies, trans. by Emily Wilson (Oxford: Oxford University Press, 2010)

Sénèque le tragique, ed. by Margarethe Billerbeck and Ernst A. Schmidt (Geneva: Fondation Hardt, 2004)

Shakespeare, William, *Complete Pelican Shakespeare*, ed. by Stephen Orgel and A. R. Braunmuller (New York: Pelican, 2002)

Share, Don, ed., *Seneca in English* (London: Penguin, 1998)

Sidney, Mary, *Antonius* in *Selected Works of Mary Sidney Herbert, Countess of Pembroke*, ed. by Margaret P. Hannay, Noel J. Kinnamon, and Michael G. Brennan (Tempe: Arizona Center for Medieval and Renaissance Studies, 2005), pp. 41–111

Sidney, Philip, *An Apology for Poetry*, ed. by Forrest G. Robinson (Indianapolis: Bobbs-Merrill, 1970)

Simon, Joan, *Education and Society in Tudor England* (Cambridge: Cambridge University Press, 1967)

Skelton, John, *Book of the Laurel*, ed. by F. W. Brownlow (Newark: University of Delaware Press, 1990)

Smith, Bruce R., 'Toward the Rediscovery of Tragedy: Productions of Seneca's Plays on the English Renaissance Stage', *Renaissance Drama*, n.s., 9 (1978), 3–37

Spearing, Evelyn, *The Elizabethan Translations of Seneca's Tragedies* (London: W. Heffer and Sons, 1912)

—, ed., *Studley's Translations of Seneca's 'Agamemnon' and 'Medea': Edited from the Octavos of 1566* (Louvain: A. Uystpruyst, 1913)

Staley, G. A., *Seneca and the Idea of Tragedy* (New York: Oxford University Press, 2010)

Tarrant, R. J., ed., *Seneca: 'Agamemnon', Edited with a Commentary* (Cambridge: Cambridge University Press, 1976)

—, 'Senecan Tragedy and Its Antecedents', *Harvard Studies in Classical Philology*, 82 (1978), 213–63

—, ed., *Seneca's 'Thyestes': Edited with Introduction and Commentary* (Atlanta: Scholar's Press, 1985)

—, 'The Younger Seneca: Tragedies', in *Texts and Transmission: A Survey of the Latin Classics,* ed. by L.D. Reynolds (New York: Oxford University Press, 1984), pp. 378–81

Taylor, A. B., 'Echoes of Golding's Ovid in John Studley's Translations of Seneca', *Notes and Queries*, n.s., 34 (1987), 185–87

—, 'The Elizabethan Seneca and Two Notes on Shakespeare and Spenser', *Notes and Queries,* n.s., 32 (1987), 193–95

—, 'Shakespeare, Studley, Golding', *Review of English Studies*, 39 (1988), 522–27

Vocht, H., *Jasper Heywood and His Translations of Seneca's 'Troas', 'Thyestes', and 'Hercules Furens'* (Louvain: A. Uystpruyst, 1913

Volk, K., and G. Williams, eds, *Seeing Seneca Whole: Perspectives on Philosophy, Poetry, and Politics* (Leiden: Brill, 2006)

Watson, Foster, *English Grammar Schools to 1660: Their Curriculum and Practice* (Cambridge: Cambridge University Press, 1908)

Winston, Jessica, 'English Seneca: Heywood to *Hamlet*', in *The Oxford Handbook of Tudor Literature, 1485–1603*, ed. by Mike Pincombe and Cathy Shrank (Oxford: Oxford University Press, 2009), pp. 472–87

—, 'Lyric Poetry at the Early Elizabethan Inns of Court: Forming a Professional Community', *The Intellectual and Cultural World of the Early Modern Inns of Court*, ed. by Jayne Elisabeth Archer, Elizabeth Goldring, Sarah Knight (Manchester: Manchester University Press, 2011), pp. 223–44

—, 'Seneca in Early Elizabethan England', *Renaissance Quarterly*, 59 (2006), 29–58

—, and James Ker, 'A Note on Jasper Heywood's "Free Compositions" in *Troas* (1559)', *Modern Philology*, 110:4 (2013) (forthcoming)

Woodbridge, Linda, *English Revenge Drama: Money, Resistance, Equality* (Cambridge: Cambridge University Press, 2010)

Works of Thomas Nashe, ed. by Ronald B. McKerrow, rev. by F. P. Wilson, 5 vols (London: Barnes and Noble, 1966)

Wright, Louis B., 'Translations for the Elizabethan Middle Class', *The Library*, 13 (1932), 312–31

Yale Elizabethan Club, '*Oedipus* Manuscript', <www.yale.edu/elizabethanclub/oedipus.html> [Accessed 30 November 2011]

INDEX

Both names (e.g. Acheron) and subjects (e.g. Tragedy) have been indexed. Some identifying information is provided here in specific entries (e.g. 'Aeacus [judge in underworld]'), unless sufficient information is already given in the notes. References below are to page numbers.

Abbreviations

Gk   Greek
Lat.   Latin
Mt   mountain
n.   in the footnotes
R.   river

Acheron (R., in underworld; 'Acheront'), 87, 150n., 197, 213, 254

Achilles (son of Peleus and Thetis; 'Achill'), 20, 25, 29, 30, 48, 73, 90–93, 94, 95, 97, 98, 99, 113, 122, 230, 231, 233, 249n., 254, 260; hides on Scyros 20, 91, 98n.; kills Trojan allies [Memnon, Penthesilea, Cycnus] 86, 90n., 92; deprived of Briseis 20, 92, 232; dispute with Agamemnon 93, 95, 96, 231n., 233n.; withholds aid to Greek troops 20, 96; armour worn by Patroclus 20, 103, 233n., 254; killer of Hector 20, 90, 92, 102, 118; ransoms Hector's body to Priam 20, 95n., 113; killed by Paris 20, 75, 87, 98, 125; armour awarded to Ulysses 127; ghost 21, 30, 52, 72, 75, 76, 86–88, 89, 90, 94, 120, 125;

demands sacrifice of Polyxena 21, 75, 88, 90, 124; tomb 21, 88, 90, 94, 99, 124, 132, 255

Adriatic sea ('gulf of Adria'), 169

Aeacus (judge in underworld), 98

Aedon, 256

Aegean sea, 84n., 91, 251n.

Aegeus (king of Athens), 84n.

Aegisthus (son of Thyestes and Pelopia; 'Aegist'), 46–48, 154n., 202n., 207n., 210, 212, 220, 222n., 223, 234–239, 235n., 238n., 239n., 259, 260n., 267n., 268, 270, 271, 273, 287, 288; as qualified model for Studley 208n.

Aeneas (Trojan warrior), 19, 74, 74n.

Aerope (wife of Atreus), 33, 168n., 239n.

Aeschylus, 11, 47, 55

Africa ('Affric land'), 224

Trojan War, 20, 23, 46–48, 73,
86, 154n., 210, 216, etc. See
also Phrygian
Trojan women, Chorus of, 19,
21, 31, 47–48, 76n., 80–83,
128–129, 220n., 253–261
Troy (also 'Troia'), Latin terms
26; building of 77n.; first
sacked by Hercules 73n.,
82n., 116, 254, 266; fall of 1,
19–21, 27–28, 47–48, 73–75,
77–79, 266n., etc.; rebuilding
of 117. See also
Agamemnon; Hecuba;
Pergamum; Priam; Trojan;
Trojan women; etc.
Tyndareus (father of
Clytemnestra), 47
Tyndaris (daughter of
Tyndareus), 132, 230, 268
Typhoeus (Giant, buried under
Mt Etna), 189
Tyranny. See kingship, tyranny
and
Tyrian (from Tyre, famous for
its luxurious purple dye), 42,
169, 194
Tyrrhenian sea (off west coast
of Italy), 246

Ulysses (Gk Odysseus), 20–21,
76, 78, 83, 91n., 95, 101–120,
124, 127, 131, 233n., 249,
255
Underworld, 12, 32, 34, 41, 44,
52, 84n., 87n., 127n., 153n.,
189n., 202n., 221n., 242n.,

261n. See also Acheron;
Avernus; Ditis; Elysium;
Erebus; Ghost; Lethe; Limbo;
Orcus; Phlegethon; Pluto;
Styx; Taenarus; Tartarus

Vegius, Mapheus, 36
Venus (goddess), 95, 140, 227
Venus (planet), 264n.
Verse form, in Seneca 14, 26–
28; in Heywood 1, 22, 25,
26–28, 31, 35, 39, 42–43, 48,
73, 115n., 141, 145, 150,
193n.; in Studley 50, 53–54,
72, 214, 216, 253n., 261n.
Vesper (Evening Star), 188
Virgil (Publius Virgilius Maro),
5n., 13, 19, 23, 35, 36, 56, 73,
87n., 149, 216

Webbe, William, 57
Westminster School, 4n., 45,
50, 218
Whitgift, John, 46
Wyatt, Thomas, 5n.

Xanthus (R., at Troy), 90, 233

Yelverton, Christopher, 143

Zeus, 47, 148n., 241n., 242n.
See also Jupiter
Zodiac, 100n., 190–91, 223.
See also Googe, *Zodiac of
Life*
Zoilus (legendary detractor of
Homer; pl. Zoili), 49, 142,
209n. 213–214

Lightning Source UK Ltd.
Milton Keynes UK
UKOW06f0154130617

303198UK00002B/230/P